FALLEN ANGEL

The Whitman daguerreotype, made November 13, 1848, by Samuel H. Hartshorn.
(Courtesy of the Edgar Allan Poe Museum, Richmond, Virginia)

FALLEN ANGEL

THE LIFE OF EDGAR ALLAN POE

ROBERT MORGAN

LOUISIANA STATE UNIVERSITY PRESS
BATON ROUGE

Published with the assistance of the John and Virginia Noland Fund

Published by Louisiana State University Press
lsupress.org

Manufactured in the United States of America
First printing

DESIGNER: Michelle A. Neustrom
TYPEFACE: MillerText
PRINTER AND BINDER: Sheridan Books, Inc.

JACKET ILLUSTRATION: Edvard Munch, *Separation* (1896).
The raven is by Édouard Manet, from *Le corbeau* (1875).

LIBRARY OF CONGRESS CATALOGING-IN-PUBLICATION DATA

Names: Morgan, Robert, 1944– author.
Title: Fallen angel : the life of Edgar Allan Poe / Robert Morgan.
Description: Baton Rouge : Louisiana State University Press, [2023] | Includes bibliographical references and index.
Identifiers: LCCN 2023020213 (print) | LCCN 2023020214 (ebook) | ISBN 978-0-8071-8045-7 (cloth) | ISBN 978-0-8071-8107-2 (pdf) | ISBN 978-0-8071-8106-5 (epub)
Subjects: LCSH: Poe, Edgar Allan, 1809–1849. | Authors, American—19th century—Biography.
Classification: LCC PS2631 .M67 2024 (print) | LCC PS2631 (ebook) | DDC 818/.309 [B]—dc23/eng/20230629
LC record available at https://lccn.loc.gov/2023020213
LC ebook record available at https://lccn.loc.gov/2023020214

for my sister, Evangeline

CONTENTS

ILLUSTRATIONS

ACKNOWLEDGMENTS

FIRST, I WOULD LIKE TO THANK MY COLLEAGUES AT CORNELL University who have done so much to support and encourage this project from the beginning, including department chairs Roger Gilbert, Caroline Levine, and Andy Galloway. A sabbatical in the fall of 2021 was crucial in the effort to complete this biography. Alice E. Murdock and Emily Louise Parsons have provided essential assistance again and again.

Equally important was the encouragement of colleagues and friends, especially Helena Maria Viramontes, Ishion Hutchinson, Paul Sawyer, Ken McClane, Lamar Herrin, Cynthia Chase, Pete Wetherbee.

A number of friends outside the Cornell Community were also helpful during the dark days of the pandemic: Edward Hower, Ron Rash, Tom Rash, Susan Weinberg, Sandy Ballard, Joseph Flora, John Lang, Michael McFee, Bill and Anne Harmon, Rebecca Godwin, George Hovis, Jesse Graves, Robert West, Randall Wilhelm, Jim Toms, David Madden, Terry Roberts, Robert Schultz, Jonathan Greene, Bhisham Bherwani, and the late Chan Gordon.

The Cornell library staff were also instrumental in providing essential research material, especially the personnel of the Library Annex during the COVID shutdown, when I depended on contactless circulation.

Because of COVID restrictions, I was unable to visit a number of archives, museums, and sites associated with Poe's life and work. Before the lockdown, I was fortunate to do research at the Enoch Pratt Memorial Library in Baltimore and visit Poe's grave there. I am also grateful to Christopher P. Semtner, director of the Poe Museum in Richmond, Virginia, who gave me a tour of the holdings in the museum, answered many questions, and provided several illustrations for this biography.

Though hampered by the pandemic, I had the good fortune to have access to many documents online and through library scans. I benefited especially from the Edgar Allan Poe Society of Baltimore website, www.eapoe.org, along with other available sites in the digital landscape.

I received significant advice and recommendations from the Poe scholar J. Gerald Kennedy and from the historian Andrew Burstein; each read the manuscript and made valuable suggestions. I am indebted to the acquisitions editor at Louisiana State University Press, James W. Long, and the staff, including Rand Dotson, James Wilson, Catherine Kadair, and Michelle A. Neustrom; Elizabeth Gratch, copyeditor; and Mary Ann Lieser, who provided the index. My agent, Liz Darhansoff, remained committed to this work throughout.

Finally, I would like to express my gratitude to my sister, Evangeline M. Freeman; my son, Ben, who assembled the illustrations; my daughters, Laurel and Katie; and my wife, Nancy, for continuous and immeasurable support.

FALLEN ANGEL

INTRODUCTION

FROM THE TIME HE PLAYED AT MARRYING HIS NEIGHBOR Catherine Poitiaux at the age of five or six, until he was engaged to Elmira Royster Shelton in the weeks before his death, Poe seemed to have a troubled fascination with the idea of matrimony. When he was seventeen, he became unofficially engaged to Sarah Elmira Royster. Later, at the age of twenty-three, he sought marriage with Mary Starr and did marry his thirteen-year-old cousin Virginia Clemm in 1836. After Virginia's death in 1847, Poe sought the hand of the poet Frances Osgood, then the poet and author Helen Whitman. He dreamed of marrying the already-wed Annie Richmond. Much of Poe's writing, both in satires, romances, and stories of horror, would concern the institution of marriage, including the failure or fear of some marriages. The poems "The Raven," "Ulalume," and "Annabel Lee" lament tragedies linked to marriage or betrothal. Stories such as "The Black Cat," "Berenicë," "Morella," "Ligeia," and "The Assignation" culminate in the death of a spouse or lover. Feminist critics have argued that many of the stories involve symbolic scenes of rape. The critic Ellen Weinauer suggests, "Marriage . . . becomes a site of Gothic terror in Poe's tales . . . [subjecting] both women and men to 'decided,' indeed often fatal, losses."

Poe's fiction can incorporate scenes of happy marriages, in stories such as "The Domain of Arnheim," "Landor's Cottage," "Hop-Frog," and maybe "Eleonora." It's also possible to see "The Murders in the Rue Morgue" as a celebration of same-sex union between the narrator and the great detective.

In "The Philosophy of Composition" Poe argues that the perfect subject for a poem is the death of a beautiful woman. In many of his poems and stories, a woman dies, usually a lover or spouse. In his own life, Poe's parents separated, and his foster parents were unhappily wed. Jane Stanard, whom he idolized in his teens, may have died from the stress of a failed marriage. We can study Poe's life in part by considering his sustained fascination with matrimony. From *Tamerlane,* published when Poe was eighteen, to "Annabel Lee," written near the end of his life, Poe struggled with the ideals and consequences of marriage or engagement and guilt and grief for the deaths of wives or lovers.

Among the major American writers of the nineteenth century, Poe remains the most enigmatic and controversial. Scores of biographers, scholars, and critics have attempted to clarify the events of his career and the relationship between his work and his life. In a famous essay, the poet and critic Allen Tate referred to Poe as "our cousin, Mr. Poe," and it is a fact that millions of readers around the world, as well as scholars and critics, feel a particular kinship with the author of "The Raven," "The Fall of the House of Usher," and "Ligeia." No one I know of has written an essay about "our cousin, Mr. Twain" or "our cousin, Mr. James." What is it about Poe that causes him to remain both mysterious and so peculiarly familiar to readers?

Some celebrated American scholars have been skeptical of Poe's achievement, while millions of readers at home and elsewhere have delighted in his writing, including important foreign authors such as Charles Baudelaire and Fyodor Dostoevsky. Alfred, Lord Tennyson proclaimed Poe "the most original genius that America has produced." Poe's position in the canon of American classics has been a subject of contention, while his place in world literature is beyond dispute.

One of the best critics of Poe, the poet Richard Wilbur, describes him as "Gnostic," that is, someone who sees the natural world as corrupted and seeks to transcend to spiritual, esoteric realms. Poe's contemporaries Ralph Waldo Emerson, Henry David Thoreau, and Walt Whitman famously celebrated the world of nature. But Poe, in many of his works, reveals a similar delight in the natural environment, with a relish, delicacy, intimacy, and love of solitude no less intense than that found in the prose and verse of his northern contemporaries, though perhaps with a southern flavor. When writing about the ocean, Poe evokes a sublime of awe and terror matched only by Herman Melville, who was in fact influenced by Poe's art.

FIG. 1. Eliza Arnold Poe ([1787?]–1811). Poe's British-born mother was a gifted and popular actress, singer, and dancer who arrived in the United States in 1796. She died in Richmond, Virginia, in 1811, when Poe was almost three. He adored her memory but was reticent about what he believed was her ethnic heritage. (Courtesy of the Edgar Allan Poe Museum, Richmond, Virginia)

Poe's life and art can be understood better if we consider the dozen or so women who had the greatest impact on him. Most important was his mother, the actress Eliza Arnold Poe (1787[?]–1811), who died on tour in Richmond, Virginia, when Edgar was almost three (fig. 1). All his life he would idolize her, defend her reputation, and carry her miniature portrait. Watching his beautiful and gifted mother die of consumption would affect Poe in ways he may not have completely understood. His response to her death informed much of his writing, his character, his ideals, and his relations with other women. The talented and dying Eliza was the beautiful mother figure Poe would search for the rest of his life, even as the failed marriage of his parents would haunt him.

It was Frances Valentine Allan (1785–1829), wife of the Richmond merchant John Allan, who took in Edgar as a foster child (fig. 2). She was also known as a great beauty. Fanny Allan protected Edgar and may have spoiled her ward, who often quarreled with John Allan, a man by turns affectionate and sarcastic. Fanny was often sick and unable to help Edgar. Because he was never legally adopted by Allan, Edgar did not quite know where he belonged. Pedigree was important in Richmond society, and Poe

FIG. 2. Frances Valentine Allan (1785–1829). Fanny Allan took the child Poe into her house after his mother's death. Affectionate and withdrawn by turns, she helped protect young Poe from her husband's rigid discipline. (Courtesy of the Edgar Allan Poe Museum, Richmond, Virginia)

FIG. 3. Sarah Elmira Royster Shelton (1810–88). Poe was engaged to Elmira twice, first in 1826, before he left for the University of Virginia, and again in 1849, just before his death. The loss of Elmira in 1827 influenced Poe's relations with women for the rest of his short life. (Courtesy of the Edgar Allan Poe Museum, Richmond, Virginia)

was never sure of his status there. He also observed from a young age the tension of the Allans' troubled union.

At about the age of fourteen, Edgar fell under the spell of Mrs. Jane Stanard (1793–1824), mother of one of his school friends. For her he wrote one of his best early poems, "To Helen," idealizing the actual woman as a classic beauty who serves as a beacon for the lost sailor-narrator. Few other poets of any age have been able to evoke the intensity and melancholy of youthful love as effectively as Poe did in this and other works. This is a major reason for Poe's enduring popularity: he reawakens the grief and yearning of adolescent love in many of his readers. And Poe must have been aware that Mrs. Stanard's unhappy marriage likely contributed to her death.

Later in his teens, Poe became unofficially engaged to a neighbor, the young Sarah Elmira Royster (1810–88) (fig. 3). They walked in the flowery garden of the Ellis family, kissed among the groves of linden trees. Their parents and guardians disapproved of the match, and Edgar was sent away to the University of Virginia. When he returned to Richmond almost a year later, Elmira, whose letters to and from him had been intercepted by her father, was betrothed to someone else. The loss of Elmira was a wound, along with other injuries, that never healed. Several of Poe's early poems, including "Tamerlane" and "Song," are responses to this humiliation, a crushing reminder of his lack of status and name in Richmond society. He would never forget the frustration of that ideal union he'd aspired to.

One of the most important women in Poe's life, after his idolized mother and the lost Elmira, was his aunt and later mother-in-law, Maria Poe Clemm (1790–1871) (fig. 4). It was with Mrs. Clemm, called "Muddy," that Edgar found refuge in Baltimore, after he got himself expelled from West Point. For the rest of his life, Poe would depend on Muddy to look after him.

In 1836, when he was twenty-seven, Poe married Muddy's thirteen-year-old daughter Virginia (1822–47) (fig. 5). Poe's idealization of the young bride, who would suffer from tuberculosis and die at age twenty-four, helped inspire many poems and stories, including "The Raven" and "Ligeia." Poe's etherealization of beautiful young women is one of the most peculiar and haunting features of his work, inspiring later writers such as Vladimir Nabokov. The critic J. Gerald Kennedy would observe that for

FIG. 4. Maria Poe Clemm (1790–1871). Both Poe's aunt and his mother-in-law, Maria Clemm was Poe's protector and confidante. When he had nowhere to go in 1831, he found a home with her in Baltimore and remained with her until the end of his life. (Courtesy of the Edgar Allan Poe Museum, Richmond, Virginia)

FIG. 5. Virginia Clemm Poe (1822–47). Poe's first cousin Virginia wed the writer in 1836. Biographers have puzzled over the marriage, but their bond seemed essential to each. Her illness and death from tuberculosis in 1847 devastated the author. (Courtesy of the Edgar Allan Poe Museum, Richmond, Virginia)

Poe "writing is a form of nympholepsy." There are signs that Poe was deeply troubled by this marriage.

Both before and after Virginia's death, Poe had several romantic attachments with literary women. One of the most important was with the poet Frances Sargent Osgood (1811–50), wife of the painter Samuel Osgood (fig. 6). There were even rumors that Mrs. Osgood gave birth to Poe's child in 1846. She and Poe wrote poems to each other, and she befriended the bedridden Virginia. Poe may have hoped to marry Fanny after Virginia's death. Mrs. Osgood would defend Poe's reputation after his death and then die of consumption herself in 1850.

Of great importance to Poe and his family was his friendship with and idealization of Mrs. Marie Louise "Loui" Shew (ca. 1821–77), who gave much-needed aid to the Poes and comforted Edgar after Virginia's death (fig. 7). Both of the poems "To MLS" and "To ——" were written for Mrs. Shew. The latter poem is a dazzling performance, apparently dashed off and only slightly revised. Mrs. Shew told Poe he must marry a woman who could keep his life in order, and Poe took her advice to heart.

Probably the most discussed among Poe's literary romances was the courtship of the Providence, Rhode Island, widow, poet, and critic Helen Whitman (1803–78), for whom he wrote a second poem called "To Helen" (fig. 8). The account of their courtship has an element of extravagance to the point of farce. They became engaged briefly, and then she broke it off because of his drinking. Yet after Poe's death, Mrs. Whitman wrote an important and perceptive memoir, defending Poe against attacks on his character.

One of Poe's most unusual relationships was with the married Mrs. Nancy Richmond (1820–98) of Lowell, Massachusetts, whom he called Annie (fig. 9). At the time he was courting Helen Whitman, he was confiding passionately in Annie Richmond. He even proposed to move to Lowell to live near her. Because she was safely married to another, Poe was free to idealize and idolize Annie as mother figure, a Madonna, and muse, from whom he sought intercession and absolution.

Before his death, in October 1849, Poe became engaged again to his childhood sweetheart in Richmond, Virginia, Elmira Royster Shelton, now a widow. Elmira was well-off and established in Richmond society. Supposedly, Poe was returning to New York to bring Muddy to Richmond before

FIG. 6. Frances Sargent Osgood (1811–50). A fashionable poet and wife of the painter Samuel Osgood, Fanny Osgood met Poe in 1845 at the height of his fame for "The Raven." They fell in love and conducted an affair in poems and in person, creating a scandal, before Mrs. Osgood moved to Providence, Rhode Island, and then to Albany, New York. After Poe's death, she defended his (and her) character. (Courtesy of the Edgar Allan Poe Museum, Richmond, Virginia)

FIG. 7. Marie Louise Barney Shew (1821–77). Daughter of a country doctor, watercolorist, and health advocate, part-time nurse Mrs. Shew cared for Virginia Poe in her last days and for Poe after his wife's death. Poe came to depend on her, but she drew away from him when told *Eureka* was "pantheistic." (From Mary E. Phillips, *Edgar Allan Poe the Man* [1926], 1264)

FIG. 8. Sarah Helen Whitman (1803–78). Born on January 19, also Poe's birthday, Mrs. Whitman, of Providence, Rhode Island, was a noted beauty, poet, and critic. She and Poe were drawn to each other in the fall of 1848 and were briefly engaged. Poe's extraordinary letters to her constitute one of the most fascinating documents of his career. (Courtesy of the Edgar Allan Poe Museum, Richmond, Virginia)

FIG. 9. Annie Richmond (1820–98). Poe formed an unusually close relationship with Mrs. Nancy "Annie" Richmond in the last year of his life. Because she was married and lived far away, in Lowell, Massachusetts, he could project onto her his highest ideals and deepest affection, making her a kind of Blessed Virgin figure to aid and guide him in the turmoil of his final months. (Courtesy of the Edgar Allan Poe Museum, Richmond, Virginia)

the wedding, when he disappeared and was found dying in Baltimore. Poe's relationship with Elmira, both in his youth and at the end of his life, is one of the most significant for our understanding of his career, personality, and imagination. For her he gave up drinking and apparently died of disease, not alcohol poisoning. Yet in his final weeks, Poe seemed to recognize that such an ideal union with Elmira was probably not possible.

In all these women, Poe sought to refind the ideal of his beautiful and dying mother. But about that ideal he was deeply divided. On the one hand, the child Edgar felt a dreadful guilt, thinking he might have caused his mother's death by something he unknowingly did. At the same time, he was angry that she'd left him alone and unprotected. This dividedness, this torturing conflict, would stay with Poe throughout his life, partly unconsciously, as he sought to recover the adored Eliza, worshipped her, then found her taken away. All his ethereal and superior heroines die, in story after story and poem after poem. He was compelled to imagine that they did not really die, but would come back, as he had to believe Eliza would return.

Poe's admirer and translator Charles Baudelaire structured his own volume of poems, *Les Fleurs du mal,* by separating the poems into groups inspired by different women. We could study Poe's life and work in a similar way, giving special attention to the women who served in turn as model, nurturer, protector, lover, and muse or bride.

While many students of Poe argue for the unity of his work and attempt to show a consistent development of his thought and art, I would also stress some of the diversity of his thought and writing. There are indeed themes that extend throughout the body of his work—his fascination with mesmerism, premature burial, the imp of the perverse, his Byronic melancholy, his relish for the funereal, his poetics of sickness and madness, his love of codes and code breaking, the attraction and dread of marriage. Poe celebrated the artificial and the otherworldly but could also pay exhilarating tribute to natural beauty. At times he delighted in reverie, dreams, the poetry of hypnogogic consciousness. At other times logic, mathematics, deduction, analysis, and encryption dominated his attention. He could be both idealistic and sarcastic, skeptical, by turns. His tone and pose of Byronic hauteur helped make him far more popular than the democratic Walt Whitman. He could be a searing critic of male writers and a rapt fan of popular female poets. With all his contradictions and inconsistencies, Poe also mirrors the contradictions and inconsistencies of his time and culture, at once the outsider and insider.

It's notable that both Emerson and Poe were born in Boston in the first decade of the nineteenth century. Each was influenced by German Romanticism and the work of Samuel Taylor Coleridge, but their careers took very different tacks. Emerson, from an old New England family, a graduate of Harvard, erstwhile Unitarian minister, followed the Wordsworthian side of Coleridge's imagination, saluting nature, confident, naturally pious. From the beginning Poe was drawn to the Byronic and Gothic brands of Romanticism, displaying a taste for the horrific and otherworldly. In the terrors of nature and history, he would most often find his sublime. Yet I will suggest that Emerson and Poe had something in common, especially when we consider Poe's *Eureka, A Prose Poem: Or the Physical and Metaphysical Universe.*

An orphan, child of itinerant actors, never adopted by his foster parents, Poe had to crash the genteel literary circles of Philadelphia, New York, and Boston, without money, family name, or a Harvard education. He had to compete with Emerson, Henry Wadsworth Longfellow, James Russell Lowell, Nathaniel Hawthorne, Evert Duyckinck, and Washington Irving. Bipolar, possibly at times schizophrenic, sometimes crippled by binge drinking and starvation, he was forced to support himself, his aunt, his young wife, by writing abrasive reviews that earned him the label of "Tomahawk man" and the enmity of other writers.

Poe's weapon against a literary society in which he was not always welcomed was his notoriety. The readers of his time delighted in his hoaxes and fantasies, his code breaking, his romances and tales of terror and detection, his scathing reviews and unforgettable poems. "The Gold-Bug" made him nationally famous in 1843, and "The Raven" made him even more a celebrity two years later. Eric Carlson suggests that "The Raven" is "the best-known poem in the Western hemisphere." Through translations by Baudelaire and others, Poe became popular in Europe. Ultimately, no American writer except Mark Twain would win such a global audience.

Richard Wilbur wrote several important essays on Poe and the Gnostic imagination. William Carlos Williams, in *In the American Grain,* celebrated Poe as more authentic and original than the New England writers influenced by Puritanism. D. H. Lawrence, in *Studies in Classic Ameri-*

can Literature, viewed Poe through the lens of Lawrence's own passions and apocalyptic obsessions. I have learned from them and many more, including Marie Bonaparte's extensive Freudian investigation of Poe and his work. In fact, Freud himself was a fan of Poe's writing.

Poe lived at the edge and sometimes over the edge. His parents were actors, and he himself was very much the actor, the "literary *histrio,*" taking on multiple roles throughout his career. Drinking played a role in Poe's story, from his time at the University of Virginia, and possibly to his death in Baltimore, but he could go for extended periods drinking nothing but water. At times he seemed to have a death wish and sabotaged some of his best opportunities. Sometimes Poe and his family were near starvation, living on bread and molasses for weeks.

Much has been made of Poe's marriage to his thirteen-year-old first cousin Virginia Clemm. It is important to explore the unusual aspects of Poe's life, including his flirtations with several married women and the poet Helen Whitman, and the way he was attracted and repelled by marriage. Some previous students of Poe biography have overlooked the depth of guilt and the role guilt about women played in Poe's poems and stories.

No biography of Poe would be complete without considering the controversy about his reputation in his native country. Immediately after his death, in 1849, his supposed executor, Rev. Rufus Griswold, blackened Poe's reputation in an obituary and then a longer memoir, portraying his late "friend" as a liar, drunkard, womanizer, ingrate, and amoral plagiarist. Griswold even altered Poe's letters to enhance his character assassination. Only years later would scholars uncover Griswold's forgeries. And in the decades since, many other American critics and literary authorities have cast a cold eye on Poe's character and his writing. Henry James is reported to have observed that a preference for Poe's writing was "the mark of a decidedly primitive stage of reflection." But James's chilling story "The Turn of the Screw" owes much to Poe's development of the tale of psychological horror. Emerson referred to Poe as "the jingle man," and Poe returned the compliment by calling the Transcendentalists "the Frog Pondians."

Yet William Butler Yeats saluted Poe as "always and for all lands a great lyric poet." Alfred Tennyson, Heinrich Heine, Thomas Hardy, H. G. Wells, Joseph Conrad, James Joyce, Friedrich Nietzsche, and Franz Kafka were admirers. Charles Baudelaire, Stéphan Mallarmé, and the French Symbolists considered Poe one of the seminal writers of the century. Paul Valéry would compare Poe to Leonardo da Vinci. Poe's reputation in Latin America is at least equal to that of William Faulkner.

It requires some nerve to think of taking on a subject exhaustively studied by so many prominent biographers, scholars, and critics. My excuse is that I will try to make some unexpected links between Poe's life and his work.

Strangely enough, many of Poe's ideas about cosmology and time in *Eureka* seem to resonate with modern theories of physics, astronomy, as well as semiotics and the psychology of consciousness. Poe is a modern, and postmodern, writer in a sense that Hawthorne, for example, is not. The critic Mark Neimeyer refers to Poe as "alive and well in the ether of postmodern meta-culture." I want to focus on some aspects of Poe's work that have been less examined: his poetry of the natural world, his study of aesthetics through landscape gardening, his enduring guilt about women, his sustained obsession about marriage, and his covert speculations and hints about his mother's ethnicity.

There is no explanation for genius. But it's still fascinating to investigate the life of the poet who wrote "Sonnet—To Science," and other canonical poems around the age of twenty, with few to encourage him. At the age of eighteen, Poe published his first book of poems and enlisted in the army. No other American poet, regardless of background and education, produced work of such quality at such an early age.

It is said heavy drinkers tend to feel sorry for themselves and yearn for a nurse and to be nursed. Alcohol is their mother's milk and the bottle the surrogate mother. But Poe was more addicted to writing than he was to alcohol. His twin demons were ink and drink.

Poe is our finest poet of first love, adolescent love, ideal love. He never outgrew the devastating sorrow of the first discovery of love and the way the young are sick with love. "Annabel Lee," one of his last poems, is a perfect expression of the solemnity of juvenile romance. Even those who smile at the poem never forget it.

There have been many biographies of Poe since John H. Ingram's landmark *Edgar Allan Poe: His Life, Letters, and Opinions* of 1880, but the classic ones, *Israfel* by Hervey Allen and *Edgar A. Poe* by Arthur Hobson Quinn, are, respectively, ninety-five and eighty years old. Mary Phillips's *Edgar Allan Poe the Man*, from 1926, is one of the longest, in company with

Marie Bonaparte's Freudian study. Though flawed and generally ignored, Phillips's work contains insights no other biographer can claim. Kenneth Silverman's *Edgar A. Poe* of 1992 is an impressive scholarly update of the work of his predecessors, but it is now over thirty years old. Jeffrey Meyers's *Edgar Allan Poe: His Life and Legacy,* also from 1992, includes an extraordinary account of Poe's influence on world literature. James M. Hutchisson's *Poe* is a valuable addition to more recent scholarship. *The Reason for the Darkness of the Night* by John Tresch, of 2021, concentrates on the importance of science in Poe's work. *A Mystery of Mysteries: The Death and Life of Edgar Allan Poe* by Mark Dawidziak, 2023, focuses on the abiding questions about Poe's death. Daniel Hoffman's *Poe Poe Poe Poe Poe Poe Poe,* from 1972, is a lively reading of Poe's work, but it is now a half-century young. In recent years there have been a number of excellent specialized studies of aspects of Poe's life and work, such as Jerome McGraw's *The Poet Edgar Poe,* from 2014. Benjamin Fisher's *Poe in His Own Time,* from 2010, gathers many important documents and excerpts from those who actually knew Poe. One of the most memorable works of Poe scholarship is *The Poe Log,* compiled by Dwight Thomas and David K. Jackson and published in 1987. John Carl Miller's *Building Poe Biography,* from 1977, is essential for any Poe scholar. The recent *Oxford Handbook of Edgar Allan Poe,* edited by J. Gerald Kennedy and Scott Peeples, is a treasury of current theoretical thought about Poe and his writing.

In recent years there has been a renaissance of Poe criticism, addressing a number of contemporary concerns such as the influence of slavery on Poe's writing, the culture of reprinting in antebellum America before there were international copyright laws, the effect of imperialist and expansionist policies on Poe's thought, Poe's implicit critique of capitalist economics and politics, and the ways Poe's writing can be understood through the approach of queer theory. Because these and other crucial studies are so numerous, I can list only a few as representative examples.

In 1992, in *Playing in the Dark,* Toni Morrison radically changed the discussion of antebellum American literature, arguing that slavery and the presence of African Americans were not marginal to American culture and literature but central: "Nothing highlighted freedom—if it did not in fact create it—like slavery." Morrison argued that even where American texts are not obviously about the African presence, they still reflect the paradox of bondage in a democratic society. She wrote, "No early American writer is more important to the concept of American Africanism than Poe."

Meredith L. McGill, in *American Literature and the Culture of Reprinting* (2003), examines the effect on American writing in the antebellum period of the practice of reprinting anything published in newspapers and in books from Britain. For example, in 1843 Poe's "The Gold-Bug" was reprinted in about three hundred newspapers, yielding the author no fees or royalties. Only when he was taken up by the Young America editors and critics in New York was Poe able to exert some control over the circulation of his writing.

Terence Whalen, in *Edgar Allan Poe and the Masses* (1999), investigates the impact of the marketplace in a capitalist culture on Poe's critical writing and his poems and stories. Far from only practicing "art for art's sake," Poe had to produce his art in a society dominated by the profit motive. Fearing to affront either northern liberals or southern slave-owning readers, Poe sought "literary neutrality." Though exhibiting "average racism" of his time in his work, Poe was far from being an apologist for the antebellum ruling elite.

In 2001 J. Gerald Kennedy and Liliane Weissberg published a collection of essays about Poe titled *Romancing the Shadow: Poe and Race*. In the introduction the authors address the issue of Poe's writing and the presence of slavery, both implicit and explicit. Several authors examine the subject of "amalgamation," or the mixing of the races. Others consider the attitude toward Blackness and whiteness in *The Narrative of Arthur Gordon Pym*, "The Murders in the Rue Morgue," and "The Gold-Bug," including scholars such as Betsy Erkkila, John Carlos Rowe, Colin (Joan) Dayan, Elise Lemire, and Leland S. Person.

David Greven, in *Gender Protest and Same-Sex Desire in Antebellum American Literature* (2014), explores Poe's work from the perspective of gender studies and queer theory. His deepest reading is of *Pym* and the figure of Dirk Peters as "male mother," and instances of gender ambiguity. Greven suggests that Ligeia in the story of that name is a phallic figure and also "nonwhite." One of Greven's claims is that Poe sees traditional marriage as "a prisonhouse of gender, oppression emanating from both restrictive gender roles *and* gender indeterminacy." Needless to say, I have learned from these and many other important students of Poe.

Though he notoriously railed against didacticism in literature, Poe is surprisingly one of the most deeply moral writers in our canon. More than any of his contemporaries, except for Melville, Poe was willing to probe the extremes and darker undersides of the human spirit as well as dire conditions of sickness and madness. Long before the Existentialists, Poe dramatized the alienation and guilt of the human consciousness and condition. And he never forgot that he was alive in a body that would soon die. Poe had courage to confront his demons and transmute them into living art.

1

ELIZA

EDGAR ALLAN POE CLAIMED DISTINGUISHED ANCESTORS ON both sides of his family. The Poes were Scotch-Irish and most likely came from Fenwick in Ayrshire, Scotland. In 1839 Poe would surprisingly assert that the Poes were originally from Germany. According to the *New Dictionary of American Family Names,* Poe means "dweller at the sign of the peacock; a nickname given to a proud or gaudily dressed man." Along with many other Protestants, the Poes removed to Northern Ireland. The first Poe we can identify by name is Edgar's great-great-grandfather David Poe, who died in August 1742. He and his wife, Sarah, produced three heirs: Alexander, John, and Anna. It was Alexander Poe who first immigrated to North America in 1730, settling in Lancaster County, Pennsylvania, near future Gettysburg. He was followed by his brother, John, who brought his wife, Jane McBride, and sons David Poe and George Poe to the British colonies around 1748. John and his family first lived in Delaware, then moved to Pennsylvania. Altogether, John and Jane would have ten children, and it was their son David ([1742?]–1816) who would become the grandfather of Edgar Allan Poe. David married Elizabeth Cairnes (1756–1835), from a Scotch-Irish family in Lancaster County, Pennsylvania.

Sometime before the American Revolution, David and Elizabeth would settle in Baltimore, where David made furniture and both spinning wheels and wagon wheels. He also took part in the rebellion against the Crown, helping to drive Loyalists out of Baltimore. Probably because of his experience in business, David Poe served as a purchasing agent for the Continental Army in 1778, with the title of "Assistant Deputy Quartermaster."

He became friends with both Washington and Lafayette. On February 18, 1780, David Poe wrote to Governor Thomas Sim Lee, "I bought grain and hay. . . . I have purchased what is done with my own money." In recognition of his services, providing supplies at his own expense, he was referred to as "General Poe." During the war Lafayette would write, "David Poe out of his own limited means supplied me with $500. to aid in clothing my troops, and his wife with her own hands cut out 500 pairs of pantaloons and superintended making them for my men." It is also said that David Poe provided two brass cannons for the siege of Yorktown in October 1781.

After the Revolution, David Poe appears to have prospered. According to the census of 1790, he owned enslaved Africans and employed nine "free white males" and "two free white females." He owned a store and in 1807 served as "fish inspector" for the city of Baltimore. It is reported that in 1814, near the age of seventy-two, he fought the British again at the Battle of North Point.

David and Elizabeth Poe would have seven children. The oldest son, David Jr., born July 18, 1784, would become the father of Edgar. The daughter Maria (1790–1871) would marry William Clemm Jr. and be both aunt and mother-in-law to Edgar. The daughter Elizabeth Poe would marry Henry Herring, who would have a troubled friendship with the poet. David Poe Sr. died October 17, 1816, but his wife, Elizabeth Cairnes Poe, would live until July 7, 1835.

On his mother's side, Poe's ancestry can be traced mostly through the history of the theater in Britain and America. Poe's great-grandfather was the actor William Smith of St. George's Parish, London, associated with Drury Lane Theatre. The records suggest that he was an accomplished actor. It is not known who Smith's wife was, though the biographer Mary Phillips believed she was Lord Montague's daughter. According to the church records of St. George's, Hanover Square, Regent Street, London, William Smith's daughter Elizabeth married the actor Henry Arnold, son of the playwright William Henry Arnold, who wrote comedies for the Drury Lane Theatre in the last decade of the eighteenth century.

Given all the composers, singers, and musicians in Edgar Allan Poe's background, it should not surprise us that he felt a special enthusiasm about music. On July 2, 1844, he would write to the poet James Russell Lowell: "I am profoundly excited by music, and by some poems. . . . Music is the perfection of the soul, or idea, of Poetry."

The records of St. George's Parish, London, show that Elizabeth Smith and Henry Arnold were married in 1784. Around 1787 a daughter, also named Elizabeth, was born to them. This Elizabeth, called Eliza, would become the mother of Edgar Allan Poe. It seems that Henry Arnold died soon after Eliza's birth, but Elizabeth Arnold had a successful career, performing throughout the early 1790s at the Covent Garden Theatre as an actress and singer, specializing in comedy.

In early 1796 Elizabeth Arnold and her daughter, Eliza, aged nine, followed a number of other actors to the United States. On the voyage across the Atlantic, Elizabeth met a pianist named Charles Tubbs, whom she married after arriving in Boston. Soon both Mr. Tubbs and young Eliza joined Elizabeth on the stage, performing concerts, comic opera, comedies, and dramas.

In those days troupes traveled along the Eastern Seaboard, performing from Savannah to Boston. The young Eliza served her apprenticeship with her mother and other accomplished actors, becoming a notable singer and dancer as well as an actress in both comedy and dramatic roles. She made a specialty of playing boy roles such as "Little Pickle" in Isaac Bickerstaff's *The Spoiled Child.* It is said that by the age of fifteen, Eliza had played around seventy different roles.

Eliza's mother apparently died of yellow fever in 1798 in the Carolinas, as they were traveling between Charleston, South Carolina, and Richmond, Virginia. Now Eliza was left alone with her stepfather, Charles Tubbs, known to be ill-tempered. But through hard work and considerable talent, Eliza soon broke away from Tubbs and made her way independently as an actress, dancer, and singer, appearing at Philadelphia's prestigious Chestnut Street Theatre.

Over the course of her short career, Eliza would perform about three hundred different roles. In some weeks she would play as many as twenty different parts. Moving from tavern room to boardinghouse, she had to constantly learn new roles, new songs and dances. If she and her fellow actors were lucky they could remain at one theater for several weeks, before moving on to the next city.

It was in Philadelphia that Eliza met a young actor named Charles Hopkins, who was a hit as "Tony Lumpkin" in Oliver Goldsmith's *She Stoops to Conquer.* When she was fourteen, Eliza began to play "Ophelia" in *Hamlet,* a part she would perform often. At the age of fifteen, she married Charles Hopkins in Alexandria, Virginia. For three years they traveled and performed together. Eliza was small in person and very pretty, with a lively manner and fine figure. There is only one miniature likeness of her, but from it we get some idea of her attractive dark-brown hair, large eyes, prominent nose. Her son would later brag, gauchely, about his own "Hebrew" nose, and he would ascribe to Ligeia, his leading heroine, "the delicate outlines of the nose—and nowhere but in the graceful medallions of the Hebrews had I beheld a similar perfection." Poe appears to have believed that some of Eliza's ancestors were Jewish. After all, acting was one of the professions open to Jews in the eighteenth century.

On April 14, 1803, Eliza would act with Matthew Sully, brother of the painter Thomas Sully, in Norfolk, Virginia. Matthew Sully's son, Robert, would later become one of Edgar's closest friends. It is believed that the miniature portrait of Eliza was painted by Thomas Sully. Eliza was especially known for her rendition of the song "Nobody Coming to Marry Me." "Heavens, what a form!" one writer in the *Norfolk Herald* exclaimed of her figure and performance.

A reviewer for the *Alexandria Times and District of Columbia Daily Advertizer* observed in 1803: "Mrs. Hopkins's interesting figure, her *correct* performance, and the accuracy with which she always commits her part, together with her sweetly melodious voice when she charms us with a song, have deservedly raised her to that respectable rank which she indisputably holds in the public favor." Later reviews would be even more enthusiastic.

Charles Hopkins died in Washington, DC, in 1805. Meanwhile, Eliza and Charles had gotten to know David Poe Jr., son of General Poe of Baltimore. David Poe Jr. had been apprenticed to study law in the office of William Gwynn but preferred acting. He had formed a Thespian Club and read plays at General Poe's house. It is thought his infatuation with Eliza drew him irresistibly to acting. After Hopkins's death, David appeared opposite Eliza in various comedies and romances. He had striking good looks and a pleasing voice but suffered from stage fright and a hair-trigger temper. Yet he was competent enough to take on a number of leading roles, before drink impaired his acting. Quick to quarrel, he threatened journalists who criticized his performances. In the spring of 1806, Eliza and David Poe married. From now on Eliza would be billed as Mrs. Poe.

A notice in the *Boston Gazette* on March 21, 1808, gives us a window into the lives of David and Eliza Poe at this time: "If industry can claim from the public either favor or support, the talents of Mrs. Poe will not pass unrewarded.—She has supported and maintained a course of characters more numerous and arduous than can be paralleled on our boards during any one season. Often she has been obliged to perform three characters on the same evening, and she has always been perfect in the text." Besides her acting and singing, Eliza Poe was also a gifted dancer: "Sometimes she danced a Polish minuet,—the feminine counterpart to her husband's hornpipes, reels, and strathspeys."

Eliza consistently outshone David on the stage. She now played "Cordelia" in *King Lear* and "Juliet" in *Romeo and Juliet.* A son, William Henry Poe, was born in Boston on January 30, 1807. On April 18, 1808, David and Eliza performed in Schiller's tragedy *The Robbers* with their friends Mr. and Mrs. Luke Noble Usher. Another son, Edgar, was born January 19, 1809, during a fierce storm, with ice floating in Boston Harbor. Eliza had continued acting until ten days before Edgar's birth, and three weeks afterward, she was back on the boards.

It is said that David Poe Sr. disowned his son after he married Eliza Arnold Hopkins. However that may be, David and Eliza had visited the Poes in Baltimore from June to September 1807. The visit must have been a welcome break from their relentless touring. According to J. H. Whitty, Boston tax records of May 1809 list the personal property of David Poe, actor, assessed at three hundred dollars (about nine thousand dollars today). In the period after Edgar's birth, David began drinking even more, and his acting grew increasingly erratic. Once he fled to his family in Baltimore. When he returned to acting, he received consistently bad reviews, as Eliza won ever more accolades.

David and Eliza visited David's parents in Baltimore more than once as they traveled between Virginia and the cities in the North. Their older son, William Henry, was left with his grandparents, while young Edgar continued to travel on the theater circuit. It does not require a lot of imagination to see how busy Eliza was at this time, learning new roles, getting better and better at her craft, moving from one furnished room to another, traveling by boat or stagecoach or carriage over rough roads, enduring bad reviews as well as good notices and sometimes small audiences, taking care of an infant, trying to calm a handsome but undependable husband.

Maria Poe, David's sister, later Mrs. Maria Clemm, remembered Eliza from her visits with the Poe family in Baltimore: "She was a lovely little creature and highly talented. I loved her most devotedly." Early in their professional association, Eliza had been paired with David Poe in several dance numbers. Apparently, David was at least a competent hoofer, but Eliza was a brilliant dancer. The many demanding roles David Poe was assigned suggest he did have some competence as an actor. There is evidence that he was particularly effective at reciting poetry, and he performed best in verse drama. It is also thought he was suffering from consumption, the disease that would probably take the life of his wife.

Around October 1810, when Edgar was about twenty months old, David Poe Jr. disappeared. It has been said he died on October 19, 1810, in Norfolk, Virginia. His name is absent from the playbills of that time, just when Eliza was busier than ever. A contemporary wrote that David and Eliza "quarreled and parted." It's possible he took his own life. The mystery of David Poe's death would be echoed decades later in the questions surrounding his son's demise. But David Poe Jr. may have simply died of consumption. The failure of the Poes' marriage would haunt their son throughout his life, expressed in story after story.

About two months after David Poe vanished, on December 20, 1810, Eliza gave birth to a daughter she named Rosalie. She was abandoned and alone with two young children. There is a legend that as a child, Edgar played Cupid in *Cinderella* on the stage in Richmond. Benefit performances were staged for Mrs. Poe and her progeny. As soon as she could, Eliza resumed acting, desperate to support her small family, now appearing in Richmond, Norfolk, and Charleston, where audiences were familiar with her and loved her. "Mrs. Poe's name is a brilliant gem in the theatric crown. . . . No one has received more than she of the public applause," one Richmond reporter wrote. Though now twenty-four, she could still play juvenile roles such as "Little Pickle." For this her petite figure was an asset. Eliza appeared a number of times, as a bride wearing white, in the melodrama *Tekeli,* a name that would later appear in Poe's novel *The Narrative of Arthur Gordon Pym.*

There is a legend that an elderly Welsh woman, who helped look after Edgar and Rosalie while their mother was engaged elsewhere, gave the children bread soaked in gin or even laudanum, to hold in their mouths to keep them quiet. So, the unlikely story goes, as early as that, Poe acquired his disastrous affinity for alcohol.

Reviewers began to notice a change in Eliza's looks. She might still be described as “an enchanting Creature!” but there was something worn about her features, as though care had robbed her of her youthful freshness. On July 26, 1811, a reporter in the *Norfolk Herald* observed, “Left alone, the only support of herself and several small children—Friendless and unprotected, she no longer commands that admiration and attention she formerly did.”

It would soon be obvious that Mrs. Poe was suffering from more than overwork and grief. In the fall of 1811, she appeared less and less on the stage in Richmond. She made her last appearance on October 11, 1811, playing “Countess Wintersen” in Kotzebue’s *The Stranger.* Eliza had to be replaced in one of her primary roles as “Rosina” in the comic opera of that name. Biographers have noted that Poe would also make his last appearance in Richmond. By November 1811 Eliza could no longer get out of bed. An appeal in the Richmond paper asked citizens to come to the aid of the well-known actress and her children. The theater manager sent a letter to her parents-in-law in Baltimore, but they offered no help.

A contemporary, Samuel Mordecai, wrote to his sister at this time: “A singular fashion prevails here this season—it is—charity—Mrs. Poe, who you know is a very handsome woman, happens to be very sick, and (having quarreled and parted with her husband) is destitute. The most fashionable place of resort, now is—her chamber—and the skill of cooks and nurses is exerted to procure her delicacies.”

On November 29, 1811, the *Richmond Enquirer* published this notice: “TO THE HUMANE HEART, On this night, *Mrs. Poe,* lingering on the bed of disease and surrounded by her children, asks your *assistance;* and *asks it perhaps for the last time.*”

In the final weeks of her life, Eliza and her two younger children occupied a second-story room in a house or tavern near the theater, called the Actors’ Boarding House, but the exact location is in dispute. Features in the newspaper describing her plight brought aid from several citizens of Richmond. It is reported that Mr. and Mrs. Luke Noble Usher helped look after the children. As death approached, Eliza gave Edgar a miniature portrait of herself and a sketch she’d made of Boston Harbor a year earlier, called “Morning 1808.” On the back of the picture, she had written: “For my little son Edgar, who should ever love Boston, the place of his birth, and where his mother found her *best,* and *most sympathetic* friends.” It is said

Poe would wear the miniature likeness of Eliza in a locket for the rest of his life. Eliza would also leave Edgar a lock of her hair and a packet of letters that Maria Clemm would later claim contained "dark family troubles that had worried Eddie." After Poe's death, Maria would burn the letters, as he had instructed.

The announcement of Eliza's death came on December 10, 1811—Tuesday: "Died on last Sunday morning [December 8], Mrs. Poe, one of the Actresses of the Company playing on the Richmond *Boards.*—By the death of this Lady the Stage has been deprived of one of its chief ornaments." Later, biographers would point out that Edgar Allan Poe also died on a Sunday.

It's not certain what Eliza died of. But given the lingering nature of her illness, it seems she was a victim of tuberculosis, "the white plague" of the nineteenth century that took the lives of so many eminent people. Called consumption, the disease had no known cure. At the time of Eliza's death, it was reported that she died of "acute pneumonia." She was buried in a grave without a marker in the Old St. Johns burial ground.

Because Eliza and her husband had quarreled and separated and Rosalie may have been born after David Jr.'s disappearance, gossip began to question Rosalie's paternity. As a woman of the theater, Eliza might have been suspect in any case. After the Mackenzies adopted little Rosalie, it was even hinted that Mr. Mackenzie might be the actual father of the girl. These charges against his mother's virtue would haunt Edgar all his life.

After David Poe Jr. deserted his family and Eliza was dying of consumption, young Edgar may have reacted in two contradictory ways. Listening to his parents argue and fight, he received an impression that marriage was a horrible state. His beautiful mother was distressed, angry with her husband, who drank and failed in his acting. It would have seemed to young Edgar that marriage was a nightmare to be escaped, resolved only by the death of his gifted mother. But on the other hand, he acquired a need, a yearning, for the security and stability of the ideal of marriage. Having led an itinerant life with an actress mother, he longed for the safety of a home, with a woman who loved him and could take care of him in a tumultuous world. His deepest desire was for a mate/mother who would cherish him and whom he could cherish. It was the best refuge he could dream of and the highest ideal. For the rest of his days, Poe would search for that perfect marriage in his life and in his writing, even as he feared matrimony.

The legacy Poe received from his father included arresting good looks, a special gift for reciting poetry, and playing roles with gravitas. But he also inherited an irresistible tendency to drink, a short temper that would not let well enough alone, self-destructive anger, and a mysterious sense of doom.

From Eliza he seems to have inherited an ability to work with extraordinary focus and intensity, when he was motivated and sober. No one who knew Poe ever doubted his genius, his blaze of originality. From his mother he apparently acquired a superb memory. He could recite poem after poem and page after page of prose. In her short career, Eliza had memorized around three hundred different roles and had played as many as twenty roles in one week and three in one day. Eliza passed on to Edgar some of her energy and discipline, her ability to concentrate, when inspired, and her courage.

From both his actor parents, Poe inherited a love of language and wordplay, a taste for the dramatic and melodramatic, the sensational, the romantic, and the quest for ethereal beauty. What they did not leave him was the means for pursuing these passions, making his way in an unsympathetic world. For the rest of his life, Poe would be unusually dependent on the support and affection of sympathetic women.

In the room where she died, possibly in a tavern on Ninth and Grace Streets, little Edgar and one-year-old Rosalie watched their lovely mother waste away as admirers brought gifts of money, clothes, food, and medicine. Among the ladies who visited, bringing meals, were Mrs. John Allan and Mrs. William Mackenzie. No doubt they were moved by the sight of the two attractive children standing or playing near the bedside.

Actors were not considered suitable for polite society in many communities. The sensitive and perceptive boy may have already begun to understand that though grown-ups made a fuss over his looks and manners, he was an outsider to the quality society that lived in brick houses with lawns in the better parts of town. He belonged to a community that entertained those who lived in houses with extensive gardens.

What happened to Edgar in that small room above the tavern would affect him and shape him and drive him in ways he would probably never entirely understand. He'd often seen his mother heavily made up for roles on the stage. He would always have a love of artifice and enhancement of the natural. The distinguished Poe critic J. Gerald Kennedy reminds us:

"Consumption . . . actually did enhance physical beauty at an intermediate stage by inducing a feverish glow." But now Eliza's face was worn, emaciated. The woman he loved, the only woman he knew, the one who loved him, whom he had seen play so many different roles yet always become herself again, was now apparently leaving him for good.

Kennedy suggests that Eliza's death instilled "in Poe a chronic fear of abandonment and dread of consequent annihilation." The loss, which must have been confusing as well as terrifying, left him with a horror of the inscrutableness of existence, the ambiguity of signs, an obsession with "the failure of interpretation itself, the unknowability of ultimate things." From his poems and stories, it's clear Poe was obsessed with the death of beautiful women. Again, J. Gerald Kennedy: "For Poe, her story could never be written; it could only be rewritten, over and over . . . like the repetition of some hideous drama of revivification." Eliza abandoned him, as John Allan would later abandon him. Almost three, Poe was at the age when an intelligent child first becomes aware of the facts of death and separation.

When traumatic events happen to children, beyond their understanding, they often believe they must somehow be responsible. A child has been corrected so often and told they have done wrong and must be punished, they cannot be sure exactly what is right or wrong. If something frightening and terrible happens, they may assume it was their fault.

A three-year-old also knows that he depends on his mother for sustenance, for protection, for warmth, for love. It's unthinkable that a mother could desert him, leaving him alone among strangers. Yet his beautiful mother grew weak and withdrew, became a corpse even as he watched.

Poe would spend the rest of his life searching for a replacement for the mother, muse, and hoping that the dead could return, as Eliza always returned after playing many roles. Yet in his combined anger and guilt, he would kill off, symbolically, all replacements. In poem after poem and story after story, he would reenact the loss of Eliza, the muse-mother, the goddess who abandoned her son.

Repressing his fear and anger, Poe would more often than not etherealize his heroines as figures of superior intellect, angelic beauty. In the early poem "Introduction," he stated:

I could not love except where Death
Was mingling his with Beauty's breath—

Or Hymen, Time, and Destiny
Were stalking between her and me.

Poe wrote those lines in his early twenties, but they contain and illuminate his biography and much of his writing. In these early verses, he gives away a significant clue to his imagination and conflicted being. The connection between romance, marriage, and death is a key to much of Poe's art and to his personality. But it is the guilt buried underneath that knowledge that is the most important clue to understanding his work. The never-ending mourning for the "lost Lenore," "Ulalume," "Eleonora," and others is a mask for repressed guilt for wanting to kill them as well as grieving for them. When we see that, we have a way to better comprehend the power of Poe's work and its odd effect upon so many readers. Tennyson would compare Poe to the Latin poet Catullus, whose most famous words are *odi et amo,* "I hate and I love."

Modern psychiatrists have shown that trauma or guilt suffered in childhood can leave devastating long-term effects on a person. "Some scientists now believe that extreme feelings of guilt in children . . . can be a strong warning sign for mental disorders such as depression, anxiety, obsessive compulsive disorder and bipolar disorder later in life," wrote Jenny Chen in the *Atlantic.* Researchers at Washington University have even found that children who experience excessive guilt have physical damage to the part of the brain "connected to controls for several different brain disorders."

Poe's art works on us in ways we don't quite understand and may be reluctant to understand. Its ethereality conceals cruelty and sadomasochistic emotions we are either unaware of or resist recognizing. Poe's gift for enacting these unconscious dramas makes him unique in American literature of his time.

In the Greek story, Oedipus kills his father without knowing it is his father and marries his mother. In Poe's stories the narrator kills or witnesses the death of the mother-muse-lover, then searches for her throughout eternity, imagining she must return. The raven, in the poem of that name, for example, is the narrator's conscience reminding him that he has loved and "killed," or betrayed, Lenore. Only near the end of his life did Poe write "Annabel Lee," in which the heroine is not harmed by the narrator. By then he had found some obscure absolution, which we will discuss later.

There are many other facets to Poe's genius, but this is an essential one, imprinted deep in his memory in that tavern room, as Eliza, who'd acted so many roles, played her last role on the stage of her son's imagination and would go on playing it in different costumes and settings for the rest of his life.

On December 1, 1835, Poe wrote to Judge Beverley Tucker: "In speaking of my mother you have touched a string to which my heart fully responds. To have known her is to be an object of great interest in my eyes. . . . I have many occasional dealings with Adversity—but the want of parental affection has been the heaviest of my trials."

Rumors that questioned Eliza's character provoked him to fury and then depression. In tribute to Eliza, he once wrote the words that would be placed on her belated monument in St. John's churchyard: "The writer of this article is himself the son of an actress—has invariably made it his boast—and no earl was ever prouder of his earldom than he of his descent from a woman who, although well born, hesitated not to consecrate to the drama her brief career of genius and of beauty."

2

FANNY ALLAN

RICHMOND, AT THE FALL LINE, HEAD OF NAVIGATION ON THE James River, where the hill country meets the coastal plain, had been settled in 1637 and became an important port of entry and shipping in the colonial era. The capital of the new state of Virginia was moved from Williamsburg to Richmond in 1779. The city served as a market, financial, and political center and place of gathering for planters, politicians, and merchants, with hotels, taverns, churches, schools, and theaters. The social life was dominated by the planter gentry, confident and at ease with their privileges and slave-owning wealth. Following the model of John Marshall, the region was "strongly anti-democratic and anti-reform." Richmond was also a major slave market for the Deep South. By 1834 the population of Richmond would include about seventeen thousand residents, with annual commerce totaling around six million dollars (about $180 million today) in tobacco, coal, iron, and other products.

It is not known whether Eliza understood, in her final days, that her two younger children, Edgar and Rosalie, would be taken into the homes of two prominent Richmond families. The older son, William Henry, was already with his grandparents in Baltimore. Jane Scott Mackenzie and Frances "Fanny" Valentine Allan had visited the actress on her deathbed and brought gifts and meals for Eliza and her children. After the mother's death, Rosalie was taken home with Mrs. Mackenzie, and Edgar was brought to the house of John and Fanny Allan, who were childless. Rosalie would be adopted by the Mackenzies, but Edgar would never be legally adopted by the Allans. The local flour mill magnate Joseph Gallego gave the

FIG. 10. Rosalie Poe (1810–74). Poe's sister, Rosalie, was adopted by the Mackenzie family of Richmond and spent much of her early life teaching handwriting in a private school. After the Civil War, she lived in poverty and died in a charity house in Washington, DC. Her only source of income had been selling pictures of her famous brother. (Courtesy of the Edgar Allan Poe Museum, Richmond, Virginia)

FIG. 11. John Allan (1779–1834). Born in Scotland, John Allan made a career as a merchant in Richmond and became a leading citizen. He never adopted the young Poe, and as Edgar grew older, they often quarreled. His treatment of Poe likely affected much of the writer's later behavior. (Courtesy of the Edgar Allan Poe Museum, Richmond, Virginia)

Mackenzies two thousand dollars (sixty thousand dollars today) to raise and educate Rosalie (fig. 10). That Poe would never be more than a foster child of the Allans would have a profound impact on his youth and later life.

When Edgar entered his household, John Allan (1779–1834) was a thirty-two-year-old merchant called "Jack" or "Jock" (fig. 11). Born in Irvine, Scotland, he'd joined his prosperous uncle, William Galt, in Richmond in his teens. Lean and energetic, strict in business, John had created his own firm at the age of twenty-one, with Charles Ellis as his partner. They had prospered with a diverse enterprise, manufacturing and repairing harness, plow points, ox yokes. They sold building materials such as plaster of paris and a wide assortment of tools. Their merchandise included things for sewing, cloth, clothes, books, mirrors, pens, makeup, medicine, and tombstones.

Allan and Ellis bought and shipped barrels of tobacco and flour, and they imported Havana cigars. Their business was both regional and national and also international. Allan and his partner kept meticulous records, so we have a wealth of information about their business. John Allan, though a hard-driven businessman, was also known for some charitable work. It was reported that he never turned away anyone in need from his door. It's possible that when Fanny Allan brought Edgar to their house, John Allan assumed it was a temporary arrangement. The Allans would take in the attractive little orphan until he could be placed with his grandparents in Baltimore. Or it's possible Allan did intend to adopt the almost three-year-old Edgar but then changed his mind. Later Allan wrote to the Poes in Baltimore promising to give Edgar a liberal education. Whatever the understanding, it did not lead to legal adoption. Allan may have taken in the boy simply because his wife urged him to do so. Without a child of her own, Fanny needed someone to care for.

John Allan had great respect for education. He'd been brought up in the commercial world by his uncle William Galt, with limited opportunities for liberal studies. But he'd learned French and read books when he had the time. The purpose of an education was to help one advance in the world. He'd devoted his life to duty, self-control, strength, and perseverance. There is some evidence that Allan would have liked to have been a writer.

In spite of his modest beginnings and lack of formal education, John Allan could associate himself with, and socialize with, the Richmond gentry, who owned great estates on the James River, with many enslaved Africans, columned mansions, stables of thoroughbreds, men who boasted university educations, and wealth from tobacco farming. John Allan enjoyed the company of the upper classes, and he had an eye for the Virginia ladies. He would father at least three illegitimate children.

Susan Archer Weiss would later report that John Allan had first proposed to Miss Anne Moore Valentine, but when she refused him, he turned his attentions to Anne's sister, Frances. We know from her portraits that Fanny Valentine Allan was a particularly beautiful woman. She was twenty-six years old when she brought Edgar into the childless Allan home. She had a slight build and was considered "girlish." Though she was efficient at looking after the housekeeping and household economy, she was given to spells of weakness and sickness. Some years of her childhood had been spent in an orphanage, and she may have had a special sympathy for orphans. But Fanny belonged to the plantation upper echelon of eastern Virginia, and in marrying her, John Allan had raised himself above his merchant status in the eyes of Richmond society. As she grew older, Fanny's health declined. From her preserved letters, it would seem she was not highly educated.

Also belonging to the Allan household was Fanny's sister, Anne Valentine, called "Miss Valentine." "Miss V." was full-figured, known to be cheerful, and she became very fond of Edgar. Fanny, who would be the second important woman in Edgar's life who would also die later of consumption, could be playful and flirtatious and sickly by turns. Some of her relatives and friends suspected that her illnesses were imaginary or at least exaggerated. She may have already been suffering from the tuberculosis that would eventually take her life.

The Allan house was a decided change from the roving world of the theater. For almost three years, Edgar had experienced travel by stagecoach, carriage, or ship, from one town to another. No doubt he'd been present at rehearsals and watched and listened as his mother and others repeated lines, hurriedly preparing one role after another, changing costumes and makeup. He'd been exposed to the gossip, antics, wit, and hyperbole of the theater. In comparison, the Allan house would have seemed ruled by arbitrary strictness. While the Allans were kind to him, especially Fanny, he had to learn rigid new standards of behavior. Allan could be handy with a switch or cane if Edgar defied him.

John and Fanny Allan appeared to raise Edgar as a gentleman in the Richmond tradition. It was what they'd promised General Poe. Though Edgar carried the stigma of being the child of strolling players, they would rear him to enter society. On December 11, 1811, he was baptized by the Rev. John Buchanan at the home of John and Mary Dixon Richard.

According to Mary Phillips, it was known in Richmond that Fanny liked to exhibit her gifted foster ward. She "gave a large dinner-party to show her friends the various accomplishments of her little son—actually standing him on the cleared table to sing and recite for her guests." One of young Edgar's set pieces was a recitation from "Lay of the Last Minstrel." On these occasions, it was recalled, little Edgar wore "a purple jacket, velvet cape, yellow linen trousers, red silk hose and velvet cap." At the Virginia Sulphur Springs resort in the mountains where the Allans spent part of their summers to escape the Richmond heat, Edgar was remembered as "a lovely little fellow with dark curls, brilliant eyes, and dressed like a young prince." He was given several pets, including a parrot that could recite the alphabet in French and a dog called "Tib."

Edgar probably saw a good bit of his sister Rosalie. From time to time the Poes in Baltimore wrote to ask after Edgar's welfare. And Edgar knew that his older brother, William Henry, lived there with his grandparents. Edgar first studied with a neighbor named Mrs. Clotilda Fisher, then later attended classes taught by William Ewing.

Edgar addressed John and Fanny Allan as "Pa" and "Ma." At the ages of three, four, five, and six, he made the adjustment to living in a very different family and community from what he had known before. To all outward signs, he was part of the family. His name had been inscribed in the Allan family Bible. Later he would mention that he once owned roller skates.

In his first years with Fanny and John Allan, Poe may have felt some of the security he so badly needed. His beautiful foster mother adored him, when she was well and not distracted by ill health. The Allan marriage seemed happy and stable. But as Edgar grew older, he must have realized not only that he had not been adopted, given a name and status in the family and society of Richmond, but that his foster parents were unhappy with each other. Fanny had not produced an heir for John Allan, so hungry for position and legacy. Mr. Allan sought comfort with other women in Richmond. Poe must have been forced to recognize that he lived in a foster family with a troubled marriage. The experience helped make him both skeptical of marriage and determined to find, later, his own ideal in marriage, if possible.

The Poes in Baltimore had not forgotten their young relatives in Richmond. On February 8, 1813, Edgar's aunt Eliza Poe wrote to Fanny Allan:

> 'Tis the Aunt of Edgar that addresses Mrs. Allan for the second time, impressed with the idea that A letter if received could not remain unacknowledged so long as from the month of July; she is induced to write again in order to inquire in her family's as well as in her own name after the health of the Child of her Brother, as well as that of his adopted Parents. I cannot suppose my dear Mrs. Allan that A heart possessed of such original humanity as your's must without doubt be, could so long keep in suspence [*sic*], the anxious inquiries made through the medium of my letter. . . . I fear I have too long intruded on your patience, will you if so have the goodness to forgive me.

From this letter it would appear that Fanny Allan had not answered requests from the Poe family about Edgar's welfare. The tone suggests the Poes viewed the Allans as of a higher social class than the Poes. Certainly, the Allans were wealthier than General Poe, who in old age had fallen on hard times and was never able to recover the dollars he'd spent for the American cause in the Revolution. At least one biographer has speculated that Fanny didn't answer letters from the Poes in Baltimore because she feared they might claim her foster son.

There are many legends about Poe's early years in Richmond. One is that he was first sent to the school of a Scottish widow dedicated to the cultivation of her garden as well as young children's minds. If a pupil invaded her garden, he was forced to wear a vegetable all day as a badge of shame. When Edgar was caught trespassing, he was made to wear an onion. To call attention to his shame, he kept the onion on his person until he returned to the Allan home. Furious that his foster son had been thus humbled, John Allan strode to the school and dressed down the teacher in warm Scottish invective. Another typical anecdote about the young Poe has him reading the newspaper to admiring adults in Staunton while on a trip to a summer resort in the mountains.

In these early years with the Allans, it is reported that Poe was frequently taken to visit his mother's grave by a nurse named Judith, who regaled him with ghost stories. There is also a tradition that he was entertained by servants in the kitchen with chilling tales and superstitions. It is possible that some of Poe's penchant for terror narratives was inspired by African and African American folklore. Poe's boyhood friend John Hamilton Mackenzie would later say that Edgar's persistent fear was of "an ice-cold hand laid upon his face in a pitch-dark room when alone at night."

Those who knew Poe as a child in Richmond remembered that he was always attracted and attractive to the opposite sex. Mary I. Dixon, in a letter of September 11, 1872, would recall: "In the nursery we played at marrying him to my little sister whom we called his 'sweetheart.'" Mary's sister was Catherine Elizabeth Poitiaux, who would figure in Poe lore as his first girlfriend. We are told that from his childhood until the end of his life, "Poe was in love with being in love." The fascination with marriage began early.

Is it possible that Edgar's experience of wrenching change, the loss of his mother at an early age, adaptation to the Allans' strange household, made him seek both the sweet escape of romance and the stability of ideal marriage? Through playacting marriage with a neighbor and later with his cousin Virginia, whom he called "little wifey," was he searching for abiding affection, a future of commitment, elusive if not unobtainable? In a world where anything could be suddenly taken away, did marriage appear to be the most likely safeguard against deprivation? These are questions we can't answer at this distance, only entertain, based on recorded witness and observation.

One anecdote of Poe's early years has him appearing as a ghost to frighten guests at a whist party where Gen. Winfield Scott was present. Another describes him pulling chairs away from friends about to sit down. When he tried the trick on a portly matron, he was whipped by Allan. Biographers and critics have wondered where Poe acquired his intimate knowledge of ships and sailing. One suggestion is that he accompanied Allan on board the ships arriving and departing at Richmond, as the merchant inspected the loading and unloading of cargoes.

In 1815, when Edgar was six, John Allan decided to expand his business to London. His partner, Charles Ellis, would look after things in Richmond, while Allan opened an office and warehouse in the British capital. The War of 1812 was over, and it seemed time to take advantage of even greater commercial opportunities. Fanny was reluctant to make the journey, fearing a crossing of the Atlantic, but John insisted that a visit of three or four years in London would be exciting and probably good for her health.

Allan sold most of their household goods in Richmond: furniture, chickens, pork, and even a telescope. About the four- or five-week voyage, Fanny remained anxious. Her health was uncertain in any case, and the prospect of storms and seasickness did not reassure her. However, Edgar did not seem disturbed by the prospect of uprooting and sea travel. John Allan wrote, "Ned cared but little about it, poor fellow."

The crossing of the Atlantic to Liverpool on the ship *Lothair* would take thirty-four days. The Allans had to bring some of their own provisions for the journey. All except John became seasick, but Edgar soon recovered and asked "Pa" to send his love to Mrs. Mackenzie and Rosalie in a letter. He also asked Allan to say, "I was not afraid coming across the Sea."

The stay in Britain would be the third major change in Poe's life by the age of six. First, he had lost his father and then his mother. Then he had to adjust to living in the Allan household. Now, after a long and uncomfortable sea voyage, he would visit Edinburgh, Glasgow, and Irvine, Scotland, where John Allan was born. For a short while, Edgar attended school there but begged to be taken on to London. Six weeks later they would move south, to 47 Southampton Row, Russell Square, London.

In the British capital, the Allans lived in style, with a housekeeper, carriage, fine wines and liquors. John bought expensive clothes. When John mentioned Edgar in a letter of October 30, 1815, he described him as "reading a little Story Book."

At first John Allan was daunted by the different manner of conducting business in London. But he had enormous drive and persistence and soon learned the advantages of bulk buying and arranging loans for large transactions. Later the family moved nearby, to 39 Southampton Row, and acquired more expensive furniture.

For his first three years in London, Edgar boarded with the "Misses Dubourg," who kept a school on Sloan Street in Chelsea. Their records show that with the Dubourgs, Edgar, now called Edgar Allan, was given a "separate bed" and a spelling book, geography, history of England, and a prayer book as well as a seat in the nearby church. The Dubourgs reported to Allan, "Your Son I am glad to say is well & happy."

Later Edgar was transferred to the Manor House School, a boarding school at Stoke Newington, then about four miles outside London, presided over by Rev. John Bransby. At Bransby's school he studied Latin, along with other basic subjects. The curriculum even included dancing lessons. It was reported that Edgar did well in his studies, reading Latin "pretty sharply." But the minister believed Allan spoiled Edgar by giving him too much pocket money. Much later, in the story "William Wilson," Edgar would describe the Bransby school in detail. But it appears he was not especially happy there. Years later Poe would tell his close friend F. W. Thomas that "his schooldays in London were sad, lonely and unhappy."

One reason Edgar may have been unhappy at the Manor House School was his lack of pedigree. J. Gerald Kennedy describes his dilemma: "If he was not the poorest boy in the school he must have been among the lowest in social standing, immersed in a culture preoccupied with rank and status." Kennedy goes on to say that the story "William Wilson" suggests Poe's "own democratic sympathies." Poe may have been more American than he sometimes realized. Much later, in 1845, Poe would argue that "in Letters as in government we require a Declaration of Independence," echoing his new Young America associates.

Added to the on-again, off-again affection of his foster mother was the awakening uncertainty for Edgar about his status in the family. As he grew older, he continued to call Mr. and Mrs. Allan Pa and Ma, but gradually he would become aware of his somewhat ambiguous position. In a sense he was privileged, with fine clothes, books, good teachers, plenty to eat, and yet there must have been hints that he didn't quite belong. Later, when they quarreled, Allan took care to remind Edgar that he, John Allan, had enjoyed no such advantages in *his* youth.

Allan's business interests in London began to founder when the tobacco market collapsed. There was a general financial crisis, and loans were suddenly hard to obtain. Allan had to ask Ellis, his partner in Richmond, to send him more money. Allan found he owed about £35,000, or around $223,000 (over $7 million in 2023 dollars). The high life in London was over. Allan had no choice but to beg his creditors to be patient and to return to Richmond to start over.

Amid the crisis, Allan himself fell ill with "bilious pleurisy" and was unable to travel until the summer of 1820. While he was incapacitated, Fanny seemed to recover her own strength to nurse him and encourage him to regain his confidence. After visiting the Allan relatives in Scotland, the family finally sailed on June 16, 1820, on the ship *Martha* for New York. Crossing the Atlantic, Fanny was seasick again and so weak that when they landed in Manhattan on July 21, she sought the care of a doctor.

There is little doubt that the period abroad added to Poe's sense of displacement and uncertainty about where he belonged. And yet the travel gave him confidence later, that he had seen London and the larger world and studied classics in an expensive boarding school. At an important time in his youth, he had not been in the United States at all. He knew how to dress and comport himself like a gentleman. In almost everything Poe wrote, he would present himself as a man of elite culture, a citizen of the world, the world of letters. The pose would be, in part, an attempt to compensate for the uncertainty of his position in all those communities. On August 7, 1820, five days after the Allans reached Richmond, John Allan's partner, Charles Ellis, wrote to his wife, Margaret, "They are a little Englishised [*sic*] but it will soon wear off." At first the Allans lived in Charles Ellis's house, but in 1821 John would move his family to their own residence on Fifth Street, between Marshall and Clay Streets. The next year they would move again, to a house on Fourteenth Street and Tobacco Alley.

Given the fact that Poe was an orphan, with no money of his own and few important connections, people, including John Allan, expected him to be humble and grateful for their favor. They could not have been more wrong. Poe fashioned an image of himself as a member of the international fraternity of the elite, gifted and damned, much like Lord Byron.

Back in Richmond, Allan had trouble getting started again in his business. He had to rely on his wealthy uncle William Galt for loans or gifts. In 1820–22 Edgar attended an academy, where he was taught by Joseph H. Clarke and studied Greek, Latin, French, English, mathematics, and science. He may also have taken instruction in accounting and shorthand. It was assumed he would join the Allan and Ellis firm. According to one fellow student, Clarke was described as a "fiery, pedantic, pompous Irishman from Trinity College, Dublin."

Clarke later left a somewhat idealized memoir about young Poe: "He was remarkable for self-respect, without haughtiness. . . . His imaginative powers seemed to take precedence of all his other faculties, he gave proof of this, in some of his juvenile compositions addressed to his young female friends." Clarke would live to attend Poe's funeral in Baltimore, and it's likely his memories of his former pupil are colored by the poet's fame.

Clarke would also say that while in his school, Edgar wrote enough verse to fill a volume. It seems John Allan considered having it printed, but Clarke advised him that such a publication might turn the young man's head. Clarke added, "The verses, I remember, consisted chiefly of pieces addressed to the different little girls in Richmond." Those who knew Poe in school later recalled his ambition and efforts to excel but would add that he was competitive and "inclined to be imperious." He was also described as "English," though we don't know whether that referred to his accent or manner.

In 1823, at the age of fourteen, Edgar began to study with William Burke, who prepared young scholars to enroll at universities. Burke was known as an accomplished classicist. From all evidence, Edgar excelled at the study of languages, especially Latin. "He won local distinction for his facility in 'capping verses' from Horace." To "cap" a verse meant "to add a line to one given, beginning it with the final letter of the previous line."

Like almost everything in Poe's life, the memories of others about his youth are contradictory. On the one hand, acquaintances such as Thomas H. Ellis would recall, "He was, indeed, a leader among boys; but my admiration for him scarcely knew bounds." Ellis would later recall that Edgar won a prize for declamation at Clarke's school. Yet others would remember that Poe was never quite accepted; after all, he was the child of strolling players, and his status in the Allan household was uncertain. One who knew Poe in those years, Dr. Creed Thomas, would remember: "[Edgar] never asked any of his school-mates to go home with him after school as other boys did to take Friday dinner and spend the night." One of Edgar's best friends was Robert Sully, whose father, Matthew, had acted with Poe's mother as a member of the Charleston Comedians. Poe was athletic, known as a swift runner and jumper.

Andrew Johnston, who also knew Poe in school in Richmond, would later leave this statement: "Poe was a much more advanced scholar than any of us; but there was no other class for him, that being the highest. . . . I dare say he liked it well, for he was fond of desultory reading, and even then wrote verses, very clever for a boy." Johnston also added: "He was the best, the most daring, and most enduring swimmer that I ever saw."

Col. John T. L. Preston, later professor of Latin at the Virginia Military Institute, would remember: "Poe, as I recall . . . was self-willed, capricious, inclined to be imperious, and though of generous impulses, not steadily kind, or even amiable . . . it was known that his parents had been players, and that he was dependent upon the bounty that is bestowed upon an adopted son. All this had the effect of making the boys decline his leadership; and on looking back on it since, I fancy it gave him a fierceness he would otherwise not have had." Preston sounds like one of those who looked down on Poe because of his uncertain rank in Richmond society. The Poe scholar Edward H. Davidson would write: "Not to bear the name of the father and mother was socially worse [in Richmond] than having no parents at all."

Edgar's friend Ebenezer Burling taught him to swim. Among his companions, Poe held the record for broad jumping. One of the legendary events of Poe's life occurred when he was about fifteen or sixteen and swam six miles in the James River against a powerful tide. He was badly sunburned but recognized as a hero among other schoolboys.

At about this time, Edgar became a lieutenant of the Junior Morgan Riflemen. Named for Gen. Daniel Morgan and a famous regiment of the Revolutionary War, the group was a kind of honor guard, apprentice militia, officer training corps, and boys club combined. Edgar was the second in command, and when the Marquis de Lafayette visited Richmond in October 1824, the Morgan Rifles took part in the parade and were reviewed by Lafayette.

As Edgar entered his mid-teens, relations with John Allan began to deteriorate. It was in this period that Edgar learned of Allan's extramarital love life. Also, Edgar exhibited more and more independence, provoked by his uncertain status in the Allan household. There exists a letter Allan wrote on November 21, 1824, to Edgar's brother, Henry:

> DEAR HENRY I have just seen your letter of the 25th ult. to Edgar and am much afflicted, that he has not written you. He has had little else to do for me he does nothing & seems quite miserable, sulky & ill-tempered to all the Family. How we have acted to produce this is beyond my conception—why I have put up so long with his conduct is little less wonderful. The

> boy possesses not a Spark of affection for us not a particle of gratitude for all my care and kindness towards him . . . but I must end and this with a devout wish that God may yet bless him & you & that Success may crown all your endeavors & between you your poor sister Rosalie may not suffer. At least she is half your Sister & God forbid my dear Henry that We should visit upon the living the Errors & frailties of the dead. . . . May [God] keep you in Danger preserve you always is the prayer of your Friend & Servant.

In his pose of piety and concern, Allan condemns the fifteen-year-old Edgar to his older brother and then slurs the reputation of their mother. While Allan was begetting illegitimate children in Richmond, he implicitly accuses Eliza Poe of adultery, to her son, on the basis of a rumor about Rosalie's paternity. Hervey Allen speculated that this letter was "an ignoble gesture . . . to seal the lips of Edgar in regard to domestic scandals then agitating the Allan household."

Because of the uncertainty of his standing in the Allan family, and therefore in the Richmond community, it must have been gratifying to Edgar to be reminded of his connection to the Poe family and the legacy of Gen. David Poe. His contacts with the family in Baltimore were sporadic, but he and his older brother corresponded, and at least once William Henry visited Edgar and Rosalie in Richmond.

3

JANE STANARD AND ELMIRA ROYSTER

A FRIEND FROM POE'S EARLY YEARS WOULD OBSERVE: "I NEVER knew the time Edgar was not in love with some one." For a while Fanny Allan would be a surrogate. She was kind and loving, then out of reach because of illness. And Nancy Valentine was also kindly but more an observer than active participant in Edgar's life. There was also Jane Scott Mackenzie, Rosalie's adopted mother. It was known that Edgar sometimes sought refuge at the Mackenzie house and called Mrs. Mackenzie his mother. In later life Poe would associate Fanny Allan with the scent of orrisroot, which she kept in the drawers of her dresser. The scent would always stir affectionate memories of a somewhat idealized Ma.

The woman who would inspire Poe most at this time was the mother of his friend Robert Stanard. Jane Stanard, in her twenties, was married to a prominent judge. In a painting, once claimed to be of her, she appears to be very pretty but with a haunted, questioning look. When Poe visited the Stanard home, she was attentive and sympathetic to him. To her he could speak of his disappointments and uncertainties, his frustrations. Later Poe would tell Helen Whitman that Jane Stanard was "the first, purely ideal love of my soul."

Jane Stanard may have had a powerful attraction for Edgar that he did not completely understand: she suffered from depression, which could have caused other illnesses. She probably sympathized with Edgar's own tendency toward depression of spirits. According to one tradition, Mrs.

Stanard as a girl had seen Eliza Poe on the stage and expressed her admiration to Edgar. Jane Stanard's marriage was far from happy. Her union with an older judge saddened her, another example to Poe of the dangers of marriage, so far from his ideal. Based on the evidence, marriage was something to yearn for and to fear.

Though Mrs. Stanard could console Edgar in his anxieties, she apparently could not console herself. Her unhappy marriage caused her to despair. Intense depression led to mental instability, and she was confined to an asylum, where she died at the age of thirty-one, on April 28, 1824. Modern scholars have thought that Mrs. Stanard may have suffered from a brain tumor. Years later Poe would explain to Marie Louise Shew that Jane Stanard was "the truest, tenderest of this world's most womanly souls, and an angel to my forlorn and darkened nature." Poe later claimed he frequently visited her grave at night.

As mentioned, Poe had already written a number of verses by the age of fifteen. He had translated from Latin, and he'd imitated Cicero, as Latin students were encouraged to do. But the admiration for Jane Stanard inspired him with new energy and ambition. One of his most famous and popular poems, "To Helen," was written as a tribute to her. Later he would say that he'd composed the poem, or an early version of the poem, at the age of fourteen. This is almost certainly not true, for the poem we know has a polish and sophistication he could not have achieved in his early teens. Likely, he did write something to honor Mrs. Stanard at fourteen or fifteen and kept revising it over the years until he published it around the age of twenty-two.

"To Helen," his first poem of that title, is one of Poe's finest lyrics in a classical mode. The classical world gave Poe an image of an ideal realm, beyond the chaotic, banal, and cruel world around him. "To Helen," in its later revised version, sings:

Helen, thy beauty is to me
  Like those Nicéan barks of yore,
That gently, o'er a perfumed sea,
  The weary, way-worn wanderer bore
  To his own native shore.

On desperate seas long wont to roam,
  Thy hyacinth hair, thy classic face,
Thy Naiad airs have brought me home
  To the glory that was Greece,
And the grandeur that was Rome.

Lo! in yon brilliant window-niche
  How statue-like I see thee stand,
  The agate lamp within thy hand!
Ah, Psyche, from the regions which
  Are Holy-Land!

With the name Helen, Poe evokes associations with Helen of Troy, the most beautiful woman in the world, a beacon to travelers, a patroness to lovers. She is perfect and remote. If we take the word *Nicéan* to mean "victorious," Helen is guiding victorious but exhausted soldiers and travelers home over a perfumed sea. No doubt Poe identified with the weary wayfarers. In his early years he had banged around with Eliza from town to town, theater to theater, boardinghouse to tavern. With the Allans he was somewhat at sea, never sure exactly where he belonged or where he was headed. He had traveled rough seas to Britain and back. Returning to Richmond, he was no more certain of his role in the Allan household than he had been earlier. No wonder Mrs. Stanard's kindness seemed a beacon of welcome. Some of Poe's most powerful writing would concern the sea and the overwhelming danger of storms at sea. In the poem "The City in the Sea," a whole civilization plunges into the sublime and infernal deep of "desperate seas."

Like most of Poe's heroines, this Helen is more a figure of art than a living, breathing person. The poet seems to identify the muse with his soul and place her in an ethereal realm, referred to as "Holy-Land," a world of dignity and repose, somewhere between life and death, a zone that would stir Poe's imagination in many later works. "To Helen" is one of the best examples of a poem that transcends attempts at explication and paraphrase. It has the peculiar authority of poetry, which we recognize when we first hear it or read it. Poe kept revising "To Helen" over the years, searching for a perfection that probably never exists, even in the greatest poetry. Poe's

Helen inhabits a state transcending life and death. She is both beautiful and dead and not dead, a combination that Poe would seek in his heroines and muses again and again.

Why do we feel, as Allen Tate said, that he is "our cousin, Mr. Poe"? We can venture one guess with respect to this early poem. Through his art Poe reawakens emotions and longings we associate with childhood and adolescence. As we grow older, we repress or forget the intensity of those fears and aspirations and the sickness of love. T. S. Eliot notoriously wrote: "That Poe had a powerful intellect is undeniable! But it seems to me the intellect of a highly gifted young person before puberty." What Eliot saw as limitation is also an essential feature of Poe's unique appeal.

WE CANNOT KNOW WHETHER THE YOUNG POE ACTUALLY VISITED Jane Stanard's grave night after night, hoping to commune with her spirit, to honor her memory, mourn her passing. What we do know is that such demonstrations of grief and loyalty and lost love were something of a fashion in the nineteenth century and in the literature of the time. And it was not only Jane Stanard who was buried in Richmond earth but Eliza Poe as well.

Though he may not have understood it at the time, or ever, the lingering near the grave of a beloved woman may have given the young Edgar the most intense emotion he would ever know. For with the dead he did not have to worry about the confusion and disappointment of the physical realm. He could worship in the imagination the ideal he sought. Near the grave he could etherealize his love on some distant star, with both his resentment for abandonment and his guilt pushed aside, as he contemplated eternal beauty and otherworldly allegiances.

Like many of the important authors of the nineteenth century, Poe was partly self-educated. Melville famously said, "A whale ship was my Yale College and my Harvard." Encyclopedias, dictionaries, and the British quarterlies would be the sources of much of Poe's knowledge. Poe had access to the books and journals the firm of Allan & Ellis imported from England, publications such as the *Quarterly Review,* which had been founded the year of Poe's birth and which published the works of Sir Walter Scott and Robert Southey. There was also the *Edinburgh Review,* which included the likes of William Hazlitt, Thomas Babington Macaulay, and Thomas Carlyle.

More important for Poe, the *Quarterly Review* printed the works of Byron. In a single issue, the young Poe could find brilliant essays, sensational Gothic tales, and sarcastic, cutting reviews, including the slashing notice of Keats's *Endymion* that some argued had hastened the poet's death.

At one time the dominant literary medium in English had been the play. In the eighteenth century the play was replaced by the novel. By Poe's time the newspapers and magazines were the most lively media, reaching an ever larger, popular audience. As Poe would write in "Marginalia," "Magazine literature [is] . . . an indication of an era in which men are forced upon the curt, the condensed, the well-digested in place of the voluminous—in a word, upon journalism in lieu of dissertation."

At about the time Poe was mourning Mrs. Stanard and writing verses to honor her memory, his relations with his foster father worsened. The inspiration of the rebellious and scandalous Byron may have been part of the cause. But given Poe's independence, the failure of John Allan to provide the legal status of adopted son, and Allan's rigid and practical outlook, it was probably inevitable that the two would clash. More and more, foster son and foster father found each other intolerable.

Because of his own humble origins, Allan had had to struggle for acceptance by Richmond society and was only rich because his uncle William Galt had left him a fortune. In the years after his return from London, and before William Galt's bequest, John Allan had labored to pay his debts and get his business back on track. No doubt Edgar seemed not to appreciate what Allan had been forced to do and sometimes returned ingratitude and sarcasm for Allan's charity.

Yet when William Galt died, in 1825, and left his nephew a fortune worth $750,000 (about $22.5 million in 2023 dollars) and vast estates in Lynchburg and Richmond, Allan, if anything, acted even less generously toward Edgar. Galt's bequest included sawmills, grist mills, many enslaved men and women. John Allan paid off his debts and bought one of the finest houses in Richmond, called Moldavia, at Fifth and Main Streets on a hill overlooking the James River. The house had ample grounds, woods and garden. Edgar was assigned a room on the second floor.

It was around this time that Edgar, with several of his friends—William Ritchie, R. C. Ambler, Creed Thomas, Robert Sully, and others—founded the Thespian Society. They performed plays in a tent on a vacant lot and charged one cent for admission. John Allan opposed *any* involvement in the theater, and Edgar may have taken part in the venture to spite his foster father. As a boy, he'd seen enough of the actor's life to know the profession was not for him. In March 1825 Poe left Burke's school and began classes with Dr. and Mrs. Ray Thomas. The Thomases may have offered special preparation for admission to the new University of Virginia.

By this time Edgar had become very close to a pretty neighbor, Sarah Elmira Royster, and before the move to Moldavia, she and Edgar had lived in the same neighborhood. Elmira was the daughter of James H. Royster, who had been a good friend of William Galt. J. H. Whitty, who knew Elmira in her later years, would recall that Elmira loved poetry and "was fond of all the boys, but liked Edgar best, while he was interested in all the girls but lingered longest with Elmira." Edgar and Elmira "roamed hand in hand through the spacious Ellis & Allan rose gardens." Since the letters between the childhood sweethearts have been lost, most of what we know about their courtship comes from Elmira's reminiscences years later. As she recalled, Poe was not very talkative when with her but could speak excitedly when he did talk. He loved music and had a pleasing voice that reminded some of his mother. Edgar drew an attractive pencil sketch of Elmira. Later she would explain that they went for walks among the flowers and trees of the Ellis estate; "a trysting place; it was spacious, a most beautiful garden, especially for roses."

In 1875, twenty-six years after Poe's death, Elmira, now the widow Mrs. Shelton, would explain to a neighbor, Edward V. Valentine, some of her memories of Poe: "He was a beautiful boy. . . . When he did talk though he was pleasant but his general manner was sad. . . . Our acquaintance was kept up until he left to go to the University, and during the time he was at the University he wrote to me frequently, but my father intercepted the letters because we were too young. . . . He never addressed any poems to me. . . . I was about 15 or 16 when he first addressed me and I engaged myself to him, and I was not aware that he wrote to me until I was married to Mr. Shelton when I was 17." To Edward M. Alfriend, Elmira would say, "I married another man, but the love of my life was Edgar Poe, I never loved any one else." Both Elmira and Edgar were musical, and they often performed together, she at the piano, he on a flute.

At this early age, Poe sought to be married, as he would many times later. Both John Allan and Elmira's father opposed any match between the lovers. Poe was without family or prospects. John Allan, now wealthy, made it clear he had no intention of legally recognizing the quick-tempered Edgar as his heir. Earlier, when Allan was in financial trouble, Mr. Royster had loaned Allan a considerable amount of money. It seems Allan wanted to send his foster son off to the university and forget about him. As several biographers have pointed out, Poe was aware of Allan's extramarital affairs and illegitimate children in Richmond. J. H. Whitty tells us, "With Mrs. Allan suspicious and jealous of her husband, the natural disposition of Poe was to side with her in family matters."

Before he left for Charlottesville, Edgar gave Elmira a small mother-of-pearl purse with their initials engraved on a plate. The engraver made a mistake, inscribing *S.P.R.* instead of *S.E.R.* for Sarah Elmira Royster. It was an error that in retrospect would seem to bode ill for their future.

At a time when many universities and colleges in the United States were church related, Jefferson had planned a nonsectarian institution, intended "to develop the reasoning faculties of our youth, enlarge their minds, cultivate their morals, and instil into them the precepts of virtue and order—and generally, to form them to habits of reflection and correct action, rendering them examples of virtue to others, and of happiness within themselves."

According to Arthur Hobson Quinn, both Anglican and Presbyterian organizations opposed Jefferson's plan, disapproving of its secular character. But construction began in 1817, and the university opened its doors in 1825. At the head of the quad, a rotunda dominated the grounds, modeled on the Pantheon in Rome. The rows of buildings of East and West Range included columns of Ionic, Doric, and Corinthian design. All structures were made of Georgian brick, much like Jefferson's alma mater, William and Mary.

In Jefferson's idealistic plans, there were no authorities to enforce discipline or order. Individual liberty was the rule. The former president set out to recruit the best scholars and educators for the new faculty. From Cambridge University he hired George Long (1800–1879) as chair of Ancient Languages. George Blaettermann, a German who lived in England, was brought aboard as chair of Modern Languages.

Library privileges at the new university seem to us unusually strict. To check out each volume, a student needed signed permission from a professor. The library was open only once a week. Card playing was forbidden, but apparently the rule was ignored. Classes began at 7:00 a.m. and, with a half-hour break for breakfast, lasted until nine thirty. The rest of the day was to be given to study and other optional activities.

Fanny Allan accompanied Poe on the journey to Charlottesville in February 1826. At the university Poe asked James Hill, the coachman and servant of the Allans, to deliver a letter to Elmira. It was probably the last letter Elmira received from Edgar for the next twenty-two years.

Except for his regret at leaving Elmira, Poe probably welcomed a chance to live away from John Allan's house. The average age for students at the university was nineteen; Edgar enrolled just after turning seventeen. Many of the other students were scions of plantation owners or prosperous merchants and professional men. They brought servants, guns, and horses with them to the university. They kept liquor and wine in their rooms and spent time playing cards and gambling, indulging in pranks. Some patronized local prostitutes and may have kept mistresses in the village.

Because Jefferson had insisted there be few rules to restrain the young scholars, fights and cruel jokes were common. Drunken students threw bricks at professors, and one hurled a bottle of urine through a professor's window. Poe was disturbed by the violence and dissolute behavior. Not only was Poe younger than the other students; he had led a more sheltered life under John Allan's roof. On May 25, 1826, he concluded a letter to Allan: "Dixon made <an> a physical attack upon Arthur Smith one of Blow's Norfolk friends—and a 'very fine fellow'—he struck him with a large stone on one side of his head—whereupon Smith drew a pistol."

On September 21, 1826, Poe wrote to Allan again. "We have had a great many fights up here lately—The faculty expelled Wickliffe last night for general bad conduct—but more especially for biting one of the student's arms with whom he was fighting— . . . It was bitten from the shoulder to the elbow—and it is likely that pieces of flesh as large as my hand will be obliged to be cut out." While students and faculty looked on, a professor cruelly horsewhipped his wife.

In 1844 Poe would write one of his best comic stories, "The System of Doctor Tarr and Professor Fether," in which inmates of a lunatic asylum take advantage of a lenient "soothing system" of treatment to overcome their supervisors and guardians and lock them in a cellar. It's possible that memories of the chaos and violence at the University of Virginia, in the absence of discipline and oversight, were one inspiration for this bizarre tale. When there was an attempt to rein in the unruly students and try them before a grand jury, many of the culprits fled to the woods. The sheriff was charged with rounding them up but with little success. In Poe's words, "This order however was very little attended to."

As it turned out, the violence and disorder were not the most serious problem for Poe in his months at Charlottesville. Allan had sent him to the university with only $110 (roughly $3,300 in current value), not nearly enough to pay tuition and room and board and daily expenses, such as laundry and wood for the fireplace in his room. Surrounded by students with large allowances, Poe had to borrow from lenders and live on credit. Hoping to cover his debts by gambling, he lost even more money. Once Allan sent him $40 (about $1,200), but it was not enough to cancel his debts. It is said that on cold nights, Poe had to burn some of his furniture to keep his room warm.

In 1831, while at West Point, Poe would write to Allan, "I will boldly say that it was wholly and entirely your own mistaken parsimony that caused all the difficulties in which I was involved while at Charlottsville [*sic*]." Allan was now one of the richest men in Virginia, but he humiliated his ward by leaving him stranded and embarrassed at the university without the means to pay his way. Arthur Hobson Quinn has pointed out that Allan, though now wealthy, gave Poe at the university less than he had paid for his elementary education years earlier in London, when the foster father was relatively poor. By the time Poe was forced by Allan to leave Charlottesville, in December 1826, he had run up debts of about two thousand dollars (roughly sixty thousand dollars today), owed to tradesmen, money lenders, and fellow students.

It's likely Poe attended Jefferson's funeral in July 1826. While it is usually assumed that Poe's descriptions of mansions, castles, and great estates are based on European and British models, it is quite possible that Jefferson's landscaping and architecture at Monticello also later inspired, in part, the concepts of "The Domain of Arnheim," and "Landor's Cottage."

All this time Edgar was waiting for a letter from Elmira, an answer to the many letters he sent back to Richmond. But week after week there was only silence, which must have contributed to "unnerving" him, though he was able to perform well in his studies. Poe joined the Jefferson Society, which sponsored debates, and demonstrated his wit and verbal ability on his feet. But there is one other factor to consider about Poe's unlucky year at the university. Because he was surrounded by older and richer students who drank heavily and often, Poe took part in the drinking and bull sessions. This may explain why he lost so much money, when he was gambling *and* drinking. Fellow students would remember that only a little alcohol would make Poe tipsy and exhibit bizarre behavior. It was a weakness that would plague him for the rest of his life and would possibly contribute to his untimely death. In a culture in which men had liquor and wine readily available and drank at all hours, Poe was at a serious disadvantage. This pattern, established at Charlottesville, would continue, broken by extended periods of sobriety, as long as Poe lived.

Poe also used tobacco for much of his life. Given that he most likely carried tubercular bacteria in his lungs, the smoking could not have helped his health. At some point he also acquired the habit of chewing tobacco, possibly while among the students at Charlottesville.

One fellow student acquainted with Poe at the university later recalled, "No one could say that he *knew* him." Yet many remembered Poe as genial and as a serious student. The college librarian, William Wertenbaker, would later write, "As Librarian I had frequent intercourse with Mr. Poe. . . . I copy from the Register a list of books which Mr. Poe borrowed while he was a student: Rollin's 'Histoire Ancienne,' 'Histoire Romaine'; Robertson's 'America'; Marshall's 'Washington'; Voltaire's 'Histoire Particulaire' and Dufief's 'Nature Displayed.'" From this list we could guess that Poe was especially interested in history, including natural history, interests later evident in both his fiction and critical writing. Wertenbaker would also remember that Poe excelled in his classes: "On one occasion Prof. Batterman requested his Italian class to render into English verse a portion of the lesson in Tasso. . . . Mr. Poe was the *only one* who complied with the request."

William M. Burwell would later recall Poe as "a very attractive companion, genial in his nature and familiar, by the varied life he had already led, with persons and scenes new to the unsophisticated provincials among whom he was thrown."

At the university Poe lived in 13 West Range. Other students would recall that he drew pictures on the walls to decorate the room, which is now a memorial to Poe. While in Charlottesville, Poe took long rambles in the woods and hills nearby. Later he would set a favorite story, "A Tale of the Ragged Mountains," in the hills around the university.

One striking memoir of Poe's time at the university was left us by Miles George, later a Richmond doctor: "[Poe] was fond of quoting poetic authors and reading poetic productions of his own . . . then suddenly a change would come over him & he would with a piece of charcoal evince his versatile genius, by sketching upon the walls of his dormitory, whimsical, fanciful & grotesque figures. . . . To calm & quiet the excessive nervous excitability under which he labored, he would too often put himself under the influence of that 'Invisible Spirit of Wine.'"

When he learned the extent of Poe's indebtedness, Allan withdrew his ward from the university. Though he had done well in his studies, Poe left Jefferson's university in disgrace. Instead of helping his foster son with his debts, his gambling, and drinking problems, Allan showed only anger and contempt. Not appreciating Edgar's excellent record in his classes, he could only condemn the foster son's dissolute ways.

To welcome her foster son home, Fanny Allan gave a Christmas party. But Poe was so disconcerted, he left the gathering and withdrew to his room. According to some accounts, a friend searched Poe out, and they repaired to a tavern. Other versions have Poe visiting Elmira's house, only to find she had been sent to relatives in North Carolina. Since Fanny Allan was Poe's most important ally in the household, the self-destructiveness of his conduct is obvious.

Because Edgar's many letters to Elmira from the university were intercepted by Mr. Royster, she had no choice but to assume he'd forgotten her. Soon after his return to Richmond, Poe learned she was betrothed to Alexander B. Shelton, a prosperous young businessman. The loss of Elmira was an injury from which he never recovered. Not only a crushing loss of the kind and beautiful Elmira; it was a put-down to remind him that among the quality of Richmond, he was an orphan, a dreamer, a nobody. For the rest of his life, Poe's peculiar relations with women would be affected by this blow to his confidence and self-esteem. Among other poems written at this time was one called "Song," in which a jilted lover witnesses the marriage of his sweetheart to another.

I saw thee on thy bridal day—
  When a burning blush came o'er thee,

Though happiness around thee lay,
  The world all love before thee:

And in thine eye a kindling light
  (Whatever it might be)
Was all on Earth my aching sight
  Of Loveliness could see.

That blush, perhaps, was maiden shame—
  As such it well may pass—
Though its glow hath raised a fiercer flame
  In the breast of him alas!

Who saw thee on that bridal day,
  When that deep blush *would* come o'er thee,
Though happiness around thee lay,
  The world all love before thee.

Besides the metrical perfection of Poe's common meter quatrains, there is irony and mystery in "Song." The poem, for all its smooth lyricism, implies a secret, a backstory.

In the American canon of the nineteenth century, no poet, with the exception of the Bryant of "Thanatopsis," ever wrote with such polish and confidence at the age of eighteen. Buried in the poem is a hint of guilt, hers, and perhaps the speaker's as well. It should be remembered that Poe's poetic canon was very different from the one we know. To him Thomas Moore and the Scottish Robert Motherwell were important poets.

Poe would not meet Elmira again for nine years. Mary Phillips tells us: "Yet, strangely, every prose and poetical allusion Poe ever made to his first, lost love seems to suggest that, in some mysterious manner, their mutual loyalty was known to each other." The scholar J. H. Whitty would record a rumor in Richmond that Elmira "created a scene in her household after finding out that Poe's letters had been kept from her." The loss of his first love would make Poe cynical about love, even as he was drawn irresistibly toward romance and marriage.

Poe's admirer in France, Charles Baudelaire, would talk of his own "*guignon*," his curse or evil star. Poe also felt such a doom or damnation hanging over him. Had Allan been more forgiving, he might have let Poe return to Charlottesville, and his subsequent life could well have been different. Some biographers have suggested that John Allan was jealous of Poe, fearing his wife loved the foster son more than him. It is also quite possible that Allan resented Poe's intellect and talent. Before Poe was taken away from the University of Virginia, he "was awarded the highest honors in both ancient and modern languages."

4

TAMERLANE AND OTHER POEMS

AFTER POE RETURNED TO RICHMOND UNDER A CLOUD OF DEBT and disgrace, creditors pursued him, and former friends avoided or belittled him. Later he would recall "taunts & abuse that followed . . . even from those who had been my warmest friends." It is said Poe was employed for a time in the accounting department of the Allan firm. Allan was furious when both students and tradesmen from Charlottesville asked *him* to cover his foster son's debts.

In March 1827 the anger and contempt between Allan and Edgar boiled to a climax. Hurt at having lost Elmira, unable to continue his studies at the university, Poe left the Allan house on March 19 and, from the Courthouse Tavern, sent a letter to Allan accusing the foster father of throwing him out of Moldavia. Assuming a tone of superiority that would characterize many later letters, Poe listed grievances against his foster father and blamed Allan for not fulfilling his promise to General Poe to educate him. Poe added that Allan had let the servants in the house treat him with disrespect. "I have heard you say (when you little thought I was listening and therefore must have said it in earnest) that you had no affection for me— . . . You suffer me to be subjected to the whims & caprice, not only of your white family, but the complete authority of the blacks." Years later Susan Weiss would write, in an article for the *Independent,* published in 1904, "The servants were forbidden to obey or attend upon him, as formerly, and a room was allotted to him which was used by the first Mrs. Allan's maid and which he refused to occupy."

Poe concluded the letter by stating he hoped to find a job in some city up north and asked Allan to send his trunk of clothes and books to the tavern and enough money to support him for a month. But he took care to leave the door open for a different outcome with a postscript: "It depends upon yourself if hereafter you see or hear from me." Allan replied in a letter of sarcasm and ridicule and sent no money.

It is not known how Edgar survived in Richmond while waiting for money and his trunk from Allan. Later he would claim that he was "every day threatened with a warrant." Perhaps he walked the streets like the character in his later story "The Man of the Crowd." As would happen so often in his life, Poe's tone would change after he cooled down and confronted the reality of his predicament. He wrote Allan again on March 20, pleading, "I am in the greatest necessity, not having tasted food since Yesterday morning. I have no where to sleep at night, but roam about the Streets."

Somehow Poe got away from Richmond around March 24, 1827. Biographers have speculated that he and his friend Ebenezer Burling signed on a ship bound for England. His brother, Henry, had been a sailor and had sent colorful letters of his adventures. Taking the alias "Henri le Rennét," perhaps to escape creditors, Poe led people to think he'd gone off to join the Greek army, like his hero Byron. Others were later convinced he'd traveled as far as St. Petersburg, Russia. Most likely, he worked his way on a coal-carrying ship to Boston. Burling deserted at Norfolk and returned to Richmond. It is possible Poe stopped in Baltimore on his way to Boston. When Fanny Allan learned that Poe had gone, it's said she "had frequent fainting spells . . . and . . . was for weeks inconsolable."

Poe landed in Boston, the city of his birth, on April 7, 1827. On the back of the sketch of Boston Harbor Eliza had given him before her death, Eliza had advised her son to "ever love Boston, the place of his birth, and where his mother found her *best* and *most sympathetic* friends." In his flight from John Allan's house, he appears to have followed his mother's admonition.

In Boston, Poe may have worked as a clerk in a warehouse for a few weeks. It was the kind of job he'd done for the Allan firm in Richmond. And then he found a position more suited to his talents in the office of a local newspaper. Some have thought he appeared on the stage in a play called *The Foundling of the Forest.* He had brought with him the poetry manuscript labored over in Charlottesville and Richmond, pouring out his frustrations and disappointment over the loss of Elmira, and he contacted a young printer named Calvin S. Thomas, who had a shop at 70 Washington Street, Boston. In June 1827 Thomas would produce a forty-page chapbook in paper wrappers titled *Tamerlane and Other Poems.* Only about forty copies were printed. The author was listed simply as "A Bostonian." As far as we know, the booklet would attract few or no reviews but was listed in the *United States Review and Literary Gazette* in August 1827. In the future this spare brochure of poems would become one of the rarest volumes, sought by wealthy connoisseurs, "the so-called 'black tulip' of American literature" for avid collectors.

Colonial America could claim the didactic religious poetry of Michael Wigglesworth's *The Day of Doom* (1662) and the metaphysical religious verse of Edward Taylor (c. 1642–1729), and in the Revolutionary period there was Joel Barlow's patriotic epic *The Columbiad* (revised in 1807) and Barlow's mock epic *The Hasty Pudding* (1796). There was Philip Freneau's satiric and romantic poems, but most of the poems read in North America were from British authors, Alexander Pope, Robert Burns, and Gray's "Elegy in a Country Churchyard," belonging to the so-called Graveyard school of poetry. Out of the latter tradition, William Cullen Bryant would fashion "Thanatopsis," which found a large audience on both sides of the Atlantic. There was also a taste for satire, irony, and wit in verse, but no one could have foreseen the way Byron's poetry and "Byronism" swept over the United States, inspiring a virtual cult among young readers in Britain and Europe.

In an essay called "Entertaining Byron in America," Susan J. Wolfson describes the vogue of Byron in the United States in the second and third decades of the nineteenth century. "Aspiring poets bid for the title of 'American Byron,' or short of this, displayed Byron, in allusions, literary style, and social affectation." The poet Fitz-Greene Halleck inaugurated himself as "The American Byron" in an edition of Byron's poems and letters he published in 1834–36. Wolfson labels Byronism as "rampant" on both the literary and social scene. Longfellow, probably the most popular poet in America at that time, wrote of Byron, "No writer has done half so much to corrupt the literary taste as well as the moral principles of our country." He further complained that "every city, town, and village had its little Byron."

Those who could afford to sometimes traveled to Italy and Greece in search of, or in imitation of, Byron. More cities in North America were named for Byron than in all the United Kingdom. The fashion took such a hold that "for a boy or man not to be Byronic [was] to be abnormal, more a mamma's boy and minister's pet."

There is another aspect to Byron's life and writing that gave him legitimacy as a hero in the United States: he not only fought for Greece's independence from Turkey and died as a martyr, but he had praised and celebrated American democracy above British monarchy. His works were sometimes called "master poems of modern democracy" and Byron a "liberalizing force that can hardly be overpraised." The young, enthralled by the notorious reputation of the poet and the poems, could always argue the poetry celebrated democratic ideals.

For the young Poe, also, the most important contemporary poet was undoubtedly Byron. After his death in Greece, in 1824, at the age of thirty-five, Byron was apotheosized as a martyr for the cause of liberty as well as a libertine and celebrity. Imagine a figure who was at once a rock star, Che Guevara, and a British lord! *Childe Harold* and *Don Juan* were read, discussed, recited, reviled, and imitated as far away as Russia. Much of Byron's poetry was considered immoral, scandalous, therefore irresistible to the young.

Poe's poems and experiments such as "Tamerlane" sound like echoes of Byron's voice and subjects. Probably "Manfred" was the work that inspired Poe most. The Byronic pose of the aristocrat, connoisseur of both good and evil, disdain for the masses, would inspire much of Poe's early writing and manners. With no money, family, position in society, Poe struggled to perform a part beyond his reach, in a country that had no place for him. Both Byron and Poe were gifted at playing roles, but in Poe's case the guilt and tragic sense were not just acting. The only feature of Byronism Poe would never share was the sympathy with radical, revolutionary causes. Poe never believed that people or society could be improved. But from the beginning of his career to the end of his life, Poe would affect Byronic sadness.

"Tamerlane" is a dramatic monologue of 406 lines, spoken by the conqueror "Timur-i-Leng," Timur the Lame (1336–1405), as he is dying. As stated, the most important model was Byron's "Manfred," and both poems feature high mountains, a holy man, a hunter, a lost love (Poe called his heroine Ada, the name of Byron's daughter) and a final confession of defeat, spoken by the hero.

Few scholars rate "Tamerlane" as one of Poe's better efforts. Yet it is a notable performance for an eighteen-year-old. No other classic American writer published anything that ambitious and impressive at the age of eighteen. In the preface to the little book, Poe claimed most of the poems were written before he was fourteen. This is almost certainly not true, but it is likely Poe had been working on some of the poems for several years.

In the title poem, Tamerlane, now dying, confesses that he fell prey to Ambition, which caused him to leave his idyllic home in the mountains, his life as a peasant, and his young Love, to conquer much of the known world. Ambition, like the snake in Eden, entered this paradise of young romance. Even as they wander hand in hand in the mountain Eden, he longs to conquer an empire to lay at Ada's feet. But in the course of his confession, it becomes clear that not only Ambition but Time has robbed him of his youth, love, and visionary power. He had sought the false glory of the outside world rather than the power of the imagination. In lines 214–33, foreshadowing the later story "Eleonora," the speaker tells us that he was drawn to become a conqueror so that his young beloved might reign as a queen:

> We walk'd together on the crown
> Of a high mountain, which look'd down
> Afar from its proud natural towers
>   Of rock and forest, on the hills—
> . . . .
> The flush on her bright cheek, to me,
> Seem'd to become a queenly throne

This conflict between ambition and ideal love would play out in much of Poe's later works and, indeed, in his life. One of the more memorable lines of "Tamerlane" is the last, the hero's lament for his choice: "A kingdom for a broken-heart." When Tamerlane returns as conqueror, his Ada is dead.

We should always take care in reading biography into poetry, for works of the imagination are rarely restricted to the author's own experience. But it's hard not to see Poe in "Tamerlane" retelling a version of his loss of Elmira. The poem is saturated with guilt for the narrator's excessive ambition and pride. Why would Poe feel guilty for the breakup with Elmira? After all, it was her father and probably John Allan who separated them. Yet it was he who had gone off to the university to enter the adult world, leaving their idyll of music and walks in the enchanted garden. To become a grown-up, educated man, he'd abandoned Elmira to fate, and when he returned, she was "dead" to him yet not dead. As far as we can tell, Poe would not learn until years later that his letters to Elmira from Charlottesville had been confiscated and destroyed. "Tamerlane" is a poem of conscience, as "The Raven" and "Ulalume" would be later.

The shorter poems in *Tamerlane and Other Poems* also reveal Poe's preoccupation with death and with a sense of his difference and alienation from the everyday world. The themes of most of Poe's later poems and some of his fiction are already implicit in this apprentice work. Byron served Poe as a model for several different reasons. Byron had famously swum the Hellespont; Poe had swum six miles down the James River against a powerful tide. Byron had lost his early love, Mary Chaworth; Poe had lost Elmira Royster. Byron had been at odds with his society, which rejected him and called him a villain, as John Allan had rejected Poe and labeled him ungrateful and unreliable. Both Byron and Poe were unusually handsome and attractive to women. Both felt guilty, gifted, and damned.

Poe had the manner and ambition of Byron, some of the same genius, sadness, and mercurial temperament, but lacked the money, the title, the connections to society, and loyal friends like John Hobhouse and Shelley and the publisher John Murray. Poe would spend much of his adult life looking for a faithful publisher. At a more intimate level, Poe may have lacked Byron's sexual gifts, his oft demonstrated potency.

A student Poe had known at the University of Virginia, Peter Pindar Pease, later reported sighting Poe in Boston in the spring of 1827. When Pease hailed him as he came out of a commercial building, Poe fled. When Pease caught up with him later, Poe insisted that he must remain incognito, for he'd run away from Allan's house.

Poe enlisted in the United States Army under the name Edgar A. Perry, on May 26, 1827. He probably chose the name Perry to prevent John Allan from learning of his whereabouts. Giving his age as twenty-two, his occupation as clerk, Poe was described as being five feet eight inches, with brown hair. His grandfather, David Poe Sr., had been honored for his service during the American Revolution. Also, Edgar had practice as the lieutenant of the Junior Morgan Rifles in Richmond. There was a side of Poe's personality that was drawn to order, discipline, and polish. We see it in his careful dress, in his formal poetry, in his bent for analytical criticism, in his love of mathematics and encryption. All his life Poe would oppose his affinity for the irrational, arbitrary, strange, and hideous, with demonstrations of logic and strict analysis. At the age of eighteen, Poe may have felt romantic about the military, as many young people do. Like other young men, he may have been drawn to the idea of military glory, of travel and adventure, or the camaraderie an army unit could provide. The biographer Jeffrey Meyers has suggested that the army might have offered Poe "escape [from] his ambiguous social status."

Poe signed on for a five-year enlistment in Company H of the First Regiment of Artillery. He held the rank of private in a fifty-man unit, with twenty-nine privates, four lieutenants, and a captain. For several months he would be stationed at Fort Independence on Castle Island in Boston Harbor. Then on November 8, 1827, his company would be shipped south to Fort Moultrie on Sullivan's Island, near Charleston, South Carolina. On the voyage south, the ship almost wrecked off Cape Cod. Edgar had been to Charleston years earlier, when his mother performed there in 1811.

Though Poe had grown up in the South, he was not familiar with the subtropical climate of the South Carolina coast, where palmettoes grew among trees hung with hoary Spanish moss. He would spend thirteen months on Sullivan's Island, and the region would leave a lasting impression, as shown later in "The Gold-Bug." With much free time in the peacetime army, Edgar was able to explore the island and nearby coastline. A famous conchologist, Dr. Edmund Ravenel, lived on the island at that time, and it's likely Poe got to know him and his work. He may have heard stories of pirate lore while stationed there.

Poe's work always displayed a taste for the bleak and desolate. Walking the beaches of the remote coastline may have thrilled him as much as the isolation depressed him. While in the region, he also seemed to acquire a taste for the sinister profusion of the southern wilderness, the moss-hung and vine-hung trees, the brush and mists of insects, standing pools of dark water. He would share with the great New England writers of his time, such as Emerson and Thoreau, a special intimacy with the natural world. But his relish would have a different tone, often glorying in the desolate and drab, as we will see in the opening paragraph of "The Fall of the House of Usher." But in "The Lake," already published in *Tamerlane and Other Poems,* we see his love for what others might find bleak and repelling. The later revision reads:

> In spring of youth it was my lot
> To haunt of the wide world a spot
> The which I could not love the less—
> So lovely was the loneliness
> Of a wild lake, with black rock bound,
> And the tall pines that towered around.
>
> But when the Night had thrown her pall
> Upon that spot, as upon all,
> And the mystic wind went by
> Murmuring in melody—
> Then—ah then I would awake
> To the terror of the lone lake.
>
> Yet that terror was not fright,
> But a tremulous delight—
> A feeling not the jeweled mine
> Could teach or bribe me to define—
> Nor Love—although the Love were thine.
>
> Death was in that poisonous wave,
> And in its gulf a fitting grave
> For him who thence could solace bring
> To his lone imagining—
> Whose solitary soul could make
> An Eden of that dim lake.

Poe's superiors liked him, and he performed his duties so efficiently that a few months after arriving on Sullivan's Island, he was appointed assistant to the commissary officer, or quartermaster. Later Edgar would become company clerk, in which position he wrote up reports for his unit and kept records. Still later, he became an "artificer," doing carpentry, blacksmithing, and other mechanical work. Some of the duties of an artificer required special skill and care, mixing gunpowder, calculating artillery trajectories. The best evidence for his success in the coastal artillery is Poe's promotion, January 1, 1829, to sergeant major, the highest noncommissioned rank in the army at that time.

By then Poe's company had moved north to Fortress Monroe, near the mouth of Chesapeake Bay. But in the winter of 1828–29, Edgar, turning twenty, began to tire of the army. After about eighteen months, he was weary of the repetition, boredom, and restrictions. The indications are that he'd continued writing, composing a long poem called "Al Aaraaf," set on a distant star. The thought of spending the next three years doing drill and company bookkeeping became intolerable. Throughout his career Poe would not enjoy any post or appointment longer than about eighteen months.

Desperate to leave barracks life, Poe confided his plight to Lt. J. Howard, with whom he had become friends. Howard explained that Edgar could only leave the army before his enlistment expired if his guardian, John Allan, would give his consent. Edgar persuaded Howard to write to Allan, which the lieutenant did through an intermediary, but Allan answered that it was better for Edgar to "remain as he is until the termination of his enlistment."

Poe wrote Allan a long letter of confession and remorse, explaining that he'd learned his lesson in the two years of military service. He begged his foster father to assure Lieutenant Howard that he and Allan were now "reconciled": "My father do not throw me aside as *degraded*[.] I will be an honor to your name."

Edgar wrote again a few weeks later. He'd come up with a proposal that he hoped might alter Allan's attitude: he asked his foster father to help him secure an appointment to the Military Academy at West Point. With such an education, he could become an officer and pursue a career, perhaps a distinguished career. After all, he'd risen to the rank of sergeant major in less than two years.

Edgar apologized for his gambling and debts at the university and conceded his own responsibility for his conduct. Whether Allan replied or not we do not know. What is certain is that as Fanny Allan's health worsened, as she approached her death on February 28, 1829, Allan's attitude toward his ward did soften. Fanny may have begged her husband to help Edgar as her end neared. We are told she desired to see Edgar once more. As far as we know, Edgar had not written to her in the two years he was away.

When Allan finally gave Edgar permission to return to Moldavia, it was too late for him to see Fanny alive. Poe reached Richmond after the burial and suffered both grief for her passing and guilt that he'd never told her of his whereabouts. He'd known that Fanny needed him, not least because of John Allan's coldness and affairs with other women.

Fanny's death affected John Allan also. His attitude toward Edgar mellowed, and he bought his foster son new mourning clothes. He claimed not to have received Poe's earlier letters and pledged to help his ward secure an appointment to the military academy. Allan even promised "to forgive all." In the rituals of nineteenth-century mourning, foster father and foster son seemed reconciled.

Obtaining the appointment to West Point took longer than Edgar expected. Actor that he was, Poe presented himself to the War Department as the adopted son of John Allan, explaining that his parents had died in the Richmond theater fire of December 1811. That seemed better than admitting his father had abandoned his family and that his mother had died a lingering death in poverty and helplessness.

A letter from Col. James House of the First Artillery on March 30, 1829, to the commanding general, F. P. Gaines, shows that Poe's petition was successful: "The said Perry, is one of a family of orphans whose unfortunate parents were the victims of the conflagration of the Richmond theatre, in 1809 [*sic*]. . . . An experienced soldier & approved Sergeant, is ready to take the place of Perry so soon as his discharge can be obtained."

On April 15, 1829, Edgar was discharged from the army. Captain H. W. Griswold had written on Poe's behalf, stating, "I have to say that Edgar Perry [Poe] was appointed Sergeant Major of the 1st Arty on the 1st of Jany. 1829. and up to this date has been exemplary in his deportment, prompt & faithful in the discharge of his duties." Back at Moldavia, Poe began the tedious process of applying to the Academy. First, he had to assemble letters of recommendation to the secretary of war, John H. Eaton. A former governor of Virginia, James Preston, father of Poe's schoolmate John T. L.

Preston, agreed to write on Edgar's behalf, calling him "a young gentleman of genius and talents. I believe he is destined to be distinguished." It would seem that Preston knew of or had read some of Poe's poems. On May 6, 1829, Allan himself wrote to the secretary of war on Edgar's behalf, taking care to distance himself from his ward. "Frankly, Sir, do I declare that He is no relation to me whatever; that I have many [in] whom I have taken an active Interest to promote thiers [*sic*] with no other feeling than that."

Poe presented his application in Washington in May and was told there was a waiting list of forty-seven candidates ahead of him, but because of resignations, dismissals, and rejections, he might still be admitted in September 1829. From Washington, Poe traveled on to Baltimore to visit his relatives there. If he had funds, he stayed in cheap hotels; when broke, he probably stayed with his aunt Maria Clemm.

When Edgar had not heard from the War Department by July 1829, John Allan urged him to visit Secretary John Eaton in person to plead his case. Edgar walked the thirty miles to the capital and was allowed an interview with Secretary Eaton, who told him he was now eleventh on the list. It was still possible he might be accepted in September. If the appointment did not come through then, it would be the following June before he could be admitted to the Academy.

Now began one of those periods of uncertainty with which Poe was already familiar. All he could do was wait, while Allan suggested he'd not tried hard enough to win the appointment. The truce between the two following Fanny Allan's death began to fray. The anger and distrust they felt for each other worked to the surface, and, predictably, they quarreled about money. Allan had sent Edgar a hundred dollars in May, but that was soon gone. Edgar explained that he was rooming at Beltzhoover's Hotel in Baltimore with his cousin James Mosher Poe, who robbed him of $46 (roughly $1,380 today) while he slept. Searching Mosher's clothes, Poe recovered $10 (about $300 today).

Edgar also needed to pay $50 (about $1,500 today) toward the $75 required to secure a substitute in his old army company. Allan challenged both of Edgar's stories, and the wrangling continued, aggravated by Poe's ambitions as a poet. Throughout the upheaval of Fanny Allan's death, leaving the army, applying to the military academy, Poe had continued to work on his poems, especially the long poem "Al Aaraaf," an otherworldly fantasy set among the stars. Edgar showed the poem to William Wirt, author, attorney general, later presidential candidate for the Anti-Masonic Party. Wirt advised him to send his poetry to Robert Walsh, whom Poe refers to as "the editor of the *American Quaterly Review*" in Philadelphia. Scholars have pointed out that Poe's spelling of *Quaterly* for *Quarterly* probably reflects the soft *r*'s of his Virginia accent.

Using what was left of Allan's money, Edgar hurried to Philadelphia, checked into the Indian Queen Hotel, and called on Robert Walsh. Walsh promised to review "Al Aaraaf" if it was published. Next, Poe took the poem to Isaac Lea, of Carey, Lea, & Carey, and explained to Lea that he was "irrecoverably a poet."

Poe was so buoyed by his contacts with these literary eminences in Philadelphia that he wrote to John Allan as soon as he returned to Baltimore, addressing his foster father as "Dear Pa." He explained that he'd shown his work to prominent literary men and the response had been encouraging. Then he asked if Allan would guarantee the costs of publishing his poems with Carey, Lea, & Carey.

Needless to say, Allan was irritated that Edgar was still wasting time on poetry, just when he needed to be getting on in the world. Allan had been ill since the death of his wife. Also, he was having an affair with a woman named Elizabeth Wills, with whom he would father twins. Allan rejected Poe's request and added, "I am not particularly anxious to see you." Poe found it difficult to accept that Allan would not forgive and continue his support, as he had in Edgar's youth at the urging of Fanny Allan. A more practical person would probably have assessed the lay of the land and made his way independently. But Edgar was still in some ways emotionally immature. The deep divisions in Poe's personality can be read in his relations with his foster father, on the one hand his anger and contempt for the merchant, on the other his need for a parent, for support, for forgiveness.

Poe would have little interest in the ways most people earn their living. Of all major American writers of the nineteenth century, except Henry James, he shows the least concern with day-to-day work. Poe's characters, like James's, somehow survive without working. When Poe was broke, we assume, he stayed with relatives, most likely with his aunt Maria Clemm, a widow who eked out a living by sewing and taking in boarders. On December 10, 1829, Poe sold a Black enslaved man for Mrs. Clemm.

Poe may have begun the poem "Al Aaraaf" while in the army, even while he was at Sullivan's Island. In Richmond and in Baltimore he continued to expand and revise it along with his earlier poems. "Al Aaraaf" was the young poet's bid to compose something "Miltonic," a poem of cosmic allegory and epic language. As a mature critic, Poe would later claim that a long poem is a contradiction of terms, the intensity and excitement of the best poems being so acute they could not be sustained for more than a few pages. But he certainly aspired to write a long poem at the age of twenty. To preface his ambitious "Al Aaraaf," he composed "Sonnet—To Science," one of his finest early lyrics. Its final revision reads:

Science! true daughter of Old Time thou art!
  Who alterest all things with thy peering eyes.
Why preyest thou thus upon the poet's heart,
  Vulture, whose wings are dull realities?
How should he love thee? or how deem thee wise,
  Who wouldst not leave him in his wandering
To seek for treasure in the jeweled skies,
  Albeit he soared with an undaunted wing?
Hast thou not dragged Diana from her car?
  And driven the Hamadryad from the wood
To seek a shelter in some happier star?
  Hast thou not torn the Naiad from her flood,
The Elfin from the green grass, and from me
The summer dream beneath the tamarind tree?

To have written such a poem at the age of nineteen or twenty was a triumph. Much of the spirit and thought of Poe's life are contained in this short work. It is a protest against what is conventionally thought of as science but also science in the larger sense of rational and practical thought, which the poet associates with materialism. To escape numbing reality, one must soar on the wings of the imagination to some faraway star.

Almost certainly, Poe knew Shelley's assertion in "A Defense of Poetry": "Reason respects the differences, and imagination the similitudes of things." "Sonnet—To Science" serves as the overture and invitation to the flight to the stars. Yet as we shall see, Poe had an enduring interest throughout his career in science, especially astronomy, and in the analytical process called ratiocination and the breaking of codes. As a child, he had looked through John Allan's telescope at the planets and stars. There were several compartments in Poe's mind, and the compartments did not always acknowledge or interact with each other. John Tresch tells us: "His deep familiarity with science was the fulcrum on which his thought balanced."

For Poe, Al Aaraaf, in Islamist mythology, was "a medium between Heaven & Hell where men suffer no punishment, but yet do not attain that tranquil & even happiness which they suppose to be the characteristic of heavenly enjoyment." Poe associates Al Aaraaf with a supernova Tycho Brahe spotted near the constellation Cassiopeia in 1572. It is a place inhabited by lower angels and some worthy people, in a realm beyond good and evil.

Like Milton before him, the young Poe found that those who sin have much more interesting stories than those who are guiltless. As the poem "Al Aaraaf" unfolds, with exotic names such as Capo Deucato and Trebizond, we encounter Nesace, the spirit of beauty, who rules this rare star. She had visited earth to purify it with fire. She then sings a song of adoration, wafted to heaven by the scent of flowers.

The verse in "Al Aaraaf" alternates between iambic pentameter couplets, octosyllabic couplets, and lyric sequences of interchanging rhymed trimeter and dimeter. Sometimes the lyric interludes are in anapestic or dactylic dimeter.

> Ligeia! wherever
>   Thy image may be,
> No magic shall sever
>   Thy music from thee.

"Al Aaraaf" is the work of a brilliant young poet, influenced by "romantic orientalism," reaching for the stars beyond his grasp. It fails as epic narrative, as drama, and as a treatise on theology and cosmology. But this longer poem of 1829 is essential to the study of Poe's life and his later work. As he will in *Eureka* later, he explores his aspiration toward the infinite, the cosmic, the otherworldly. And like Blake before him, he revels in paradox and in song that must be silent if it is celestial. "For what (to them) availeth it to know / That Truth is Falsehood—or that Bliss is Woe?"

As in Byron's poems, the personae in Poe's works are almost always doomed and damned. In "Al Aaraaf," in this universe of faraway stars, of Nesace, the spirit of beauty, of purification and flowers and perfume that lifts the goddess to heaven, we encounter the semi-divine, semi-human Angelo and Ianthe, guilty of passion. They are fallen angels because they commit the folly of love.

> What guilty spirit, in what shrubbery dim,
> Heard not the stirring summons of that hymn?
> But two: they fell: for Heaven no grace imparts
> To those who hear not for their beating hearts.

The name Ianthe, meaning "hyacinth," might have been taken from Shelley's "Queen Mab." Angelo is the spirit of Michelangelo in the afterlife. Poe would have known the story of Michelangelo's infatuation with the Italian noblewoman and poet Vittoria Colonna. This theme of fall through human desire is very much Poe's own. Milton's Adam and Eve fall from paradise because of disobedience to God, not passion. Desire and love for Elmira had yielded Poe grief and embarrassment.

By 1829 Poe seemed to have, at times, a horror of physical love, perhaps of his own desire, even as he idealized marriage. In both his poetry and his later fiction, passion is seen as an evil lurking in the garden. In "Eleonora" it is passion that destroys the idyll of the Valley of Many-Colored Grass. Incestuous passion destroys the House of Usher. Much of Poe's creative energy would be devoted to escaping to a safer realm, to the stars, to dreams, to the intellect, to the imagination, though he remained obsessed with marriage to a beautiful woman. In "Al Aaraaf" it turns out again that the true enemy is Time. Time destroys love and beauty. The failure of "Al Aaraaf" would inspire Poe to develop a poetics declaring the long poem impossible, a contradiction in terms. But Poe would continue to cherish the name Ligeia.

One source of controversy about Poe's poetry and poetics in the modern era has been the seeming conventionality of his versification. Ezra Pound famously admonished, "Make it new." But for Poe and many poets of his time, the ambition was also to make a poem seem "old." In the words of the critic Michael C. Cohen, "Far from being signs of aesthetic failure, conventionality and derivativeness [were] now seen as signal achievements of nineteenth century poetic language, because they generated and maintained an ever-expanding audience in the first era of mass communication."

Meredith McGill goes even further, stating that Poe's poetry "asserts its originality by highlighting its secondariness." Later Poe would stress originality in poetry, but that originality would always be expressed in conventional forms and rhetoric. We must remember that Poe's canon was very different from ours. Only in the twentieth century would the experimental, irregular, obscure, formless, and fragmentary become poetic virtues.

Tamerlane, Al Aaraaf, and Minor Poems was brought out by Hatch & Dunning of Baltimore in December 1829. Poe had managed to publish an excerpt from the book in John Neal's *Yankee and Boston Literary Gazette.* Neal gave Poe what was probably his first critical response, describing the poetry as "though nonsense, rather exquisite nonsense." He held out hope that Poe "might make a beautiful and perhaps a magnificent poem. There is a good deal here to justify such a hope."

As he waited for news of his appointment to the Academy and begged a skeptical John Allan for more money, this encouragement from Boston must have felt like manna from the stars. In the history of literature, especially poetry, most writers come in pairs or clusters. There might not have been a Shakespeare without a Marlowe and other Elizabethan poets and playwrights. We can't think of Wordsworth without Coleridge, a Byron without a Shelley, Thoreau without Emerson, Elizabeth Bishop without Marianne Moore. As they become poets, every poet must have a reader. All that's required is one. Poe would later declare that Neal's comments were "the very first words of encouragement I ever remember to have heard."

Poe signed his second book of poems as by "Edgar A. Poe," the name he would use for his writing from then on. This volume of seventy-one pages would actually attract some attention. A bookseller in Richmond named R. D. Sanxay advertised it in a local paper. It is remotely possible that John Allan paid for publication of the book or arranged for the ad in the Richmond paper. There were at least four reviews of "Al Aaraaf," some favorable, some not. A Baltimore critic recognized the quality of the short poems but referred to the versification as "a pile of brickbats" and claimed "Al Aaraaf" to be so obscure that "all our brain-cudgeling could not *compel* us to understand it." A reviewer in the *American Ladies' Magazine and Literary Gazette* of Boston remarked: "A part are exceedingly boyish, feeble, and altogether deficient in the common characteristics of poetry, but then we have parts and parts too of considerable length, which remind us of no less a poet than Shelley."

We can guess that Poe was gratified by a notice in a Baltimore newspaper in which the reviewer commented that American critics were typically looking for some great poet on these shores but usually ignore work such as Poe's. "We view the production as highly credible to the Country. Throughout, there runs a rich vein of deep and powerful thought, clothed in language of almost inimitable beauty and harmony. His fancy is rich and of an elevated cast." These were the words of encouragement and recognition Poe had been longing for. It's possible he wrote them himself.

Somehow Edgar survived the winter and spring of 1830 in Baltimore. John Allan may have sent him more money. Edgar may have returned to Richmond for some of those weeks and months, for Allan's records show him buying hose and four blankets for Edgar. It was almost certainly Allan who persuaded Powhatan Ellis, a brother of his former business partner, now a United States senator from Mississippi, to write a letter in support of Poe's application to West Point. It is said that Gen. Winfield Scott also recommended Poe's appointment to the Academy. Later a copy of Poe's early poems was found in General Scott's library. Allan himself wrote again to Secretary of War Eaton. The acceptance came through quickly, and Poe was directed to report to the Academy in June. Now that the appointment was secured, he was allowed to stay at Moldavia, but it was not a happy reunion. Allan accused Edgar of lying about paying his army substitute, Sgt. "Bully" Graves, the money he owed him.

Poe made a mistake when he replied to Graves, explaining that though he had asked repeatedly, Allan had never given him the money. It was possibly a lie, and then he added, to make his statement more convincing, "Mr. A. is not very often sober." This letter to Graves would later cost him far more than seventy-five dollars, for Graves would petition Allan for the money and reveal to him Edgar's letter, just when Edgar needed Allan's support at the military academy.

It is said that after the death of Fanny, John Allan proposed to her sister, "Aunt Nancy" Valentine, but she rejected him for a second time. It is also reported that Poe supported Aunt Nancy in this refusal, which action could not have endeared him to his already estranged foster father.

5

WEST POINT

THERE IS AN OLD JOKE AT WEST POINT: WHEN UPPERCLASSMEN explain the rules of protocol to arriving freshmen, the "plebes," they say there are only three permitted responses to a superior at the Academy, "Yes, sir," "No, sir," and "Nevermore, sir!"

Many of the most distinguished leaders in our history have attended West Point, including Ulysses Grant, George Armstrong Custer, Dwight Eisenhower, George Patton, but none is more famous or notorious than Edgar Allan Poe. Poe entered the Academy in June 1830 and would be discharged the following February. Poe's months there would become part of West Point legend, and American literary history.

Some things seemed to go badly for Poe almost as soon as he reached the Point. John Allan sent him a letter accusing him of stealing books and other items from Moldavia. Edgar fired back that he had taken "nothing except what I considered my own property." Poe had proven three years earlier that he could excel at soldiering, at military drill and discipline, when he put his mind to it. He was older than the other plebes, and he did well on the entrance exams. But discipline at West Point was strict, especially for first-year cadets. Edgar wrote Allan that out of 130 admitted each year, only 30 to 35 would graduate. Cadets rose at five in the morning and were expected to study until breakfast at seven thirty. Classes ran from eight until noon. In late afternoon there were drills and parade. After supper cadets were expected to study until lights-out at nine-thirty. Poe roomed in No. 28 South Barracks.

Cadets were directed to concentrate on two subjects at a time. Edgar would study French and mathematics and do well in each. He already had a background in both subjects and placed third in French and seventeenth in math.

The most distinguished general in the United States Army at that time was Winfield Scott, hero of the War of 1812. Edgar wrote John Allan that Scott was "very polite and attentive" to him. Scott would certainly have known of Poe's foster father and his grandfather Poe. John Allan's second wife, Louisa, was a relative of General Scott's spouse.

Poe's fellow cadets would later remember that he assumed a "Byronic" air of one damned from birth, having lived a mysterious but adventurous life of travel to exotic places. To some he claimed to be the grandson of Benedict Arnold, replacing General Poe with the notorious traitor who had once commanded the fortress at West Point. Poe led his classmates to believe that he'd sailed to South America and the Far East and had graduated from a college in England, incorporating in his stories details from his brother William Henry's travels as a sailor.

A cadet named Thomas W. Gibson later recalled Poe not only as a storyteller but as a poetaster. He shocked other cadets with hoaxes, scaring them with a bloody goose that he claimed was the head of someone he'd killed. He also wrote satirical doggerel about instructors at the Academy.

Edgar did not conceal from his fellow cadets the fact that he'd published poems. He very likely showed some a copy of *Al Aaraaf, Tamerlane, and Other Poems.* One cadet would quote "Sonnet—To Science" to his mother, the editor Sarah Joseph Hale. That poem would be reprinted in the October 1830 issue of the *Philadelphia Casket.* During the summer of 1830, Poe seemed to do well enough at the Academy. He admired Col. Sylvanus Thayer, the commandant.

Everything began to change in the fall, when he learned that John Allan had remarried on October 5, 1830. The second Mrs. Allan was Louisa Gabriella Patterson of Elizabeth, New Jersey. Allan was fifty-one and his bride two decades younger. Allan had illegitimate children in Richmond but no heirs. With this second marriage, it was possible, even probable, that he would sire legal offspring. Edgar's chances of inheriting from his foster father were now even less likely. Nevertheless, he wrote to Allan, sending his "respects to Mrs. A."

At West Point, Poe's time was filled with rigid, arbitrary restrictions.

A day was taken up with drill, parades, trivial protocol. But worst of all was Edgar's realization that he could never fit in, even if he wanted to. He was older than the other cadets and different. He was also far more accomplished and experienced. Sometimes he could escape to Benny Haven's nearby tavern for relief from the deadening routine.

Many of Poe's classmates were given adequate and even generous allowances. Clothes and everyday necessities had to be paid for. Some cadets received visits from members of their families. Poe could not conceal, even with his fantastic stories of adventure, that he had no money beyond his meager pay. He might display a Byronic air, but he could not hide his lack of means and outside support. Allan did not answer Poe's letters, and now the foster father had started a new family.

Poe could not accept that Allan had abandoned him. In a most essential way he was alone, as he had been so often before. An interesting memoir of Poe at West Point can be found in a letter Allan B. Magruder wrote to the biographer George Woodberry on April 23, 1884: "He was very shy and reserved in his intercourse with his fellow-cadets—his associates being confined almost exclusively to Virginians. . . . His wayward and capricious temper made him at times utterly oblivious or indifferent to the ordinary routine of roll-call, drills, and guard duties. These habits subjected him often to arrest and punishment."

In 1829 Poe had written in the album of Miss Lucy Holmes of Baltimore a poem called "Alone," along with another poem by "W. H. Poe," his brother. The poem "Alone," oddly, was never included in any of the four collections of poems Poe published in his lifetime. Yet it is one of his most memorable early poems and one of the most revealing.

From childhood's hour I have not been
As others were—I have not seen
As others saw—I could not bring
My passions from a common spring—
From the same source I have not taken
My sorrow—I could not awaken
My heart to joy at the same tone—
And all I lov'd—*I* lov'd alone—
Then—in my childhood—in the dawn

Of a most stormy life—was drawn
From ev'ry depth of good and ill
The mystery which binds me still—
From the torrent, or the fountain—
From the red cliff of the mountain—
From the sun that 'round me roll'd
In its autumn tint of gold—
From the lightning in the sky
As it pass'd me flying by—
From the thunder, and the storm—
And the cloud that took the form
(When the rest of Heaven was blue)
Of a demon in my view—

One of the acute ironies of American literary history is that the supposedly "democratic" poet Walt Whitman, who dreamed of writing of and for the masses, found mostly a learned, urban audience in his lifetime, while Poe, who saw himself as an elite genius, superior to the mob, became one of the most widely read and popular poets of his century. This poem "Alone" may offer a clue to Poe's popularity. Paradoxically, Poe, with his sense of alienation and difference, speaks for each of us, for most experience just such a sense of isolation. In our hearts and deepest selves, we feel alone and in some ways are thrilled by that separation, by the mystique of being exceptional. By tapping into the guilt and sense of difference, Poe makes us feel, strangely, *connected* to humanity. And we all love to read about drama more than placidity.

The poet was stranded at the United States Military Academy. He'd taken an oath to serve for five years. Day after day, he no doubt pondered how he could escape this penitentiary above the Hudson, whose routines held no further charm for him. Other cadets had grown up with firearms and horses and were excited by practice with artillery, bayonet drill, athletic training, military history, tactical manuals. After he'd made such an effort to secure the appointment, Poe probably felt guilty also for wasting his time, knowing he was destined for other things, greater things.

There is at least one other factor to consider with Poe's difficulties at West Point: his health. Hervey Allen, one of the most important, though not always reliable, chroniclers of Poe's life, argued in his best-selling biography *Israfel* that by the time Poe arrived at the Academy, starvation, stress, and maybe congenital defects had weakened his heart and general health. He simply lacked the strength and stamina to perform the drills, athletic exercises, and physical work required of cadets. For the rest of his life, Poe would experience periods of extreme fatigue, dizziness, headaches. Some afflictions may have been imagined but not all. It is also quite possible that he was infected with tuberculosis, from so much exposure to it, but that his immune system somehow kept the disease in check.

Edgar was looked down on by his fellow cadets because he'd served in the ranks, evidence that he was not officer material, despite his pose as a Byronic man of the world. And then, he was the son of actors and was forced to borrow money to pay for necessities. Still, he was handy with a bottle, and after only one drink, Edgar became wild and unpredictable, entertaining fellow cadets, but also quick-tempered, sarcastic, haughty.

If Poe had any prospect of assistance from John Allan, it was shattered when Sgt. Samuel "Bully" Graves, who'd never recovered the dollars he'd loaned to Poe, wrote directly to Allan and appealed to the foster father for payment. Graves let Allan know that Poe had described his foster father as "not very often sober." Allan sent Edgar a furious letter, asserting that he wanted "no further communication with yourself on my part."

Edgar replied to Allan that he *had* made the remark to Graves when he was upset, embittered by accusations Allan had made. No matter how many times he'd quarreled with Allan, Poe expected to be taken back, as he had been when a boy. It was a part of the mystery, part of the doom, and probably an essential component of his unusual genius.

There is also a further factor to be considered in Poe's stress at West Point. Poe was undergoing the hazing all plebes experienced at the Academy. First-year cadets were expected to perform trivial, arbitrary tasks for upperclassmen, answer ambiguous questions, endure sarcasm, and never complain or tattle. Older than the other plebes, Poe must have found it insufferable to have to submit day after day to demeaning treatment from upperclassmen two or three years younger than he. As far as we know, he was never targeted for particular hazing, though he was teased about his age. A joke went the rounds that it was Poe's son who had won the appointment to West Point but the father had taken the son's place.

As 1831 began, Poe composed the longest letter he'd ever sent to Allan. Now he had nothing to lose, and he unburdened himself of things he'd waited years to say. The pent-up rage blazed from his pen. "Did I, when an infant, sollicit [*sic*] your charity and protection, or was it of your own free will, that you volunteered your services in my behalf? It is well known to respectable individuals in Baltimore, and elsewhere, that my Grandfather (my natural protector at the time you interposed) was wealthy, and that I was his favourite grandchild. . . . Under such circumstances, can it be said that I have no *right* to expect any thing at your hands? . . . If I had been the vilest wretch on earth you could not have been more abusive . . . it was my crime to have no one on Earth who cared for me, or loved me."

As the letter gained momentum, emotions long suppressed surfaced. Poe reminded Allan that he had not been called to Richmond in the spring of 1829 until it was too late to see his foster mother alive. "If she had not have died while I was away there would have been nothing for me to regret—*Your* love I never valued—but she I believed loved me as her own child." Edgar added that he did not expect to live much longer. "My future life (which thank God will not endure long) must be passed in indigence and sickness. I have no energy left, nor health."

In concluding his long letter of confession and accusation, Poe reminded Allan that he needed his consent to withdraw from the Academy. However, if consent was not forthcoming, he would leave anyway. "From the time of writing this I shall neglect my studies and duties at the institution—if I do not receive your answer in 10 days—I will leave the point without—for otherwise I would subject myself to dismission."

Allan did not answer the letter but jotted on it, "I do not think the Boy has one good quality. . . . I cannot believe a word he writes."

Biographers have usually judged John Allan harshly. His failure to support his ward at the university and at the military academy caused Poe humiliation and grief. The loss of Elmira Royster, compounded with disgrace at Charlottesville and West Point, yielded psychological damage from which the poet never completely recovered. And Allan's snarls about Poe's family and aspersions cast on Eliza's character stung Edgar deeply. One explanation for Allan's behavior has been that the merchant had a very different temperament and could not understand the sensitive, volatile, gifted young poet. On the surface, this is undoubtedly true, but underneath there was a deeper bond between foster father and foster son. Otherwise, they would not have kept accusing and torturing each other. The young Edgar always believed, somehow, that the older man would come to his rescue, if only he could make Allan understand how wretched he was. And Allan did come to his aid, later covering a debt of eighty dollars (about twenty-four hundred dollars today) in Baltimore, paying for the substitute in the army, helping him to secure the appointment to West Point. It is even possible that Allan had subsidized the publishing of *Tamerlane, Al Aaraaf, and Other Poems* in December 1829.

Part of the tension between Edgar and Allan may have been that Poe was what Allan would have liked to be. When young, Allan, too, had dreamed of becoming a man of culture, possibly a writer, who moved in the best society. In 1814 Allan had written to a correspondent, "What would I not give, if I had [Shakespeare's] talent for writing! and what use would I not make of the raw material at my command." Instead, he'd apprenticed himself to business, without the benefit of a liberal education. Yet he wrote every day, letters and detailed accounts. He learned French; he saved all letters, including Edgar's, and for years read and reread and wrote comments on Edgar's missives. Part of Allan's anger at Edgar could have been jealousy of the poet's talent. Allan deeply admired and resented Poe's gifts and independence. His harshness was fueled in part by fear that had *he* been less dedicated to material things, he, too, might have been a poet or gifted essayist like those he read in the British quarterlies. This combination of admiration and envy forced Allan to grudgingly come to Edgar's aid and then betray him once more. Poe had a kind of courage that Allan lacked. The older man liked to think the world had been too harsh toward *him* and that he had spoiled Edgar. Encountering Poe's confidence in his abilities aggravated an old self-doubt.

Poe made good on his threat to get himself expelled from the Academy by neglecting all his duties, refusing to attend classes or take part in drills. He did not attend chapel. A legend at the Point, probably apocryphal, is that he did appear once on the parade ground at the designated time. The order of the day was to wear a dress sword for the exercise. Taking the order literally, Poe appeared on the field wearing only his sword!

On January 5, 1831, a court-martial was convened to try the case of Edgar and others, but proceedings were postponed until January 28. At the later date, Poe was charged with "Gross Neglect of Duty" and "Disobedience of Orders." He was found guilty of all charges and dismissed from the Academy as he had hoped. Between January 31 and February 18, Poe apparently spent some time confined in the guardhouse. He raised a little travel money by selling off things he'd accumulated at the Academy and took a steamboat for New York City on February 19, 1831. It is said he left West Point with only twenty-four cents ($7.20 in today's money).

Many years later, the United States Military Academy at West Point would recognize the memory of Edgar Allan Poe with "a marble doorway, inscribed with verse honoring Poe, in the Cadet Library." To add to the irony, we are told the doorway leads nowhere.

Some biographers claim Poe had traded his cadet uniform for cheap civilian clothes. But this is unlikely since he chose to appear in the uniform in Baltimore later that year. He would also wear his cadet overcoat, it seems, for the remaining eighteen years of his life. He arrived in the city on February 20, in cold wet weather, with few coins in his pocket, suffering a fever. But while at the Academy, Poe had not neglected his writing. Beside satiric doggerel to amuse the other cadets, Poe had polished his earlier poems and written "To Helen" and other new poems. He'd won a contract for a new book of verse with the New York firm of Elam Bliss. The way Poe pulled off this coup was to persuade many cadets at the Academy to subscribe to the forthcoming volume. The cadets understood the book as a kind of prank, with lampoons and satires about the faculty and officers at the Academy. Only a few had seen the kind of poems Poe wrote seriously, but Poe collected $170 (about $5,100 today) from the cadets. A. B. Magruder would later explain: "The cadets, especially from the South, generally subscribed at seventy-five cents [$22.50 in current money] a copy, which the superintendent allowed to be deducted from our pay."

Poems by Edgar A. Poe: Second Edition was issued in New York soon after Poe arrived. The volume was 124 pages long and dedicated "To the U.S. Corps of Cadets." It is said that most of the cadets were disappointed, even angry, when they saw the book for which they had subscribed. The legend is that some threw their copies into the Hudson. The book appeared hurriedly and cheaply produced. But for discerning readers, and for posterity, the publication was a milestone. Many of the earlier poems had been revised and improved. The volume contained "Tamerlane," "Al Aaraaf,"

"Sonnet—To Science," and others refined by revision. And there was the masterpiece "To Helen," already described, and "The Doomed City," later called "The City in the Sea," which some would label Poe's finest poem. And Poe introduced the poems with a short essay-like "Letter to B—" in which he began to further define his poetics and aesthetics, drawing on his reading of Coleridge's *Biographia Literaria* to proclaim: "A poem, in my opinion, is opposed to a work of science by having, for its *immediate* object, pleasure, not truth." Throughout his career Poe would argue that a poem exists for its own sake, echoing Kant's "definition of the work of art as possessing the quality of purposiveness without purpose." But in fact, Poe's poems reveal far more than their aesthetic surfaces might imply.

One poem Poe did not revise or improve was the earlier lyric "Romance" from his volume of 1829. Instead, he incorporated the older poem into a longer confession and meditation that, while not one of his best poems, is one of his most revealing. The new poem, called "Introduction," begins by quoting the first stanza of the earlier "Romance."

> Romance, who loves to nod and sing,
> With drowsy head and folded wing,
> Among the green leaves as they shake
> Far down within some shadowy lake,
> To me a painted paroquet
> Hath been—a most familiar bird—
> Taught me my alphabet to say—
> To lisp my very earliest word
> While in the wild-wood I did lie
> A child—with a most knowing eye.

In this tribute to romance, as opposed to science, the speaker presents himself as a child, similar to the speaker of "Alone," in the forest, with heightened perception and understanding. It is the third stanza that tells us most about the speaker, a passage he would never publish again.

> For, being an idle boy lang syne,
> Who read Anacreon, and drank wine,
> I early found Anacreon rhymes

Were almost passionate sometimes—
And by strange alchemy of brain
His pleasures always turn'd to pain—
His naivete to wild desire—
His wit to love—his wine to fire—
And so, being young and dipt in folly
I fell in love with melancholy,
And used to throw my earthly rest
And quiet all away in jest—
I could not love except where Death
Was mingling his with Beauty's breath—
Or Hymen, Time, and Destiny
Were stalking between her and me.

In this poem, written before he was twenty-two, Poe states one of the major paradoxes and inspirations of his art. It may be as close as he would ever come to understanding his own gifts and limitations. He conceded that his speaker "could not love except where Death / Was mingling his with Beauty's breath." Equally important, he admits the threat of "wild desire." This is an essential key to Poe's work in both prose and poetry. All the heroines, all the beloveds in his writing, are dying or already dead. All are idealized as the epitome of beauty. It was the threat and thrill of mortality that stimulated Poe's imagination and released his creative energy. This stanza encapsulates much of Poe's emotional and imaginative geography. The lines "And used to throw my earthly rest / And quiet all away in jest" define the way so much of Poe's work negotiates a fine line between satire, parody, burlesque, and elegiac elevation, confusing many readers. Poe often undercuts his most serious work with a wink or wisecrack.

One of the most unusual poems in the 1831 *Poems* is "Israfel," which in its revised version begins with the epigraph: "And the angel Israfel, whose heart-strings are a lute, and who has the sweetest voice of all God's creatures. —KORAN." The poem ends:

If I could dwell
Where Israfel
  Hath dwelt, and he where I,

He might not sing so wildly well
  A mortal melody,
While a bolder note than this might swell
  From my lyre within the sky.

Since so much of Poe's poetry and prose seems to aspire toward heavenly and angelic beauty, this poem may come as a surprise, appearing to defend human efforts at song here on earth, the earthly struggle for the sublime. It is the mortal experience, "In a world of sweets and sours," that has the most meaning, escaping passion.

In his comments on the poetry of Amelia Welby in *Marginalia* of December 1844, Poe would write, "A passionate poem is a contradiction in terms." The poet of the earth must sing rebellion and reach for the sublime through conflict, whirlwind, and vortex. Because of the epigraph of "Israfel," many readers and commentators over the years have understood the poem as the inverse of its actual meaning.

One of the finest poems in the volume of 1831, if not the very best, is "The Doomed City," which later became "The City in the Sea." The final version of the poem begins, and ends:

Lo! Death has reared himself a throne
In a strange city lying alone
Far down within the dim West,
Where the good and the bad and the worst and the best
Have gone to their eternal rest.
There shrines and palaces and towers
(Time-eaten towers that tremble not!)
Resemble nothing that is ours.
Around, by lifting winds forgot,
Resignedly beneath the sky
The melancholy waters lie.

. . . .

But lo, a stir is in the air!
The wave—there is a movement there!

. . . .

The waves have now a redder glow—

The hours are breathing faint and low—
And when, amid no earthly moans,
Down, down that town shall settle hence,
Hell, rising from a thousand thrones,
Shall do it reverence.

"The City in the Sea" may be the poem by Poe about which there is the least critical consensus. Some have read it as a narrative of transcendence to a heavenly state, called Hell, similar to an escape to a distant star. All agree on its apocalyptic nature. The critic Edward H. Davidson has seen the poem as illustrating the difference between Coleridge's Primary Imagination, which attempts to make sense of the world, and the Secondary Imagination, which creates the radical and new by destroying the familiar. In Poe's imagination, the sea devours the human. It is possible that for Poe this was a supremely erotic poem, in which Death, the consummation of the sexual act, drowns each in the dark, deep mystery of the female body, swallowing all in its triumph. We will see this ravenous, erotic, and sublime oceanic depth again in "MS. Found in a Bottle," "Descent into the Maelström," and other later works. In Poe's writing, death is never final but leads to some other state, a return to the lost Atlantis.

6

MARIA CLEMM AND BALTIMORE

IN NEW YORK, POE BECAME ACUTELY ILL, POSSIBLY FROM exposure, but slowly recovered. His trials at West Point had likely further weakened him. After he collected his copies of *Poems* in New York and whatever royalties were owed him, Poe made his way to Baltimore. With three books of poetry to his credit, an exceptional gift for writing, it would have seemed natural for him to seek work in New York, which offered many opportunities for someone with his talents. One of the many mysteries about Poe is why he found employment so hard to obtain, both at this time and later. There is a legend that in Baltimore he labored for a short while in a brickyard. On February 21, 1831, Poe had written yet another letter to John Allan, explaining his misery, ill health, and poverty. Poe's letters of wretchedness might be considered among his most accomplished works of art.

Edgar returned to Baltimore and to his brother, Henry, and his aunt Maria Clemm. It was she who had likely shown affection and taken him in while he waited to enter the military academy. His grandfather, Gen. David Poe, was dead. His grandmother, Elizabeth Cairnes Poe, was an invalid cared for by Mrs. Clemm.

According to the 1830 census, the population of Baltimore was 80,620. As a port for shipping tobacco and grain, near the northwest head of Chesapeake Bay, the city had become a major commercial and industrial center. After the war of 1812, Baltimore experienced an explosion of growth as the gateway to the National Road to the West, and after 1827 it had become the terminal of the Baltimore & Ohio Railroad. Because of its harbor and international trade, the city was more culturally diverse than most other southern port cities.

Maria Clemm, the younger sister of Poe's father, was born in Baltimore on March 17, 1790. At the age of twenty-seven, she had married William Clemm Jr., a widower with five children. Maria and Mr. Clemm would have two surviving children of their own, a son named Henry, born September 10, 1818, and a daughter named Virginia, born August 15, 1822. When William Clemm died, in 1826, he left Maria no money. What property he had was willed to the children of his first marriage.

The Irish novelist Mayne Reid would later leave one of the most vivid portraits of Maria Clemm: "She was the ever-vigilant guardian of the house, watching it against the silent but continuous sap of necessity, that appeared every day to be approaching closer and nearer. She was the sole servant, keeping every thing clean. . . . She was also the messenger to the market; from it bringing back, not 'the delicacies of the season,' but only such commodities as were called for by the dire exigencies of hunger."

Maria's son, Henry, about whom little is known, was a stonecutter but given to drink. It's reported that he soon "went West." Besides her invalid mother, Maria had taken in Edgar's older brother, Henry, dying of tuberculosis and far gone with alcoholism. Also in the house was little Virginia, now nine years old. It's possible that Maria's son Henry was still living there, for a while. Maria sometimes took in boarders to help pay the bills.

Frederick W. Thomas (1806–66), a popular novelist and songwriter, who would later prove a loyal friend to Poe, knew both Mrs. Clemm and Henry in Baltimore, while Poe was stationed on Sullivan's Island. After Poe's death, he would leave a memoir of his relations with the Poe family: "I was intimate with Poe's brother in Baltimore during the year 1828. He was a slim, feeble young man, with dark inexpressive eyes, and his forehead had nothing like the expansion of his brother's. His manners were fastidious. We visited lady acquaintances together."

With two alcoholic young men in the house on Wilks Street, Maria probably welcomed Edgar to help manage things. It seems she'd always had an affection for him, which only grew over the years. Maria loved Edgar as a mother and forgave his faults. She took him in when he had nowhere else to go. She could not be a muse; she was large and kindly and almost masculine. She was known for her tidiness and strict cleanliness.

In the worst of times, Mrs. Clemm fed the family from her basket. Setting out with the container on her arm, first in Baltimore and later in Philadelphia and New York, she would make her rounds to neighbors, friends, storekeepers, and even strangers, telling stories of hardships, bills unpaid, sickness, near starvation, and piety and would collect gifts of money, bread, vegetables, whatever people had to give. She could be shameless in her begging. At grocery stores, she might collect things thrown away or about to be thrown away.

Mrs. Clemm devoted her life to helping others, but we know from her letters that she was a whiner and manipulator. Later she would petition editors to publish or employ "Eddie." She would embarrass him after he became famous by promising mediocre poets he would write favorable reviews of their work in return for gifts of cash or other necessities. But Poe's life cannot be imagined without Muddy. She provided the unconditional love he searched for and may never have found elsewhere. Without Maria Clemm, Poe might have died much earlier or passed a short life of drudgery in a newspaper office.

When Poe arrived in Baltimore, he moved into a third-story room with his brother, William Henry. Like Keats and William Blake before him, Poe nursed his brother until he died five months later. Death from consumption was common in the nineteenth century, and the disease seemed especially prevalent in writers' families, including the Brontës. Henry Poe had published both short stories and poems in magazines and newspapers. There are some poems on which the brothers appear to have collaborated.

By the summer of 1831, Henry was so weakened with consumption there was little to be done except to try to make him comfortable. Alcohol and laudanum probably helped, when they could be afforded. Baltimore is witheringly hot in summer, and there could have been little ventilation in the room as Henry coughed blood and gasped. While looking for work, Edgar apparently stayed with his brother, doing what he could through those wretched days and nights. He must have seen that all Henry's travels and different jobs had not helped him much as a writer. Henry's death may have encouraged Poe to concentrate on his writing and let Mrs. Clemm prevent him from starving. And he may have hoped that he could still wheedle money out of John Allan if he had to. At least one Poe biographer believed that Allan still gave Poe "a small annuity," though that seems unlikely.

On May 6, 1831, Poe wrote to William Gwynn, editor of the *Federal Gazette and Baltimore Daily Advertiser*, seeking help in obtaining employment: "Dear Sir,—I am almost ashamed to ask any favour at your hands after my foolish conduct upon a former occasion—but I trust to your good nature. . . . I write to request your influence in obtaining some situation or employment in this city." Gwynn had known Poe's father when David Poe Jr. was a law student.

William Henry Poe died August 1, 1831, and the funeral took place the next day at Maria Clemm's residence. There was little doubt that Henry's drinking had hastened his end, though it may have mitigated his suffering. Edgar had described his brother in 1829 as "entirely given up to drink & unable to help himself, much less me." Henry died at the age of twenty-four, as had their mother.

Poe's time in Baltimore between 1831 and 1835 has been called by some "the mysterious years" or "the lost years." Hervey Allen believed that Poe took opium while he worked in Maria Clemm's attic, beginning to write the stories of fantasy for which he became renowned. It's true there are few explicit records for this period. And Poe himself would sometimes claim that he had shipped out to exotic places, much as his brother, Henry, had. And yet we have enough facts to provide a general sense of Poe's activities during these four years. What he was doing was what inspired young writers do: he was writing. He sat in his room on the third floor, in air tainted with tuberculosis bacteria, freezing in winter, sweating in summer, reading and writing and dreaming. He tried one idea and then another and found that prose is just as hard, or perhaps harder, to master than verse. In poetry you have the meter and line length and rhyme to guide you. In prose you launch out into imagined space with nothing to direct you but a voice of narration and what you can visualize. He'd tried the university, he had worked as a clerk, and he'd experienced the army. Only his pen could save him, if he could be saved. Besides, he knew that Maria Clemm would have something on the table when he descended the stairs each morning.

The Baltimore that Poe immersed himself in, in the early 1830s was hardly a literary desert. As the third most populous city in the United States, Baltimore was a rapidly growing center of commerce because of its harbor and connections to several highways, the Chesapeake and Ohio Canal, the Potomac Canal, and the new B&O Railroad. The city claimed a vigorous culture, including theaters, lecture halls, and at least seventy-two periodicals founded between 1815 and 1833. Some had names implying classical learning: *Baltimore Athenaeum, Baltimore Minerva and Emerald, Baltimore Monument.* Two new theaters were established in 1829 and 1830, respectively.

The catastrophic cholera outbreak in Baltimore in 1832 may have later helped inspire Poe's "Masque of the Red Death." An unusually bright meteor shower over the city on November 13, 1833, could have added to the awe of the heavens Poe would demonstrate in *Eureka* and other works.

Between 1816 and 1825, leading citizens of Baltimore met weekly as the Delphian Club to discuss literary and other topics of interest. Mostly doctors and lawyers, they gathered to enjoy refreshments and each other's company and to learn from the conversations, in the tradition of "coterie societies" such as Joseph Addison's Spectator Club. Members would include the author and politician William Wirt, the editor John Neal, and Tobias Watkins, editor of *Portico.* Poe would satirize the gatherings in *Tales of the Folio Club.*

Based on the advertisements for books in the newspapers of the time, it seems there were many bookstores in the city, offering "a surprising number and variety of works." It has been claimed that in the 1830s Baltimore's intellectual life "was at high tide."

In 1832 the *Baltimore Saturday Visiter* would be established by Charles Cloud and Lambert Wilmer. Wilmer would become a close friend of Poe. After Poe's death, Wilmer would defend the poet's character. John Hewitt became editor of the *Visiter* around 1833. Hewitt, a sometime musician, sign painter, and music teacher, had previously edited the *Baltimore Minerva and Emerald* and the *Minerva and Saturday Post.*

The most distinguished member of the Baltimore literary community was John Pendleton Kennedy (1795–1870) (fig. 12). Kennedy would serve in the House of Representatives from 1841 to 1845 and later be appointed secretary of the navy by Millard Fillmore. He had belonged to the Delphian Club and edited a periodical called *Red Book.* Among his many publications were the classic novels *Swallow Barn* and *Horse-Shoe Robinson.* Kennedy was a board member of the B&O Railroad and the Peabody Institute,

FIG. 12. John Pendleton Kennedy (1795–1870). A Baltimore lawyer and author of novels set in the Old South, Kennedy served as a judge for the *Saturday Visiter* prize awarded to Poe in 1833. An early supporter of Poe, Kennedy recommended the young writer to the editor of the *Southern Literary Messenger* in 1835. (Courtesy of the Edgar Allan Poe Museum, Richmond, Virginia)

forerunner of Johns Hopkins University. He was a lifelong opponent of slavery. As one of the judges for the *Baltimore Saturday Visiter* fiction prize who chose "MS. Found in a Bottle," Kennedy was a valuable supporter of Poe's early career.

Dr. Joseph Evans Snodgrass (1813–80), founder of the *American Museum,* was a friend of Poe and would later play a significant role in Poe's life, and death. There are rumors that Poe would join a group of literary bohemians from time to time at the Seven Stars Tavern, with disastrous results for Maria Clemm to address.

Poe's "mysterious years" in Baltimore remind us of questions Shakespeare's biographers have always faced: why are there so few records? Yet there is the work, which suggests that Shakespeare, whoever he was, spent most of his time writing. The same is likely true of Poe in 1831–35, for we know the result of those long years of apprenticeship. The editor and writer L. A. Wilmer would later recall strolling in the countryside with Edgar, "long and frequent walks together in the beautiful undulating country around Baltimore."

In the *Poems* of 1831, Poe had published a poem that provides a special key to much of his fiction writing. Later it would be revised as "The Sleeper," but the 1831 version is called "Irenë." He would describe it to James Russell Lowell as one of his best poems, and there are many who would agree. In its final version, "The Sleeper" has one of the most songlike beginnings of any of Poe's poems.

At midnight, in the month of June,
I stand beneath the mystic moon.
An opiate vapour, dewy, dim,
Exhales from out her golden rim,
And, softly dripping, drop by drop,
Upon the quiet mountaintop,
Steals drowsily and musically
Into the universal valley.
. . . .

The lady sleeps! Oh, may her sleep,
Which is enduring, so be deep!
Heaven have her in its sacred keep!
This chamber changed for one more holy,
This bed for one more melancholy,
I pray to God that she may lie
Forever with unopened eye,
While the pale sheeted ghosts go by!

The most important feature of "The Sleeper" is that the subject is both alive and dead. She may lie in her tomb, never decaying, but is always alive for the narrator. For Poe the poem must have evoked an exquisite erotic guilt, foreshadowing the stories he would write about romance and marriage, and death.

In Mrs. Clemm's attic, first at Mechanics Row, Wilks Street, then at 3 Amity Street in Baltimore, Poe apprenticed himself to the art of the tale or short story. Some have called him the inventor of the detective story and the first theorist of modern short fiction. In many ways the short story is the most difficult of all narrative genres. To be effective, a tale must be executed as perfectly as a poem. Novels may contain many flaws and still succeed, but a story must grab its readers from the first and never let go. A story must surprise the reader with its turns and yet seem inevitable at the end.

The fiction writer Hollis Summers once said, "The point of the story is always the point beside the point." Peripheral vision is essential to a story. The significant clue is always there, but the reader does not notice it until near the end. Think of the "one-third" rule in photography: the center of attention in a photograph should not be at the physical center of the picture but about one-third from the margin.

Even gifted novelists find the short story a formidable challenge. Every short story has its own logic and must be consistent within that logic as well as maintaining its tension and curvature. A story has to fall into place like a poem, landing on its feet as surely as an Olympic gymnast. The short story is a kind of miracle, combining the art of narrative with the perfection of a lyric.

Emerson says in the poem "Merlin I" that the poet must "mount to paradise / By the stairway of surprise." A story without surprise is hardly a story at all, a mere anecdote. In literary history it's rare for a fiction writer to be equally good at writing both poems and short stories: maybe D. H. Lawrence? Poe is unique in that he broke new ground in at least three genres: poetry, short fiction, and criticism.

Poe had a number of models when he began writing stories in the early 1830s. America had produced the sensational Gothic novels of Charles Brockden Brown, and the English quarterlies published ghost stories and tales of lurid melodrama and sensation. There were the tales of Washington Irving.

Poe turned to the short story at about the time Hawthorne, in Salem, Massachusetts, began writing his tales, and for the same reason. Publication in magazines and annuals was almost the only outlet for an American writer. Most novels brought out in the United States were reprinted editions from abroad. But there were dozens of magazines in cities such as Baltimore, Philadelphia, New York, and Boston, as well as newspapers and annuals, that published poems and stories. The short fiction market was hard to break into then, as it is now, but it was about the only market there was.

A further problem for American writers then was that anything published in a magazine or newspaper could be reprinted in other publications, with no royalties paid. It was an age of reprinting. As Meredith L. McGill tells us, "Achieving proprietary control over the circulation of his writing largely eluded Poe until he was taken up by an influential group of literary nationalists, the Young Americans." But that would not be until 1845.

On May 28, 1831, the *Saturday Courier* in Philadelphia advertised that it would award a hundred-dollar prize for the "best AMERICAN TALE." Poe submitted several stories but did not win. Yet on January 14, 1832, he had the pleasure of seeing what was probably his first story, "Metzengerstein," published in the *Saturday Courier*. It's possible "Metzengerstein" was not Poe's very first published fiction. A short piece called "A Dream," printed in the *Saturday Evening Post* on August 13, 1831, and signed P., was discovered in 1917 by the Poe specialist Killis Campbell. Many scholars think it was written by Poe, probably while at West Point or just after he arrived in Baltimore. The narrator dreams he is a Pharisee who drove nails into Jesus's flesh on the cross. It's a story of guilt and punishment, and unending horror, until the narrator wakes. It would seem the young Poe had already found his subjects.

The prize offered by the *Saturday Courier* went to Delia Bacon, who would later promote the Baconian theory about the authorship of Shakespeare's plays, for her story "Love's Martyr." "Metzengerstein" was published anonymously, and Edgar would have only the pleasure of seeing his work in print. But for a young author that is no small satisfaction.

Poe's story resembles many stories published in the quarterlies at that time, yet it displays the unmistakable Poe touch. Metempsychosis was a common theme in those days, but migration of souls was only a springboard for Poe's imagination. The setting is Hungary, and two families, the Berlifitzings and the Metzengersteins, have adjoining estates. The princely families have been enemies for centuries, and there is an ancient prophecy: "A lofty name shall have a fearful fall when, as the rider over his horse, the mortality of Metzengerstein shall triumph over the immortality of Berlifitzing." Along with "Metzengerstein," Poe submitted several other stories to the *Saturday Courier*. They were part of a projected volume of eleven stories he called *Tales of the Folio Club*. They included "The Duc de L'Omelette," a romp of grotesque humor, and "A Tale of Jerusalem," an attempt at comedy in which a joke is played on Jews by feeding them pork when they expect lamb.

Of the comic tales Poe wrote at this time, the most impressive may be "A Decided Loss," which later became "A Loss of Breath." Several Poe scholars have suggested it's a story about sexual impotence. It is certainly a story of grotesque self-punishment and guilt. In the second version the narrator has just been married, and the morning after the wedding night he abuses his wife relentlessly: "'Thou wretch!—thou vixen!—thou shrew!' said I to my wife on the morning after our wedding, 'thou witch!—thou hag!—thou whipper-snapper!—thou sink of iniquity! . . . to my extreme horror and astonishment, I discovered that *I had lost my breath.*" "A Decided Loss" has been viewed as Poe's first story about the horrors of marriage. There is a hint that the new bride has been unfaithful. The critic Ellen Weinauer tells us that the story, in its "postnuptial setting," evokes "the institution of marriage, which functioned precisely to create new (and arguably unnatural) entities."

Humor often does not age well. The jokes of one era fall flat in another. Humor depends on context and expectation. Cartoons that were hilarious a hundred years ago may seem pointless to us. Poe's comic writing was not especially successful in his own time. Now much of it just seems absurd. But for students of Poe's mind, his humorous sketches have been a trove for insight into his personality and thought. Many of his ideas of what was funny appear bizarre and cruel to us. But a story such as "Loss of Breath" opens the window a little on his secret life, his horror of sexual desire and marriage, his alternating lust and repression, his intense need for a wife-mother-muse-lover, and his feared inability to perform. For Poe, burlesques and parodies often became expressions of rough cruelty, sarcastic sadism, both masking and displaying his own anxieties, especially about marriage. The critic Daniel Royot tells us, "Poe's black humor is a form of bravado designed to articulate genuine fears and partly allay such fears."

While Poe was living in Baltimore, in Maria Clemm's attic, he paid court to several young women who would remember him later. He wrote poems to his cousin Elizabeth Herring, who was fourteen years old, but her family discouraged his interest. At one point he became enamored of a girl who lived next door, Mary Starr, and little Virginia Clemm carried notes between Edgar and Mary. Long after Poe's death, Mary would recall her relations with the writer next door, which lasted from the summer of 1831 to the summer of 1832.

> My intimacy with Mr. Poe isolated me a good deal. In fact my girl friends were many of them afraid of him and forsook me on that account. . . . He despised ignorant people, and didn't like trifling and small-talk. He didn't like dark-skinned people. When he loved, he loved desperately. Though tender and very affectionate, he had a quick, passionate temper, and was very jealous. . . . He was not well balanced: he had too much brain. He scoffed at everything sacred, and never went to church. . . . He believed he was born to suffer, and this embittered his whole life. *Mrs. Clemm also spoke vaguely of some family mystery, of some disgrace. . . .*
>
> We used to go out walking together in the evenings. We often walked out of the city and sat down on the hills. . . .
>
> Our final lovers' quarrel came about in this way. . . . He said he had met some cadets from West Point. . . . They were old friends, and took him to Barnum's Hotel, where they had a supper and champagne. He had gotten away as quickly as possible, to come and explain matters to me. A glass made him tipsy. . . .
>
> I went and opened the door and sat on the stoop with him in the moonlight. We then had a quarrel, about whose cause I do not care to speak. . . .
>
> He sent me a letter by Virginia. . . . and upbraided me in satiric terms for my heartless, unforgiving disposition. . . . My uncle was very indignant, and resented Mr. Poe's letter so much he wrote him a very severe, cutting letter . . .
>
> Mr. Poe was so incensed at the letter . . . that he bought a cowhide [whip], and went to my uncle's store one afternoon and cowhided him. . . . My aunt and her two sons rushed into the store, and in the struggle to defend my uncle tore his assailant's black frock-coat at the back from the skirts to the collar. Mr. Poe then put the cowhide up his sleeve and went up the street to our house as he was, with his torn coat, and followed by a crowd of boys. . . . I had been called down-stairs, and when Mr. Poe saw me, he pulled the cowhide out of his sleeve and threw it down at my feet, saying, "There, I make you a present of that!"

Some Poe biographers, including Arthur Hobson Quinn, have discounted Mary Starr's story. It was published in an article called "Poe's Mary," by Augustus Van Cleef, Mary's nephew, in *Harper's New Monthly*

Magazine in March 1889. Van Cleef calls her Mary Devereaux, to conceal her identity. Yet there is probably considerable truth in Mary's memories of Poe. Poe later saw a good bit of Mary after she was married, in Philadelphia, and at her home in New Jersey, and in Virginia's last days, Mary visited the Poes more than once. That does not mean that every statement by Mary Starr should be believed literally. For example, she may have taken his teasing about church attendance too seriously. The story of the cowhide is much too good to be true. More likely, the angry Poe threatened to buy a cowhide and chastise the insulting uncle.

Most convincing is that Edgar, as his courting of Mary grew more serious, made sure to find a way to end it. Drink was his refuge and his means for avoiding the horror of a commitment that loomed closer. With Mary Starr, Poe exhibited both his attraction to marriage and his repulsion. He dreamed of wedding his beautiful neighbor but found a way to break off the relationship before it proceeded further. He was fascinated with matrimony and terrified of marriage. There seemed to be no practical middle ground.

While his romantic life may have been in turmoil, Poe made significant headway with his art. A local newspaper, the *Saturday Visiter*, announced in 1833 a prize of fifty dollars (fifteen hundred dollars today) for the best story submitted by October 1 and a prize of twenty-five dollars for the best poem.

With painstaking effort, Poe printed by hand a copy of his *Tales of the Folio Club* for the contest. This group of stories was modeled in part on Benjamin Disraeli's *Vivian Grey*. He also included a poem called "The Coliseum." The three judges, one of whom was the novelist John Pendleton Kennedy, chose a story called "MS. Found in a Bottle" by Edgar A. Poe.

Besides Kennedy, the judges for the contests were Dr. James H. Miller and John H. B. Latrobe, an inventor and lawyer. Dr. Miller founded the Washington College Hospital, where Poe would later die. Latrobe was the son of Benjamin Latrobe, architect of Washington, DC. According to Latrobe's later account, they met one afternoon on his back porch and, fortified with wine and cigars, began to read the submissions. At first they could find no fiction worthy of a prize. And then one of them opened a manuscript in which the writing "was in Roman characters—an imitation of printing." As Latrobe began reading the entry aloud, suddenly the others listened.

"I had not proceeded far before my colleagues became as much interested as myself. The first tale finished I went to the second, then to the next and did not stop till I had gone through the volume. . . . And finally the committee selected *A Ms. Found in a Bottle.*"

After choosing the best story, the committee had to select the winning poem for the twenty-five-dollar prize. Poe had submitted the poem "The Coliseum," but the judges decided not to award both the fiction and the poetry prizes to the same person. Instead, they picked "The Song of the Winds" by "Henry Wilson," who turned out to be none other than John H. Hewitt, the editor of the *Saturday Visiter.* Hewitt had given the *Al Aaraaf* volume of 1829 a harsh review. Poe confronted Hewitt, and they almost exchanged blows, but others separated them.

After the prize for "MS. Found in a Bottle" was announced, Poe called on each of the judges to thank them. Later Latrobe left an account of his young and grateful visitor: "His figure was remarkably good, and he carried himself erect and well, as one who had been trained to it. He was dressed in black, and his frock-coat was buttoned to the throat. . . . Coat, hat, boots, and gloves had very evidently seen their best days, but so far as mending and brushing go, everything had been done, apparently, to make them presentable." Poe described to Latrobe a story about a voyage to the moon on which he was working.

Winning the *Saturday Visiter* fiction award proved a significant turn in Poe's fortunes. When the prize was announced, the three judges expressed their admiration for the young author in print: "We . . . can not refrain from the expression of the opinion that the writer owes it to his own reputation, as well as to the gratification of the community, to publish the whole volume. These tales are eminently distinguished by a wild, vigorous and poetical imagination, a rich style, a fertile invention, and varied and curious learning."

It's not hard to imagine the lift this prize and praise gave to Poe after two years of working relentlessly in obscurity. "MS. Found in a Bottle" was a significant advance over "Metzengerstein." The story begins like an essay, establishing the practical common sense of the narrator. Poe already knew that in effective fantasy, an air of authenticity and realism is essential. We are drawn step by step from the ordinary to the fantastic along a seamless trail of detail and comment. Sailing from Java, the narrator, a restless and inveterate traveler, describes the approach of a terrible storm. Unable to sleep, he goes up on deck at midnight, just as a cataclysmic wave sweeps over the ship, breaking the masts and killing all on board except our speaker and an old Swede. "The hulk flew at a rate defying computation, before rapidly succeeding flaws [gusts] of wind, which, without equalling the first violence of the Simoon, were still more terrific than any tempest I had before encountered."

Poe's talent for evoking the violence and terror and wonder of the ocean, to be developed further in "Descent into the Maelström" and *The Narrative of Arthur Gordon Pym,* is on full display here. For Poe the ocean often represents at once horror, the irrational, and the sublime. The narrator staggers to the rear but is thrown into the rigging of a giant ship when the two crafts crash. "To conceive the horror of my sensations is, I presume, utterly impossible; yet a curiosity to penetrate the mysteries of these awful regions, predominates even over my despair." The narrator has found pen and paper in the captain's cabin and records his nightmare journey. At the final moment, he will place his account in a bottle and fling it into the ocean.

"Oh, horror upon horror!—the ice opens suddenly to the right, and to the left, and we are whirling dizzily, in immense concentric circles, round and round the borders of a gigantic amphitheatre. . . . The circles rapidly grow small—we are plunging madly within the grasp of the whirlpool—and amid a roaring, and bellowing, and thundering of ocean and of tempest, the ship is quivering—oh God! and—going down!" The ship spins faster as the circle closes, as ice skaters, drawing in their arms, begin to blur.

Daniel Hoffman points out, in *Poe Poe Poe Poe Poe Poe Poe,* that the story recounts a dangerous and horrifying return to the womb. Yet to what extent is Poe playing games with the reader? In the final seconds, the ship is whirled in concentric circles, "screwing" beyond control into the thrilling depths. The climactic moment in several of Poe's stories is approached at the edge of an amphitheater. The world is indeed a stage.

In a story such as "MS. Found in a Bottle" Poe was able to bring out into the light of fiction his fascination and his terrifying secret. The mother womb was the suppressed wonder whose name could not be spoken. Poe's awe and love for the beauty and power of the ocean are also a measure of his awe and love for mother nature. Daniel Royot suggests the story comes from a liquor bottle and is a drunken fantasy. The novelist Joseph Conrad would later say of "MS. Found in a Bottle": "A very fine piece of work—about as fine as anything of that kind can be—and so authentic in detail that it must have been told by a sailor of a sombre and poetical genius."

Maria Clemm provided Edgar with what he'd never known since Eliza's death: unconditional affection. No matter if he piddled away hours writing poems and stories, if his clothes were falling to pieces, no matter if he told white lies or got in a fight, no matter if he was sick day after day, no matter if he made himself ridiculous flirting with women, Muddy still loved him and fed him and gave him a home.

From Mrs. Clemm's point of view, Eddie must have been a godsend. She'd lost a husband, who left her no money. Her stepchildren were hostile. Her son was an alcoholic. She was alone, caring for her young daughter and her dying mother. Her only means of support were taking in boarders and sewing. Eddie was the brightest person she'd ever known. He could explain anything, and charm anyone, if he chose to. He was her brother's son, and his weaknesses were the weaknesses of the Poes.

Muddy was a widow, without much affection in her life, and there was little chance she would marry again. Eddie was in need of motherly affection. What is certain is that he had found a family. Later, as his interest turned elsewhere, she may have encouraged his attentions to Virginia, as her daughter grew into her teens, to keep him at her side. Muddy may have been more necessary to Poe than Virginia, and Poe was essential to Muddy in her difficult and discouraging life. She had to keep him with her. Neilson Poe may have suspected something unnatural in the relationship and tried to rescue Virginia in 1835 from such an unusual home. Muddy was the real wife, at least for a time.

Little Virginia delighted in her older cousin, who took time to tell her stories, recite poems, play with her, and send her on errands. And Muddy may have believed that with his extraordinary wit, charm, and good looks, Eddie just might be a success someday. In the years after Poe's death, Muddy would explain: "I attended to his literary business, for he, poor fellow, knew nothing about money transactions. . . . I even bought his clothes for him. . . . he was very charitable, and would empty his pockets to a beggar."

In the so-called Mystery Years, 1831–35, the arrangement became a way of life. As he won the *Saturday Visiter* prize and sold a few additional pieces to newspapers, Poe presumably helped with the family finances, though he never cared much for money as such. He was always willing for Muddy to manage whatever funds he scrounged. And day by day, Muddy did her fanatical cleaning, nursed the sick, took her basket out to buy or beg for their supper. Eddie did his scribbling and played with Virginia. Virginia did her homework and played with the cat and occasionally with other children.

As Virginia grew older and the dependence of the three on each other deepened, it was far from clear at times how they would survive. But the little household of Maria Clemm and Virginia and himself satisfied Poe in ways he may not have entirely understood. He was protected and safe there from humiliations and embarrassments of the outside world. At home with them, his sexual anxieties and excitable nature were no problem. To them he was not only acceptable; he was a hero. He could no more leave Muddy and Sister, or "Sissy," as he called Virginia, than he could live without breathing. Yet he likely felt guilty for depending on them. As the man of the house, supremely gifted, he was required to make his way in the larger world.

It is probable that the happiest times and most productive periods in Poe's adult life were the days and months and years when he lived alone with Muddy and Virginia. Day after day Muddy struggled to find something to eat. There is a rumor that they once lived for weeks on bread and molasses. In summer they endured the blistering city heat in second stories and attics. In winter they huddled around small stoves and wrapped themselves in blankets and overcoats, while Eddie scribbled and sulked by turns. There is no doubt that Poe was, in modern terms, bipolar. He could work feverishly for days and weeks and then lapse into depression and indolence. If he got drunk, it could take days to recover. He did not like to drink, and yet when depression deepened, he could not help himself.

If he was at his best alone with Virginia and Muddy, Poe was at his worst when he fled their sanctuary and joined friends or strangers at a tavern. To some he might seem the life of the party, for a while. But soon his behavior became so bizarre people would think him insane. He insulted friends and those who could help him. He fought with his fists or challenged men to duels.

Poe carried within him a deep sense of guilt and a belief that he was damned, for reasons almost too subtle for him, and for us, to understand.

His sense of being condemned was so profound it could best be expressed in his writing. But when drinking, his belief in his own mystery and doom surfaced. Mary Starr saw the rage, and years later she would see the fear and confusion also. She would recall that "Mrs. Clemm also spoke vaguely of some family mystery, of some disgrace."

When a new magazine began publication in Richmond in 1834, John Pendleton Kennedy suggested to T. W. White, the editor, that he feature Poe's stories and poems and commission the young writer to contribute reviews and articles. On March 15, 1835, Poe asked Kennedy to recommend him for a teaching position in Baltimore. To discuss the matter, Kennedy invited Poe to dine with him. In return the older writer received this note: "Dear Sir,—I cannot come—and for reasons of the most humiliating nature [in] my personal appearance. . . . If you will be my friend so far as to loan me $20 [about $600 today] I will call on you to morrow—otherwise it will be impossible, and I must submit to my fate."

Kennedy not only sent Poe money for decent clothes; he offered the young author the use of a horse "for exercise." It was a magnificent gesture, of one gentleman to another, designed to boost Poe's confidence just when he needed it most. Years later Poe would remember Kennedy's kindness to him: "Mr. Kennedy . . . was the first true friend I ever had. I am indebted to him *for life itself*." Kennedy would leave a posthumous assessment of Poe's character: "He was debauched by the most grovelling appetites and exalted by the richest conceptions of genius."

In those hard years in Baltimore, Poe had not been completely out of touch with John Allan. When about to be arrested for an eighty-dollar debt (about twenty-four hundred dollars today), Poe had appealed once again to his estranged foster father, and, belatedly, Allan came to his rescue. On December 15, 1831, Poe wrote to Allan, "I feel at the very bottom of my heart that if you were in my situation . . . how differently I would act." There are conflicting stories of visits, or attempted visits, to Richmond and encounters with the second Mrs. Allan. Though wealthy and father of young children with his new wife, Allan had fallen ill. Susan Weiss tells us Miss Valentine sent money to Poe from time to time. According to J. H. Whitty, Poe kept in touch with some of the older Allan servants, who informed him of the goings-on in Richmond.

Back in October 1831, Poe had written to Allan, hanging on to the belief that the older man still considered him his son. "When I think of the long twenty-one years that I have called you father, and you have called me son, I could cry like a child to think that it should all end in this."

John Allan Jr. had been born in August 1831. Probably Allan had less interest than ever in hearing from his foster son. Poe could not give up the hope that Allan would one day make him his heir. Usually a gifted young man, who had been treated as Poe had been, would have looked for a job and made his own way in the world. It would have been the practical way, the Ben Franklin way. Instead, this struggling young man holed up in an attic in Baltimore, scribbling and dreaming. And from time to time, he would humble himself and appeal to Allan again for support, confess his past mistakes, and imagine that somehow Allan still cared for him.

When looked at from this distance, we can see that Poe had made a decision: he would follow his imagination. Other young men *would* have found a day-to-day job, teaching or writing for a newspaper, and never contacted John Allan again. But Poe had a special kind of courage to go his own way. And if that required him to humble himself again to his foster father to get out of some crisis, then it was worth it to appeal to the old skinflint. Besides, he'd found Maria Clemm and knew he would not really starve. Even the most impractical genius usually has a way of sustaining itself, whether in Nathaniel Hawthorne's upstairs room in Salem or William Blake's humble quarters on a London back street. When his aunt and Virginia moved to Amity Street in Baltimore in the spring of 1833, Edgar moved with them.

It is thought that Poe tried to visit Moldavia in early 1834, after learning of John Allan's illness. According to one account Allan suffered from dropsy so severe he could not lie down but remained in a chair and could only stand or walk with help. The story goes that when Edgar came to the house, the second Mrs. Allan tried to prevent him from seeing the invalid foster father, but Edgar rushed upstairs to Allan's room. At the sight of his prodigal foster son, Allan raised his cane and shouted for Edgar to leave. Only a month later, Mrs. Allan stepped into the sickroom and found her husband dead in his chair. The date was March 27, 1834.

John Allan died as one of the most prominent men of Richmond. A commanding tombstone was erected in Shockoe Cemetery with a glowing inscription: "Blessed with every social and benevolent feeling, he fulfilled the duties of Husband, Father, Brother, and Friend, with surpassing Kindness, supported the ills of life with Fortitude, and his Prosperity with Meekness."

Because of inconsistencies in Allan's will, Louisa (Mrs. Allan) let the court settle the estate. Most of Allan's considerable wealth went to her and his legitimate sons. An annuity of three hundred dollars was left to sister-in-law Nancy Valentine. No mention was made of Edgar A. Poe. It is reported that Edgar traveled to Richmond to see Louisa Allan after his foster father's death, but she refused to receive him. As fate would have it, the only reason John Allan or any of his family are remembered is their connection to the cast-off foster son, who preferred to write books rather than keep them. On August 20, 1835, Poe would write to William Poe about John Allan: "I have accordingly been thrown upon my own resources . . . the blow has been a heavy one, and I had nearly succumbed to its influence, and yielded to despair."

7

RETURN TO RICHMOND

IN THE SPRING OF 1835, JOHN PENDLETON KENNEDY ANSWERED an inquiry from Thomas Willis White (1788–1843), editor of the *Southern Literary Messenger:* "Dear Sir,—Poe did right in referring to me. He is very clever with his pen—classical and scholarlike. . . . I have no doubt he can be made very useful to you; and, poor fellow! He is *very* poor. . . . This young fellow is highly imaginative, and a little given to the *terrific.*"

Poe had begun to send poems and stories to the new magazine published in Richmond. As historians have pointed out, this was a boom period for magazines and newspapers in the United States. Because of public education, there were more readers than ever. Because of railroads and better roads, steamboats and canals, distribution was now easier. Because of improved presses, printing was cheaper and faster. According to Kenneth Silverman, between four and five thousand magazines would be launched in the United States in the 1830s and 1840s and 1850s. Most would be short-lived, but a few would make an impact on the culture. The content of magazines has been described by Sandra M. Tomc as "literature . . . meant to be consumed immediately and forgotten promptly."

Though most publishing would occur in the cities of the Northeast, in Boston, New York, and Philadelphia, a number of attempts would be made in the South to establish and foster literary culture. The most prominent of the southern literary magazines would be the *Southern Literary Messenger*

FIG. 13. Thomas Willis White (1788–1843). Trained as a printer, Thomas White founded the *Southern Literary Messenger* in 1834. In 1835 he hired Poe as an editor. A kind man, he objected to Poe's drinking and harsh reviews of other writers and let the young editor go in 1837. (Courtesy of the Edgar Allan Poe Museum, Richmond, Virginia)

issued from Richmond. In the 1850s there would be others, such as *Russell's Magazine* of Charleston, South Carolina.

The first issue of the *Southern Literary Messenger* had appeared in August 1834. Thomas W. White proclaimed his mission "to stimulate the pride and genius of the south, and awaken from its long slumber the literary exertion of this portion of our country" (fig. 13). White's ambition was to inspire both writers and readers of the region, to steer the discussion toward artistic and cultural things. Too many northern journals were edited by abolitionists, in White's opinion.

White started out with high expectations, but after a year he'd secured only about a thousand subscribers. There were too many magazines, mostly in the North, competing, not to mention the prestigious British quarterlies and monthlies available by subscription. And newspapers could reprint anything they chose from both foreign and domestic publications.

White's education had been an apprenticeship to a printer, but he was ambitious, and he had good intentions, to produce a quality publication for the better segment of the population. He'd hired in succession two editorial assistants, but now the second, Edward V. Sparhawk, was moving on. Poe began a correspondence with White, diplomatically suggesting that successful magazines, like those from Britain, depended not just on good taste and what White called "Virginia simplicity." To woo subscribers, a magazine must have vigorous criticism and sensationalistic fiction. Poe even suggested that White improve the typography of the *Messenger.*

At the age of twenty-five or twenty-six, though he had no experience at editing a magazine, Poe knew how to speak with confidence and authority. As he would later say of his style of detective writing, it was not so much his method as his *air* of method. All his life Poe had read magazines and newspapers, and he seemed to have a knack for knowing what would appeal to the public. For all his aristocratic manner, in his writing and in his person, Poe also had the common touch. He was intellectual, but he also knew how to entertain.

Besides sending White tales and poems, Poe began to review books for the *Messenger.* And he wrote some features promoting the Richmond magazine in the Baltimore newspapers. Following a line of argument that would be echoed by writers and editors south of the Mason-Dixon Line in the future, he declared, "It is indeed a subject of general congratulations that the South has at length aroused herself from her lethargy in these matters, and ventured to erect a periodical literature of her own." Poe sought the outlet the *Messenger* provided as well as the modest honoraria for his contributions. He needed a profession, and a professional home, and luckily, at this time, Thomas W. White was badly in need of an editor or editorial assistant.

With Kennedy's recommendation, Poe had submitted his *Tales of the Folio Club* to the firm of Carey & Lea of Philadelphia, but it had not offered either money or a contract. Poe had published the story "The Visionary," later called "The Assignation," in the *Godey's Lady's Book,* also in Philadelphia, in January 1834. The story, inspired by a Byronic figure, included the poem "To One in Paradise," his tribute to Elmira. It was one of his first tales of a bitter, doomed marriage, and lovers, ending in suicide.

One of the books Poe sought to review for the *Southern Literary Messenger* was Kennedy's novel *Horse-Shoe Robinson.* But as it turned out, Poe was too ill and weak to do the book justice. Some biographers think Poe was already suffering from the frail heart that would hamper his work later.

Determined to break into the fiction market, Poe wrote stories more and more sensationalistic. David Leverenz has observed, "Antebellum readers' avidity for sensationalism hurt Poe into writing great short fiction." Teresa A. Goddu suggests, "Slavery serves as a significant social context for the discourse of sensationalism." Such events as flogging were common in a slavery culture. In that society Poe became "both analyst and symptom."

Around this time Poe sent the story "Berenicë" to White. Though White found it distasteful, he printed it anyway, with this explanation: "Whilst we confess that we think there is too much German horror in his subject, there can be but one opinion as to the force and elegance of his style." Though not long, "Berenicë" is one of Poe's most intense and revealing stories. It is the second of Poe's stories about "marriage." "Morella," "Ligeia," "Eleonora," and "The Fall of the House of Usher" would follow. But Poe would never write a narrative more grisly than "Berenicë."

The name Berenicë was pronounced in the nineteenth century to rhyme with "very icy." It is the name of two Jewish Herodic princesses, both of whom married cousins and were involved in political intrigue. One was accused of an incestuous relationship with her brother. The narrator of Poe's story is named Egaeus, and the tale begins with a short discussion of the interrelationship of the beautiful and the horrible. The essay-like beginnings of stories by Poe and Hawthorne show the pedigree of nineteenth-century short fiction in the essays of writers such as Joseph Addison: "Misery is manifold. The wretchedness of earth is multiform. Overreaching the wide horizon as the rainbow, its hues are as various as the hues of that arch." The real bond of kinship between the short story and the informal essay is that they both belong to the world of newspapers and magazines, the new media.

Egaeus confesses the perverse nature of his character. He and Berenicë are cousins who grew up together and become engaged. She is lively and happy, loving the outdoors of the great estate of Arnheim. Arnheim would be the name of Poe's paradise on earth, as described in the later tale "The Domain of Arnheim." *Heim* means "home" in German, and John Ingram, Poe's first major biographer, speculated that Poe imagined an ancestral estate incorporating the name of the Arnolds, Poe's mother's family. Suddenly this healthy young fiancée is stricken with an illness that changes both her person and her personality. Berenicë suffers from "epileptic" trances. Beyond his control, Egaeus seems hypnotized by the features of the sickened Berenicë.

The narrator admits, grimly, that he never loved Berenicë when she was healthy. As the date of the marriage of Berenicë and Egaeus approaches, he's frightened and fascinated to see his bride-to-be sickened and hideous. Her "emaciation was excessive, and not one vestige of the former being lurked in any single line of the contour." But it is her teeth in the emaciated face that his eyes fasten upon in monomaniacal obsession. A story had appeared in the *Baltimore Saturday Visiter* about graves robbed to extract teeth.

All night the narrator meditates upon this obsession and fantasy about teeth. Near dawn he hears screams and is informed that Berenicë has expired in an epileptic seizure. The story then slips forward to the night after the interment. Egaeus sits alone in the library, knowing he has done something horrible but not being able to remember exactly what atrocity he has committed. A little box that belongs to the family physician lies on the table near him.

A servant enters and whispers that Berenicë's grave has been violated and her body mutilated, even though she was *still alive!* Egaeus notices that his hands are scratched by human nails. The servant directs his attention to a spade. With a scream, Egaeus pounces on the box on the table, knocking it to the floor, where the contents spill out, dental instruments and thirty-two small teeth. In his madness Egaeus has opened Berenicë's grave and extracted all her teeth while she still lived!

"Berenicë" is by no means Poe's best horror story, but for the student and biographer, it is one of the most significant. As far as we know, Poe never harmed a woman in his forty years on earth. But the turmoil in his mind and in his blood came out in stories such as "Berenicë" and "The Back Cat."

Psychologists and biographers long ago connected Egaeus's obsession with Berenicë's teeth to the unconscious fear the male suffers of the vagina dentata, the vagina with teeth, which threatens castration, devouring the male. The womb the male desires to return to is also terrifying, and yet it's the destiny of the male to go there, or attempt to return. The prospect is so frightening that the beautiful woman must be killed to prevent the horror of consummation. And in "Berenicë" the narrator is driven to extract the teeth from the mouth/vagina. The sight of the bloody teeth at the end of "Berenicë" is so revolting that the reader forgets or hardly notices the other horror: the bride has been placed in the grave while she still lives. Poe will return to the theme of premature burial, one feature of his Gothic arsenal. But in "Berenicë" premature interment serves a particular purpose, besides creating a multiple horror. The threatening body of the bride-to-be must be disposed of, hidden in the earth, even while she lives. And yet Egaeus's fear is so great, he must dig it up to extract the threatening teeth. Marie Bonaparte labels the story as an example of "sado-necropilia."

In no other story, except perhaps "The Black Cat," would Poe make his dilemma and guilt more explicit. He was near the beginning of his career as a fiction writer in 1835, but Poe was already learning to disguise his essential fears in romantic settings and costumes, in Gothic atmospheres, to make erotic sadism and necrophilia bearable, entertaining, and acceptable to a Victorian audience. But the deep psychological dramas would always be there in his best work, revealing the horror of marriage and the female body. A number of feminist critics have found Poe's stories especially relevant when examined from the woman's point of view. As the critic Ellen Weinauer writes, "Marriage, in short, becomes a site of Gothic terror in Poe's stories."

The *Southern Literary Messenger* received letters of protest about "Berenicë." Friends complained to White about the bad taste of the story. But in a famous letter to White, Poe defended himself and explained how such fiction drew readers: "The history of all Magazines shows plainly that those which have attained celebrity were indebted for it to articles *similar in nature*. . . . You may say all this is bad taste. I have my doubts. . . . To be appreciated you must be *read*." Patrick Quinn has said there are only two kinds of plots in Poe's stories, analysis and obsession. "Berenicë" includes elements of each and is, in fact, as J. Gerald Kennedy points out, a story of "self-detection." There are many kinds of horror, but one horror Poe could not avoid was the seductive crime of marriage.

Poe wrote to White on June 22, 1835: "I have been desirous, for some time past, of paying a visit to Richmond, and would be glad of any reasonable excuse for so doing." Poe traveled to Richmond that August, hoping for a job as a teacher or employment on a newspaper. As it turned out, he and White seemed to hit it off, and he was offered a position on the *Messenger* as an editorial assistant. After four years in Muddy's house in Baltimore, Poe would be paid, at first, $10 a week, or $520 a year ($15,600 today), barely enough to live on but still more than he'd been earning in Muddy's attic.

Thrilled to have employment in the city of his childhood and youth, Poe must have felt some trepidation also. John Allan's heirs still lived in

Richmond, and they had made known Edgar's many quarrels with his foster father, his ingratitude, his bad temper, and his failure to pay debts. People remembered his reputation for drinking. And we should not forget that Elmira lived there, now married to Alexander B. Shelton. White was warned that association with Poe might hurt his magazine but hired him anyway. Two former schoolmates of Poe, when they heard he'd been invited to a party, would refuse to attend.

Poe plunged into his new role. In his first weeks on the staff of the magazine, he published a poem titled "To Sarah," a tribute to Elmira, using only her first name. Though living in the same town as Elmira, he could not call on her. But he could recall their love in a thinly disguised poem, hoping she would see it. His association with the *Southern Literary Messenger* gave Poe new boldness and vigor. But White would never make Poe full editor.

SUDDENLY POE'S NEW CONFIDENCE WAS SHATTERED BY A LETTER from Maria Clemm pleading that she felt abandoned in Baltimore, without money, family, or friends. The thrust of her letter was the news that Neilson Poe, Edgar's cousin, had offered to take Virginia into his house and educate her. Neilson Poe had married Josephine Clemm, Virginia's half-sister, who objected to the idea of Poe marrying Virginia. Apparently, there had been talk among the Poes that Edgar intended to wed Virginia when she was a little older. Neilson's intentions were to prevent such a marriage, or at least delay it until Virginia was more mature. Even in 1835, there was a hint of scandal about first cousins marrying, not to mention Virginia's tender age. Yet Neilson had married his own first cousin in 1831. Neilson may have made a mistake in not offering to take in Muddy also. Her letter to Poe was an act of manipulation. One factor to consider in these events was the death of Muddy's mother, Elizabeth Cairnes Poe, on July 7, 1835. With her mother's death, a meager pension came to an end.

The news of Neilson's offer shocked and terrified Edgar. What would seem on the surface a generous and helpful gesture on Neilson's part was taken as a judgment and attack by Poe and perhaps by Muddy also. The offer was an assault on their little family. Edgar had never been entirely accepted among the Baltimore Poes, and his recent behavior had not reassured them.

Another factor to consider in Poe's interactions with his Baltimore relatives was their attitude toward his beloved mother. As Marie Louise Shew would later write to the biographer John Ingram: "Mr. Poe's (Edgar's) animosity towards some of his relatives was from their disrespect, (in one or two cases) of his mother, and her profession."

But Edgar's ties to Muddy and Virginia were deeper than the other Poes may have understood. Or if Neilson understood, he must have thought the bond should be broken for Virginia's sake. A marriage between first cousins, with a girl so young, would be frowned upon, though Neilson himself had made a similar match.

Neilson could also have known Edgar well enough to have understood that consanguinity may have been part of the attraction Virginia presented for Edgar. After all, he called her Sister, or Sissy, and would for the rest of his life. Those who knew Virginia would describe her as anxious to please, perhaps a little spoiled. There is much about the relationship of Poe and his cousin that we cannot know. But it seems that as his interests turned elsewhere, first to Mary Starr, and later to Eliza White, Muddy encouraged Poe's attentions to Virginia. It was a way to hold him. She knew he would love her as a mother but never as a wife. From Poe's letters, we see that he addressed Virginia as "little wifey" and "darling little wifey." It seems that Edgar and Virginia had played at being wed, perhaps childlike but possibly physically. We do not know how far Poe had gone with his little cousin. But somehow Muddy had a hold over Poe and, by threatening to let Virginia go to Neilson Poe's house, brought about a wedding pledge between Poe and Virginia. There is no doubt that Poe loved Virginia and idealized her in his poems and stories. But there is also a good bit of evidence that he felt trapped in the marriage, and he hated marriage and feared marriage, as dramatized in story after story. There is also a possibility that Muddy made up the story of Neilson's offer to frighten Poe.

From his day to the present, Poe's marriage to his thirteen-year-old cousin has served as a notorious and delicious feature of his legend. The figure of the child bride, the nymphet, would inspire the Nabokov of *Lolita* and other authors. The marriage to, and the early death of, Virginia would become so much a part of the legend of Poe that it's impossible to imagine his life without Sissy. Virginia referred to Edgar at times as "Buddy," or brother.

The first thing Poe did when he received Muddy's letter was to flee, to the bottle. Just when things were looking up for him, it seemed the worst possible news had come thundering down. Up to this point Poe himself may not have understood the depth of his dependence on Virginia and Muddy. The letter he wrote on August 29, 1835, to Muddy, likely in his cups, is one of the most revealing documents of Poe's emotional makeup.

> I am blinded with tears while writing thi[s] letter—I have no wish to live another hour. Amid sorrow, [manuscript torn] and the deepest anxiety your letter reached—and you well know how little I am able to bear up under the pressure of grief. . . . I love, *you know* I love Virginia passionately devotedly. I cannot express in words the fervent devotion I feel towards my dear little cousin—my own darling . . . you have driven me to the grave—for love like mine can never be gotten over. It is useless to disguise the truth that when Virginia goes with N. P. that I shall never behold her again. . . . Pity me, my dear Aunty, pity me. . . . I am among strangers, and my wretchedness is more than I can bear. . . . If she had truly loved me would she not have rejected th[e] offer with scorn? . . . [page 2] If she goes with N. P. what are you to do, my own Aunty?
>
> [Oh G]od have mercy on me. What have I *to live for?* Among strangers with *not one soul to love me* . . .
>
> I would send you on $5 now—for White paid me the $8 2 days since . . .
>
> The tone of your letter wounds me to the soul—Oh Aunty, Aunty, you loved me once—how ca[n] you be so cruel now . . .
>
> Adieu my dear Aunty. I *cannot advise you.* Ask Virginia. Leave it to her. Let me have, under her own hand, a letter, bidding me *good bye*—forever—and I [m]ay die—my heart will break—but I will say no more.
>
> E.A.P.
>
> Kiss her for me—a million times[.]
> For Virginia,
> My love, my own sweetest Sissy, my darling little wifey, thi[nk] [w]ell before you break the heart of your cousin. Eddy

I have quoted this letter at length because it's important to understanding much in Poe's subsequent life. However Poe's marriage to Virginia may have appeared to others, it answered some essential need for him and her at that time. The despair in these lines seems all too real. The fear of losing Sissy devastated him. This terror is at the heart of any study of Poe's life and art, as is the wee hint of role-playing we will see more of later.

Even in his anguish, he asked about a notice of the *Messenger* in a Baltimore paper. Virginia was everything to him, but so was his new career as an editor. On September 11, 1835, he wrote to Kennedy, his mentor and patron in Baltimore, another letter of despair: "My feelings at this moment are pitiable indeed. I am suffering under a depression of spirits such as I have never felt before. I have struggled in vain against the influence of this melancholy. . . . My heart is open before you—if it be worth reading, read it."

In the letter to Kennedy he does not mention the threat of losing Virginia, or his fear of marriage, only his deep despair. For it was not only Neilson Poe's offer to take in Virginia that was troubling Poe at this time. The stress of being alone in Richmond, of finding his way as a reviewer and editor for the *Messenger,* had already driven him to the bottle. The commitment he had made to Virginia filled him with dread. By 1835 Poe must have known he was almost helpless when he began drinking. On September 29 White wrote a letter to his new assistant editor:

Dear Edgar,

> That you are sincere in all your promises, I firmly believe. But, Edgar, when you once again tread these streets I have my fears that your resolves would fall through—and that you would again sip the juice, even till it stole away your senses . . .
>
> If you should come to Richmond again, and again should be an assistant in my office, it must be expressly understood by us that all engagements on my part would be dissolved, the moment you get drunk.

From this letter we construe that White had fired Poe, who'd returned to Baltimore, to his sanctuary with Muddy and Virginia. But White's letter must have elicited the right response, for in October 1835 Poe was back at work on the *Messenger,* starting a new chapter in his life, and he'd brought Maria Clemm and Virginia to Richmond. They were living in the boardinghouse of Mrs. James Yarrington on the corner of Twelfth and Bank Streets. Now he was back at work, and his stories and poems were appearing in the

Messenger. He had his family with him, and he was earning a modest wage. He had also become good friends with White's daughter Eliza, to whom he wrote a poem. There were rumors of a romance between Miss White and Poe. They were both fervent dancers and were seen at parties as dance partners. One Bell Lynes would recall: "Mr. Poe was the most enthusiastic dancer I ever saw, although he remained cold and calm, showing his delight only in his eyes." The poem Poe addressed to Eliza White had earlier been given to his cousin Eliza Herring. Later it would be repurposed for Fanny Osgood. It is said that Mr. White discouraged the flirtation. When Poe was sober, White got far more than his money's worth. It was in this period that Poe honed his skills as a reviewer and essayist and became known for the acid in his critical notices.

One challenge Poe faced in Richmond in 1835, and indeed for the rest of his life, was that he daily encountered men for whom drinking was a social and professional bond. He was offered drinks and was expected to tender drinks in return. Few understood that he could not have even one drink of wine without disastrous consequences. A Richmond acquaintance said: "[Poe] resisted more temptations in a day than most men do in a year."

Sadly, Poe would later write: "I have absolutely no pleasure in the stimulants in which I sometimes so madly indulge. It has not been in the pursuit of pleasure that I have periled life and reputation and reason. It has been in the desperate attempt to escape from torturing memories, from a sense of *insupportable loneliness,* and a dread of some strange, impending doom."

There have been rumors that Edgar and Virginia were privately married in Baltimore before he brought her and Muddy to Richmond. Hervey Allen, in his entertaining and imaginative *Israfel,* stated that the marriage took place on September 22, 1835, at St. Paul's Episcopal Church in Baltimore, and indeed a marriage license was issued on that date. But there seems to be no record of such a ceremony. Muddy may have demanded that he obtain the license as a pledge to marry Virginia when she was a little older.

Joseph Wood Krutch, in his biography of 1926, *Edgar Allan Poe: A Study in Genius,* was the first major biographer to suggest that the marriage of Edgar and Virginia was never consummated. Several scholars since have come to agree with Krutch. After Poe's death, Maria Clemm is supposed to have stated that the relationship between Edgar and Virginia had never been physical: they had slept in separate rooms. This may have been true in the first years of their marriage. Whether it remained true throughout their married life is another question. It is also possible Muddy was covering up some family secret. Since the marriage is so much a part of the "enigma" of Poe's life, it is important to consider its nature, insofar as we can.

If Edgar was never able to live with Virginia in the usual sense of man and wife, why had the threatened loss of her devastated him to such a degree? From the evidence it seems he could not contemplate living without her. And yet we know he later expressed deep guilt to Helen Whitman for marrying his thirteen-year-old cousin. The question is: why was Virginia so necessary to him? What essential need did Sissy fulfill at this time? A further question we may ask is why did they need to *marry*? If the relation between them was truly that of brother and sister, why was it so important that they wed? As cousins, it would have been perfectly respectable for them to live in the same house with Muddy. No one would have questioned the propriety of such an arrangement. Yet Poe refers to Sissy as "darling little wifey." So much of Virginia's behavior toward Poe seems not "sisterly" but intimate and affectionate. One biographer tells us that "Virginia once kissed Poe in public so passionately that at least one onlooker was shocked." An acquaintance who knew the Poes well implied that the marriage was unconsummated, but only for the first two years. The plain fact is that we cannot know what the physical relations between Poe and Sissy were either before or after their marriage. They had lived in close quarters since she was nine years old. Was there an unmentionable secret between them? Had Poe taken liberties with his little cousin about which Muddy was or was not aware? Whatever it was that bound them together, neither could bear to break it off.

In his relations with Virginia, we see Poe's fixation on marriage, the institution he always yearned for. True, he knew marriage was often a nightmare but also an ideal state, hopefully a perfect union. The idea of marriage brought out romance in Poe that overrode all the risk, even though the actual state would clash with the ideal. Marriage was an aspiration he could not resist then, or later, a promise of home and stability.

It has been argued that Muddy was more important to Poe than Virginia, for she protected him and nursed him in his sicknesses, and that the real marriage was to Muddy. She was the most satisfying mother figure he had yet found to replace Eliza Poe. But his love for Virginia was undoubtedly real and painful. Since we cannot look into anyone's heart or know the dynamics of a marriage from outside, we can only make informed guesses. Virginia's later illness and death would drive Poe to the brink and over, into madness.

Poe's painful guilt about Virginia may have been rooted in part in his knowledge that he used her in some way. By the age of twenty-six, he knew quite well that while he was passionately drawn to women, obsessed with women, devoted to women, he could not always physically perform. He likely blamed himself for this dysfunction, as he blamed himself for his drinking. It was all part of the curse on him, the doom he'd been born with. As much as he admired women, desired women, adored women, lusted after women, he often expressed his love best in writing.

But there was a much deeper guilt also, for the other side of that frustrated love was anger and resentment, anger at the mother who had abandoned him, anger at beautiful women who attracted and repelled him at the same time. There was a darker passion in Poe that he tried to ignore and conceal, a passion that surfaced in his poems and stories, in which the beautiful women all sickened and died, were buried prematurely, or worse, had their bodies mutilated. The anger often appeared in the cruel humor of stories such as "Loss of Breath."

Sweet and trusting Virginia was as necessary to Poe as breathing. She protected him—from himself. She was possibly too young for a physical union at first and then, after 1842, too ill. We don't know when Poe first realized she had consumption, but likely, he suspected it long before her first hemorrhage in 1842. With Virginia, Poe found a kind of security he badly needed, but he was also trapped. His romantic and spiritual nature would always be drawn to women, gifted intellectual women, and ultimately embarrassing and sometimes absurd flirtations. But he could return to the comfort and safety of the household with Muddy and Virginia. And between 1838 and 1842, he may well have enjoyed, at times, a physical union with Sissy. Some have suggested that the story "Eleonora" is evidence that when Virginia was about fifteen, their marriage became physical. A rereading of that story reinforces the argument.

An alternate explanation for Poe's marriage to Virginia has been offered by John Walsh in his study *Plumes in the Dust*. Walsh argued that in his panic and desperation, alone in Richmond in August 1835, Poe promised to marry Sissy. After he brought Muddy and Sissy to Richmond, he regretted his impulsive proposal, as he fell in love with the beautiful and more mature Eliza White, ten years older than Sissy. But Muddy intervened, demanding that he honor his commitment to Virginia, and so the wedding took place on May 16, 1836.

Poe devoted much time to educating Virginia himself, and he spent money on her music lessons in Richmond and later. Muddy would write to Neilson Poe after Poe's death: "Eddie finished Virginia's education himself, and, I assure you, she was highly cultivated. She was an excellent linguist, and a perfect musician, and she was so *very beautiful.*"

Edgar's actual sister, Rosalie, who had been taken in by the Mackenzies of Duncan's Lodge, also lived in Richmond. Rosalie had remained childlike but taught handwriting at the school conducted by the Mackenzies. She followed Poe around at times, much to his annoyance. She and Virginia played together, like young girls.

It is the word *genius* that even Poe's most hostile critics usually concede to him. And his genius is undeniable, evident on several fronts, in different genres and activities. But overall, as we understand the adversities Poe encountered, the scars from the relationship with John Allan, the bad luck that seemed to pursue or waylay him repeatedly, it's his tenacity and courage that seem most notable. Given the emotional turmoil he lived with much of the time, the cruelty of his weakness for alcohol, the wonder is that Poe accomplished anything, much less the seminal work, in at least three fields of literature.

It was in this period of upheaval and settling in Richmond that Poe wrote some of his finest early stories. He was back among the scenes of his boyhood, exploring deeper and deeper into his memory and imagination. He was at work on a play called *Politian,* some of which was published in the *Messenger.* Though set primarily in Rome, the unfinished verse drama was modeled on the so-called Beauchamp Kentucky Tragedy, a lurid story of seduction, betrayal, murder, and suicide. Poe also published selections from his notebooks called "Pinakidia."

Soon after completing "Berenicë," Poe wrote "Morella," one of his very best stories and more typical of his "arabesques." It is in "Morella" that Poe introduced the heroine who is not only fabulously beautiful but boasts extraordinary learning in mystical philosophy and lore. It is also in "Morella" that he introduced in fiction the lover who dies and does not die, the figure he had begun to explore in "The Sleeper."

The narrator of "Morella" is guided by his learned wife in the study of taboo subjects that awaken a "forbidden spirit enkindling within me." They plunge so deeply into this esoteric philosophy it scares him. "And thus, joy suddenly faded into horror, and the most beautiful became the most hideous, as Hinnom became Ge-Henna." The esoteric lore that Morella expounds to her lover may include, like the vast learning of Ligeia in the later story of that title, Kabbalah and other mystical writing. Several times throughout his career, Poe would refer to Kabbalah. In "Marginalia" Poe would write, "We dote upon records, which, in the main, lie; while we discard the *Kabbala,* which, properly interpreted, do *not.*" Morella is the second of Poe's "dark ladies." The name Morella is derived from *Moor,* with Arabic and Semitic overtones.

When Morella begins to understand that her voice and obscure studies repel her lover, she sickens. As she dies, Morella asserts that though her husband does not love her, he will love her child with a painful and immoderate love. The daughter Morella gives birth to, just as she expires, grows prodigiously in intellect and maturity. The narrator loves the daughter with an intensity he would formerly have thought impossible. She develops so quickly it frightens him. The daughter is like her mother in both intelligence and kindness. Finally, at the age of ten, she must be given a name.

A perverse, perhaps demonic, impulse causes the narrator to whisper the word *Morella* to the priest. The daughter turns her eyes to heaven and says, "I am here," and then dies. For the narrator nothing lies ahead but bitter wandering, and when he carries the young Morella to the family tomb, he finds there no trace of the first Morella.

The story repeats the theme of the revenant, the lover who dies but returns, the lover whose passion is so intense she comes back from beyond the grave. "Morella" also introduces the theme of the non-Christian name the narrator is reluctant to pronounce. But buried underneath this repeated figure in his stories is the complex memory of Eliza's death and perhaps the hint and repression of Eliza's heritage. He feels both sorrow and guilt for his young mother's passing, and yet he cannot concede that she will remain dead forever. Eliza played many different roles, in many different costumes, in her life and then in her son's imagination. For Poe all deaths were inconclusive and all burials premature. In "Morella" the barrier between life and death is breached.

While he printed and reprinted his stories and poems in the *Southern Literary Messenger*, the bulk of Poe's work for the magazine was writing articles and reviews. Day after day and week after week, he reviewed the books that arrived, not only fiction and poetry but books of science, history, travel, biography, and philosophy. Out of this flood of review writing, two significant traits would emerge. He would become notorious for wounding critical comments, leading to his reputation as "the literary Comanche." And he would discover in himself a fury to appear logical, rational, superior, analytical, and "scientific." Students of Poe have long recognized and investigated the contrary tendencies of his imaginative work and his critical writing. He might disparage the scientific and rational in poems such a "Sonnet—To Science" and "The City in the Sea," but by 1835–36 he had discovered in himself a penchant for the mathematical, the analytical, and delight in pointing out illogical, ungrammatical, and factual errors in other writers' work. He was also thrilled to find evidence of plagiarism, though he himself plundered other writers for plots, names, phrases, and ideas.

The concern with logic and precision may have grown partly out of Poe's fear of madness and disorder. Often when distraught or under the influence of alcohol, he behaved erratically and self-destructively. The pursuit of the cold and analytical may have reassured him that he could demonstrate sanity and superior intellect. His gifts at mathematics, ciphers, languages such as Latin and French, helped to balance his propensity for fantasy and dreaming, his crippling lack of business sense, his volatile temperament, and taste for the perverse and weird.

Poe would prove to be one of the leading literary critics of his time. Among all the filler and hack work, he produced essays, passages, phrases, and concepts that would influence the discourse about poetry and poetics as well as the short story for generations to come. He could be diabolical in his comments about contemporary male writers, but with a few exceptions, his opinions have stood the test of time. Of women authors he would famously assert: "Where the gentler sex is concerned, there seems but one course for the critic—speak if you can commend—be silent, if not."

Once he had the megaphone of the *Messenger*, in 1835 and 1836, Poe the analytical critic was off and sprinting. It was a role he would cherish for the rest of his life, and it was as a critic that he would first become well known. One of his favorite terms would be *ratiocination,* by which he meant the use of logic, mental powers, along with intuition, to solve apparently insoluble mysteries.

In 1769 a Hungarian nobleman, Baron Wolfgang von Kempelen, had created for the Empress Maria Theresa a supposedly mechanical chess player called "the Turk." It included a large figure dressed as a Turk seated behind a box with a chessboard on top. The Turk would take on all challengers and became a sensation when J. N. Maelzel brought it to the United States in 1820. The Turk usually won against competitors but not always. Among others, the chess player had defeated Benjamin Franklin and Napoleon Bonaparte. There were many attempts to debunk the Turk, which purported to be an *Android.*

In 1827, about the time Poe was joining the army, the chess player was exhibited in Baltimore. Two boys, hidden on a roof, saw a living man come out of the Turk. On Friday, June 1, 1827, an article in the *Baltimore Gazette,* "The Chess-Player Discovered," exposed the fraud. A man named William Schlumberger was one chess master who performed inside the Turk. Schlumberger traveled with Maelzel but was never seen while the Turk played chess. Later the Turk was purchased by Dr. John K. Mitchell and placed in the Chinese Museum in Philadelphia, where it would be destroyed by fire in 1854. Poe sought to demonstrate by observation and details from all previous reports that the Turk could not be mechanical. He compared Maelzel's chess player to the calculating machine of Charles Babbage to make his logic clear. Poe would present seven points, each of which proved that the Turk was not a machine. But the heart of his argument was that the Turk was inconsistent in both timing and choice of moves. A machine would be consistent. Much of Poe's reasoning in the essay was derived from David Brewster's *Letters on Natural Magic,* though not all. Implicitly, Poe's essay is a celebration of showmanship.

In this period, while he was debunking Maelzel's chess player, Poe began exhibiting a habit of quarreling with scholars and pretending to erudition in history, languages, and science he did not possess. In the moon voyage tale "Hans Pfaall," he lifted whole paragraphs from the work of the astronomer J.F.W. Herschel. In the grab bag of quotations and comments, often about ancient history, called "Pinakidia," a Greek word meaning "tablets," he relied mostly on encyclopedias and other reference sources. His quotations from languages other than English sometimes reveal an imperfect understanding of the foreign tongues.

The scholar Stephen Rachman, in an essay called "The Marginal Center," argues that one aspect of Poe's genius was his "investment in literary derivation, recycling, intertextuality, and the conscious calculations of the working literary artist." A certain kind of creative talent depends on "conscious adoption and adaptation . . . replication and reduplication with change occurring through gradual, traceable variations." One of Poe's most important sources was Isaac Disraeli's *Curiosities of Literature,* which taught Poe "a process in which attractive notions and phrases were subject to chains of literary appropriation, reappropriation, and misappropriation."

What is most unusual about Poe's essays is that he would become notorious for accusations of plagiarism, especially against the poet Longfellow. The high standards he espoused were those he aspired to, not those he always practiced. We can think of his attacks on Longfellow as unconscious confessions, indictments of himself.

Yet Poe's strictness as a reviewer was much needed at the time. In the so-called Era of Good Feelings following the War of 1812, American reviewers tended to be gentle with American authors. Even the smiling Emerson called in "Self-Reliance" for a new candor: "Check this lying hospitality and lying affection."

While working for the *Southern Literary Messenger,* Poe described the style of a best-selling novel by Theodore Fay as "unworthy of a school-boy." Some of his harshest criticism was directed at the South Carolina novelist William Gilmore Simms, whose grammar he parsed mercilessly. Poe's slashing reviews in the *Messenger* helped establish new standards for criticism in the United States, and they made him feared and admired. Critics of Poe's own work would be delighted ever after to find the bold critic had committed many of the sins he'd condemned in others. Poe knew he was fighting against the disdain of British and European critics for literature published in the United State. In the *Edinburgh Review* the critic Sydney Smith had notoriously proclaimed: "In the four quarters of the globe, who reads an American book?"

Poe reserved some of his most severe criticism for American male poets, including Joseph Rodman Drake and Fitz-Greene Halleck, explaining that easy praise of native work hindered rather than aided the growth of

American literature. One of his most quoted comments concluded, "We . . . often find ourselves involved in the gross paradox of liking a stupid book the better, because, sure enough, its stupidity is American."

In 1850 Herman Melville would publish an exuberant tribute to Hawthorne, "Hawthorne and His Mosses," and sign the article as "by a Virginian Spending July in Vermont." Was Melville hoping to suggest that his salute to Hawthorne echoed the work of the greatest critic of his time, Edgar Allan Poe, who often referred to himself as a Virginian and had earlier written with appreciation of Hawthorne?

Reviewing inspired the manic side of Poe's personality. Like Walt Whitman after him, he reviewed some of his own work favorably. Once he put on the critic's mantle, Poe was fearless and elated, the opposite of Poe in his dreamy ethereal mood, the author of "Eleonora" or, later, "The Domain of Arnheim." In fact, if we did not already know it, we might find it hard to guess that the author of many of the reviews could be the poet of "To Helen," "Sonnet—To Science," and "Dream-Land." Several biographers have pointed out that if you examine the famous daguerreotypes of Poe, you see the division and asymmetry of his face, the sensitive dreamer on one side, the jaded, irreverent skeptic on the other.

There is an element of paradox about Poe's critical writing, as about almost every aspect of his career. While he introduced a new rigor in reviews and essays, he was also forging a kind of criticism for a large popular audience, creating a precedent for later writers such as Margaret Fuller, Edmund Wilson, and maybe Joan Didion. Inspired by the essays in the British quarterlies, Poe attracted readers with prose that was at once sophisticated, memorable, trenchant, and accessible. Modern critics have also argued that Poe was "the first original literary theorist America produced."

The exacting criticism Poe wrote for the *Messenger* helped make the magazine increasingly noticed. The number of subscribers rose steadily. The magazine was read beyond the South. One Boston magazine declared, "*The Southern Literary Messenger* is equal in interest and excellence to any Monthly Periodical in the country." In some of his reviews, Poe began to appear sensitive about the attitude of northern critics toward southern authors, a theme he would return to later.

The critic Colin (Joan) Dayan has reminded us that while Poe edited the *Southern Literary Messenger*, in 1835–36, he passed slave markets "two blocks away from the offices," where enslaved men and women were considered "things" to be sold, not people. In recent years a whole new school of Poe criticism has evolved to address the issue of slavery in Poe's works. It was probably initiated by Toni Morrison in the book *Playing in the Dark* (1992). Morrison argued that "even, and especially, when American texts are not 'about' Africanist presences or characters or narrative or idiom, the shadow hovers over by implication."

Following the lead of Morrison, a number of scholars and critics began to investigate the implicit presence of slavery and African Americans in Poe's writing. Some have pointed out that Richmond, in the period when Poe was growing up there, was a center "for distribution of slaves to the Deep South." One of the most important critics is Terence Whalen, in his study called *Edgar Allan Poe and the Masses* (1999). While Whalen does not defend Poe's racism, he attempts to put it in historical perspective, arguing that Poe, writing for a northern as well as a southern audience, aimed for "literary neutrality" about the subjects of race and slavery. Whalen suggests that Poe exhibited an "average racism" of his time, common in both North and South. Insofar as he could, Poe avoided the controversial subject of slavery. Yet he did not argue even for "gradual elimination" of the institution. As a literary journalist, Poe preferred to "sidestep the entire question."

In 2001 J. Gerald Kennedy and Liliane Weissberg published a volume of essays called *Romancing the Shadow: Poe and Race*. The collection contains some of the most incisive writing about race and slavery in Poe's work. In the introduction the editors wrote, "Poe endeavored to ignore the terrible contradiction between slavery and the American credo of equality." Several contributors point out that the orangutan in "The Murders in the Rue Morgue" and the apelike Dirk Peters in *The Narrative of Arthur Gordon Pym* are meant to suggest African Americans and reveal Poe's actual fears about race.

Elise Lemire, in "Amalgamation Discourses and the Race Riots of 1838 in Poe's Philadelphia," examines the implied issue of "amalgamation," or race mixing, in "The Murders in the Rue Morgue." Leland S. Person tells us that "race lurks behind walls and screens in Poe's writing." He compares the presence of race to "buried corpses" in "The Cask of Amontillado," "The Tell-Tale Heart," and "The Black Cat." Like Morrison and others, Person believes that race and slavery are implicit in much of Poe's writing: "He clearly embedded dramas of color in his psychological romances." In the stories "Ligeia," "The Back Cat," "The Murders in the Rue Morgue," and "Hop-Frog," Person discovers "the revenge of blackness as a critical fascination of white psychology." "Poe's philosophy of amalgamation turns on a philosophy of white male racism."

J. Gerald Kennedy suggests that Poe, like many others of his time, viewed slavery as a "lamentable system upon which the economy of the South had come to depend." Kennedy reprints a letter of conveyance showing Poe represented Muddy in the sale of an African American in 1829. These scholars and others have demonstrated the intimate, troubling, and often hidden connection between Poe's writing and the subject of slavery in antebellum society.

AS STATED EARLIER, POE WAS MARRIED TO HIS FIRST COUSIN Virginia Clemm on Monday, May 16, 1836, with Rev. Amasa Converse officiating. On the marriage bond, Virginia was listed as twenty-two years old. She was not yet fourteen and was described as "plump" by one observer. The fact that they inflated Sissy's age shows that both Poe and Muddy were sensitive about the appearance of the marriage with one so young and to a first cousin. Yet such marriages were not unknown in the Poe family. Another relative, "Washington Poe of Macon, Georgia, married Selina Shirley Prince when she was fourteen as well."

Years later Poe would tell Helen Whitman that he married Virginia out of a sense of obligation, not to please himself. There is probably some truth in that statement, for Poe owed much to Virginia's mother, Muddy, for taking him in in 1831. But from his letter of August 1835, it's clear that Virginia was essential to him, like a part of himself. She was the childlike muse at home, to idealize and transform in his imagination.

A Richmond neighbor named Jane Foster, who was Virginia's contemporary and friend, would recall Virginia as a playmate. She was surprised and awed by the marriage of her young friend to the older cousin: "For in that short ceremony of a few minutes she was picturing her little companion of the day before suddenly transported into matured womanhood."

Edgar and Virginia traveled to nearby Petersburg for their honeymoon, staying for several days in an apartment over Hiram Haines's Coffee House, before resuming life in Richmond. But with the marriage official, Edgar was now the legal head of the house, as he established himself as an authority in the world of letters. Two years earlier, he'd been penniless and unknown. Now he had both position and the beginnings of fame. Neighbors later reported that each evening when Poe returned from work, Virginia "ran out to the sidewalk to embrace her husband." Some days Poe and Virginia took long walks to the Shockoe cemetery, where Jane Stanard was buried.

In 1836 the now-married Poe published in the *Southern Literary Messenger* two articles titled "Autography," using facsimiles of actual signatures of prominent figures. The first article began with a burlesque in which a Mr. Joseph Miller flees after handing the narrator a packet of fictitious letters from well-known authors signed with authentic signatures. After each item there is a comment on the character of the author as revealed by the handwriting. "Autography" foreshadows Poe's later gossipy efforts such as "The Literati of New York City." Of Theodore S. Fay he comments: "The MS. . . . has an air of *swagger* about it and there are too many dashes—and the tails of the long letters are too long . . . and . . . *all* his tales are too long."

Poe's meager salary seemed to slip away. They lived in the boardinghouse owned by Martha Yarrington, and it is thought Poe's income for his first year in Richmond was about thirteen hundred dollars (about thirty-nine thousand dollars today), counting his salary and what he was paid for other writing. He cast around for additional ways to make money. Once he borrowed one hundred dollars (about three thousand dollars today) from his cousin George Poe Jr., who was a banker in Mobile, Alabama. The money would enable Muddy to open and maintain a boardinghouse. Nothing came of the plan, and it's unlikely George Poe Jr. was ever repaid.

A more likely prospect came from White himself, who bought an expensive house in Richmond and suggested renting the house to Muddy, who would then board the White family as well as her own. White's wife, we are told, was an invalid. Enthusiastic about the plan, which promised to solve at least some of his financial problems, Poe purchased two hundred dollars (about six thousand dollars today) worth of furniture for the new house, only to discover there was scarcely room there for the Whites. He applied, without success, to Kennedy for a loan of a hundred dollars (roughly three thousand dollars today). In this period Poe even petitioned the federal government for repayment of funds loaned by his Grandfather Poe to the army during the Revolution but did not succeed with that appeal either.

One source of anxiety in Richmond must have been rumors the Allan family had spread about him. It was claimed that when Poe had returned to Richmond after Fanny Allan's funeral in 1829, he had swiped silverware and fine linen from Moldavia. He was also accused of rudeness to the second Mrs. Allan and being driven from the house by servants. But now that the foster father, his tormenter, was no more, Edgar tried to put the relationship in a more respectable light. He told others that he *had* been adopted by Allan. Married and employed as an editor and critic, Poe tried to counter the Allan family rumors with an appearance of optimism and confidence. To explain why he'd inherited nothing from Allan, he stated, "No will was found among his papers."

The biographer Kenneth Silverman has argued that Poe never escaped his anguish about the relationship with John Allan. In much of his writing, Poe would weave the *al* sound into the names of characters, in Al Aaraaf, Lalage, Pfaall, needing so badly a sense of a father and a family. Yet from 1831 he signed his work as "Edgar A. Poe."

Elmira Royster, now Mrs. Alexander Barrett Shelton, still lived in Richmond. In later life Elmira would say that during Poe's tenure as editor of the *Southern Literary Messenger,* he was invited to a party at one of the prominent houses in Richmond. He'd heard that Elmira would be there, and he arrived early. A grand stairway in the house led to the second-story drawing room. In an alcove at the top of the stairs, Edgar waited for Elmira to appear. When she came up the stairs, she did not see him at first, but when she did notice him staring at her, she was overcome with emotion. As the childhood sweethearts gazed at each other, Mr. Shelton stepped forward and led his wife away. It is said that one of Elmira's best friends, Mary Winfree, told Poe in 1835 that Elmira had never loved Alexander Shelton.

Elmira was so shaken by this chance meeting with her former betrothed she was ill for several days. Mr. Shelton promised serious consequences if Poe came near his wife. As far as we know, Poe did not see Elmira again for more than ten years. But thirteen years later, Elmira would concede to Muddy that she had been stung by jealousy seeing Poe with Virginia.

There is a traditional story in Richmond that Poe's flirtation with White's daughter Eliza, caused tensions between the two men. We have seen the letter White wrote to Poe in September 1835, warning that if he ever got drunk again he would be fired. Though he seemed to like Poe and at times treated his assistant almost as one of the family, White was a printer and businessman, neither a writer nor an intellectual. Starting a literary magazine in the South was as risky then as it is now. White had taken a great gamble in launching the *Messenger* at all, and hiring a temperamental editor like Poe proved both his greatest asset *and* liability.

Convention holds that there *was* a flirtation, or close friendship, between Poe and White's attractive daughter Eliza. Eliza would later visit the Poes in Philadelphia and then in New York. She and Poe would remain friends to the end of his life, and she would never marry.

Over the course of about eighteen months, Edgar and his boss quarreled and yet somehow tolerated each other. Some of Poe's critical attacks on other authors were considered libelous, including comments about James Fenimore Cooper and the novel *Norman Leslie* by Theodore Fay, already referred to. Since Fay was an important editor and literary figure in New York, Poe made enemies who would never forget the caustic comments by the upstart in the South.

From time to time Poe was drinking again, though he probably did not show up at the office intoxicated. Poe considered White's tastes sentimental and banal. In many ways White represented exactly what Poe was struggling against in his criticism, attempting to forge new literary and critical standards for his time.

Poe had not forgotten his ambition to produce a volume of fiction. His efforts to see *The Tales of the Folio Club* into print had come to nothing. In his capacity as editor of the *Southern Literary Messenger* he made the acquaintance of the powerful and distinguished New York author James Kirke Paulding, one of the most successful writers in New York. Of Poe's review of the poetry of Drake and Halleck, Paulding had written, "I think it one of the finest specimens of criticism ever published in this country." At Poe's request, Paulding agreed to submit a volume of Poe's stories to Harper Brothers. Complaining the stories were "too learned and mystical," the firm declined the volume but added, as almost any publisher would in the present day, that a book-length narrative would be more likely to sell than a collection of shorter pieces. Paulding advised Poe to write a novel, and the young editor set to work immediately on a longer story.

8

NEW YORK AND PHILADELPHIA

BY CHRISTMAS OF 1836 THOMAS WHITE HAD HAD ENOUGH OF POE. Not only had Poe taken to drink from time to time, breaking his pledge to the printer and publisher, but White found Poe irritating in other ways as well. True, Poe had performed a prodigious amount of work, writing whole issues and lengthy and biting reviews, reading proof, soliciting contributions from distinguished authors, offering his own poems and stories. Subscriptions had increased, not fivefold, as Poe later claimed, but from about thirteen hundred to over eighteen hundred. Yet White had been embarrassed by several of Poe's severe reviews. White wanted a respectable magazine that sold well and offended no one. The attraction between Poe and his daughter may have worried White also.

Biographers have tended to be sympathetic to Poe and less tolerant of the publisher who hired and fired him. My guess is that while working with Poe week after week and month after month, Poe's arrogance would begin to grate on anyone, however generous and admiring they had been at first. Because of his many failures and his poverty, Poe sought to bolster his self-esteem by assertion, pronouncement, and overreacting to slights or criticism. Poe would sulk and disappear from the office for days. With White and the *Southern Literary Messenger,* Poe established a pattern he would follow for most of his career. Broke and desperate for work, he promised to be sober and industrious, easygoing and dependable, and he lived up to his commitment for months at a time. But gradually he became disaffected and bored, with growing contempt for the taste of his employer, and often perceived some slight to his own authority and genius. He would absent himself from the office and, when found, plead illness. He would become "ill" more often, nursed by Muddy and Virginia. And sometimes he was genuinely ill, for Poe had a weak heart and may, even then, have been infected with tuberculosis kept in check by his immune system. And as many have commented, a few drinks left him ill for days. Poe later characterized White as an "illiterate and vulgar, although well-meaning man." No wonder that the January 1837 issue of the *Messenger* included a notice that Poe was retiring from the magazine. That issue also included the first two installments of the novel *The Narrative of Arthur Gordon Pym.*

Poe set his sights on New York, which he hoped would provide more opportunities than Richmond. He already had a certain reputation as a critic and reviewer and editor, and he had high hopes for the novella he was composing for Harper and Brothers. Much of Poe's life can be viewed as a series of flights or fugues. In 1827 he'd fled Richmond for Boston and then left Boston for the army. He'd fled the ranks for West Point and the military academy for New York and then Baltimore. He left Baltimore for Richmond, coming full circle. He had a very American footloose, desperate belief that just over the horizon, in the next town, things would begin to improve. He had the nerve of a gambler, bluffing his way, playing poker with fate. After eighteen months in Richmond, it was time to try his luck among other players.

Some might argue that in each case Poe was not so much fleeing as searching for a home. But if we look at his many departures, it seems both opinions are true. In the literary world, he was a kind of Daniel Boone, willing to pick up and explore new territory, no matter the bankruptcies and debts left behind. New York beckoned with its teeming commerce, deep harbor, rapid growth, and uncertainty.

Little is known about the Poes' first residence in New York. Edgar and Virginia and Muddy arrived in February 1837 and would remain in Manhattan until May 1838. But the record of their stay there is almost nonexistent. Poe had been invited by Dr. Francis Lister Hawks to write for the *New York Review,* especially review essays. Dr. Hawks had written to Poe, "I wish you to fall in with your *broad-axe* amidst this miserable literary trash that surrounds us." But the *New York Review* folded soon after Poe's arrival, though not before Poe had contributed an impressive review essay of John L. Stephens's *Incidents of Travel in Egypt, Arabia Petraea, and the Holy Land.* The Poes first lived in Greenwich Village, at Sixth Avenue and Waverly Place, and later at 113½ Carmine Street. At Waverly Place the Poes got to know a Scotsman named William Gowans, a bookseller who boarded in their apartment. Gowans would leave a memoir about Poe, correcting some of the exaggerations of early biographers: "I never saw him the least affected with liquor, nor even descend to any known vice, while he was one of the most courteous, gentlemanly and intelligent companions I have met with . . . he had a wife of matchless beauty and loveliness. Her eye could match that of any houri, and her face defy the genius of a Canova to imitate. . . . She seemed as much devoted to him and his every interest as a young mother is to her first-born."

The arrival of the Poes in New York happened to coincide with an economic collapse, a severe depression, which made it much harder to survive on freelance work. In May 1837 the Bank of New York closed. Andrew Jackson's and then Martin Van Buren's financial policies had destabilized the economy. Somehow the Poes kept themselves alive, but except for a few reviews, the only known publications by Poe at this time, besides the Stephens review article, are the tales "Von Jung, the Mystic" and "Siope—A Fable." The first is a satire about a con artist who takes advantage of others through pretensions of wisdom and learning. Some of the humor for Poe may have been that he was partly satirizing himself.

"Siope—A Fable" is one of Poe's finest prose poems and also one of his strangest. Later writers such as H. P. Lovecraft have cherished it. The narrator tells of a "Demon" who, speaking from the shadows of a tomb, tells of the horror of existence without imagination. Set in the Congo, the fable describes a man seated on a rock in a world of poisonous flowers, fetid water, a stagnant river. When fierce animals are summoned, the man is shaken but does not move. Like God tempting Job, the Demon calls forth hurricanes, but still the man on the rock does not flee. It is only when the Demon makes all, including the moon and clouds, stand still that the man can tolerate it no longer and escapes in terror. The critic Louis Renza anagrammatizes the word *Siope* as "is Poe."

"Siope" illustrates Poe's theme that the greatest horror is not pain, disease, filth, and danger, but nonbeing, loss of existence. In a world bereft of imagination, being becomes unbearable. As the critic J. Gerald Kennedy would observe, for Poe writing was an effort to escape silence, or nonexistence. On March 30, 1837, Poe attended a Booksellers' Dinner, where he would have seen local luminaries such as William Cullen Bryant and Washington Irving. It is recorded that he proposed a toast: "The *Monthlies* of Gotham—Their distinguished Editors, and their vigorous Collaborateurs."

It's not clear when or where Poe met the Antarctic explorer Jeremiah N. Reynolds, whose writing would influence *The Narrative of Arthur Gordon Pym,* but the meeting may well have occurred in New York while Poe was struggling to survive and complete the novel. In January 1837 he had reviewed Reynolds's work in the *Southern Literary Messenger.*

In the spring of 1838, Poe took Virginia and Muddy to Philadelphia, at the time a major publishing center. In the eighteenth century, Philadelphia had been the center of Enlightenment learning in North America, home of the polymath Benjamin Franklin, the Peale family of artists and their museum, John Bartram the botanist, and his son William, explorer, artist, and author, the bird painter Alexander Wilson, and the most famous physician in the United States, Benjamin Rush.

At first the Poes lived in a boardinghouse managed by a Mrs. C. Jones at 202 Mulberry (or Arch) Street, but in September 1838 they moved to a modest house on Sixteenth Street near Locust. It would be Christmas of that year before Poe was able to pay Mrs. Jones what he owed for rent. Poe scrambled to make a living by obscure hackwork. He appealed to James Kirke Paulding, now secretary of the navy, to help him find a clerkship in the government, but nothing came of that.

During his first year in Philadelphia, Poe became acquainted with the English-born writer James Pedder, who published juvenile fiction and books on agricultural subjects. Pedder helped the Poes get settled in the Quaker City, and he likely provided contacts with the literary community there. Pedder's daughters, Anna and Bessie, aided the Poes in their most desperate months in the city. It was Pedder who would arrange for Poe's involvement with *The Conchologist's First Book.*

The conventional wisdom has been that Poe's efforts on the book on conchology were primarily a matter of hackwork and plagiarism. Certainly, he made use of an earlier text, with new illustrations. But in 1995 the scientist Stephen Jay Gould, in *Dinosaur in a Haystack,* would argue that Poe's work on mollusk shells was a "breakthrough" because Poe had arranged his subjects in sequence from simplest to more complex, foreshadowing Darwin's work on evolution. It was probably in this period that Poe considered learning the trade of lithography but soon gave it up. In his correspondence with Paulding, Poe bragged that he had completely stopped drinking. It was a pledge he would repeat many times.

The novel *The Narrative of Arthur Gordon Pym,* postponed for a year because of the financial crisis, was Poe's only book-length work of fiction. He'd published the first two installments in the *Southern Literary Messenger,* though the remainder of the story would be rejected. Poe argued later that the finest and most intense works in both prose and poetry are those that can be read at one sitting. He'd tried to write longer poems in "Tamerlane" and "Al Aaraaf," with questionable results. In *Pym* he attempted the most popular and commercial literary form of his time, and ours, the novel.

The Narrative of Arthur Gordon Pym is a freewheeling adventure story. In the preface Poe explains that Pym was urged to write an account of his extraordinary voyage to the South Seas. Pym requested that Poe compose a fictional narrative based on his memoirs but then realized that a plain factual account of his exploits would sound like fiction anyway, what would later be called science fiction, or speculative fiction. Yet Pym died before he could complete his narrative. Much of *Pym* is intended to sound like travel writing gone hallucinogenic. As mentioned, Poe was inspired in part by the writing of Jeremiah N. Reynolds, who had adapted a theory from one Capt. John Symmes that "the earth was hollow and inhabited and that holes leading into the earth's interior were to be found at the poles."

The story begins with Pym and his friend Augustus Barnard somewhat drunk, taking Barnard's sailboat out for a cruise in the middle of the night. They crash into a whaling ship and are saved by the crew of the whaler. Eighteen months later, the teenage Pym is hidden by Augustus in the hold of a whaling ship captained by Augustus's father. J. Gerald Kennedy reminds us that escaping enslaved men and women often hid in the holds of ships. Before Pym can emerge safely from his hiding place, a mutiny occurs. Only the intervention of the half-Indian from the Black Hills, apelike Dirk Peters, saves Augustus and Pym from murder. A catastrophic storm overturns and almost destroys the ship, called the *Grampus.* The mutineers are overpowered and thrown overboard.

Surviving weeks with almost nothing to eat or drink, three of those left, Pym, Augustus, and Peters, kill a fourth named Parker and consume him. Then Pym watches Augustus sicken and become "a mass of putrefaction." Clinging to the bottom of the overturned ship, eating barnacles, Pym and Peters are eventually rescued by the schooner *Jane Guy.* Looking for seals and a mollusk called *biche de mer,* the *Jane Guy* sails even farther south, toward the Antarctic, on seas more and more mysterious.

Pym began his voyage in June 1827, the same time and at the same age Poe enlisted in the army as Edgar A. Perry. The narrator is troubled by guilt for disobeying his father, for his deceptions. There are passages that include some of Poe's finest writing about the ocean. The details of shipping, the vocabulary of ship structure, the atmosphere of the hold, are impressive. Poe claimed to disapprove of allegory, but all of *Pym* seems allegorical, the ocean a metaphor for nature, terrifying nature and time, in the storm called life. Both Marie Bonaparte and Patrick Quinn have observed that Pym's narrative concerns a "passionate and frenzied search for the Mother . . . and . . . revolts against the Father." But in the words of John T. Irwin, "Pym's voyage to the pole is a symbolic quest for the origin of writing."

There are inconsistencies throughout. For example, how could Pym possibly write in his diary while clinging for his life to the ship in a cataclysmic storm? But the descriptions of wildlife on the strange island where they land are particularly fine. Much of Poe's depiction of rookeries was taken from Benjamin Morrell's *A Narrative of Four Voyages.*

Literary theorists have had great fun with *Pym,* finding within its contradictions and inconsistencies opportunities for profound investigations of semiotics, the limits of language, and "the unreadability of lived experience." Some have described the novel as "a voyage to the end of the page." More recent critics, such as Colin (Joan) Dayan and Terence Whalen, read the novel as a response to slavery. The unfinished state of the story creates many occasions for ingenious speculation, similar to the case of Melville's *Pierre.* Poe himself, in his praise for Jean-François Champollion, celebrates an "extraordinary combination of analytic method and imagination."

Like all good science fiction writers, Poe enhances his fantasy with lavish realistic detail and a factual tone. He quotes chunks of material from encyclopedias and Jeremiah N. Reynolds's history of exploration of the South

Seas. Like Melville, who learned from *Pym,* Poe includes catalogs of fish and little essays on wildlife. As the *Jane Guy* sails farther south, hoping to reach the southern pole, the sea gets warmer, rather than colder, and even hot. Great white animals like polar bears are spotted. The whiteness of the ocean could suggest warm mother's milk, or, as David Greven suggests, semen.

When the crew lands on an exotic island, they are welcomed by very dark natives and the chief Too-wit. Everything on the island, including the soil and rocks, is black. We are told the water there is purple. Nothing terrifies the natives like whiteness—white linen, white sails, white skin. For the critic Sidney Kaplan, "'Tsalal is Hell,' because the black people of the earth are, in Poe's mythology, damned." Enticed inland to the village of Klock-Klock, all the crew are buried in a narrow valley by an arranged avalanche of soil and rock, except for Pym and Peters, who happen to be exploring a narrow crevice, where they are protected. They are "entombed alive" in "living inhumation." Eventually, they escape by carving footholds in the soapstone-like rocks with their bowie knives. "We alone had escaped," Pym tells us.

When the natives see something white, they shout: "Tekeli-li! Tekeli-li!" Eliza Poe had appeared as a bride, wearing a white dress, in the 1806 melodrama *Tekeli* by Theodore Edward Hook. Tekeli is the Turkish name of a Hungarian patriot and must have had some special resonance for Poe. H. P. Lovecraft would later have the character Danforth scream "Tekeli-li!" at the end of his novel *At the Mountains of Madness,* suggesting both horror and the sublime.

Critics have long been fascinated by the chasm markings in *Pym,* figures cut into the cave walls. Inspired by H. W. F. Gesenius's *Hebrew and Chaldee Lexicon to the Old Testament,* the inscriptions seem to suggest racial contrasts, "to be shady," "to be white," functioning as runic signs of the apparent chasm and clash between white people and Black people. The glyphs appear to echo the racial subtexts in other works of Poe, including "The Journal of Julius Rodman," and the growing tensions in the United States about slavery and emancipation. It is significant that the seemingly primitive Dirk Peters can read the signs more readily than the supposedly educated Pym. People of color appear to understand the racism of whites better than the whites themselves.

Forcing the native named Nu-Nu to help them, Pym and Peters escape from the island in a large canoe. Carried farther south by a mysterious, powerful current, they approach a vast cataract plunging into an abyss. Because the final chapters of Pym's account were never written, we don't learn how he survived to return to the United States. Instead, the narrative ends with an apocalyptic scene of approach to the lip of the chasm:

"And now we rushed into the embraces of the cataract, where a chasm threw itself open to receive us. But there arose in our pathway a shrouded human figure, very far larger in its proportions than any dweller among men. And the hue of the skin of the figure was of the perfect whiteness of the snow." John T. Irwin has argued that the looming figure in vapor at the end of the narration "evokes the transfiguration," as portrayed in the Gospels.

Richard Kopley has suggested that much of the imagery of horror in Poe's writing seems to have been inspired by that ultimate vision of the destruction of the world, Revelation. For example, this passage from the first chapter of John's vision: "His head and his hairs were white like wool, as white as snow; and his eyes were as a flame of fire" (Revelation 1:14).

Pym is Poe's most extended poem of Mother Earth, her oceans and eerie places, dangers and horrors, and "regions of novelty and wonder." Pym is finally drawn ever southward at "hideous velocity." What draws him is the ultimate horror, the abyss, which is the womb of earth. The ocean is warm and white as mother's milk. It is a narrative, as Edward H. Davidson tells us, of the horror of origins, and endings. The account must break off with the approach to the brink and the ghostly figure that looms over the plunge back into the mother. Pym survives to write his tale but then dies before it's finished, ten years later. As in "MS. Found in a Bottle," the great secret almost learned can never be expressed. *Pym* is Poe's deepest exploration of desire for, and repulsion from, the female body, a threat Daniel Hoffman calls both "fatal and foetal." But underlying the novel is the implicit fear of an uprising of people of color, in a world in which slavery was a way of life.

When *The Narrative of Arthur Gordon Pym* was published by Harper and Brothers in 1838, delayed by the financial disturbances, Poe had already moved on to Philadelphia. He'd hoped the book would make his name and fortune, but his powerful symbolic voyage aroused only critical interest at the time and made him little money. However, it was republished in London and sold well enough to warrant a second printing but yielded the author no royalties. The English were more responsive to stories of voyages and cataclysmic ocean storms than Americans.

Many of the themes and motifs of the novel resurface in later fiction such as "Descent into the Maelström." The powerful, short, apelike figure of Dirk Peters would be seen again in "The Murders of the Rue Morgue" and "Hop-Frog." The lovingly detailed descriptions of geology and vegetation appear again in "The Gold-Bug" and other stories. Poe is a poet of nature in his prose, nature in all its beauty, horror, bleakness, mystery, and glory.

The novella would receive over twenty reviews. Both style and content would be compared to *Robinson Crusoe.* Because of the way the story is introduced, many readers and reviewers didn't realize Poe was the author. But reviewers appreciated the richness of detail and the thrilling adventures of Pym. One notice in the *New Yorker* called the novella "a work of extraordinary, freezing interest beyond anything we ever read. It is more marvelous than the wildest fiction, yet is presented and supported as sober truth. . . . Those who delight in the wonderful and horrible have a feast before them."

One might expect that after the critical success of this longer work of fiction, Poe would have been inspired to write other novels. He was only twenty-nine years old and could have penned a series of adventure novels. But he had to make a living, and he received little money for the novel, neither from Harper and Brothers nor the British edition.

It is also true that Poe was drawn to the shorter, swerving, quicker form of the tale. When he proposed in his review of Hawthorne that the ideal tale must have unity of effect and could be read at one sitting, he was also defining the kind of fiction he excelled at. In a way we are lucky that Poe did not go on writing adventure novels after *Pym.* Had he done so, we might not have the great detective short stories. Poe's distinct affinity for poetic narrative is demonstrated in both his own fiction and his critical writing: "Plot, . . . properly defined, is *that in which no part can be displaced without ruin to the whole.*"

Despite the extreme struggles his family experienced in their early months in Philadelphia, Poe would enjoy his most fertile period as a writer in the city where the nation was born. Among his many bread-and-butter projects, there was a column for the Baltimore magazine the *American Museum of Science, Literature, and the Arts* called "Literary Small Talk" in which he gathered anecdotes from Gibbon's *Decline and Fall of the Roman Empire* and other sources. More notoriously, as mentioned, he gave his name and an introduction to *The Conchologist's First Book,* written by the English-born Thomas Wyatt. Poe was paid fifty dollars (fifteen hundred dollars today) for the use of his name, but this venture would prove embarrassing over the years as he accused others of plagiarism and was himself attacked in turn. He also published "The Psyche Zenobia," a satire or burlesque of the typical sensationalistic tales seen in the British magazine *Blackwood's.*

Soon Poe moved on from this hackwork to more substantive productions. He even composed a new poem called "The Haunted Palace," his first effort in verse in some time. The poem constitutes a ballad-like description of the mind as a palace or house "haunted by phantoms." Written for the most part in a tripping trochaic meter, it is intended to be hypnotic.

In the greenest of our valleys
  By good angels tenanted,
Once a fair and stately palace—
  Radiant palace—reared its head.
In the monarch Thought's dominion—
  It stood there!
Never seraph spread a pinion
  Over fabric half so fair!

"The Haunted Palace" is one of Poe's most significant poems, dramatizing the breakdown of a mind from stately order and "a lute's well-tunéd law" to rout, flight, and chaos. The collapse of the mind is presented with lyrical exactness and allegorical picturesqueness. Later Poe would incorporate "The Haunted Palace" in "The Fall of the House of Usher" as the work of the inspired but deranged Roderick Usher.

At this time Poe wrote what he and many others consider his finest story, "Ligeia," at the beginning of his most productive period. "Ligeia" is his most memorable "dark lady" tale and tale of marriage, the glory and horror of marriage. Some of the best Poe scholars and critics have expressed very different opinions about its meaning. On the surface the story seems to be a romance. The longer it's studied, the stranger the tale becomes. For this arabesque Poe concocted an epigraph that he ascribed to the seventeenth-century writer Joseph Glanvill: "Man doth not yield himself to the angels, nor unto death utterly, save only through the weakness of his feeble will."

The epigraph is later quoted in the body of the story, and those who interpret "Ligeia" as a study of vampirism or metempsychosis have a point. The story is yet another example of Poe's interest in the theme of women who seem to die but do not die. The name Ligeia was used by Poe in "Al Aaraaf" for a spirit of light and love. Daniel Hoffman has pointed out that *Ligeia* rhymes with and suggests *idea*.

From the name alone, we associate Ligeia with music and the muse. From the first sentence, we are plunged into the strangeness of this tale. "I cannot, for my soul, remember how, when, or even precisely where, I first became acquainted with the lady Ligeia." What an odd way for the speaker to introduce the story of his great love, for whatever else "Ligeia" may be, it's also a story of overpowering and frightening love.

In "Ligeia" the narrator is very precise in describing the heroine's face, hair, voice, and eyes, especially the eyes, yet he cannot recall her last name, though she came from an ancient and distinguished family. He depicts her as a connoisseur might describe a special work of art. Leland S. Person has observed that Poe "[created] female characters by anatomizing and idealizing parts of their bodies." The narrator can remember "her rare learning, her singular yet placid cast of beauty, and the thrilling and enthralling eloquence of her low musical language" but has only a vague sense that he met her in "some large, old, decaying city near the Rhine." This connection to Germany is important, for later the narrator will stress Ligeia's mastery of what we might assume is German transcendental thought. As in most Poe stories, the narrator admits that the romance and marriage with Ligeia were "ill-omened."

Poe portrays Ligeia as statuesque, her "majesty, the quiet ease, of her demeanor, or the incomprehensible lightness and elasticity of her footfall. She came and departed as a shadow." There is something ghostlike about Ligeia, and her voice is music. She has the radiance of an opium dream. Poe loved to quote a Francis Bacon maxim: "There is no exquisite beauty without some *strangeness* in the proportion." Ligeia's high forehead and skin are perfection itself, as are "the raven-black, the glossy, the luxuriant and naturally-curling tresses." An important clue, sometimes overlooked by Poe critics, occurs in the description of Ligeia's nose. "I looked at the delicate outlines of the nose and nowhere but in the graceful medallions of the Hebrews had I beheld a similar perfection."

Both Ligeia and Roderick Usher are described, awkwardly, as having

"Hebrew" noses. In an unpublished self-portrait, Poe described his own nose as "Hebrew." Poe's description of Roderick Usher, with his "nose of a delicate Hebrew model," is essentially a would-be self-portrait. The most intense and intimate details of Ligeia's person are given to her eyes, which remind the narrator of "the beauty of the fabulous Houri of the Turk. The hue of the orbs was the most brilliant of black."

Since the narrator cannot define precisely what was most significant about Ligeia's wisdom and beauty, he relies, as all poets must, on analogy and metaphor. Poe, in "Ligeia," hints at some profound secret that language cannot utter. In Kabbalistic texts the transcendent, hidden God "remains forever beyond the grasp of the human mind."

For the narrator, Ligeia has only one flaw, and that is her passion. "And of such passion I could form no estimate, save by . . . the fierce energy . . . of the wild words which she habitually uttered." The speaker is in awe of Ligeia's physical beauty and intellect but appalled and frightened by the strength of her desire. "She was the most violently a prey to the tumultuous vultures of stern passion." The speaker still wants to worship at her feet and learn from her, as from a mother/muse.

The great learning and intelligence he ascribed to Ligeia might well be Jewish scholarship and mysticism, the Kabbalah of Zohar. When the speaker refers to the ancient pedigree of her family, most readers have assumed he was referring to a European noble family. Poe had once claimed his ancestors were from Germany! But what family could have more distinguished roots than one from the yeshivas and synagogues of Germany, with the blood of Abraham, Moses, and David in their veins?

The Poe textual scholar Thomas O. Mabbott noted in 1969: "[Ligeia's] lack of remembered family name, despite her noble ancestry, suggests she may have been of Jewish origin. . . . Ligeia is described as resembling the poet's mother, Elizabeth Arnold Poe, who had a Hebraic nose and large dark eyes."

Ligeia must die, wasting away, as Eliza Poe did. She must die because she has been consumed with the sin of sexual pleasure. Throughout his life Poe took out the miniature of Eliza, mesmerized by her large dark eyes, as Laban of the Bible stared at the eyes of his teraphim (Genesis 31:30). Ligeia's eyes were both hypnotic and seductive. It is the eyes that provoke glossolalia and mesmeric trance in ecstatic rituals. As she is dying, Ligeia asks the narrator to recite a poem she has written earlier, called "The Conqueror Worm." As she passes away, she is aghast at the defeat of the mind and will in death.

The narrator flees the Rhine and marries a petite, blonde English girl, Lady Rowena Trevanion of Tremaine, the opposite of Ligeia in every way. In other words, he seeks to be conventional, wed to an English girl of good family. (Poe knew well a novel by Plumer Ward called *Tremaine.*) Ligeia has left him considerable wealth, and he restores an abbey in a remote part of Britain. Burton Pollin has pointed out that Byron's grandmother was named Sophia Trevanion.

Much of the rest of the story is taken up with descriptions of the decor of the abbey. This suggests that while life with Ligeia was more mental, emotional, and spiritual, as well as sexual, the new life with Rowena is materialistic, superficial, dominated by graven images. Rowena makes normal sexual demands on the narrator, and he recoils in disgust. Being an aesthete, he devotes himself to interior decoration. The bridal chamber is described in minute, exotic detail. The room has the shape of a pentagon, which has mystical significance, and contains sarcophagi, like those Poe saw as a boy in London.

The details of the bridal chamber, which becomes the death chamber, heighten the tension and thrill as the story approaches its climax. Of course, the marriage with Rowena is doomed, and she sickens, unloved by the narrator. It has been pointed out by Thomas Mabbott that Poe probably took the name Rowena from Sir Walter Scott's *Ivanhoe.* But we should also remember that the other heroine and rival to Rowena in that novel is the Jewish Rebecca, another clue to the identity of Ligeia and her heritage. We might also recall that William Makepeace Thackeray published a novel called *Rebecca and Rowena,* a sequel to *Ivanhoe,* in which the hero eventually marries the Jewish Rebecca. David Greven refers to Rebecca as the "sensual Jewess."

Rowena suffers a horrendous struggle to die, as the narrator longs for the lost Ligeia. He brings Rowena a goblet of wine, ostensibly to revive her, and then sees "three or four drops of brilliant and ruby colored fluid" fall into the goblet. The drops are apparently poison, for now Rowena lies still, though she revives and lies still several times.

In the dawn the corpse stirs again, and the face flushes with new life.

Suddenly the body, bound in the shroud, rises from the bed and steps into the middle of the overdecorated chamber. In terror and confusion, the narrator notices that the figure is much taller than Rowena. The bands of the graveclothes fall away. "And there streamed forth, into the rushing atmosphere of the chamber, huge masses of long and disheveled hair; *it was blacker than the wings of the midnight*. . . . 'Here then, at least,' I shrieked aloud, 'can I never—can I never be mistaken—these are the full, and the black, and the wild eyes—of my lost love—of the lady—of the LADY LIGEIA!'"

Like most great art, "Ligeia" can mean different things to different readers. It is both a romance and a horror story of marriage. It can be seen as an account of mental illness. To some it means the restoration of an ideal love through strength of will. With the contrived "quote" from Joseph Glanvill, Poe wanted to suggest that. To others it is the story of the return of the feared superior woman who demands sexual gratification the narrator cannot provide. In that way it is a double or triple horror. And there are many other ways this prose poem can be explicated.

But for Poe it was his most intense imagining of the mother, lover, muse, who can be worshipped but not with the body. The features he ascribed to Ligeia are those he saw in the miniature of Eliza and found in the reviews and personal memories of the actress. All except the height—Eliza was small of stature but *very* tall to the two-year-old and in Poe's imagination. To him that heritage of intellect, scholarship, mystical learning, beauty, and song represented his own distinct identity, genius, heritage, and otherness, and was both a blessing and a curse. Throughout his career Poe had shown a special interest in Eugene Sue's novel *The Wandering Jew*. Ligeia is both the Wandering Jew *and* Aphrodite or Astarte. She must die, and yet she cannot die, and she haunts the narrator forever.

However we choose to interpret "Ligeia," it is Poe's most memorable and most tortured tale of the terrors of marriage. The brilliant Ligeia intimidates the narrator with her intellect, learning, beauty, and sexual passion. The conventional Rowena disgusts him. Both wives die, but Ligeia returns, for purposes we don't know. The drug-addled narrator may be a murderer or witness to a demonic miracle. Each marriage is a calamity.

9

WILLIAM BURTON

FOR "LIGEIA" POE WAS PAID BY THE BALTIMORE *AMERICAN Museum* ten dollars (three hundred dollars today), or about fifty cents per manuscript page. It may have been his finest story, or one of two or three of his finest stories, but since he left the *Southern Literary Messenger,* Edgar, Sissy, and Muddy had been living precariously, week by week. Philadelphia was a quieter, cleaner city than Manhattan, more conducive, probably, for writing, but it was not much cheaper.

The Poes continued to live at the western side of the city, almost in the country, on Sixteenth Street near Locust Street. Sissy was offered a pet fawn, which they could not accept. They did not have a house to themselves but lived in a kind of annex built onto the main house. But there was a wide yard with flower beds and a fence that gave a sense of privacy. A garden was important for all three, for the vegetables as well as the flowers and shrubs growing there. Poe always had a special delectation for shrubbery.

As it turned out, Mary Starr, now married to a tailor in New York named Jennings, visited the Poes at their home and would remember how tidy Muddy kept the place, though their poverty could not be disguised. She would recall that Sissy, now seventeen, remained plump and childlike but had a particularly sweet singing voice. Mary would sing "Come Rest in This Bosom" at Poe's request. All his life Poe passionately loved music and was drawn to women with fine voices, like Eliza Poe. The Poes were also visited by another woman he had courted in Baltimore, his cousin Elizabeth Herring. For a time, Poe's uncle by marriage, Henry Herring, lived in

FIG. 14. William Evans Burton (1802–60). An actor as well as editor and publisher, the British-born Burton hired Poe to edit *Burton's Gentleman's Magazine* in Philadelphia in 1839. Burton seldom allowed Poe to make editorial choices, and the two men clashed almost from the beginning. He fired Poe in 1840 but later recommended him to his successor. (Courtesy of the Edgar Allan Poe Museum, Richmond, Virginia)

Philadelphia with his daughter Mary from his second marriage, and the Poes and the Herrings saw a good bit of each other.

It would be an English actor, resident in Philadelphia, William Evans Burton (1802–60), who would rescue Poe. Burton, a large, blustery man, specialized in comic roles, playing Irishmen, ne'er-do-wells, bums (fig. 14). Another actor would describe him as "an enterprising man but a vulgar indecent actor." Most people called him "Billy Burton." Besides acting, he'd tried his hand at journalism, also writing fiction and plays and editing collections of humor.

Burton tried to live the life of a high-roller. He'd been divorced at least once. In 1837 he had begun publishing *Burton's Gentleman's Magazine* in Philadelphia, with features on sports, hunting, and sailing as well as fiction and poetry. Burton wrote many reviews of current books, and he had given *Pym* an especially cutting notice, calling the novella a hoax, an "impudent attempt at humbugging the public."

Poe had a long memory for slights to his person and his writing, but he was desperate for work and applied to Burton for an editorial position. The fact that Burton was an actor, from England, may have seemed a favorable sign to Poe. If such was the case, Poe was badly mistaken, for he and Burton would find themselves at odds almost from the beginning. Burton's gruff, heavy-handed manner would grate on Poe's fastidious sensibility. And it's apparent that Poe aggravated Burton also. Poe could be arrogant and independent, then cooperative and courteous by turns. From the beginning Burton was nervous about Poe's slashing reviews, and Poe had nothing but contempt for Burton's vulgarity and lack of taste. Burton would write to his young editor: "I am sorry you have thought it necessary to send me such a letter. Your troubles have given a morbid tone to your feelings which it is your duty to discourage."

Burton offered Poe ten dollars (about three hundred dollars today) a week for his editorial services, beginning in June 1839. The actor promised that the magazine work could be completed in two hours each day. It was less than he'd been paid at the *Messenger,* but Poe was in no position to quibble. Billy Burton considered himself a self-made man and jack-of-all-trades. Instead of the sympathy Poe was accustomed to, from Sissy and Muddy, Burton brusquely ordered Poe to get on with his duties. Poe was listed as "Assistant Editor."

Given his small salary and the amount of article writing, reviewing, letter writing, and proofreading Poe was expected to do, the position at *Burton's* was little better than serfdom. And yet this was Poe's period of greatest productivity. Working with compulsion, he reviewed books on every subject that came his way. He gave special praise to Fouqué's *Undine,* which delighted and thrilled him. Like Coleridge, and others before him and after him, Poe filled his copy with passages paraphrased from other sources, especially Reese's *Encyclopedia,* not to mention other magazines and newspapers. Many of his reviews of established literary figures such as Fitz-Greene Halleck, Washington Irving, and William Cullen Bryant were particularly severe, even for Poe. He declared both Irving and Bryant overrated. The months of hunger in New York and Philadelphia had given an extra sharpness to his pen and attitude. Writing in 1840, Poe said, "I intend to put up with nothing that I can *put down.*"

But it was Henry Wadsworth Longfellow who seemed to provoke Poe's worst spleen. Poe would wage a long and sustained attack on the best-selling popular author that would make Poe notorious and cost him friends and supporters later. Since Poe and Longfellow had much in common as poets, at least superficially, it's curious that Poe was so offended by the much-loved Boston poet. In reviewing *Voices of the Night,* Longfellow's volume of 1839, Poe declared the poet "singularly deficient in all those important faculties which give artistical power." But the core of his attack was on plagiarism, "too palpable to be mistaken; and which belongs to the most barbarous class of literary robbery."

Biographers and critics have, over the years, attempted to explain Poe's persistent and growing animosity toward Longfellow. By turns Poe would praise Longfellow and then begin slashing again. Poe seemed to be at war with the Harvard professor of languages, who had married an heiress and lived in a mansion in Cambridge.

New England always irritated Poe. Though he'd been born there, that fact had done him little good. Poe had been forced to be a wanderer. That was *his* legacy. There was something about Longfellow, and Emerson too, that really got under Poe's skin. "When I consider . . . Mr. Emerson, I am lost in amazement at finding in him little more than a respectful imitation of Carlyle."

Yet Poe probably felt guilt for his repeated attacks on the respected Longfellow. When Poe was thinking of founding his own magazine in 1841, he wrote to Longfellow: "It would be desirable that you should agree to furnish one paper each month,—prose or poetry—absolute or serial—and of such length as you might deem proper." This on-again, off-again concern with Longfellow will be discussed later.

Working furiously for Burton, Poe published the dialogue "The Conversation of Eiros and Charmion." There is a cosmic strain in Poe's work, beginning with "Al Aaraaf," set among the stars, and culminating in *Eureka* in 1848. Again, Poe's imagination is similar in many ways to William Blake's. Both poets thought in terms of moon and stars, time and eternity, and cosmic forces. The names Eiros and Charmion are taken from the devoted handmaidens of Cleopatra. The voices are speaking from the afterworld, in a posthumous dialogue after Earth has been destroyed by fire. Charmion had passed into Aidenn earlier and is curious about the details of the end of the world, destroyed by a comet.

As the amount of oxygen increased in the atmosphere, living things experienced a euphoria, even as the horror approached. Eiros concludes the account: "A furious delirium possessed all men; and . . . they trembled and shrieked aloud. . . . For a moment there was a wild lurid light alone, visiting and penetrating all things. Then . . . there came a shouting and pervading sound, as if from the mouth itself of HIM; while the whole incumbent mass of ether in which we existed, burst at once into a species of intense flame. . . . Thus ended all."

It was in the offices of *Burton's Magazine* that Poe met Thomas Dunn English, a writer and editor who would figure later in Poe's life in both good and disastrous ways. According to English's later statement: "I was favorably impressed with the appearance and manners of the author . . . in plain, rather worn suit of black, carefully brushed, and linen . . . notable for its cleanliness. We went out of the office together, and in conversation as we walked along Chestnut Street, and parted above Third, well pleased with each other. . . . I became a frequent visitor to his family." It would be English who introduced Poe to his friend Henry Beck Hirst, a writer and lawyer who may have advised Poe on copyright and libel law.

Also in 1839, Poe wrote what many consider to be his finest story, "The Fall of the House of Usher." From the time the story was published in *Burton's Gentleman's Magazine* in September 1839, critics have celebrated its eerie power, unity of effect, and the poetry of its narration. It might be pointed out that Eliza Poe had close actor friends named Luke Noble Usher and Harriet Ann L'Estrange Usher, whose children, James Campbell Usher and Agnes Pye Usher, were orphans and known as eccentrics, or neurotics.

Poe was particularly good at beginning stories in a way that draws the reader into the mood and atmosphere of a tale. Probably he wrote no more effective opening than the long first paragraph of "Usher."

> During the whole of a dull, dark, and soundless day in the autumn of the year, when the clouds hung oppressively low in the heavens, I had been passing alone, on horseback, through a singularly dreary tract of country; and at length found myself, as the shades of the evening drew on, within view of the melancholy House of Usher. I know not how it was—but, with the first glimpse of the building, a sense of insufferable gloom pervaded my spirit. . . . I reined my horse to the precipitous brink of a black and lurid tarn that lay in unruffled lustre by the dwelling, and gazed down—but with a shudder even more thrilling than before—upon the remodelled and inverted images of the gray sedge, and the ghastly tree-stems, and the vacant and eye-like windows.

There is no sighing of wind in the skeletal trees, no birdsong, no chattering of squirrels. The narrator has entered the world of the dead.

Critics have attempted to read "The Fall of the House of Usher" as autobiographical. There is no doubt that Poe projected onto Roderick Usher many features of his own person and personality. Usher belongs to an ancient and distinguished family, but he and his sister, Madeline, are the last of the line. Their house is decaying, and the building itself, with windows like eyes, has a barely discernible crack down the middle. Poe lets us know early on that Usher, for all his gifts and sensibility, is "cracked," doomed. The narrator is shocked by the looks of his childhood friend: "A cadaverousness of complexion; an eye large, liquid, and luminous beyond comparison; lips somewhat thin and very pallid, but of a surpassingly beautiful curve; a nose of a delicate Hebrew model."

A glance at any of the photographs of Poe will persuade us that the author is, at least in part, describing himself. The wide forehead, the "Hebrew" nose, are unmistakable. And the description reminds us very much of Ligeia. It is the way Poe saw himself. In Richard Wilbur's words, "'The Fall of the House of Usher' is a journey into the depths of the self." In his portrait of the character John Hermann, later left out of "Mystification," Poe would again describe his own idealized face: "The forehead was massive and broad. . . . The aquiline nose, too, would have done honour to a Hebrew medallion." Among celebrities of the nineteenth century, only Richard Wagner would have such a wide forehead. Usher's twin sister looks very much like him and is tall, even statuesque, like Ligeia. Like Poe himself, Usher lives with unspecified guilt and cannot be comforted. He suffers from hyper-neurasthenia and feels "the sentience of all vegetable things."

Much has been written about Poe's use of the double, the doppelgänger, in his fiction. But what we have in "The Fall of the House of Usher" is not a double but a quadruple. For Poe is the narrator attempting to analyze Usher, who represents himself and is identical with his twin sister, Madeline. Through the merciless lens of fiction, Poe studies himself: "The now ghastly pallor of the skin, and the now miraculous lustre of the eye, above all things startled and even awed me. The silken hair, too, had been suffered to grow all unheeded, and as, in its wild gossamer texture, it floated rather than fell about the face." The gossamer-like hair suggests a spider, but it floats like the hair of Coleridge's ecstatic poet who has fed on honeydew and "drunk the milk of paradise."

Poe gives minute attention to the physical House of Usher: "Perhaps the eye of a scrutinizing observer might have discovered a barely perceptible fissure, which, extending from the roof of the building in front, made its way down the wall in a zigzag direction, until it became lost in the sullen waters of the tarn." Early in the story we understand that the house is the mind of Roderick Usher, who lives in guilt and terror to the point of madness.

There is so much to say about "The Fall of the House of Usher" and its relevance to Poe biography that I can only summarize and suggest. The effect of the story lies in its pacing and atmosphere of dread and depression that gradually overtake the narrator. It is especially useful to consider "Usher" in conjunction with "Ligeia." They are probably Poe's best two tales, other than the detective stories, and they inform each other.

If the character Ligeia is Poe's most frightening portrayal of the ideal lover-muse-mother figure and Roderick Usher shares so many features with Ligeia, we begin to see what Poe is doing here. To put it plainly, the narrator of "Usher" represents the rational, analytical side of Poe's personality, examining Usher, the poetic, visionary, sometimes mad, side of himself. Madeline Usher, the twin sister, who looks exactly like her brother, and therefore like Ligeia, is the Jungian anima, lover, mother, muse, the poet has longed to be reunited with.

Roderick Usher knows he is a dreamer who can't, or won't, awaken; he's doomed. And the house by the tarn is doomed. He and the Lady Madeline have lived too long in the decaying mansion of their forbidden romance. Madeline is ill, but Roderick does nothing to help her. She haunts the house like an apparition, passing silently in the hallway. She suffers from a disease, like all Poe's heroines, sometimes passing into epileptic states, between life and death.

The feminine side of Usher's personality had been suppressed. We can assume that the narrator has been concerned with reasonable and practical things, while his double has buried himself in mystical and forbidden studies, obscure volumes of forgotten lore. Since we know that Poe took great care with names, we might ask why the tall, mysterious sister-lover is named Madeline, a version of Magdalen. With her Hebrew features, Lady Madeline reminds us of Eliza Poe, who was accused by some of adultery. Many thought of actresses, in any case, as little better than harlots. In "Marginalia" Poe sought to rehabilitate the fallen woman: "We have no reason to believe that Mary Magdalene ever sinned as supposed."

One day, while the narrator is attempting to help his host through a crisis of conscience and fear, Usher tells him that his sister has died, after he has recited the poem "The Haunted Palace," describing a mind's descent into madness. Instead of burying his sister, Roderick will place her in a coffin in the dungeon, a former torture chamber of the house, hoping to avoid premature burial in one of her cataleptic states, and maybe to avoid grave robbers. There she will lie between life and death.

Poe describes in detail the chamber where the coffin is taken, far down in the cellar of the castle, directly below the narrator's sleeping chamber, that is, in his unconscious. It's only as he looks upon the face of Madeline, before the lid is placed on the coffin, that the narrator learns she and Roderick are twins. And he notices a faint blush upon her skin but, strangely, says nothing. After Lady Madeline is left in the dungeon, the coffin lid screwed on, Roderick's behavior becomes more bizarre. "There were times, indeed, when I thought his unceasingly agitated mind was laboring with some oppressive secret, to divulge which he struggled for the necessary courage." Later in the story the narrator repairs to his bedroom and is disturbed by a storm and the stirring of the draperies in the room. He is bothered by low and indistinct sounds he cannot interpret. Then Usher knocks on his door and enters, looking even more disturbed than before. Usher hurries to the window and opens the casement to the storm.

To calm his host, the narrator reads to him from an archaic romance called "Mad Trist" of Sir Lancelot Canning. But as he reads, Usher seems preoccupied by his own fears, and there are noises in other parts of the house. The sounds continue, and the story of Ethelred's fight with the dragon only heightens the tension, as Usher appears to be demented. The sounds grow louder, and Roderick exclaims: "'Not hear it? yes, I hear it, and *have* heard it. Long—long—long—many minutes, many hours, many days, have I heard it—yet I dared not . . . speak! *We have put her living in the tomb!* . . . Do I not distinguish that heavy and horrible beating of her heart? Madman!'—here he sprang furiously to his feet, and shrieked out his syllables, as if in the effort he were giving up his soul—*'Madman! I tell you that she now stands without the door!'*" "Madman" may be addressed to either the narrator or Usher, or both.

The Lady Madeline does indeed appear at the door, exhausted and bloody from her struggle to escape from the coffin and climb the stairs:

"Then, with a low moaning cry [she] fell heavily inward upon the person of her brother, and in her violent and now final death-agonies, bore him to the floor a corpse, and a victim to the terrors he had anticipated." According to David Leverenz, Madeline's "self-birthing [from her coffin] becomes self-murder."

The narrator flees the house and watches the building split along the fissure and sink "like the voice of a thousand waters" into the tarn in the light of a "blood-red moon." In Acts 2:20 it is predicted the moon will turn to blood at the end of time. With this apocalyptic ending, Poe also echoes Revelation 1:15: "and his voice as the sound of many waters."

"Usher" may be Poe's most extreme dramatization of guilt. Usher's secrets are never fully revealed, but he has lived with his sister like a pharaoh, and his mind and character have decayed. Worst of all, he has placed her prematurely in the vault, as though to bury evidence of his guilt. Rather than helping Madeline in her illness, he composes refined dirges and indulges in voluptuous narcissism. The "marriage" of brother and sister ends in catastrophe.

Usher is Poe looking at himself with a cold and critical eye, articulating his self-destructive, neurotic genius and love and hate for his mother and for all women, including Virginia. "Usher" is Poe's confession of guilt for marrying his cousin, whom he calls "Sister." The narrator, the rational side of his personality, does escape from the collapsing mansion and Usher's madness, but Usher, even as he approaches death, screams that the narrator is also a madman.

"Usher" is Poe's recognition that finally logic, analysis, ratiocination, code breaking, do not solve the sickness of the soul and the cruel splendors of being. In fact, with his pretensions to rationality in a chaotic and irrational and doomed universe, in which the feminine component of the self is denied, the narrator may be the maddest of them all. For the House of Usher is not only the mind of Roderick Usher (and Edgar Allan Poe); it is the whole universe, which will ultimately self-destruct, as Poe will tell us later in *Eureka*. "Usher" may be Poe's most bizarre tale of the punishment of marriage. Washington Irving wrote to Poe: "I am much pleased with a tale called 'The House of Usher,' and should think a collection of tales, equally well written, could not fail of being favorably received."

"William Wilson," another of Poe's best stories, written the same year as "Usher," is Poe's finest contribution to the genre of the double, or doppelgänger, and it may well be Poe's most elegant study of guilt, perversity, and the war within one's own mind and heart. Here Poe comes close to writing allegory, which he would disparage in writers such as Hawthorne as clumsy and outdated. The narrator of "William Wilson," from an affluent family, was sent to a boarding school near London, modeled on Reverend Bransby's Manor House School at Stoke Newington, which Poe had attended: "My earliest recollections of school-life are connected with a large, rambling Elizabethan house, in a misty-looking village of England, where were a vast number of gigantic and gnarled trees, and where all the houses were excessively ancient. In truth, it was a dream-like and spirit-soothing place."

The elderly headmaster rules with a "Draconian" hand. The story is a confession. "In truth, the ardor, the enthusiasm, and the imperiousness of my disposition, soon rendered me a marked character among my schoolmates." The only student Wilson cannot dominate and intimidate is also named William Wilson, the same age as the narrator, who arrived at the school the same day as the speaker. This other William Wilson frustrates the intrigues of the arrogant and malicious narrator. The reader soon realizes that this mirror image of Wilson is none other than his conscience.

The second William Wilson, born the same day as Poe, January 19, infuriates the speaker so much that he intends to attack him in his sleep. But when he lowers the lamp and sees the otherness in the familiar face, he is so shocked he flees the school, only to encounter the double again at Eton College. At Eton the narrator begins a life of dissipation, but again he is confronted by the other who dresses like him and appears at awkward moments to sabotage his schemes of malice. There is no escaping this nemesis, who reappears at Oxford. The narrator absconds to the Continent for a life of decadence and exploitation of others. Poe may have been reminded of how he'd been taken in card games at the University of Virginia.

The final confrontation with the hated double occurs during Carnival in Rome. The narrator is engaged in seducing the young wife of the elderly Duke Di Broglio but is interrupted at the ball by the second William Wilson, dressed exactly like himself. They fight. "In a few seconds I . . . plunged my sword, with brute ferocity, repeatedly through and through his bosom." When the narrator sees himself in a mirror, he recognizes the other William Wilson, now defeated, bloody, speaking the words of his dying conscience: *"You have conquered, and I yield. Yet, henceforward art thou also dead . . . how utterly thou hast murdered thyself."*

The story is one of Poe's most original. Later writers such as Dostoevsky, Conrad, Kafka, and Robert Louis Stevenson would be inspired by it. "William Wilson" was published in *Burton's Gentleman's Magazine*, October 1839, and reprinted in the annual called the *Gift*. The story is a caricature of some of Poe's own weaknesses and an admission of guilt for tendencies he'd worked to overcome. Poe had once again contradicted his critical dicta, writing a clearly moral tale.

It was while editing *Burton's Gentleman's Magazine* that Poe began to create the legend of himself as a code breaker. For a few extra dollars, Poe wrote articles about codes for *Alexander's Weekly Messenger* and acquired a reputation as an expert on decryption and encryption. People were drawn to the subject and sent him an overwhelming number of puzzles and ciphers. What Poe and his readers were experimenting with were "elementary substitution ciphers," in which other symbols replaced the letters of the alphabet and text sources were familiar, such as the Book of Common Prayer. Writing in codes was appealing because it promised privacy from the Mob. It seems that what Poe knew about code breaking came from *Reese's Encyclopedia* and the *Encyclopedia Britannica,* but to readers of the magazines, he appeared to be a wizard. His challenges to readers to send him encrypted texts to decipher increased the circulation of the magazine significantly. Poe's articles on ciphers may have been the most popular of all his magazine and newspaper features.

Poe's mind was unusually quick, and appearing analytical and penetrating was a role he relished. Later Poe would demonstrate his gift for decryption in the detective stories and, in *Eureka,* attempt to break the code of God's creation. Poe would take great pride in what the critic Shawn James Rosenheim would call "the analytic sublime."

In December 1839 the Philadelphia firm of Lea & Blanchard, which had turned down Poe's *Tales of the Folio Club* years earlier, brought out *Tales of the Grotesque and Arabesque* in an edition of 750 copies. The two volumes contained twenty-five tales, including "Berenicë," "Ligeia," and "William Wilson." Readers at the time, and critics to this day, have trouble deciding exactly which stories are "grotesques" and which are "arabesques." The problem may be that Poe did not intend us to see some stories as all grotesque and others as only arabesque. Many of the stories contain elements of both. Certainly, stories such as "The Loss of Breath" have more of the grotesque than the arabesque. For *arabesque* suggests delicacy and intricate design, like the decor of mosques, the fantasy of *The Arabian Nights,* the subtlety of Arabic mystical poetry. A story such as "Eleonora" would be almost completely arabesque.

In his preface to the tales, Poe made some of his most memorable comments about fiction writing. It irritated him that critics and readers associated his stories with "Germanism" and the Gothic tales of E.T.A. Hoffmann. Poe knew the originality of much of his work and was determined to assert his independence and distinctness of voice. "If in many of my productions terror has been the thesis, I maintain that terror is not of Germany, but of the soul."

Along with Hawthorne's *Twice-Told Tales* of 1837, *Tales of the Grotesque and Arabesque* brought American fiction to a new level. The native of Salem, Massachusetts, and Poe, of Richmond and Philadelphia, set the standard for the short story in the United States. Poetry, drama, the novel, and the essay had their origins elsewhere. But the modern short story as we know it has roots in American soil, in the commercial world of newspaper and magazine publishing. In the tales of both Poe and Hawthorne, we see the manner of the eighteenth-century essay as practiced by Joseph Addison and Richard Steele and the nineteenth-century essays by William Hazlitt and Charles Lamb, adapted as lead-ins for narratives. Both Poe and Hawthorne sometimes began stories as essays on madness or fate and wrote prose so rich and allusive that their best stories are poems. Each would create a standard and inspire those who came after to write "Bartleby," *The Turn of the Screw,* the Civil War stories of Ambrose Bierce, the science fiction of H. P. Lovecraft.

10

PENN MAGAZINE

POE'S EXPECTATIONS FOR *TALES OF THE GROTESQUE AND Arabesque* were indeed high. He knew that he'd touched the sublime in "The Fall of the House of Usher" and "Ligeia" as well as in *The Narrative of Arthur Gordon Pym.* Several reviewers did appreciate the power and artistry of his tales. One reviewer wrote: "To say we have *read* this production attentively, is not enough. We have *studied* it. . . . He has placed himself in the foremost rank of American writers."

Like all authors, Poe yearned for praise and approval. For all his posture of superiority and indifference to fashion and the Mob, he may have longed for recognition even more than most authors, craving legitimacy, acceptance. Though as a critic he'd lashed out at contemporaries such as Longfellow, Poe was extremely sensitive to criticism of his own writing. When the *Boston Morning Post* observed of *Tales of the Grotesque and Arabesque* that "a greater amount of trash within the same compass it would be difficult to find," Poe's resentment of New England snobbery was renewed. The *Boston Notion* echoed the *Boston Morning Post:* "We have read a goodly number of these tales, and verily must say that they fall below the average of newspaper trash."

As stated, Poe was not above reviewing himself. In the periodical called *Alexander's* and in the pages of *Burton's Gentleman's Magazine,* he praised himself anonymously. In one instance he created an epigram to puff himself: "Why ought the author of the 'Grotesque and Arabesque' to be a good writer of verses? Because he's a poet to a *t.* Add *t* to Poe makes it a Poet."

In May 1840 Poe published in *Burton's Magazine* an oft-neglected piece called "The Philosophy of Furniture." Along with the later "Landscape Garden" and "The Domain of Arnheim," it is one of Poe's significant explorations of design and aesthetics. Poe deplores "the aristocracy of dollars, the *display of wealth*," that encourage "over-furnishing" and vulgarity in American decoration. In 1845 Poe would add: "Appallachia [*sic*]" would be a better sounding name for the United States. Later, in "Marginalia," Poe would write: "There should be no hesitation about 'Appalachia.' In the first place it is distinctive . . . in the second place . . . indigenous, springing from one of the most magnificent and distinctive features of the country itself."

Poe tells us that "the soul of the apartment is the carpet," and he warns of the excessive glitter of too much cut glass on display and too many mirrors in a room. The purpose of decoration is to relax, hearten, and assure. "*Repose* speaks in all." Poe's own walls and floors were probably bare, but he could visualize the perfect quarters for living.

In 1840 Poe began to think seriously of founding his own magazine. He was thirty-one, and he'd worked as a low-paid assistant on two magazines for which he'd written hundreds of pages of articles and reviews. He'd often quarreled with his employers over issues of taste and critical rigor. He was embarrassed by the low literary standards of *Burton's Magazine.*

Poe's critical reviews and astute editing had increased the circulation of both the *Messenger* and *Burton's*. What he needed was a forum, a platform, from which he could reach the larger public, unimpeded by the conventional tastes of a White or Burton. In the words of J. Gerald Kennedy, "It appears that ownership of a literary periodical became the dominant compensatory fantasy of Poe's adult life."

In the twenty-first century, it's hard for us to understand the importance of magazines and newspapers in the nineteenth. Editors like Horace Greeley and William Cullen Bryant wielded vast influence on politics and public opinion. All his life Poe had read the prestigious British monthlies and quarterlies such as *Blackwood's* and the *Edinburgh Review* in which distinguished writers such as Macaulay and Carlisle raised their eloquent voices about history, culture, and the issues of the day.

Given the freedom of his own journal, Poe could surpass New England and perhaps the British journals. A popular editor in those days had the influence and prestige of a network commentator, a media celebrity, self-help guru, and television evangelist of our day combined. Though he disdained the populism and provincialism of the United States, Poe, too, was a man of his time. For all his sense of irony and caustic wit, Poe, too, would be subject to the enthusiasm and vigor of the movement called Young America, celebrating the new republic, as we shall see.

We are told by the scholar Meredith L. McGill that "many of the periodicals in which Poe's texts appeared vastly exceeded the print runs of his published books." And through unregulated reprinting in other publications, his work reached an even larger audience. Poe argued that magazines should not be limited to domestic themes. "A foreign theme is, in a strictly literary sense, to be preferred." Or as McGill states, "Poe calls for an investment in variety and elaboration" in magazines, not nationalist limits.

Poe grew increasingly disillusioned with Billy Burton. The actor and publisher had announced several large prizes of $250 ($7,500 today) and $200 ($6,000) for the best essay and tale, respectively, submitted to his magazine. When Poe discovered that Burton had no intention of paying the prize money but intended to publish the articles and tales submitted without compensating the authors, he lost all respect for the man. Burton had been attempting to sell his magazine without telling Poe, and then Burton discovered that Poe intended to establish his own *Penn Magazine* while still on the staff of *Burton's*. Each accused the other of treachery. Burton was planning to build his own theater in Philadelphia with whatever funds he could raise.

In a June 1, 1840, letter to Burton, Poe detailed many of his accumulated grievances: "Sir: I find myself at leisure this Monday morning, June 1, to notice your very singular letter of Saturday. . . . your attempts to bully me excite in my mind <nothing> scarcely any other sentiment than mirth. . . . If by accident you have taken it into your head <by any sad accident> that I am to be insulted with impunity I can only assume that you are an ass." After a long list of his financial and professional grievances, Poe concluded: "The charge of 100 $ I shall not admit for an instant. If you persist in it our intercourse is at an end, <and I shall refer you to an attorney>."

Burton put around the story that Poe's drinking had caused his troubles. We can't be sure that Poe didn't drink while working for Burton, but in general he was sober during this period of intense writing and planning for his new magazine. Poe famously pledged in a letter to his Baltimore friend Joseph Evans Snodgrass, April 1, 1841, that in all the time he worked for Burton, "*nothing stronger than water ever passed my lips.*"

Poe did not spare the epithets when he attacked his former employer as a "buffoon and a felon" and "a blackguard and a villain," "a scoundrel," and "the basest of calumniators," known for "his chicanery, arrogance, ignorance, and brutality." Given the amount of work he'd done for the magazine, Poe cannot have fallen off the wagon very often. Poe knew that Snodgrass was a lecturer on temperance.

In the 1840s magazine after magazine was founded and then folded. Poe had to believe that his own venture would be the exception. The hurdle, of course, was finding seed money to start. Poe gave himself half a year to collect the necessary funds to launch *Penn Magazine.* He bought an ad in the *Saturday Evening Post* on June 6, 1840: "PROSPECTUS OF THE PENN MAGAZINE, A MONTHLY LITERARY JOURNAL, TO BE EDITED AND PUBLISHED IN THE CITY OF PHILADELPHIA, BY EDGAR A. POE."

Poe promised the highest critical standards in the new magazine. "Its aim, chiefly, shall be *to please;* and this through means of versatility, originality and pungency." The *Penn Magazine* would cost $5 a year ($150 today), and the first issue was promised for January 1841. Poe had many copies of the prospectus printed as a broadside, and using the backs of the broadsides for letters, he wrote to authors, editors, and publishers, asking for names and addresses of subscribers. He needed at least five hundred dollars (fifteen thousand dollars today) to get started. To meet the January deadline, he would have to get the first issue to the printer in December 1840.

We, with the advantage of hindsight, could predict no *Penn Magazine* would appear. Poe's explanation was "illness," which kept him in bed for the whole month of December. The illness was almost certainly aggravated by drink and a long hangover. He may have raised some money, and he may have assembled some contributions for the inaugural issue.

On the surface there was no reason why Poe should not have been successful at establishing and sustaining his own national magazine. He was the foremost literary critic of his time. But when confronted with business, he retreated to rationalization, drink, and the comfort and sympathy of Muddy and Sissy. For the rest of his life, Poe would dream of editing and publishing his own magazine, first in Philadelphia and then in New York and Richmond. But none of the plans came to anything in the end. This likely had something to do with his relations with John Allan, who'd belittled Poe in his teens as impractical, a dreamer, a liar. The damage to Poe's confidence about practical matters is incalculable. What he was good at was writing and thinking and dreaming. Allan could not take that away from him. In Poe's nightmares, in deepest hell, John Allan taunted him.

One of the projects Poe had begun to publish in *Burton's* was a narrative called "The Journal of Julius Rodman," in which an explorer claims to cross the Rocky Mountains before Lewis and Clark. Similar to *Pym* in some ways, "The Journal of Julius Rodman," after several installments, was abandoned. Yet the six chapters he did publish gave Poe an opportunity to indulge his love of natural description, of forests and rivers, of weather and open spaces. As the ostensible editor of the fictive journal noted, Julius Rodman "was possessed with a burning love of Nature, and worshiped her, perhaps, more in her dreary and savage aspects, than in her manifestations of placidity and joy." One of the most unexpected features of "Rodman" is that the hero is probably Jewish. Poe hints as much in a footnote: "He was a remarkably vigorous and active man. . . . His physiognomy was of a Jewish cast."

Drawing on the journals of Lewis and Clark, Irving's *A Tour of the Prairies, Astoria,* and *The Adventures of Captain Bonneville,* and other sources, Poe created diary entries of a fictive explorer, and commentary of a fictive editor, to capture the exuberance of exploration of new territory. The account describes the members of the crew, including the Black servant Toby, probably inspired by York of the Lewis and Clark expedition. The events take place in 1791–92, more than a decade before the Lewis and Clark journey to the Pacific. With realistic detail, Poe establishes an air of authenticity, acknowledging previous explorations, describing methods of survival such as preparing pemmican. He lists the varieties of vegetation found, especially different grasses. The techniques of river navigation are explained. Rodman insists he is not exaggerating and asserts his enthusiasm, "At the moment I seemed possessed of an energy more than human."

"Rodman" is a celebration of the natural world to compare with "The Domain of Arnheim," "Landor's Cottage," and "The Isle of the Fay." The depictions of Indian mounds, the methods of trapping fur-bearing animals, the lives and behaviors of beavers, confirm the good use Poe made of his sources. The reader shares the tension of a confrontation with the Sioux as well as the camaraderie of the team. "We were all like brothers." We feel the "intense excitement with which I surveyed the wonder and majestic beauty of the wilderness."

The team passes a cliff "carved over with hieroglyphical devices." They see the Black Hills, the mouth of the Yellowstone, and hope to reach "The Aregan (Oregon)." With fine particularity, Rodman tells how to dig a cache for hiding pelts. The journal ends with a fight with two grizzly bears. The abrupt break-off is literally a cliff-hanger. It is our loss that Poe did not complete the Rodman story. It could have been one of his best works on landscape and nature.

"The Journal of Julius Rodman" is significant in ways many readers have not realized. John Carlos Rowe, in "Edgar Allan Poe's Imperial Fantasy and the American Frontier," recognizes that Poe, in "Rodman," displayed an American "rhetoric of imperial power that reinstates many of the racial hierarchies recognizable in nineteenth century British imperialism." This is especially evident in the depiction of the enslaved man Toby.

As far as we know, Poe never saved money. Most of what he earned was turned over to Muddy for household expenses. When he could afford to, he bought pretty things for Virginia. And he cared a great deal about his looks, about his clothes. And Poe was reputed to be generous to the needy, when he had funds. But once he left *Burton's,* Poe had no steady income at all. Much of their furniture had to be pawned. Muddy and Virginia took in sewing. Yet he dreamed of editing a magazine for the educated upper classes, writing to Kennedy, "I need the countenance of those who stand well in the social not less than in the literary world." But he could not afford a healthy diet for his wife and mother-in-law. Some of Poe's physical and emotional problems may have been exacerbated simply by the lack of proper nourishment. Sometimes he drank because he was hungry.

Poe had a number of friends in Philadelphia, but none was wealthy. He applied to Nicholas Biddle, one of the richest citizens of Philadelphia, who'd served as president of the Second Bank of the United States, for help with *Penn Magazine.* Biddle had many scholarly and literary interests. Among other projects, he'd edited and published an edition of the Lewis and Clark journals in 1814. Biddle was cordial to Poe and subscribed to the magazine but offered no other support. Poe may have known that Biddle, when a young man, had copublished, with Joseph Dennie, his own magazine, called *Port Folio.*

On February 4, 1841, the United States Bank stopped payments in cash, and panic spread in Philadelphia and elsewhere, as other banks suspended transactions. Without adequate financial backing, there was never a chance for *Penn Magazine.* But we should not lose sight of Poe's disadvantages as an outsider. Those familiar with him knew his great gifts as a poet, story writer, critic, and conversationalist. But they also knew his quick temper, his slowness to pay debts. He spoke with a Virginia accent; he was the child of actors. As the British might say, Poe was not "clubbable." In the words of Sandra Tomc, "Poe belonged mainly to the category of the dispossessed."

Yet Billy Burton, when he sold *Burton's Gentleman's Magazine* to a young Philadelphia publisher named George Rex Graham in late 1840, wrote to Graham, "There is one thing more, I want you to take care of my young editor." Graham was only twenty-seven, but he had a knack for business and already published a magazine called the *Casket* (fig. 15). He'd worked as a cabinetmaker, studied and practiced law, but his special enthusiasm was publishing. He planned to combine the *Casket* and *Burton's Gentleman's Magazine* into a popular periodical.

Graham would prove to be one of the better friends Poe had in the publishing world, though he would later, oddly, reject "The Raven," or an

FIG. 15. George Rex Graham (1813–94). Graham was the publisher of several magazines in Philadelphia, including the *Saturday Evening Post.* After he acquired *Burton's Magazine,* in 1840, he hired Poe the next year as editor. His relationship with Poe was mostly amicable, but Poe grew tired of the "namby-pamby" quality of *Graham's Magazine* and left in 1842, though he continued to contribute to the magazine. (Courtesy of the Edgar Allan Poe Museum, Richmond, Virginia)

early version of the poem. After Poe's death Graham would defend him vigorously against the libels and fabrications of Rufus Griswold (as would Billy Burton). His ideas for the new *Graham's Magazine* included engravings by John Sartain, one of the foremost engravers in Philadelphia or the nation. Graham also planned to pay writers at a higher rate than most magazines. It is said that the "Graham Page" became the benchmark for remuneration for magazine writing of the period.

Graham's taste for sentimental poetry and pious comment would irritate Poe from the first, but having been unemployed for eight months and unable to get *Penn Magazine* off the ground, Poe was happy to accept Graham's offer of a post, and the two liked each other. Graham was also a publisher of the *Saturday Evening Post* and had promoted Poe's plans for *Penn Magazine* in that periodical.

Graham hired Poe in February 1841, and while he listed Poe as editor, Graham would make most editorial decisions himself. What he wanted from Poe was someone to ask famous writers for contributions, answer letters, check proofs, and write reviews. For Poe's own stories and poems that appeared in the journal, he would be paid extra, at $4 a page ($120 today). Poe even continued his series of articles about codes, then gave it up because the response was too great to manage. Poe bragged that no one had ever sent him an authentic code he could not decipher.

It appears that Graham gave Poe a free hand in writing reviews, at least at first. This may have been liberality on Graham's part, but he also knew that Poe's abrasive reviews drew readers and subscribers and increased the fame of his magazine. Poe proved to be particularly brutal when writing about the poems of Rufus Dawes and Cornelius Matthews at this time. In Matthews's *Wakondah: The Master of Life,* which he reviewed for *Godey's Lady's Book,* Poe claimed to find "*no* merit whatever; while its faults . . . are of that rampant class which, if any school boy *could* be found so uninformed as to commit them, any schoolboy should be remorselessly flogged." Of Dawes's *Geraldine,* Poe would state in *Graham's Magazine,* "It is a mere mass of irrelevancy, amid the mad *farrago* of which we detect with difficulty even the faintest vestige of a narrative."

About a third of Poe's reviews for *Graham's* were favorable. And in his most slashing notices, there was usually some important insight. Even Henry James, who later found Poe's reviews "pretentious, spiteful, vulgar," would concede that they "contain a great deal of sense and discrimination as well."

Like almost everything else about Poe, his career as a critic is paradoxical. He knew the critical writings of Coleridge and the contributions to the British quarterlies and monthlies. He also knew something of the aesthetic criticism of the famous German authors such as August Wilhelm Schlegel, who had influenced Coleridge. Schlegel stressed unity and overall impression in a work of art. Poe's ambition as a critic was second only to his ambition as a poet. In an essay called "Exordium," he asserted: "Criticism is *not*, we think, an essay, nor a sermon, nor an oration, nor a chapter in history, nor a philosophical speculation, nor a prose-poem, nor an art novel, nor a dialogue. In fact it *can be* nothing in the world but—a criticism." Poe's articles for *Graham's* laid the foundation for what would later be called "formalism" by Marxists and the New Criticism in the twentieth century. "A book is written—and it is only *as the book* that we subject it to review. With the opinions of the work, considered otherwise than in their relation to the work itself, the critic has really nothing to do."

Poe's understanding of criticism was that it was primarily evaluative. Writing of Hawthorne's short fiction, he declared the prose tale the work of "highest genius," next to rhymed poetry. A tale was short enough to maintain its high intensity, unlike a novel. All subsequent theorists and practitioners of the short story have had to reckon with Poe's formulations.

Though in many ways Poe was socially and professionally an outsider to his time, he was also in some pertinent ways very much an insider, which helps account for his growing popularity. Even his otherworldliness was fashionable. As both poet and critic, Poe could speak affectingly of angels, and there is no doubt that he thought of poetry as an angelic medium, like music.

Even while unemployed and dreaming of establishing *Penn Magazine* as the arbiter of taste in America in 1840, Poe had written distinctive pieces. But the masterpiece of that year was "The Man of the Crowd." It is one of Poe's most original and most memorable stories. The tale has hardly any plot. The narrator, resting in a coffeehouse, relishes the diverse pageant of humanity passing before the window. He especially notes a nondescript older man passing and then re-passing. His curiosity piqued, he decides to follow the wanderer, who leads him on and on through the crowds and streets, far into the night, never pausing. The narrator speculates that the odd character who draws him onward suffers so intensely from guilt for a crime or crimes that he cannot rest and seeks to lose himself in the anonymity of crowds. It is a story not of horror but of guilt and terror. But the man of the street is Everyman, and his plight is the human condition.

In "The Man of the Crowd" we can see the origins of the kind of fiction Dostoevsky, Conrad, and Kafka would produce, all of them admirers of Poe. The critic Patrick Quinn tells us that "The Man of the Crowd" reveals Poe's recognition that "a kind of Dr. Jekyll foresees the Mr. Hyde he will become." Poe draws on his youthful memories of London.

After he was hired by Graham, in 1841, Poe wrote several of his finest prose poems. It was a genre in which he combined his gifts for colorful phrasing, sensuous detail, exotic language, with characters of mystery and the tension of drama or narrative. In steady succession he produced "A Descent into the Maelström," "The Island of the Fay," "The Colloquy of Monos and Una," "Eleonora," "The Oval Portrait," "The Masque of the Red Death," "The Pit and the Pendulum," and, in 1842, the important essay "The Landscape Garden." Added to all that, he completed his finest and possibly his best story of ratiocination, "The Murders in the Rue Morgue," introducing the prototypical sleuth C. Auguste Dupin.

In his essay on Hawthorne's *Twice-Told Tales,* Poe had reserved for the highest literary status the rhymed poem. "We have said that the tale has a point of superiority even over the poem. . . . But Truth is often, and in a very great degree, the aim of the tale. . . . Its products are never so rich, but infinitely more numerous, and more appreciable by the mass of mankind." Of Hawthorne he would write: "We look upon him as one of the few men of indisputable genius to whom our country has as yet given birth."

Poe claimed not to be satisfied with the end of the tale "Eleonora," his most ethereal and fairy tale–like story. This short work of poetic prose lacks the obvious macabre ending we find in "Ligeia," "The Fall of the House of Usher," "Morella," and other arabesques. In fact, for most readers the tale seems to have a happy ending. The narrator of "Eleonora" concedes from the beginning that he may be mad but wonders, as others have, whether so-called madness might not be the same as great intelligence. "They who dream by day . . . obtain glimpses of eternity, and thrill, in awaking, to find that they have been upon the verge of the great secret." This motif Poe explored in "Ligeia" and elsewhere, the sense of mystery almost solved, the clue, almost revealed, that slips away at the last instant. Poe may have chosen the name Eleonora because of its similarity to Elmira.

The narrator and his first cousin Eleonora grow up in the remote Valley of the Many-Colored Grass. Like Edgar and Sissy, they live with the narrator's aunt and Eleonora's mother, by the River of Silence, gazing into its limpid depths. The valley is lush with flowers of all kinds, including the "ruby-red asphodel." Fantastic trees sway in the wind like "giant serpents of Syria doing homage to their Sovereign the Sun."

In this paradise the cousins roam hand in hand until the God Eros enters the valley when Eleonora is fifteen and the narrator twenty. Sexual passion threatens the young lovers with the fiery spirit of their ancestors. A luminous cloud settles over them. The ruby-red asphodels multiply and proliferate. Stirred by this new aspect of their love, they explore "its inmost recesses" as they "discoursed of the mighty changes which had lately taken place therein." The story suggests that the Poes' marriage had been physically consummated when Virginia was about fifteen. As the intense sexual passion causes Eleonora to sicken and die, she extracts from the narrator the promise that after her death he will never marry "any daughter of Earth." He solemnly vows to never wed, knowing a betrayal of his oath will incur a penalty too awful to be revealed to the reader.

After Eleonora is gone, the speaker is comforted by her presence in the wind, in the perfume that seems to waft from "the censers of the angels." But here the story takes a turn, and the speaker warns that what he says henceforth may be the testimony of insanity. The Valley of the Many-Colored Grass is altered as bright colors fade and the luminous cloud floats away.

The narrator, suffering from loneliness, leaves the valley for the vanities and vulgar challenges of the outside world, where he meets the ethereal and extraordinary Ermengarde and falls desperately in love. They marry, and the reader expects the terrible curse for his betrayal of Eleonora to descend on the narrator. Instead, "in the silence of the night, there came through my lattice the soft sighs which had forsaken me; and they modelled themselves into [her] familiar and sweet voice, saying: 'Sleep in Peace!—for the Spirit of Love reigneth and ruleth, and, in taking to thy passionate heart her who is Ermengarde, thou art absolved, for reasons which shall be made known to thee in Heaven, of thy vows unto Eleonora.'"

Some critics suggest that Ermengarde is Eleonora returned from the grave. Others have read the story as the work of a more romantic and less damned Poe, the Poe who would later write "Landor's Cottage" near the end of his life. But I suspect Poe intended us to take more seriously the caveat at the beginning of the piece: "Men have called me mad; but the question is not yet settled." And then the narrator warns us again halfway through the story, "I feel that a shadow gathers over my brain, and I mistrust the perfect sanity of the record." We can read the ending of the story as an expression of the bliss of someone who has completely lost his connection to the actual world.

After savoring the prose poem many times over the decades, I believe Poe intended it to be a celebration of pure love, like "Annabel Lee," love that to the rational world can seem much like insanity. The narrator's love for Eleanora is so intense it draws him to the edge of madness and maybe beyond. And in his mad vision he meets the celestial, perfect Ermengarde. The reader realizes that the punishment is insanity, but he does not. In this reading the ending is charged with dramatic irony and is one of the most chilling Poe ever wrote. Edgar had another trick up his sleeve for the cognoscenti, and besides, he'd warned us in the first paragraph. The story may also be read as Poe's fantasy that Elmira had absolved him of his marriage to Virginia.

The name Ermengarde is associated with a twelfth-century patron of troubadours, suggesting royalty, and literally means "Universe," or wholeness, safety, or protection. Thus, Ermengarde connotes total refuge or security. In his mad dream of marriage to Ermengarde, the narrator of "Eleonora" is safe and happy, in the asylum of the imagination. There is an erotic warmth to "Eleonora" virtually unique in Poe's arabesques, most likely inspired by the youthful, tender Sissy at his side and his memories of the nubile Elmira of the enchanted garden.

ALL HIS LIFE POE CHERISHED SOLITUDE, ESPECIALLY IN FOREST settings. It is one of the ironies of American literary history that writers such as Emerson, Thoreau, Whitman, and Dickinson are rightly esteemed for their portrayals of the natural world while Poe is thought of only as the poet of madness and Gothic interiors. Nowhere is Poe's love for the natural better illustrated than in the short prose poem "The Island of the Fay." Pretending to be a study of a fairy on a tiny islet in a stream, it is much more a celebration of solitude and the cycles of time and life.

"The Island of the Fay" begins as a kind of essay or meditation on the solitary enjoyment of music, and then Poe echoes *The Reveries of a Solitary Walker* by Jean-Jacques Rousseau: "But there is one pleasure still within the reach of fallen mortality. . . . I mean the happiness experienced in the contemplation of natural scenery."

As he penned "The Island of the Fay," Poe may have heard in the back of his mind Emerson's assertion in *Nature:* "In the tranquil landscape, and especially the distant line of the horizon, man beholds somewhat as beautiful as his own nature." Thoreau would title one of the finest chapters of *Walden* simply "Solitude." In the tiniest blade of grass, Poe sees the connection to the cosmic and timeless. And he glimpses the cycles of all process in nature, signs that lead us to spiritual perceptions and to the mind of deity: "As we find cycle within cycle without end—yet all revolving around one far-distant centre which is the Godhead."

After the long transcendental introduction, the narrator describes wandering in a remote region of mountains, where he comes upon an island in a small stream. As he observes the islet, he notices how different the eastern end is from the western. The western side "was all one radiant harem of garden beauties." The trees there are erect and colorful and the air filled with butterflies like petals.

But the eastern end is dark and shadowy; everything there seems "mournful," "solemn," "spectral." The ground "had the aspect of graves." In his reverie the narrator thinks of the passing of the race of the Fays, who once enchanted the forest, the theme of the earlier "Sonnet—To Science." But while musing, he sees a tiny fairy appear from the shadows, standing in a fragile canoe and paddling it. She seems joyous but then sorrowful as she circles back into the shade. The speaker imagines that these cycles of light and dark are fairy years.

The second half of the sketch becomes a picturesque fable, illustrating the brevity of our time in the scheme of things. There is something southern about the vegetation and landscape—much like the Blue Ridge Mountains of Virginia—and the somber recognition of mortality. Overall the piece stresses humility, not the egotistical sublime of Wordsworth and

Emerson. "The Island of the Fay" reminds us of the many ways in which Poe was like his New England contemporaries and ways in which he was not. The prose poem might also suggest the lure of the West.

In this very rich period of his writing, the ocean still stirred Poe's imagination, for the high seas are a wilderness more untamed and dangerous than the wildest landscape. "A Descent into the Maelström" is one of Poe's most powerful symbolic stories. It was published in *Graham's Magazine* in May 1841. Like Conrad after him, he told the tale as a story within a story.

The narrator is escorted to the summit of a cliff high over the ocean by an elderly looking Norse sailor who says he only appears to be old. Three years earlier, an event occurred that changed his dark hair to white. As they sit on the mountain called Helseggen, the Cloudy, looking far down on the sea and the Lofoden Islands, the sailor points to the place of the deadly Maelström, a whirlpool caused by tides and currents, powerful enough to suck any ship close by into its vortex and into the abyss.

The Norse sailor tells his story with all the color and precision of Homer describing troop deployments on the plains of Troy: "In five minutes the whole sea, as far as Vurrgh, was lashed into ungovernable fury. . . . Here the vast bed of the waters, seamed and scarred into a thousand conflicting channels, burst suddenly into phrensied convulsion—heaving, boiling, hissing—gyrating in gigantic and innumerable vortices."

Both the narrator and the old sailor go into precise and clinical detail describing the causes and actions of the Maelström. When our expectations and awe are at their highest pitch, the sailor calmly commences his account: "It is now within a few days of three years since what I am going to tell you occurred. It was on the tenth day of July, 18–."

The sailor and his two brothers in their smack are surprised by the force of a hurricane. The younger brother is washed overboard immediately. The masts on their boat break, and the sailor has to lie on the pitching deck holding to a ringbolt, but when that brother crawls to grasp the ring, the sailor is forced to hold to a cask. Conceding that he cannot be saved, the sailor finds himself calm, even curious to observe the fury of wind and water around him and the walls of the feared Maelström. The old Norse sailor speaks some of Poe's finest poetry of the sublime.

The sailor notices that on the walls of the whirling Maelström, cylinders sink slowest of all objects. He lashes himself to the barrel he clings to, cuts it loose, and as the boat and his brother plunge into the horror below, he is saved as the great whirlpool finally slows and fills and tosses him to the now calm surface. The fishermen who rescue him hardly recognize him, he is so altered and aged.

In this period of his career, employed by the respectful Graham, supported by a number of friends in Philadelphia, Poe's creative energies seemed endless. Review after review, story after story, streamed from his pen. He drank little, if any, and night after night sat up writing while Muddy made coffee and kept the house spotless. It was probably the best period of Poe's life. Visitors to the Poe house would recall being entertained by music, Virginia at her harp or piano, accompanied by Poe's fine tenor voice or his flute.

With respect to his larger audience, Poe's most popular tale of this descent into the horror of darkness may be "The Pit and the Pendulum," one of the stories most likely to appear in high school textbooks and anthologies. Some critics have described "The Pit and the Pendulum" as a conventional horror story. The tale is indeed like those popular tales of sensation of the early nineteenth century, with all the trappings of dungeon, castle walls, rats, pit, and instruments of torture.

Like Shakespeare, Poe could take the clichés and conventions of his time and raise them to the level of high art. Things that lift "The Pit and the Pendulum" above the conventions are effective use of darkness and sense deprivation to confuse and break the will of the victim and the implied horrors of the pit into which the narrator almost plunges. It is the awful *silence* of the dungeon that unnerves the narrator most and the sensory starvation of the blackness.

Like a character in a Kafka story, the narrator's guilt is assumed. It is from the pit that the rats emerge. And later, when there is light, when he looks into the pit, what he sees is too horrible to share. The pit terrifies like the abyss in "A Descent into the Maelström" and "MS. Found in a Bottle" and the plunge into the chasm at the end of *The Narrative of Arthur Gordon Pym.*

When he wakens later and finds himself strapped on his back to a wooden frame, there is enough light for him to see a large figure of Time staring down at him. Time holds a heavy pendulum, which begins to swing back and forth, with a razor-like blade at the end. As the terrible pendulum sweeps and begins a slow descent, the rats crawl over him, and he feels their cold lips on his lips. As the pendulum whispers closer, he can smell the sharp steel. The narrator has one free hand, and when he reaches for the meat the rats haven't finished, he feels a surge of hope.

He smears the remains of his repast on the band, and sure enough, the rats gnaw through it. The blade of the pendulum is already cutting into his clothes, threatening castration, when he slides from the platform. His torturers stop the pendulum and haul it up. But his ordeal is far from over. Through cracks and holes, he sees the chamber is surrounded by fire. The walls are getting red hot and closing in on him. Soon he will be forced into the pit too horrible to describe. Teresa A. Goddu has suggested the horror of the pit echoes the condition of slavery. At the very last instant, he's saved by General Lasalle and the French army's arrival in Toledo.

"The Pit and the Pendulum" is one of the finest dramatizations of the horror and torture of time. The pendulum is part of the big clock that will strike all down in the end. Caught between the pit, or womb, of death and the blade of time, a human has little choice. In another story, "The Psyche Zenobia," a character is threatened with decapitation by the hands of a giant clock. Time itself is the Grim Reaper.

Even while writing one masterpiece after another in Philadelphia, Poe was still determined to start his own magazine. In May 1842 he left *Graham's*. In a letter written July 6, 1842, to Daniel Bryan of Alexandria, Virginia, Poe announced: "I feel that *now* is the time to strike. . . . My conduct of 'Graham' has rendered me better and (I hope) more favorably known than before. . . . I shall make war to the knife against the New-England assumption of 'all the decency and all the talent' which has been so disgustingly manifested in the Rev. Rufus W. Griswold's 'Poets & Poetry of America.'"

11

RATIOCINATION

ONE OF THE MOST TRAUMATIC EVENTS OF POE'S LIFE OCCURRED in January 1842, when Virginia began to bleed at the mouth while singing. Poe would insist she had "ruptured a blood-vessel" in her throat, but that was just a euphemism. He would not concede that she had tuberculosis. He'd watched his mother die of consumption, and his foster mother had died of consumption. He'd nursed his brother, Henry, as he also succumbed to tuberculosis in 1831. As Keats, who had nursed his own dying brother, said of himself, when he first spat up blood, the bleeding was Virginia's "death-warrant."

Virginia was only twenty years old. However irregular their marriage appeared to others, Sissy had provided Poe with some stability and the affection he required. It is quite possible that from the age of fifteen until the onslaught of the disease, their relationship was physical. The prospect of witnessing a long, painful life-in-death brought back memories of Eliza Poe and made him frantic. In the seven years remaining to him, Poe would never again find the stability he'd known in Philadelphia at that time.

In the weeks following Virginia's hemorrhage, Poe hovered over her. He wouldn't let anyone speak of consumption and insisted her condition was caused by a broken blood vessel. He began drinking again and wrote two of his most gruesome tales, the miniature "The Oval Portrait," in which an artist in effect kills his muse and model by forcing her to pose until the painting is perfect, and "The Masque of the Red Death," in which the blood of the plague conquers all. Both stories may suggest the depth of guilt Poe carried, fearing that his art and his poverty were somehow responsible for Sissy's suffering.

"The Masque of the Red Death," published in *Graham's* in May 1842, is one of the most perfect story-poems of this period, or any period. Almost certainly inspired by Virginia's hemorrhaging, drawing on many sources, the tale is a parable. The main character, Prince Prospero, reminds us with some irony of the hero of *The Tempest.* The idea of a group of revelers retreating from the plague surely had its source in Boccaccio's *Decameron.* The plague of the fourteenth century was called the Black Death, but Poe names this pestilence the Red Death. The prince's name suggests prosperity.

Prince Prospero, with many merrymakers, withdraws to his remote palace, a former abbey, to party while the plague rages in the city and countryside. Much of the body of the story is taken up with description of the decor of the seven rooms of the palace and the costumes of the revelers. Safe in the sealed fortress, they indulge in a prolonged orgy of excess. For many readers the seven rooms of the palace suggest the seven seals of Revelation. Or we might also consider the seven deadly sins.

A masque is of course a kind of play or pageant, put on by a cast of amateurs. Poe is punning on the word *mask,* for the festivities at Prospero's palace include an extended masked ball. The narrator calls it "a voluptuous scene, that masquerade." The seven rooms of the former abbey are arranged at angles so one has to wind to the right and to the left to go from one chamber to another. The configuration appears in many of Poe's story-poems. One does not progress linearly into reverie, into paradise, or revelation, approaching the great mystery of a woman's body, or the secret clue of death. There must be a zigzag, or winding in.

All is revelry until the ebony clock strikes midnight and a tall, masked figure appears. The mask is that of a corpse, splattered with blood to resemble the Red Death. Drawing a dagger, the prince confronts the fearful stranger but suddenly dies himself "on the sable carpet." In terror the merrymakers rush the tall intruder, only to find no one at all behind the mask of a corpse. The Red Death has reached their inner sanctum, and one by one they expire and the flames of the torches go out. "And Darkness and Decay and the Red Death held illimitable dominion over all."

Critics from Poe's day until our own have speculated on the code of colors of the seven rooms. Perhaps most significant are the red and black of the westernmost room, the site of greatest drama and horror. At some deep level Poe equates sexual consummation with death, as the poets of the Renaissance had. In several of Poe's other stories, the greatest horror is associated with an entrance into the blood-lit darkness of the womb. However a Poe story might begin, it will often circle back to that feared and thrilling site, sometimes seen as the abyss, sometimes as the apocalypse.

The Georgia poet Thomas Holley Chivers, who had a medical degree, would visit the Poes in Philadelphia and leave this portrait of Sissy in her illness: "She addressed [Poe] with the endearing appellation of *My Dear!* . . . At irregular intervals . . . she was attacked with a terrible paroxysm of coughing whose spasmodic convulsions seemed to me almost to rend asunder her very body. This was so severe at times as to threaten her with strangulation." This horrifying struggle Poe witnessed every day.

Poe's heavy drinking, beginning in the winter of 1842, may have undermined his relations with Graham. Poe was divided between his love of reverie and dreams, of escaping to the realm of angels or to an earthly paradise, and the exhilaration of his mental powers of analysis, logical method, the process of deduction and decryption, with a complement of intuition, which he liked to call ratiocination. William F. Friedman, the celebrated cryptanalyst of World War II, would say of Poe: "It is a curious fact that popular interest in this country in the subject of cryptography received its first stimulus from Edgar Allan Poe."

In 1841 Poe wrote the first of the four stories in a genre that would make him famous around the world and for all time. We cannot say exactly that he invented the detective narrative. But there is no doubt that Poe perfected the mystery *story* and created the type of the cool, eccentric, genius detective in Monsieur C. Auguste Dupin that would inspire Sherlock Holmes, Lord Peter Wimsey, and scores of other literary sleuths and aesthetes.

The detective story suited Poe's genius perfectly. He loved to demonstrate mental agility; he relished the lurid descriptions of violence, the realism of the crime scene, and the challenge of unraveling the seemingly inexplicable. In the detective story, some dire wrong in the world could be put right, or at least explained. The detective story allowed Poe to indulge in his flair for the exotic, the mysterious, the obscure, along with the hard realism of crime solution. In a story of ratiocination, Poe could create rich atmospheres and solve puzzles at the same time. The story of ratiocination seemed a stay against the horror of disorder and moral confusion. In J. Gerald Kennedy's phrase, the detective story for Poe was "a powerful counter-fantasy to mortal terror."

In a letter to his southern friend Philip Pendleton Cooke in 1846, Poe comments on his hero Dupin and the detective story: "You are right about the hair-splitting of my French friend [Dupin]:—that is all done for effect. . . . I do not mean to say they are not ingenious—but people think them more ingenious than they are—on account of their method and *air* of method."

The most important phrase in this quotation is "*air* of method." Poe knew that it was his "air" of method that made his stories so seductive and convincing. The exact detail and realism and authority of narration make even the most unlikely events riveting. There are passages in "The Murders in the Rue Morgue" that are far too ingenious to be believed outside the context of the story. Think of the instance in which Dupin follows the narrator's train of thought and association through many steps to demonstrate that he knows exactly what his companion is thinking. Most of Dupin's surmises are arbitrary at best. But in the story, in the pacing of the narrative and in the voice and personality of Dupin, it all seems to work. Peter Thoms has suggested that the name Dupin "reflects his acts of duping."

Already Poe understood that the seemingly insoluble crime is the richest basis on which to concoct a story. Later this kind of story would be known as a "locked room mystery." The writer begins with a crime that seems impossible to commit, much less solve, and then proceeds to break the mystery down step by step. Poe knew that any reliance on the supernatural or scientific hoax would spoil the effect of a story of ratiocination.

The title "The Murders in the Rue Morgue" is one of Poe's best. There is no Rue Morgue in Paris, but the name is vivid in the imagination, connecting the words *murders* and *rue*. The narrator meets Monsieur C. Auguste Dupin at "an obscure library in the Rue Montmartre." They strike up an acquaintance that leads to friendship. They are kindred souls.

The narrator, who is better fixed financially, invites Dupin to live with him "in a retired and desolate portion of the Faubourg St. Germain." The two become recluses, needing only each other's company. One of Dupin's many eccentricities is that he prefers night to day and avoids daylight. But when night returns, "we sallied forth into the streets, arm in arm," . . . looking for "that infinity of mental excitement which quiet observation can afford." Much like a composition of music, the mystery story must unfold at the correct tempo, introducing motifs, embellishing themes, revealing clues, in appropriate places.

In the "Gazette des Tribunaux" there is the headline "EXTRAORDINARY MURDERS—This morning, about three o'clock, the inhabitants of the Quartier St. Roch were aroused from sleep by a succession of terrific shrieks, issuing, apparently, from the fourth story of a house in the Rue Morgue, known to be in the sole occupancy of one Madame L'Espanaye, and her daughter, Mademoiselle Camille L'Espanaye."

A number of neighbors gathered to break down the street door. They discover the daughter's bruised and bloody body shoved up the chimney feet first, like a child emerging from the womb. Looking out a closed window, they spy Madame L'Espanaye's nearly decapitated body lying on the paving stones below. All the windows are locked.

Adolphe Le Bon, a bank clerk who had delivered four thousand francs to Madame L'Espanaye three days earlier, has been arrested and charged with the crime, since the police have no other suspect. Le Bon is a friend of Dupin's, and Dupin owes him a favor. It was said that Madame L'Espanaye told fortunes for a living, but who could explain her fate?

The narrator and Dupin visit the crime scene, but the narrator sees nothing that explains what took place there. On the way back to their house, Dupin places a notice in a newspaper but doesn't tell why. It's obvious by now that Dupin has already solved the mystery. Dupin explains that the murderer could not have been human. The tuft of red hair and the size of the finger marks on the victims suggest the murderer was an orangutan. Then he describes how someone could have climbed up the lightning rod on the house and entered the apartment through an open window. He had also discovered that the window could be closed and spring-locked by someone exiting through the window. He also announces that he is awaiting the arrival of someone and suggests that he and the narrator arm themselves with pistols.

A sailor shows up, just as Dupin knew he would, and the poor man is forced to explain how he brought the primate back to France to sell, how it tried to imitate him by shaving itself, and how it ran away with the razor.

When the orangutan climbed into Madame L'Espanaye's apartment at three in the morning, the two women panicked. Their shrieks excited the animal, which shoved the daughter into the chimney and threw the old woman from the window. Climbing out, it slammed the window shut and a spring locked it. As the story winds up, Le Bon is freed from prison, and the orangutan is caught and sold to the Jardin des Plantes. The tale ends with a dig at the police inspector, who "denies what is and explain[s] what is not."

The real subject of "The Murders in the Rue Morgue" is the analytical ability of Dupin, who sees what is obvious to him but unnoticed by others. The dynamics of the story lie in the demonstration of a problem that appears impossible to solve, then after it is unraveled, we are shown step by step how the solution was inevitable. The narrator represents us, the readers, the ordinary minds that see no hope of a solution until Dupin leads us little by little to understand what occurred.

In an important sense, a main character of "The Murders in the Rue Morgue" is the orangutan, for the beast represents the irrational, the arbitrary, and dangerous intruder in the world that the mind of a Dupin must neutralize. Most of Poe's best stories confront the irrational, in ourselves and in the world at large, the factor that even when explained cannot be tamed or completely understood.

Equally important is the partnership between the narrator and Dupin. The warm relationship of the narrator and Dupin is part of the charm and meaning. The narrator provides a home and a sympathetic ear to Dupin the genius, but he needs everything explained to him, and we are the beneficiaries of that explanation. "The Murders in the Rue Morgue" is a narrative of companionship, a lifestyle of books, eccentricity, conversation, of instruction and exploration of ideas and the city, friendship of a kind Poe probably never knew. The story is another arabesque, an intellectual and entertaining tale of a partnership Poe may have longed for. The story might be read as Poe's homage to another kind of marriage, in this case a same-sex union, though he would not have used that term. The story is a variation on Poe's permanent quest for models of marital happiness. Later Sir Arthur Conan Doyle, creator of Sherlock Holmes, would write, "Edgar Allan Poe was father of the detective tale, and covered its limits so completely I fail to see how his followers can find ground to call their own."

It's not clear from the correspondence exactly what caused the break with Graham. But Poe's success with *Graham's* is part of his legend. When he joined the magazine, its circulation was around fifty-five hundred; by March 1842 it was about forty thousand. On May 18, 1842, the *Public Ledger* reported, "E. A. Poe, Esq, has retired from the editorship of *Graham's Magazine,* and has been succeeded by Rev. R. W. Griswold." Poe would describe publishers as "men whose imbecility was evident to all but themselves."

After Poe's death, Graham would write: "He had the docility and kind-heartedness of a child. No man was more quickly touched by a kindness, none more prompt to atone for an injury. . . . he was always the same polished gentleman. . . . This, of course, was in his better days, and by them *we* judge the man."

Still, Poe dreamed of editing his own magazine, perhaps with Graham as publisher. After all, Graham already owned several publications, had the business experience, a printing press, and managerial ability. Why would he not back a magazine edited by his gifted former assistant? Given the amount of copy he produced for the *Southern Literary Messenger, Burton's Gentleman's Magazine,* and *Graham's Magazine,* Poe may have worn himself out at all three magazine posts. Famously, he wrote to his friend Frederick Thomas on July 4, 1841, "To coin one's brain into silver, at the nod of a master, is to my thinking, the hardest task in the world." And yet Poe knew he had a special gift for magazine writing and editing. Two weeks earlier, on June 21, he had written to Washington Irving, "The brief, the terse, the condensed, and the easily circulated will take [the] place of the diffuse, the ponderous, and the inaccessible."

On May 25, 1842, it seems the Poe family moved out of the house on Sixteenth Street. By September 12 of that year, they had taken up residence on Coates Street, in the Fairmont District. Hoping to launch his own journal with Graham's backing, Poe wrote to Longfellow, Washington Irving, Cooper, Bryant, and other prominent authors and poets, asking each celebrated figure to contribute a piece every month for a year. But once again, Poe's plan came to nothing. Graham apparently cooled to the idea of the new magazine. Poe had no choice but to rely on freelance writing, which, according to one biographer, paid less than a common laborer's wages.

During this period in Philadelphia, Poe met one of the friends who would prove most loyal and helpful, Frederick W. Thomas (1806–66), a

FIG. 16. Frederick William Thomas (1806–66). A journalist and minor politician, Thomas became one of Poe's most loyal friends. In 1842–43 he tried unsuccessfully to win Poe an appointment to a government position that would enable him to found his own magazine, called *Penn Magazine*, and later the *Stylus*. (American Antiquarian Society)

popular novelist and songwriter (fig. 16). Thomas had known Poe's brother, Henry, years earlier, in Baltimore, and through Henry, Thomas had met both Muddy and Virginia. Sometimes Thomas drank to excess and had lectured on temperance, attempting to overcome his own weakness.

In September 1842 Frederick Thomas visited the Poes at Coates Street, North Fairmont, and left this description: "I met Poe in Philadelphia during September, 1842. . . . His wife entertained me. . . . Her pale complexion, the deep lines in her face and a consumptive cough made me regard her as the victim for an early grave. She and her mother showed much concern about Eddie . . . and were anxious to have him secure work . . . he had been to New York in search of employment and also had made effort to get out an edition of his tales but was unsuccessful." Unlike Poe, Thomas was involved in politics and campaigned for the Whig Party. As a reward, he was given a clerkship in the office of the secretary of the Treasury. The position left him time for his writing. Why shouldn't Poe have a similar sinecure?

It is thought that Poe had had some contact with President Tyler earlier, while editing the *Southern Literary Messenger*. Perhaps that slight connection might help him with an appointment. The president's son Robert wrote poetry, and one poem, *Ahasuerus,* had impressed Poe. On February 6, 1842, Thomas wrote to Poe, "Robert Tyler expressed himself highly gratified with your favorable opinion of his poem." But the fact was that Poe was not a political person. He'd not campaigned for Whigs nor written editorials nor given money to those running for office. Nevertheless, Thomas was determined to help Poe. As a minor clerk, he knew he himself had little influence in Washington. He encouraged Poe to come to the capital to speak to the president in person.

By far the longest story Poe wrote in this interval was a follow-up to "The Murders in the Rue Morgue." Hoping to capitalize on the success of that earlier tale of ratiocination, Poe would base "The Mystery of Marie Rogêt" on the reported death of one Mary Rogers of New York City. All the newspapers had carried the sensational story of the beautiful "cigar girl" Mary Rogers, whose body had been found floating in the Hudson River off New Jersey. "The Mystery of Marie Rogêt" is a slightly longer and more complex narrative than Poe's first detective story. Though it was never as popular with the general public as its predecessor, connoisseurs of mystery fiction have been fascinated by the intricacies of the latter story. Richard P. Benton, writing about "The Mystery of Marie Rogêt," described it as "caviar for the gourmet."

Dupin's deductions in "The Mystery of Marie Rogêt" are impeccable in procedure, though he does not solve the crime with the facts available to him. Dupin blamed the "man of dark complexion." In this story of ratiocination, Poe was inspired in part by the subject he considered most appropriate for a poem, the death of a beautiful woman. According to all reports, Mary Rogers was a stunning beauty.

On December 19, 1842, Poe filed for bankruptcy in the District Court of the United States in Philadelphia, and his petition was granted January 13, 1843. At this time Poe's debts totaled over two thousand dollars (about sixty thousand dollars today). His assets are listed as "his wearing apparel and a few hundred Sheets [of paper], of no use to any one else." Financially and emotionally, the winter of 1842–43 may have been one of the most difficult periods in Poe's life.

Poe had developed a friendship with young James Russell Lowell, who initially contacted Poe around 1841 (fig. 17). Lowell belonged to a prominent Boston family, was a graduate of Harvard, and, though only in his

FIG. 17. James Russell Lowell (1819–91). From a prominent Boston family, Lowell admired Poe's poetry and criticism. The two were friends in the early 1840s, but the younger man became disillusioned by Poe's drinking and his continued attacks on Longfellow. (Courtesy of the Edgar Allan Poe Museum, Richmond, Virginia)

early twenties, had begun to publish poems in leading magazines such as *Graham's*. Poe had criticized the awkwardness of Lowell's early verse but believed Lowell might become one of the country's leading poets. On October 19, 1843, Poe would write to Lowell, "No poet in America has done so much. . . . Mr. Longfellow has genius, but by no means equals you in the true spirit."

Lowell planned to start a magazine in Boston, much like Poe's projected *Penn Magazine* and the later *Stylus*. Given what we know about Poe's defensiveness toward New England intellectuals, we can understand how pleased he was to be in touch with a Lowell who admired him. Lowell believed that Poe was the leading literary critic in the United States, and he rated Poe's early poems as second only to Shelley's. He invited Poe to contribute anything he could spare to his new magazine, called the *Pioneer*.

By Harnden's Express, Poe sent Lowell an essay on versification called "Notes upon English Verse," his first exploration of the mysteries of meter and poetics, later to be expanded into "The Rationale of Verse." He also sent the *Pioneer* "The Tell-Tale Heart," which had already been rejected by the *Boston Miscellany*. Through Lowell, Poe hoped to get some revenge on Boston editors who'd snubbed him.

Like other Poe stories, "The Tell-Tale Heart" can be read as a dramatic monologue narrated by a madman. But the narrator believes himself to be far from mad. In fact, he asserts that his disease has made him smarter. The narrator resides in a house with an old man. They are friends, but he is obsessed by one of the old man's eyes. "One of his eyes resembled that of a vulture—a pale blue eye, with a film over it."

Most of the story is taken up with the step-by-step planning and preparation for murder. The narrator intends to kill the old man to get rid of the "Evil Eye." Arthur Robinson has suggested that the Evil Eye implies an "evil I," revealing the self-accusation of the narrator. The old man is a father figure, perhaps related to John Allan, and the eye of surveillance and judgment must be put out.

Our mad narrator not only means to kill the old man to escape the eye; he wants the old man to *know* he is being killed. The surprising thing about the story is the sadistic joy taken in the old man's horror that he is about to die. The narrator savors the old man's anguish in the dark and prolongs the torture. The old man shrieks and is suffocated with the featherbed.

Calmly, our madman cuts up the corpse and buries it under the floorboards of the bedroom. However, the old man's shriek had been heard, and three policemen arrive. Confidently, the narrator explains that the old man is away visiting in the country. But as he talks, the narrator hears a sound like a watch ticking. The sound grows louder, until the narrator can control himself no longer. "They heard!—they suspected!—they *knew!*—they were making a mockery of my horror! . . . I could bear those hypocritical smiles no longer! . . . 'Villains!' I shrieked, 'dissemble no more! I admit the deed!'" Poe may not have been the first author to tell a story from the point of view of a madman and murderer. But "The Tell-Tale Heart" is certainly one of the most notorious examples. Later there would be Fyodor Dostoevsky, Ambrose Bierce, Jim Thompson, and others, writing as though from the mind of a murderer.

"The Tell-Tale Heart" was published in Lowell's *Pioneer*, but Lowell soon found himself deep in debt and unable to pay the promised ten dollars (about three hundred dollars). Poe told Lowell not to worry about it, writing on March 27, 1843, "I am poor, but must be very much poorer, indeed, when I even think of demanding them." Later, when Poe was desperate for funds, he had to ask Lowell to pay up, and the young poet did.

No sooner had Poe written "The Tell-Tale Heart" than he began a third story of ratiocination, one that doesn't feature M. C. Auguste Dupin. "The Gold-Bug" is said to be Poe's only story based on American folklore, in this case the legends of Captain Kidd's buried treasure. Washington Irving had already treated the subject in the story "Wolfert Webber," as had Robert M. Bird in the novel *Sheppard Lee.*

Poe would be able to indulge his taste for natural description in "The Gold-Bug" also, for one of the glories of the new story was its scenery. While stationed on Sullivan's Island in 1827–28, he'd spent much time exploring the beaches, the forests and thickets on the island, and the woods on the nearby mainland. In "The Gold-Bug" he found occasion to summon up his memories of the hours and days and weeks he'd spent in the southern wilds.

After Poe finished "The Gold-Bug," he sold it to *Graham's.* But when a start-up Philadelphia magazine called the *Dollar Newspaper* offered a hundred-dollar prize for a new story, he withdrew the piece and gave Graham other articles in its place. The story won the hundred-dollar prize, and in the June 21 and June 28, 1843, issues of the *Dollar Newspaper,* "The Gold-Bug" appeared and was quickly reprinted in about three hundred other newspapers.

The hero of "The Gold-Bug," like Dupin, has a French name, William Legrand. He belongs to an old Huguenot family of the South Carolina Low Country but has lost all his money. He retires to a hut on Sullivan's Island with a servant, a free Black man named Jupiter. It is thought that the Legrand family had assigned Jupiter to look after the reclusive and depressed Legrand. Jupiter is a stereotypical character from the fiction and minstrel shows of the time, a humorous but kindly figure, so devoted to Legrand that he even threatens to whip the young man if he does not behave, reversing the usual roles of master and servant. Jupiter is one of the few explicitly African American characters to be found in Poe's stories.

Since Poe grew up in the antebellum South, with enslaved men and women and slavery all around him, critics and biographers have wondered why so few Black people appear in his writing. As a child, he was surrounded by African servants. Their absence in his stories may suggest that he was, at the very least, uneasy about the issue of slavery and mostly avoided explicitly mentioning it. A favorable review of a book defending slavery, published in the *Southern Literary Messenger* while Poe was editor there, was once thought to have been written by Poe, but most scholars now believe it was the work of Judge Beverley Tucker. Poe's disparagements of abolitionists seem more about regional rivalry than the actual issue of slavery, however much we regret Poe's lack of sensitivity. Terence Whalen, as we have seen, recognizes Poe's "average racism" of his time. Since he was writing for a northern audience as well as a southern readership, he probably wanted to appear impartial on the issue of slavery. Modern writers, including Toni Morrison, have shown that while race and slavery may not be explicit in Poe's work, they are implicit in much of it.

"The Gold-Bug" is one of Poe's happiest stories, for it tells of a return to the seashore and forest of the South, of digging into the Mother Earth for undreamed of wealth, enough to restore the Legrand family fortune, and of the cunning to solve an old mystery. The narrator visits Legrand's hut on an especially cool October day. (Many significant things in Poe's writing happen in October, a time of both beauty and threatening change.) Wandering with Jupiter, Legrand has discovered an unusual gold beetle. He has also found a scrap of parchment that, when held to the fire, reveals a skull inscribed on it.

About a month later, Jupiter seeks out the narrator in Charleston and delivers a letter from Legrand begging the narrator to hurry to his hut. Legrand is so obsessed with a mission he has in mind that the narrator, who may or may not be a medical doctor, consents to accompany him and Jupiter to humor his friend. With spades, scythes, and lanterns, they set out and journey inland for about two hours. To the narrator it seems "a region infinitely more dreary than any yet seen": "It was a species of table land, near the summit of an almost inaccessible hill, densely wooded from base to pinnacle, and interspersed with huge crags that appeared to lie loosely upon the soil. . . . Deep ravines, in various directions, gave an air of still sterner solemnity to the scene."

The hills and ravines near the coast of South Carolina exist only in Poe's imagination. What he has done is combine his memories of the hills and mountains of Virginia with the coastal plain of South Carolina, merging two different southern landscapes. "The Gold-Bug" is in part an ode to the southern wilderness, both the coast and the ridges around Charlottesville. Poe also combines the two regions of the South in the character of Jupiter, who speaks the dialect of Blacks in Virginia, not the Gullah speech of Charleston and the Sea Islands.

Everyone knows that Legrand finds an enormous tulip poplar looming above the surrounding oaks. Jupiter must take the gold-bug, tied to a string, and climb the mammoth tree to the seventh branch, where he finds a skull nailed to the limb. He drops the gold-bug through the supposedly left eye socket, and where the insect lands, Legrand drives a peg. By running a line from the base of the tree to the peg and out fifty feet, he marks a spot to dig. All three men shovel and find nothing. They start back to the hut in defeat, but Legrand thinks to ask Jupiter which is his left eye and discovers that Jupiter has confused left and right.

Hurrying back to the tree, Legrand moves the peg three inches and runs the line out from the tree again for fifty feet. This time they dig and find skeletons, uniform buttons, and a box three feet by three and a half feet and two feet deep. When they open the chest, they discover wealth beyond their imagination. What follows is a catalog of the treasure discovered in coins, jewels, watches, diamonds, sapphires, crucifixes, censers, a golden bowl. "We estimated the entire contents of the chest, that night, at a million and a half of dollars [forty-five million dollars today]; and, upon the subsequent disposal of the trinkets and jewels (a few being retained for our own use), it was found that we had greatly undervalued the treasure."

No work of Poe has inspired more enthusiastic and imaginative criticism than "The Gold-Bug." The Freudian Marie Bonaparte sees it as Poe's tapping into unconscious memories of infancy and, thinking of the bug as a dung beetle, sees the mother's body yielding both the gold of dung and a younger sister. In any case the story shows Poe remembering the southern forests and thickets and delving into the mother earth, fearing and finding the pit but discovering there not horror but untold wealth of memory and kinship. It is a story of recovery of family riches, position, and tradition, even the selling of gems.

Poe liked to think he was descended from illustrious people on both sides of his family. The cosmopolitan treasure unearthed in the soil of South Carolina could well symbolize the treasure of a tradition of wealth, diamond cutting and jewelry, and intellectual authority. It was a fortune found by following signs, decoding a text, and delving into the body of maternal earth. When the coffer of treasure is uncovered and counted, the story is only halfway over. We must find out how Legrand learned about the treasure and found his way to it. The greatest wealth lies in the intellect and imagination, and craft.

The remainder of the story is taken up with ratiocination, as Legrand explains how he discovered that the parchment, when heated, displayed encrypted writing. He demonstrates how he broke the code, step by step. Poe made some mistakes in his account of the decryption, but for most of us, the demonstration is convincing. A picture of a goat on the parchment suggested it was a document left by Captain Kidd and that the text was in English. When the message is deciphered, it reads: *"A good glass in the Bishop's hostel in the Devil's seat—twenty-one degrees and thirteen minutes—northeast and by north—main branch seventh limb east side—shoot from the left eye of the death's-head—a bee-line from the tree through the shot fifty feet out."*

Legrand explains that the "Bishop's hostel" is a high rock, and from a seat on the rock, through a telescope, one can find a skull on the distant, giant tulip tree. A bullet dropped through the left eye of the skull would mark the direction of the beeline from the tree. To tease Jupiter and the narrator, Legrand had used the gold-bug instead of a bullet.

As it turns out, the gold-bug, or scarab beetle, is only incidental to the discovery of the exotic treasure. Critics have pointed out that the scarab beetle has symbolized both wisdom and life itself. For Marie Bonaparte the scarab suggests the dung beetle, for she is preoccupied with the infantile fascination with excrement. "The Gold-Bug" is a story of deep reading and delving into the mother earth of memory for the filthy and glorious lucre buried there. On May 28, 1844, Poe wrote to James Russell Lowell, "of 'The Gold-Bug' (my most successful tale) more than 300,000 copies have been circulated."

In 1842 Charles Dickens first visited America. Poe had admired Dickens for years, and he sought a meeting with the celebrated novelist. Poe had given more time to reviewing Dickens than to any other fiction writer. When discussing an early installment of *Barnaby Rudge,* Poe solved part of the mystery long before the later chapters were available. It is said that printers, or their assistants, waited on the docks in New York or Boston for the next installment of a Dickens novel, rushing to get into print a pirated edition.

Poe wrote to Dickens and sent him copies of his tales and several reviews of Dickens's novels. The novelist invited Poe to visit him at his hotel on March 7, 1842. Dickens was promoting copyright laws that would protect writers such as himself from piracy. Surprisingly, Poe read to Dickens Emerson's poem "To the Humble Bee," not one of his own poems. And he asked Dickens to help him find an English publisher for *Tales of the Grotesque and Arabesque.*

Dickens, it appears, did submit the tales to the London publisher Edward Moxon, who explained that stories by an unknown writer would not sell. Later Poe would blame Dickens for a review of a book of American poets in which he mentioned Emerson's "To the Humble Bee" but left out any reference of Poe's own poetry. Predictably, this cooled Poe's enthusiasm for Dickens's later novels.

One of the saddest incidents of this period occurred in June 1842. Poe traveled to New York to find a publisher for a new volume of his tales. The year before, Lea & Blanchard of Philadelphia had refused a proposed second edition of *Tales of the Grotesque and Arabesque,* pleading that the firm had not yet sold all the first edition. Several who saw Poe in New York at that time noted his odd behavior, which he later explained was caused by drinking. A poet from Kentucky named William Rose Wallace (1819–81) plied Poe with juleps, and as a result, he wandered around the city disturbed and disoriented.

Mary Starr, now married to New York tailor James Jennings, lived across the Hudson in Jersey City. Mary had kept in touch with the Poes and even visited them in Philadelphia. Poe called at Mr. Jennings's tailor shop to find out Mary's home address, but on the ferry across the river, he realized he'd forgotten the residence. Not knowing where to go, he remained on the ferry, crossing and recrossing the river and asking other passengers if they might know where Mary Jennings lived. He eventually acquired her address and showed up at her door.

Years later Mary would recount the visit:

> When Mr. Poe reached our house I was out with my sister, and he opened the door for us when we got back. . . . He said to me: "So you have

> married that cursed —— [referring to my husband's business]. Do you love him truly? Did you marry him for love?" I answered, "That's nobody's business; that is between my husband and myself." He then said, "You don't love him. You do love me. You know you do."
>
> Mr. Poe staid to tea with us, but ate nothing; only drank a cup of tea. . . . After tea he asked me if I would not play and sing for him, and I sang his favorite song again. He then went away. A few days afterward, Mrs. Clemm came to see me, much worried about "Eddie dear." . . . She did not know where he was, and his wife was almost crazy with anxiety. . . . A search was made, and he was finally found in the woods on the outskirts of Jersey City, wandering about like a crazy man. Mrs. Clemm took him back with her to Philadelphia.

A few weeks later, Poe returned to New York, probably looking for work as an editor. Again, he met the poet William Wallace, who offered him drinks. Poe offended friends such as Thomas Holley Chivers and was forced to apologize to editors when he returned to Philadelphia. "Will you be kind enough to put the best possible interpretation upon my behavior while in N-York . . . but the simple truth is that Wallace would insist upon the *juleps,* and I knew not what I was either doing or saying."

12

WASHINGTON, DC

BY 1842–43 POE UNDERSTOOD THAT AMONG ALL HIS GIFTS AND achievements, he harbored within himself a self-destructive flaw he would call "the imp of the perverse." In the story of that title, and in the classic "The Black Cat," he would dramatize a kink of character that he knew well. On a visit to Philadelphia in September 1842, Frederick Thomas, as we have seen, persuaded Poe that Robert Tyler, the president's son, was enthusiastic for Poe to be appointed to a post in the Customs House in Philadelphia. Poe knew that Thomas was arriving for a visit, but he'd been drinking, and late in the morning he was just getting up. The usually well-groomed Poe was disheveled. Thomas later recalled, "His dark hair hung carelessly over his high forehead, and his dress was a little slovenly."

Poe confessed he had been drinking, but he agreed to meet Thomas the next morning at the Congress Hall Hotel. The following day Poe did not show up and later explained that he'd been so ill Virginia and Muddy forbade him from going out. Even so, Poe later called at the Philadelphia Customs House, expecting news of his appointment. The collector told him to come back later. When Poe did return, the collector brushed him off with, "I will *send* for you, Mr. Poe." For all Thomas's lobbying, and with the apparent support of the president's son, no position at the Customs House materialized.

Desperate to find new sources of income for his projected magazine, Poe hunted for a wealthy patron once more and applied to the poet Thomas Holley Chivers, a Georgia plantation owner (fig. 18). But Chivers was

FIG. 18. Thomas Holley Chivers (1809–58). Son of a Georgia planter, Chivers wrote mystical, rococo verse that may have influenced "The Raven." Because Chivers was wealthy, Poe hoped his fellow southerner would support the founding of the *Stylus,* but Chivers only offered Poe a home and help to overcome his drinking. (From S. Foster Damon, *Thomas Holley Chivers: Friend of Poe* [1930], frontispiece)

mourning the death of his three-year-old daughter and had little interest in funding a magazine in Philadelphia.

Besides growing up in the antebellum South, Poe and Chivers had other things in common. Each wrote poems about the death of beautiful women. While Poe was skeptical about much of Chivers's poetry, he recognized an affinity with the Georgia bard, both Chivers's ideas and his mellifluous versification. When Poe began lecturing on American poetry, he often quoted passages by Chivers in his presentations. Because Chivers was wealthy, Poe always hoped the Georgia poet would become his partner in founding an independent magazine. But such support was not forthcoming. Chivers was a teetotaler and had found Poe drunk in Philadelphia, ready to pick a fight with another editor, and Chivers had to lead him home to Muddy. Chivers would offer Poe a "home" in Georgia and assistance in overcoming his dependence on alcohol.

Poe had decided to call his projected magazine the *Stylus,* instead of *Penn Magazine.* The *Stylus* suggested something incisive, even surgical, reviews written with a steel point. The *Stylus* would "far surpass all American journals of its kind."

In March 1843 Poe decided that his best chance for securing a government appointment was to travel to Washington, DC. Surely if he met officials in the capital, including President Tyler, the appointment could be won and he could proceed with the *Stylus*. Poe lacked the money to travel and had to borrow enough for a ticket to the capital. When he arrived at Thomas's hotel, he found his friend too ill to accompany him to the offices of important people. Already broke, Poe had to write back to Philadelphia asking for another loan from his friend Thomas C. Clarke. Clarke had promised to help launch the *Stylus*, and Poe assured him, "I believe that I am making a *sensation* which will tend to the benefit of the Magazine."

The cruel irony was that Poe was indeed making a sensation in Washington: he was making a spectacle of himself. Away from Muddy and Sissy, he'd started drinking as soon as he arrived in the District. Thomas, too sick to leave his room, asked a writer and poet named Jesse Dow to look after Poe. But there was little Dow could do to restrain Poe. In his cups Poe offended Thomas, Dow, Dow's wife, Robert Tyler, and Thomas Dunn English (fig. 19). English would retaliate by satirizing Poe in a novel. The legend is that Poe was seen inebriated and wearing his West Point overcoat wrong side out and had to be escorted away. He was broke, and his clothes were in disarray. He later wrote an apology to Dow on March 16, 1843: "My dear fellow—Thank you a thousand times for your kindness & great forbearance, and don't say a word about the cloak turned inside out. . . . Also, express to your wife my deep regret for the vexation I must have occasioned her."

Poe expected to meet with President Tyler, but no invitation came. One day on Pennsylvania Avenue, Poe ran into John Hewitt, former editor of the *Baltimore Saturday Visiter*, with whom he had once quarreled. Intoxicated and broke, Poe asked for Hewitt's help: "[He was] seedy in his appearance and woe-begone. He came boldly up to me, and, offering me his hand, which I willingly took. . . . He . . . begged me to lend him fifty cents to obtain a meal. . . . I gave him the money."

Dow wrote to Clarke in Philadelphia asking him to come rescue Poe but not to tell Muddy and Virginia about Poe's condition. After about a week of chaos and embarrassment, Dow managed to get Poe on the train for Philadelphia. Needless to say, Poe was ashamed of his behavior. Worst of all, he had deeply upset Virginia, already weakened by consumption. And he was afraid his friend Clarke, who had promised support for the

FIG. 19. Thomas Dunn English (1819–1902). A lawyer and physician as well as man of letters, English became Poe's friend in Philadelphia but was deeply offended by Poe's behavior and the remarks an intoxicated Poe made about him. English satirized Poe in two novels, *The Doom of the Drinker* (1843) and *1844, or The Power of the S.F.* (Courtesy of the Edgar Allan Poe Museum, Richmond, Virginia)

Stylus, would learn of his shenanigans. Poe tried to put the best face on his debacle in Washington, but in May 1843 Clarke, a temperance man, did indeed withdraw his support for the new magazine.

In April 1843 the Poe family moved again, this time to a house at 234 North Seventh Street, in the Spring Garden District, at the northern edge of the city. From that location Poe could easily take long walks into the countryside. On June 15, 1843, Poe's cousin William Poe, a banker in Augusta, Georgia, sent him a kindly letter of advice: "There is one thing I am anxious to caution you against and which has been a great enemy to our family . . . 'a too free use of the Bottle.'"

Over the years students of Poe have tried to explain his self-destructiveness. Some have sought to gloss over it, blaming the times and the Victorian mores that made Poe a victim. Some have blamed his dipsomania or, in the case of Hervey Allen, his supposed opium addiction. But the facts are too plain to be ignored: again and again Poe sabotaged opportunities.

Poe was a man of extraordinary intelligence and sensitivity, yet guilt and lack of confidence overtook him in the most crucial circumstances. There was something in his character that feared success because he did not believe he deserved it. When confronted with responsibility and possible victory, he may have heard Allan's voice taunting and accusing him and his actor parents.

That Poe understood these aspects of human nature is indicated by a story such as "The Black Cat," published in the *United States Saturday Post* on August 19, 1843. The story had been written earlier, as Poe was waiting for the appointment to the Philadelphia Customs House. Like Poe himself, the narrator of the story loves cats. He has a black cat of his own named Pluto. As the tale begins, we learn that the narrator is about to be hanged; the story is his confession: "For the most wild, yet most homely narrative which I am about to pen, I neither expect nor solicit belief. . . . But to-morrow I die, and to-day I would unburthen my soul."

One of the most surprising features of this horror story is that the narrator calmly tells us his account is "homely," a "series of mere household events." In the twentieth century Hannah Arendt, writing about Adolf Eichmann and the Holocaust, would notoriously refer to the "banality of evil." The narrator of "The Black Cat" makes a similar observation. Far from considering himself of a cruel or violent temperament, the narrator informs us: "From my infancy I was noted for the docility and humanity of my disposition. My tenderness of heart was even so conspicuous as to make me the jest of my companions." The story is framed so that we see lurking in even the kindest people, and in ourselves, the potential for extraordinary cruelty.

Things go smoothly in the household until the narrator begins to drink; then he becomes abusive and violent to his wife and to the cat Pluto. One night, returning home drunk, he grabs the cat, and Pluto bites him. Furious, the narrator takes his penknife and cuts out one of the cat's eyes. After that the cat does indeed avoid him, and poisonous guilt overcomes the narrator. "It was this unfathomable longing of the soul *to vex itself*—to offer violence to its own nature . . . that urged me to continue."

Hating himself, the narrator hangs the black cat that he had mutilated. That night his house burns, and an image of the hanged cat is seared onto the standing plaster wall. The narrator is ruined financially and morally. While drinking in a tavern, the speaker notices another black cat similar to Pluto, which follows him home. It might be a reincarnation of Pluto, since it too has only one eye. But the pet only disgusts him, once established in his home. Part of the horror is caused by a white patch on the cat's chest in the shape of a gallows. One day when the cat nearly trips him on the stairs, the narrator takes up an axe in fury to kill the cat, but his wife attempts to stop the blow. "I withdrew my arm from her grasp and buried the axe in her brain."

Once more a woman has died in a Poe story, her only sin that she was kind and loyal and that she attempted to persuade the narrator to control his perverse cruelty. Ellen Weinauer calls the murder a "figurative rape scene." A marriage has become a nightmare. The narrator decides to hide the corpse behind the cellar wall, "as the monks of the middle ages are recorded to have walled up their victims." Carefully, he loosens the bricks of the basement wall, thrusts the body inside, then replaces the bricks and covers them with plaster. The body hidden, he looks for the cat, intending to kill it, too, but the cat has disappeared. "It is impossible to describe, or to imagine, the deep, the blissful sense of relief which the absence of the detested creature occasioned in my bosom."

"I looked upon my future felicity as secured." It is only on the fourth day that the police come to investigate the disappearance of his wife. Confidently, he shows them around the house and leads them into the cellar. The police are satisfied and are leaving the cellar when the narrator, driven by forces he does not understand, hears himself bragging about how well constructed the house is.

"'I rapped heavily, with a cane which I held in my hand, upon the very portion of the brick-work behind which stood the corpse of the wife of my bosom." There is a cry, like a moan, "like the sobbing of a child, and then quickly swelling into one long, loud, and continuous scream." The police quickly tear apart the wall on which he has knocked, and the bricks fall. "The corpse, already greatly decayed and clotted with gore, stood erect before the eyes of the spectators. Upon its head, with red extended mouth and solitary eye of fire, sat the hideous beast."

With great skill Poe seduces the reader into participating in the crime, exposing the Imp of the Perverse in us all. Leland S. Person tells us, "We identify with the Imp and his Perverseness precisely because we know we should not." Some think the story reveals Poe's unconscious resentment for his marriage to the gentle Sissy. Once again, we have a tale of the depravity of marriage. Flawlessly structured, the tale suggests that perversity, cruelty, even murder, are not exceptions but inherent, integral to the human condition, especially in marriage. Each of us is capable of the cruelest deeds. Deep in the unconscious is the desire to kill what we love, to hurt what has done us no wrong. To borrow the title from one of Poe's other stories, "Thou Art the Man." Teresa A. Goddu has argued that the black cat symbolizes slavery and the way enslaved humans were viewed as dangerous animals.

It seems inescapable that Poe, perhaps unconsciously, writes in "The Black Cat" of the fear of the enslaved people and the cruelty of masters toward Black human beings. The black cat is part of the household and is given a classical name, as so many enslaved individuals were in the fiction of the nineteenth century. The drunken narrator blames the Imp of the Perverse, almost as an excuse for his irrational, murderous violence. The ending suggests that ultimately the slave master will be punished.

The range of Poe's imagination was such that around the same time he wrote the nightmare of "The Black Cat," he composed the idyll called "Morning on the Wissahiccon." As I have stressed, Poe is also the poet of the forest, the riverbank, the peace of the countryside. The Wissahiccon is a small stream that empties into the Schuylkill. In the 1840s it wound its way through the countryside toward the edge of the city. Likely, Poe spent many hours in the woods beside the Wissahiccon, away from pen and paper, far from his creditors, from the pain of Virginia's declining health. In the forest he loved to dream, to reach the state he called reverie.

For Poe and other poets of the time, the word *reverie* was charged with special meaning. Like the surrealists of a later era, they believed that a source of the imagination was the unconscious, or subconscious, the place from which dreams are summoned. The poet, the artist, can access the imagination in a hypnogogic state, at the edge of sleep. It's a semi-passive condition, in which the poet lets the imagination have its way. Poems are acts of discovery and reception as well as constructions.

Later Poe would stress how consciously and mechanically he'd planned "The Raven," how he had designed and constructed that poem the way a builder might fashion a building or a cryptographer would fabricate a cipher. But the essay "The Philosophy of Composition" is probably not a completely accurate account of how he actually wrote a poem. In a more candid mood, Poe knew poetry is a gift as well as an invention. The conscious mind can be forceful, but the metaphoric imagination has its own obscure methods, and the poet learns to trust and follow them and to shape what is given.

"Morning on the Wissahiccon" was written to accompany an illustration in *The Opal for 1844* by J. G. Chapman. The sketch begins by comparing the American landscape with European scenery. Like Jefferson before him and Thoreau after him, Poe boasts of the natural splendors of the North American continent. Though he had never seen it, except in the writing of travelers, Poe describes the Valley of Louisiana as "the most voluptuous natural scenery upon earth."

Poe, who shared Thoreau's love of walking, was writing in Philadelphia, where the Bartram botanical gardens were still in business. William Bartram had published his *Travels* in 1791, celebrating his exploration of the pristine southern wilderness in the 1770s, a work that inspired Wordsworth and Coleridge and other Romantics. Though he had not seen the vistas of the prairies and high plains nor the glory of the Rocky Mountains, Poe could evoke the reverie in forests, the Edenic drama of rivers, as did his best contemporaries.

The sketch "Morning on the Wissahiccon" continues with the narrator floating downstream and relishing both the light and sounds of the wooded banks. The narrator observes that smaller streams are often more satisfying than larger rivers. The Wissahiccon is the perfect example, intimate, refreshing.

For Poe the route into reverie, into the imagination, is always winding, never direct, to reach the vista, the epiphany. The truest beauty of the Wissahiccon is not to be seen by moonlight or even romantic twilight but in the full light of noon, when detail and variety are bitingly clear. The narrator tells us that on a recent hot day, he floated down the Wissahiccon and, because of the warmth, drifted into "half-sleep," in which he thought of the stream in the days before white men arrived. As though he has floated back in time, he spots a lofty cliff not noticed before: "I saw, or dreamed that I saw, standing upon the extreme verge of the precipice . . . one of the oldest and boldest of those identical elks which had been coupled with the red men of my vision."

As the narrator watches, feeling he has been transported back to the pristine wilderness, a Black man appears and puts a halter on the animal. It turns out the elk is a pet of a family living nearby. Poe shares with us a Daniel Boone fantasy of entering the primeval woods, as known only to the Indians, and then snaps us back to the present with a wink and a smile.

FIG. 20. The McKee daguerreotype, before 1843. In the earliest known daguerreotype of Poe, he wears side-whiskers, fashionable at the time. His expression may have more to do with holding still for the exposure than his mood. The absence of a mustache is disconcerting to those familiar with Poe's later, more famous portraits. (Courtesy of the Edgar Allan Poe Museum, Richmond, Virginia)

Like many writers of his time, Poe was fascinated by the new art and science of photography, the daguerreotype, which was less than four years old in 1842, when he first posed in Philadelphia (fig. 20). Over the next seven years Poe would sit for at least eight photographic portraits, leaving a vivid record of his aging. Poe described the new invention as "the most important, and perhaps most extraordinary triumph of modern science": "For in truth, the Daguerreotyped plate is infinitely (and we use the term advisedly) is *infinitely* more accurate in its representation than any painting by human hands." In the daguerreotype taken in the early 1840s, Poe appears morose, distracted, though that attitude may have been caused in part by having to remain fixed while the plate was exposed. In 1842 he sports fashionable side-whiskers but no mustache. Poe was not pleased with his appearance in some of his portraits. About a steel engraving of a drawing, he wrote to Thomas on February 25, 1843: "I am ugly enough God knows, but not *quite* so bad as that" (fig. 21).

In the biographical portrait of himself published in the *Saturday Museum* in February 1843, Poe presented the life he wanted the public to see, declaring descent from ancestors "noted in British naval history and claiming kindred with many of the most illustrious houses of Great Britain." In this sketch, written by Henry Hirst, from material provided by the subject, Poe explained that he had attended school in Britain for five years and studied at the University of Virginia for three years as well as at West Point.

Shaving two years off his age, Poe maintained he'd been born in 1811 and that Allan had adopted him and made him his heir. He recorded his athletic feats in jumping and added that *The Narrative of Arthur Gordon Pym* had gone through many editions in Britain. Like Byron, he had tried to join the Greek fight for independence from the Turks, and he'd traveled to St. Petersburg. We cannot read Poe's autobiographical sketches without being touched by his hunger for a pedigree and distinguished heritage. He relished performing the role of Edgar A. Poe, which he revised as he went along. Later he would claim to have been born in 1813, to make himself appear even more a prodigy.

While enrolled at the University of Virginia, Poe had spent hours rambling in the nearby hills, called the Ragged Mountains, as he grieved over the apparent break with Elmira Royster. "A Tale of the Ragged Mountains" is the only narrative Poe explicitly set in the southern Appalachian Moun-

FIG. 21. Steel engraving by Thomas B. Welch and Adam B. Walters, 1843. Based on a watercolor by A. C. Smith. Of the portrait, Poe complained to James Russell Lowell, "It scarcely resembles me at all." The engraving appeared in *Graham's Magazine* in February 1845. (Courtesy of the Edgar Allan Poe Museum, Richmond, Virginia)

tains. It's a story in which Poe explores the subject of mesmerism, or hypnosis, as well as metempsychosis, or the transmigration of souls. It's interesting that Poe twice suggested, once in "Marginalia," that Appalachia would be the most appropriate name for the United States.

A young man named Augustus Bedloe has formed a close relationship with a mesmerist named Dr. Templeton. Bedloe, suffering from "neurasthenic attacks," has come to depend on Templeton's treatment, sometimes called "magnetism." Bedloe also takes morphine, on which he has come to depend. One day in late November, Bedloe sets out on a walk but does not return at the expected time. At about eight o'clock that evening, he suddenly appears, excited and anxious to tell what has befallen him. He had entered a gorge in the mountains and wandered through many twists and turns, as all Poe's heroes do as they approach reverie or revelation.

"I followed the windings of this pass with much interest. The scenery . . . had about it an indescribable, and to me, a delicious aspect of dreary desolation." As he winds into a remote and secluded ravine, Bedloe feels that he is the first to ever behold, to "penetrate," the primeval recesses. A thick mist hangs over the forest: "This path was excessively sinuous, and as the sun could not be seen, I soon lost all idea of the direction. . . . In the meantime the morphine had its customary effect—that of enduing all the external world with an intensity of interest."

In this reverie state, he sits beneath a tree and recognizes it as a palm tree. The humid air has become unbearable. He hears many human voices as wind clears the fog away and finds himself beside a wide river and a majestic "Eastern-looking" city, which we find out later is Benares. As he descends into the city, he is swept up in a riot, and Bedloe is hit by a poison arrow. As he dies, he feels a violent shock: "In an instant I seemed to rise from the ground. . . . Beneath me lay my corpse, with the arrow in my temple." Bedloe finds himself again in the Ragged Mountains, transported from India to an Indian Summer day. He can only call his experience a dream, yet it was much too real for a dream.

"Nor was it [a dream]," Dr. Templeton says. "Let us suppose only, that the soul of the man of to-day is upon the verge of some stupendous psychal discoveries." Templeton shows Bedloe and the narrator a miniature portrait of someone who looks remarkably like Bedloe, his friend Oldeb, who was killed by an arrow in Benares years ago.

A week later a notice of Bedloe's death appears in the Charlottesville, Virginia, paper. The narrator discovers that his name was spelled *Bedlo, Oldeb* in reverse. It turns out Bedlo was killed by a poisonous leech Dr. Templeton applied to his temple by mistake. There is no such thing as a poison leech, but the horrifying idea works well in the story. Since we know that Bedlo was wealthy, we wonder if Templeton does not become his heir. Perhaps the doctor himself is the poison "leach." We can be sure Poe leaves us wondering, as Dr. Templeton has suggested, if we are on the threshold of "stupendous psychal discoveries."

In July 1843 Poe and William H. Graham tried another manner of publishing Poe's stories. A pamphlet containing "The Murders in the Rue Morgue" and "The Man That Was Used Up" was issued under the title *The Prose Romances of Edgar A. Poe* as the first installment of a "Uniform Serial Edition." But sales were so poor no other volumes would appear. Surprisingly, given Poe's stature as a fiction writer, one ongoing struggle of his career was to find a publisher for his tales.

One of the most important and fated acquaintances Poe made in his Philadelphia years was Rev. Rufus Wilmot Griswold (1815–57) (fig. 22). Griswold has been a favorite target of Poe's biographers and defenders, but his relationship with Poe was complex and difficult to summarize. Perhaps our modern word *frenemies* is one to keep in mind.

Griswold was both a respected and representative figure of his time, though except for his connection to Poe, Griswold would have been forgotten long ago. What probably first brought the two men together was Griswold's anthology *The Poets and Poetry of America* of 1842. Griswold later claimed that Poe had first called on him. Poe wanted to be included in the anthology, and Griswold hoped to cultivate favor with the most feared literary critic of the time. Griswold was six years younger than Poe, something of a dandy in dress, with a flair for literary conversation.

In some ways we could almost see Griswold as Emerson's self-reliant, self-made man, "who in turn tries all the professions . . . in successive years, and always, like a cat, falls on his feet." There was indeed something feline about Griswold, secretive, calculating. He'd grown up in rural Vermont in a large family. Apprenticed to a printer, he became close friends with a journalist and musician named George Foster. When the two friends split up, Foster wrote Griswold a letter, which Griswold kept for the rest of his

FIG. 22. Rufus Wilmot Griswold (1815–57). Griswold, a self-made editor and journalist, published several popular anthologies of poetry and prose. Though Poe was irritated by Griswold's lack of taste and intellect, he knew he needed the anthologist. Claiming to be Poe's executor after the poet's death, Griswold blackened Poe's reputation with false accusations about the late poet's character but brought most of Poe's work back in print. (Courtesy of the Edgar Allan Poe Museum, Richmond, Virginia)

life: "I have loved often and deeply . . . and yet I have never felt towards any human being—man or woman—so strong and absorbing an affection as I bear to you. . . . Farewell—farewell—come to me if you love me."

Griswold later worked as an associate of Horace Greeley. He was licensed to preach as a Baptist minister, acquired a Doctor of Divinity degree, and married Caroline Searles at the age of twenty-two. By the time Poe met him in Philadelphia in 1841, Griswold had come to Philadelphia to edit an anthology of American poetry, his wife and children remaining in New York. Oliver Wendell Holmes Sr. wrote of Griswold, "He seems to be a kind of naturalist whose subjects are authors, whose memory is a perfect fauna of all flying and creeping things that feed on ink."

Since the *Poems* of 1831, Poe had mostly concentrated on writing prose. He'd always disdained what he called "the didactic" strain in Wordsworth and other poets. He believed strongly that the purpose of poetry was to create and celebrate Beauty. And the Beauty of poetry actually transcends the natural Beauty, reaching for the "supernal," the ethereal. As Poe's translator Baudelaire would say, poetry is "the infinite in the finite."

Though Poe was not in any conventional sense a religious poet, he would be influenced in subtle ways by the aftereffects of what was called the Second Great Awakening. The rhetoric and figures of the New Testament, especially Revelation, would resonate, as we have seen, in much of his writing. The biblical scholar William Mentzel Forrest would write in 1928: "Such quotations, allusions, phrasings, and stylistic features as abound in Poe indicate considerable knowledge of the Bible."

While decorated with exotic Arabic, Persian, and other oriental names, the visionary quality in much of Poe's writing has its sources in the messianic and apocalyptic rhetoric he was exposed to in his childhood and youth. Thus, when he really wants to describe the exhilaration of the poetic imagination, his image is "an ecstatic prescience of the glories beyond the grave."

In the early 1840s, Poe's reputation was based on the tales and especially on his reviews and articles on encryption. He submitted three poems to Griswold, and his work was placed near the end of the large anthology. The volume would include scores of minor poets, most now forgotten, but it was a publishing triumph and sold out three editions in the months after appearing in August 1842. In all the anthology would appear in over twenty print editions. Griswold gave a very large space to his friend Charles Fenno Hoffman. Griswold's taste in poetry ran to the sentimental, fashionable, and facile. He was certain to be a success.

With his biography in the *Saturday Museum,* Poe included twenty of his earlier poems, many partially revised. The earlier "To Helen" became the version we are now familiar with. Poe's poems, as well as his stories, had always been concerned with death, but Virginia's illness made the theme even more relevant as Poe stared at death every day.

To be included in a prominent and best-selling anthology was encouraging, even if Poe was marginalized at the end of the volume. Poe and Griswold became rivals as arbiters of taste, as they would later become rivals for the affections of Fanny Osgood. Poe's resentment of Griswold's success and mediocre standards stimulated him to think more rigorously about poetry and poetics, a process that would lead to the composition of his best later poems and several important essays on poetry and poetics. Griswold and his anthologies would infuriate Poe, but they also provoked and inspired him to begin a new phase of his creative life.

One of Griswold's many sins was that he was from New England and favored New England poets in his collections and in his reviews. Griswold admired and feared Poe as a critic and paid him to review the first anthology of 1842. Poe took the money and then under-praised the anthology. Griswold acquired a reputation for cunning and aggressive self-promotion. Years later the artist and editor John Sartain would recall the Reverend Griswold as "a notorious blackmailer, and I myself had to pay him money to prevent abusive notices of Sartain's Magazine."

As bad as Griswold's taste was, Poe understood that by making a popular anthology of American poetry, the Baptist preacher had done something significant, and Poe was willing to say so in print, calling the anthology "*the most important addition which our literature has for many years received.*" Over the next few years, Poe would continue to write tales, but from now on, until the end of his life, Poe's imagination would be more concerned with poetry and poetics. As much as we may despise Rufus Griswold, we should give him some credit for that.

Griswold became the book review editor of *Graham's,* sitting in Poe's old chair. It is said that Griswold even visited the Poes at home, and he would leave this description of his visit: "When once he sent for me to visit him, during a period of illness caused by protracted and anxious watching at the side of his sick wife, I was impressed by the singular neatness and the air of refinement in his home. . . . For this and for most of the comforts he enjoyed, in his brightest as in his darkest years, he was chiefly indebted to his mother-in-law, who loved him with more than maternal devotion and constancy."

Notice the sly hint of incest at the end of the last sentence. Yet for all their differences, there was an affinity between the two men. For one thing, Griswold had a preoccupation with death, similar to Poe's. According to Joy Bayless, in her biography of Griswold, when Griswold learned his wife, Caroline, had died, he rushed back to New York and held her body in his arms for thirty hours. "I kiss her cold lips, but their fervor is gone," he wrote. Later, at the cemetery, he would not leave her grave until led away.

In many ways Griswold resembled a character in a story by Poe, one of his grotesques. Everything about Griswold was extreme, his piety, his perfidy. He never forgot a slight; he knew well the Imp of the Perverse. He devoted more effort to American poetry than anyone else of his time. He put the title of "Reverend" before his name in his publications. His behavior was erratic, not to say self-destructive. Forty days after her funeral, Griswold revisited his wife's grave and left this account: "The vault where she is sleeping is nine miles from the city. I went to it. . . . I kneeled by her side and prayed, and then, with my own hand, unfastened the coffin lid, turned aside the drapery that hid her face, and saw the terrible changes made by Death and Time. I kissed for the last time her cold black forehead."

After initially praising Griswold's anthology of American poetry of 1842, Poe later gave his more honest assessment of Griswold's talents in another review: "That he has *some* talents we allow, but they are only those of a *mediocre* character. . . . As a critic, his judgment is worthless. . . . The [prefatory] biographies are miserably written . . . simply because reason and thinking are entirely out of Mr. G.'s sphere."

Strangely, Poe may have appointed him his literary executor. Griswold would collect and publish a substantial first edition of Poe's works, for no remuneration whatever. There was a bond between Griswold and Poe that biographers have found difficult to explain. Griswold's own biographer gives us another insight into the complex relationship between Poe and the anthologist: "Griswold had been reared on a hilly farm in the backwoods of Vermont . . . Poe had been surrounded by the best which money could buy. . . . The self-made man is seldom able to excuse the inefficiencies and failures of the prodigal who wastes his golden opportunities."

Poe, on his part, was irritated to the point of fury by the success of *The Poets and Poetry of America*. He may have wished *he* had thought of compiling such an anthology. To assemble such a collection, however bad it was, Griswold must have read hundreds of dreadful books of verse and written thousands of letters, gathered biographical material and bibliographical information. Editing the anthology had put Griswold in contact with, and made his name known to, hundreds of poets, many of them pretty young women.

Griswold's anthology inspired Poe to find a new outlet for his talents in lecturing. Then and now, it's possible to make more money and reach a larger audience by reading poems and lecturing on poetry than by simply writing and publishing poetry. Poe had always been an eloquent speaker. Emerson and many others had proven how lucrative the platform could be, and oratory was a fashionable art, practiced at the time from pulpit, lyceum, and local club.

It was the occasion of the publication of Griswold's *The Poets and Poetry of America* that gave Poe his opportunity: from the lectern he could say things he'd not been able to say in reviews, first in Philadelphia on November 21, 1843, to an overflow audience, and then in Wilmington, Delaware, and later, on March 13, 1844, in Newark, Delaware; Baltimore; and Reading, Pennsylvania. Poe was witty and sarcastic, and by reading the worst poems in Griswold's anthology, he could entertain his audience. On the lecture stage, Poe found yet another facet of his identity as the "literary *histrio.*" For the rest of Poe's life, lecturing would be his most dependable source of income.

After the onset of Virginia's illness, Poe had begun drinking again. Several of his acquaintances would later recall rescuing him from the gutter during his binges. It was related that Poe would "wander about the streets for hours; proud, heart-sick, despairing, not knowing which way to turn or what to do, while Mrs. Clemm would endure this anxiety at home as long as she could, then start off in search of him."

Years later, on January 4, 1848, Poe would describe in a letter to his new friend in Maine, George W. Eveleth, the horrors he'd experienced after Virginia fell ill with almost certainly fatal consumption: "Her life was despaired of. I took leave of her forever & underwent all the agonies of her death. She recovered partially and I again hoped. . . . During these fits of absolute unconsciousness I drank, God only knows how often or how much."

But all was not gloom, even after the onset of Virginia's disease. Poe's lawyer and poet friend Henry Beck Hirst called often (fig. 23). Eight years younger than Poe, he kept a pet store, specializing in birds, and authored a volume titled *A Book of Cage Birds.* Hirst also owned a pet raven. Hirst "would come, during these early Philadelphia days, for Sunday morning breakfast with [Poe] and family; then the two men would spend the day in country strolls."

One of the most controversial episodes of Poe's Philadelphia years occurred in either the summer of 1842 or 1843. According to one source, Poe traveled to the spa at Saratoga, New York, in the summer of 1842 "'to arrange for the treatment of his wife' then rapidly failing, and to recuperate his own health." Since they could only afford travel for one, Poe went alone to scout out the potential for a cure at the fashionable watering place. According to Peter Pindar Pease, Poe had suffered "heart failure" himself in the winter of 1841–42.

FIG. 23. Henry Beck Hirst (1817–74). Hirst became a close friend to Poe in Philadelphia. The two took long walks in the countryside, and Hirst published a sketch of Poe in 1843 in the *Saturday Museum*. A lawyer as well as owner of a pet store, Hirst kept a pet raven. (From Mary E. Phillips, *Edgar Allan Poe the Man* [1926], 695)

There grew the legend that Poe had composed "The Raven" at Saratoga. There may even be an element of truth to the tale. Poe would later tell Susan Talley Weiss that he'd worked for more than ten years on the poem. There is a legend that Poe was encouraged to leave Philadelphia at this time because of a scandal not caused by his drinking or quarrels but by the trip to Saratoga Springs in 1842 or 1843. The best-known version of the legend was included by Hervey Allen in his best-selling biography *Israfel*. To quote Allen: "In the summer of 1842, Poe was seen at Saratoga Springs . . . driving in a handsome carriage with a married woman from Philadelphia, well enough known to have her name worth talking about." Supposedly, Poe even showed a draft of "The Raven" to a reporter from the *New York Mirror*. Mrs. Ann Barhyte of Saratoga would later claim to have offered Poe advice while he worked on "The Raven" in the summer of 1843.

13

NEW YORK, "THE PURLOINED LETTER"

IN APRIL 1844 POE AND VIRGINIA WOULD MOVE AGAIN TO New York. They could not afford to bring Muddy but promised to send for her when they were settled in Manhattan. The six years Poe had spent in Philadelphia had been fabulously productive, the most fertile of his life. When he left the City of Brotherly Love, he was famous for "The Gold-Bug" and other stories of ratiocination. And he was becoming established as a lecturer and authority on poetry.

Why would Poe have wanted to return to the city on the Hudson? His career had been made in Philadelphia, and he'd found many friends there. George Graham still published his work and paid him well. Poe had enjoyed long walks in the countryside around Philadelphia. But Poe may have thought a change of scenery would be good for the ailing Virginia.

He and Sissy traveled by train and boat to Manhattan, and the morning after arriving, he sat down to write Muddy one of his most memorable letters. This document of Sunday, April 7, 1844, is one of our most intimate peeks into the private life of Poe and Sissy.

> We have just this minute done breakfast, and I now sit down to write you about everything. . . . Last night, for supper, we had the nicest tea you ever drank, strong & hot—wheat bread & rye bread—cheese—tea-cakes

> (elegant) [page 2] a great dish (2 dishes) of elegant ham, and 2 of cold veal, piled up like a mountain and large slices—3 dishes of the cakes. . . . For breakfast we had excellent-flavored coffe [*sic*], hot & strong—not very clear & no great deal of cream—veal cutlets, elegant ham & eggs & nice bread and butter. . . . Sis is delighted, and we are both in excellent spirits. She has coughed hardly any and had no night sweat. She is now busy mending my pants which I tore against a nail. . . . The very instant I scrape together enough money I will send it on. . . . Sissy had a hearty cry last night, because you and Catterina weren't here. . . . Be sure & take home the Messenger, [to Hirst]. We hope to send for you *very* soon.

The description of the food on the table gives us a hint of their struggles in the past for necessities. The attention to Sis's health adds to the vividness: she is mending his pants torn on a nail. What courage it must have required to set out with so little money, no solid prospects of employment, and a tubercular wife. Instead of returning the file of the *Southern Literary Messenger* to Hirst, Muddy sold it to Leary's bookstore, causing a rift between Poe and Hirst.

To raise money, Poe hurriedly wrote the story called "The Balloon Hoax." Talk of lighter-than-air travel was popular then, but there had been no successful crossing of the Atlantic by balloon. Poe loved hoaxes and puzzles, and he composed a story to pass off as a piece of factual reporting. As was his habit, he drew on a number of sources for his narrative, including a publication called *Remarks on the Ellipsoidal Balloon propelled by the Archimedean Screw, described as the New Aerial Machine,* published in 1843 in London by Monck Mason. Poe recognized the significance of the use of the propeller to drive the balloon in the desired direction.

"The Balloon Hoax" actually fooled people, for a few days, into believing that such a journey from Britain to Charleston, South Carolina, had been made in three days. Poe always loved to blur the line between fact and fantasy (and life and death). News from Charleston would soon prove it all a journalistic prank. But by then Poe had had his laugh and a fee from the *New York Sun.* There is much in "The Balloon Hoax" that is credible, including the propeller. If the jet stream moved from east to west instead of west to east, the story would be even more plausible. Poe's images of how the land and ocean would look from thousands of feet above are a tour de force. The journal kept by the aeronaut is vivid:

> The last nine hours have been unquestionably the most exciting of my life. I can conceive nothing more sublimating than the strange peril and novelty of an adventure such as this. May God grant that we succeed! I ask not for mere safety to my insignificant person, but for the sake of human knowledge and—for the vastness of the triumph. And yet the feat is only so evidently feasible that the sole wonder is why men have scrupled to attempt it before. One single gale such as now befriends us—let such a tempest whirl forward a balloon for four or five days (these gales often last longer) and the voyager will be easily borne, in that period, from coast to coast. In view of such a gale the broad Atlantic becomes a mere lake. . . . The immense flaming ocean writhes and is tortured uncomplainingly. The mountainous surges suggest the idea of innumerable dumb gigantic fiends struggling in impotent agony. In a night such as is this to me, a man *lives*—lives a whole century of ordinary life—nor would I forgo this rapturous delight for that of a whole century of ordinary existence.

"The Balloon Hoax" shows why Poe is so important in the history of science fiction. With all the technical details based on actual geography and the science of his times, he demonstrates the method of the speculative fiction of the future.

In late 1843 or early 1844, Poe had written "The Purloined Letter," the fourth and last of his stories of ratiocination and the one many call his best. The story was published in the annual *Gift* magazine, for the year 1845. Unlike "The Murders in the Rue Morgue" and "The Mystery of Marie Rogêt," there is no horror in "The Purloined Letter" and little violence. It is a story of intellect pitted against intellect and imagination against imagination. The plot is at once simple and complex.

Monsieur G—, prefect of the Paris Police, is baffled by an obvious crime he can't solve. There is no mystery about the perpetrator of the crime. Unscrupulous Minister D— has stolen a compromising letter from the chamber of a royal lady and uses the letter to blackmail the lady for political leverage. Much of the story is taken up with the prefect's description of the way Minister D—'s apartment has been thoroughly searched but no letter found.

A large portion of "The Purloined Letter" is also devoted to Dupin's discussion of how one matches wits with an opponent. First you have to judge the intelligence of the rival and adapt your methods to the antagonist's ingenuity. Because the police can only think in logical ways, they have been outsmarted by Minister D—, who is also a poet, with imagination. Monsieur G— assumes that all poets are fools.

Dupin, it turns out, is a poet also, and he can put himself in Minister D—'s mind. What is required is intuition and sympathetic imagination, essential gifts for a poet. Dupin knows that Minister D— would place the letter where the police will never look. A large reward is offered for the return of the letter, and halfway through the story, Dupin claims the reward and hands the prefect the stolen letter. The rest of the story is taken up with Dupin's explanation of how he obtained the letter, which the clever Minister D— had folded wrong side out, readdressed, and left in plain sight.

We learn that Dupin has reason to get revenge on Minister D—, who had offended him once in Vienna. Not only must he even the score, but D— must know who defeated and ruined him. There is no doubt D— will destroy his own career, still believing he has the advantage of the letter in his possession. The similarity of the names Dupin and D— suggest they are kin, or even two facets of the same person.

(Poe might be amused and pleased by the French psychoanalyst Jacques Lacan's elaborate and elusive "Seminar" essay on "The Purloined Letter" and Jacques Derrida's incisive deconstruction of Lacan's essay in "The Purveyor of Truth" as well as the several brilliant responses to the essay and the story by eminent theorists such as Barbara Johnson and Shoshana Felman, collected in *The Purloined Poe* of 1988.)

It is especially interesting that the story of "The Purloined Letter" depends on the use of a letter compromising the honor of a lady. Remember that Poe had carefully preserved damaging letters by or to or about his mother, which he asked Muddy to destroy in case of his death. With this story, Poe reached the pinnacle of his narrative writing.

In New York, Poe began thinking more of ultimate things, of life, death, and the cosmos. In a long letter to Lowell written July 2, 1844, he touched on the subjects that would inspire him to write *Eureka* three years later: "The unparticled matter, permeating & impelling, all things, is God. Its activity is the thought of God—which creates. Man, and other thinking beings, are individualizations of the unparticled matter. . . . which individualizes him. . . . What we call 'death' is the painful metamorphosis."

Apparently, Muddy joined Sissy and Edgar in New York in May or June 1844. For a short while Poe shared a room in a boardinghouse at 4 Ann

Street with Clark C. Curtis, while Muddy and Sissy either lived in an adjoining room or remained at 130 Greenwich Street. For reasons of Sissy's health and his own peace of mind, and perhaps for the sake of economy, Poe moved them out of the city in early July, about five miles north, to a farm owned by the Patrick Brennan family near Bloomingdale Road.

The Brennan farm was located on two hundred acres overlooking the Hudson River. During the American Revolution, George Washington had once made the house his headquarters. The Brennan family grew apples and vegetables and raised cattle. There were several streams and ponds on the tract and a thrilling view across the river to New Jersey from a rock outcrop called Mount Tom. According to the daughter Susannah Brennan, whom Poe called "Little Lady," Poe enjoyed sitting by the Brennans' pond. Sometimes the Brennan children would accompany him as he walked along the river. Poe and Sissy and Muddy lived in part of the two-story house, the Brennan family in the rest. Muddy had a room on the first floor, and Poe's study and the bedroom he shared with Sissy were on the second floor. Poe and his family would stay there through the summer and fall of 1844. The sojourn at the Brennan farm was mostly a happy period for Poe, before the shadow of Virginia's illness closed further in.

Mrs. Brennan would later remember Poe "as a shy, solitary, taciturn person, fond of rambling alone through the woods . . . often observed . . . gesticulating wildly, and loudly and excitedly soliloquizing." To pay off his debts, Poe did an extraordinary amount of routine journalism, even serving as correspondent for a small-town paper in Pennsylvania called the *Columbia Spy* and for the *Columbian Magazine* in New York City. During this period Poe began compiling for the *Democratic Review* a series he called "Marginalia." Ostensibly, the pieces were notes written in his books over the years. But Poe's library had never been large. Most of the entries for "Marginalia" were filleted from his earlier reviews and the series from the *Southern Literary Messenger* called "Pinakidia."

On July 2, 1844, Poe wrote to James Russell Lowell: "My life has been *whim*—impulse—passion—a longing for solitude—a scorn of all things present, in an earnest desire for the future." Given the interest the future has shown him, Poe achieved his desire. Poe's concession to *whim* echoes Emerson in "Self-Reliance": "I would write on the lintels of the doorpost, *Whim*."

It was while living on the Brennan farm that Poe began writing more and more for the *Evening Mirror*, edited by Nathaniel P. Willis. Willis would prove to be one of Poe's most loyal friends, both while Poe lived and afterward. Willis was one of the most successful writers and editors in the United States at that time, associated with the Young America movement. After a five-year stay in Europe, he had the manners of a cosmopolitan intellectual, and he dressed like a dandy. In "Literati of New York City" Poe would describe Willis's play *Tortesa* as "the best play ever written by an American."

But Willis's air of sprezzatura, the ease of a gentleman, was partly a pose and a mask. While Poe lived at the Brennan farm, sauntering in the woods and fields and contributing odd pieces to Willis's *Evening Mirror*, Willis would experience one grief after another. In a short period both his mother and younger sister died, and then his wife died in childbirth, along with the new baby. His brother had been imprisoned in Ohio.

At some point in the fall of 1844, Poe began to work as an editor for the *Evening Mirror*, commuting daily the five miles from the Brennan farm to the city. According to one story, it was Muddy who appeared in Willis's office and told the celebrated editor her son-in-law badly needed a job. Willis was willing to extend a helping hand, but all he had to offer was a position as assistant editor, a "mechanical paragraphist," someone to polish and rewrite features. After years of unemployment, Poe was happy to accept the position.

Willis paid Poe fifteen dollars a week for his work at the *Evening Mirror*. From time to time Poe had criticized Willis in print as a lightweight and a trifler. But he also respected the man as a generous professional, writing, "A more estimable man, in his private relations, never existed." After Poe's death, Willis would remember him as dependable and hardworking. Poe was famous for his reviews and stories, such as "The Gold-Bug," but he labored as assistant editor of the newspaper without resentment or complaint, though Willis would recall that "he never smiled."

While Poe was busy in the office of the *Evening Mirror*, he was able to do little of his own work, though in his first year in New York he did complete "The Raven" and turn out two or three satiric stories, "The Angel of the Odd: An Extravaganza," "The Literary Life of Thingum Bob, Esq.," sending up the world of magazine publishing, and "The Thousand-and-Second Tale of Scheherazade," poking fun at contemporary exuberance about technical progress such as trains, steamboats, telescopes, and other modern improvements. Modern theorists have found Poe's burlesques a goldmine for analysis and debate as well as insight about his thought and personality.

It was in this period, soon after arriving in New York, that Poe worked on two or three of his finest later poems. The first was the poem called "Dream-Land," first published in *Graham's Magazine* in June 1844. From the first line, we can hear that Poe had found his poetic voice again. We are whisked into a realm to which only Poe seemed to have a map and visa. The poem concludes:

> For the heart whose woes are legion
> 'Tis a peaceful, soothing region—
> For the spirit that walks in shadow
> O! it is an Eldorado!
> But the traveller, travelling through it,
> May not—dare not openly view it;
> Never its mysteries are exposed
> To the weak human eye unclosed;
> So wills its King, who hath forbid
> The uplifting of the fringed lid;
> And thus the sad Soul that here passes
> Beholds it but through darkened glasses.
>
> By a route obscure and lonely,
> Haunted by ill angels only,
> Where an Eidolon, named NIGHT,
> On a black throne reigns upright,
> I have wandered home but newly
> From this ultimate dim Thule.

For Greek geographers Thule was the realm of the extreme far north, an imagined land of ice and desolation, and for this speaker a realm beyond space and time.

"Dream-Land" is one of Poe's most memorable poems. Once you hear it, you can never get the variable meter and rhymes and repetitions out of your mind. Its mesmeric doublings irritate some readers, used to the flatness of modern free verse. Like Dupin with his green glasses, the traveler to dreamland must view the bleak world through darkened lenses or, better yet, through closed eyes, in trance, in sleep, or perhaps in death, or something like death. Of course Poe would know Paul's assertion in 1 Corinthians 13:12: "For now we see through a glass, darkly."

At this time and later, Poe was fascinated by hypnosis. There was a great deal of interest in the medical and psychological and even spiritual applications of hypnotic trances, sometimes called "magnetic sleep," as hypnosis itself was publicized as "animal magnetism." There was a feeling in this era that through hypnosis the "sleep-waker" might touch the supernatural and timeless, and Poe was happy to exploit this suggestion in stories, which many people would accept as factual reporting.

Through hypnosis and morphine, Bedlo traveled across thousands of miles and many years to enter the mind of someone who'd lived and died decades before him. Mesmerism appeared to be a doorway into the spiritual, to unknown realms, possibly a window into the eternal. Poe was deeply influenced by a book by Chauncy Hare Townshend called *Facts in Mesmerism,* published in London in 1840.

In "Mesmeric Revelation," in *Columbian Magazine* in August 1844, Poe imagined hypnosis as a way of exploring the experience of death and the world beyond death. "Mesmeric Revelation" is one of several stories, including "The Power of Words" and "The Facts in the Case of M. Valdemar," in which Poe addressed cosmic issues and images, in the world beyond time. "Mesmeric Revelation" is presented as an essay on hypnosis and an account of treating a particular patient named Mr. Vankirk. Vankirk, as he weakens, asks the narrator to put him in a hypnotic trance to further study the nature of "sleep-waking." When Vankirk is deeply asleep, the interrogation begins. The conversation is succinct and elemental.

> P. Is not God spirit?
> V. While I was awake I knew what you meant by "spirit," but now it seems only a word—such for instance as truth, beauty—a quality, I mean.

Vankirk tells the narrator: "Yes; for mind, existing unincorporate, is merely God. To create individual, thinking beings, it was necessary to incarnate portions of the divine mind." With a smile "irradiating all his features," Vankirk dies, and the narrator realizes that he must have been speaking "from out the region of the shadows."

Better known than "Mesmeric Revelation" is "The Facts in the Case of M. Valdemar," because the latter is a classic horror story. The tale appeared in the *American Review* for December 1845. The occasion is similar to that of "Mesmeric Revelation." A patient, near death, requests to be hypnotized. When asked if he feels pain, M. Valdemar answers, "No pain—I am dying."

M. Valdemar is left to rest and die in peace. The details of his face are graphic: "The upper lip, at the same time, writhed itself away from the teeth. . . . So hideous beyond conception was the appearance of M. Valdemar at this moment, that there was a general shrinking back from the region of the bed." M. Valdemar, in his extreme condition, can still answer questions, but in a voice unlike anything the narrator has ever heard. "It impressed me . . . as gelatinous or glutinous matters impress the sense of touch."

M. Valdemar, the sleep-waker, is left undisturbed for nearly seven months. At last the attending physician demands that they try to wake him. But when the hypnotic spell is broken, M. Valdemar, in the unearthly voice, cries, "For God's sake!—quick!—quick!—put me to sleep—or, quick!—waken me!—quick!—*I say to you that I am dead!*"

As the mesmeric spell is ended, what occurs is almost too horrible to describe: "His whole frame at once . . . crumbled—absolutely *rotted* away beneath my hands. Upon the bed, before that whole company, there lay a nearly liquid mass of loathsome—of detestable putridity."

"Mesmeric Revelation" and "The Power of Words" may be more profound discussions of the nature of the universe and timelessness, but "The Case of M. Valdemar" is the story readers remember. Its ending has been imitated in a thousand later stories of horror. Filmmakers have re-created the revolting final image again and again.

In the *Democratic Review* for November and December 1844, Poe published further installments of the series of odds and ends titled "Marginalia." The biographer George Woodberry would comment about "Marginalia": "As one reads them and the later collections, which continued to be published until Poe died, one cannot but admire the audacity of their author, who could thus resell clippings from his old book reviews."

While working on his stories of mesmerism and death, and life after death, and adding to "Marginalia," Poe continued to polish the poem that would become, by far, his best-known work. Though he would later write an essay explaining how he had cunningly contrived "The Raven" to create just the desired effect, we understand that "The Philosophy of Composition" is, in part, another of Poe's hoaxes. He labored on the poem for many months, even years, experimenting intermittently with voice, refrain, and form. Poe told F. W. Thomas yet another version of the composition of the poem: "'The Raven' was written in a day." Some would say "The Raven" is the most memorized poem because you can't get the wretched thing out of your mind once you hear it and experience the bizarre sound and eerie atmosphere and endless overlapping phrases and repetitions.

Over the years scholars have found dozens of sources that influenced Poe in the composition of "The Raven." There is probably some truth to Thomas Holley Chivers's claim that Poe took ideas and metrical patterns for "The Raven" from him. Later Chivers would be accused of plagiarizing from Poe's poetry and prose. Writing to William Gilmore Simms, Chivers would assert: "But all these things are mine. . . . I am the Southern man who taught Mr. Poe all these things . . . long before 'The Raven.'"

Another important influence on "The Raven" is almost certainly Elizabeth Barrett Browning's poem "Lady Geraldine's Courtship," with its rollicking trochaic meter. But it's safe to say that none of the sources that inspired Poe achieves anything like the effect, or the success, of Poe's poem. Certainly, "The Raven" is one of the most mournful of the Graveyard school poems of that era, which began with Gray's "Elegy in a Country Churchyard." But no other poem in the school is quite so quotable or so easy to parody. People who don't care for poetry and never read the stuff can recite lines from "The Raven." Susan Weiss would later claim Poe informed her that he originally intended to write a poem about a wise owl and labored over the poem more than a decade.

After Poe encountered Elmira at a party in 1836, he had been so excited that he wrote a poem called "To Zante," in which he lamented the loss of bliss with the bride of his choice: "No more—no more upon they verdant slopes! / *No more!* alas, that magical sad sound." With the phrase *no more,* Poe rings the bell of mourning for the loss of his first love, anticipating "The

Raven." Elmira remains in his memory and imagination, an island oasis, a marriage that might have been.

The audience for "The Raven" was prepared for the sentiment of what they heard. But nothing had prepared them for the mesmeric rhyme and cadence, the tide of repetition, the mournful imagery, the colloquy between the grieving lover and the unlikely, torturing bird. American poetry has never been the same since "The Raven" was published in the *American Review* in February 1845, signed by the name "Quarles," after first appearing in Willis's *Evening Mirror* on January 29, 1845.

In its final form "The Raven" comprised eighteen stanzas, each with five lines of trochaic octameter, plus a final line of trochaic tetrameter. The trochaic foot, one accented syllable followed by an unaccented syllable, was considered by the Greeks to be a high-stepping, marching meter, more assertive and stirring than iambic meter, its obverse. The shorter sixth line of each stanza always ends with a refrain echoing "Nevermore," so the effect is not unlike responsive reading. Because of the echoing of whole phrases, the poem incorporates incremental repetition, giving it a litany effect.

> Once upon a midnight dreary, while I pondered, weak and weary,
> Over many a quaint and curious volume of forgotten lore—
> While I nodded, nearly napping, suddenly there came a tapping,
> As of some one gently rapping, rapping at my chamber door—
> "'Tis some visitor," I muttered, "tapping at my chamber door—
> Only this and nothing more."
>
> Ah, distinctly I remember it was in the bleak December;
> And each separate dying ember wrought its ghost upon the floor.
> Eagerly I wished the morrow;—vainly I had sought to borrow
> From my books surcease of sorrow—sorrow for the lost Lenore—
> For the rare and radiant maiden, whom the angels name Lenore—
> Nameless *here* for evermore.

One important clue to "The Raven" is Poe's poem "Lenore," published first in 1842, then revised in 1844. The grieving lover of the lost Lenore is named Guy de Vere. The lament contains a confession of guilt, urging that

Lenore's angelic soul be allowed to ascend to heaven without any tolling bell from "the damned earth."

> "How *shall* the ritual then be read—the requiem how be sung
> By you—by yours, the evil eye—by yours the slanderous tongue
> That did to death the innocence that died and died so young?"

Guilt for the cruel treatment of the lost Lenore permeates "Lenore," as it does "The Raven." Guy de Vere accuses himself, as well as the world, for her tragedy and death. When we read "evil eye" we can remember that the phrase can be heard as "evil I." By comparing "The Raven" with "Lenore," we understand that the speaker of the latter poem is trying to forget not just his grief but, more importantly, his guilt. "The Raven" was not only Poe's most popular poem; it was the poem he could not let go of. For the rest of his life, he would continue to revise and perfect it. The final version of "The Raven" would be published in Richmond in the *Semi-Weekly Examiner* on September 25, 1849, just days before his death.

One of Poe's earliest biographers, William F. Gill, noted in "The Raven" "an exaggerated sense of wrong done to his lost loved one . . . exciting the most irrational remorse. . . . His remorse also forbade him any hope of meeting her in the distant Aidenn." It helps if we remember that the raven, which enters the narrator's chamber and refuses to leave, is the narrator's conscience and memory, black as a judge in judicial robes. The narrator has tried to escape the horrors of his guilt by reading ancient and obscure lore. We can associate Lenore with the raven-haired beauty Ligeia, with her beautiful Hebrew nose, who also died young. And we should remember the speaker of "Berenicë," who has tried to repress his horrible deeds. "The Raven" implies the story of a love or marriage that ended badly. David Leverenz suggests that the raven represents a Black body torturing the narrator.

But the poem "Lenore" has given us another insight into the identity of the lost Lenore. Some critics have pointed out that in 1845, Poe was already grieving and horrified by the approaching death of Virginia, and that seems relevant to this poem. But buried deep in Poe's memory, and in all his stories and poems of death, is the image of Eliza Arnold Poe, the archetypal dead beauty. In "The Philosophy of Composition" Poe would celebrate poetry as "*Mournful and Never-Ending Remembrance.*" But the most thrilling element of the remembrance is guilt for the lover's (and mother's) death.

It is interesting that in line 38 the Raven is described as "of the saintly days of yore." We can only construe that the narrator is thinking of the time of innocence, before he committed the deed he struggles to forget. In line 89 he will cry, "*Is there, is* there balm in Gilead?" Students of the Old Testament know that Gilead was a place of refuge. The narrator is a fugitive from his conscience, and from judgment.

In "The Philosophy of Composition" Poe explains his intentions in "The Raven" by referring to "the human thirst for self-torture" and "the luxury of sorrow." And though the essay is not always credible, Poe gives away much that is authentic in this explanation of how to write a poem. As he entertains himself and the reader, Poe lets slip the meaning of his poetic covenant: "the human thirst for self-torture."

Like other Poe narrators, from "Berenicë" to "The Imp of the Perverse," the narrator knows that he is both guilty and damned. Since the rare and radiant maiden has gone to heaven, he confesses he is condemned to the other place. "The Raven" achieves the hypnotic effect Poe had sought in many of his poems. It is a poem of ceremony and ritual, a dervish dance, a ghost dance, whirling through rhyme and repeated phrases to induce a trance beyond any prophecy or interpretation. It's a plea for absolution for the human condition, a prayer for resolution of the burden of conscience and memory, a confession of an unpardonable sin never defined or explained, having to do with the sin of marriage or betrothal, the grief of marriage.

"Be that word our sign of parting, bird or fiend!" I shrieked,
upstarting—
"Get thee back into the tempest and the Night's Plutonian shore!
Leave no black plume as a token of that lie thy soul hath spoken!
Leave my loneliness unbroken!—quit the bust above my door!
Take thy beak from out my heart, and take thy form from off my door!"
Quoth the Raven "Nevermore."

And the Raven, never flitting, still is sitting, *still* is sitting
On the pallid bust of Pallas just above my chamber door;
And his eyes have all the seeming of a demon's that is dreaming,

And the lamp-light o'er him streaming throws his shadow on the floor;
And my soul from out that shadow that lies floating on the floor
Shall be lifted—nevermore!

It is said that Poe liked to close the curtains and dim the lamps before he recited "The Raven" in parlors and salons. He was the child of actors, the literary *histrio.* All his life he'd been preparing to write "The Raven" and recite it to hushed audiences. Poe had achieved his ambition of composing for a vastly popular audience a poem that would also engage some of the most distinguished critics and readers of the next two centuries. Yet buried in the vagueness, in the indefiniteness, is a confession, a recognition at the very heart of his best work: the burden and never-ending pain and torture of guilt, somehow related to the yearning for and torture of marriage.

While there is no one model for the heroines of Poe's poems and stories, including "the lost Lenore," there is some evidence, as mentioned, that Poe had Elmira Royster in mind as he composed and revised "The Raven." In two of the poems he composed for her in the 1830s, "To One in Paradise" and "To Zante," he used this phrase *no more* repeatedly. He clearly associated the tolling sound of *no more,* which evolved into *nevermore,* with the Elmira of the enchanted garden and his guilt for losing her.

But beyond all Poe's heroines looms the figure of Eliza Poe. She appears under many names, as the young Eliza appeared on stages in so many guises and with many different names. Underneath the costumes and makeup, it is the same mother-muse-beauty-lover torturing and inspiring the imagination. "The Raven" is the confession of one damned, and inspired.

For thirty-six years Poe had sought fame. He'd found it first with "The Gold-Bug." But it was the bleak, gray shadow of "The Raven" that would make him a celebrity, a kind of nineteenth-century rock star. As he would write to his friend Frederick Thomas, "The bird beat the bug, though, all hollow." All his life Poe had believed he was both doomed and destined for greatness. He wished to be the arbiter of taste for his time, the ratiocinator par excellence, the poet of the age. Be careful what you wish for—the Fates may be listening. For "The Raven," Poe's most famous poem, he was paid $9 ($270 today). It is said his lifetime earnings were about $6,200 ($186,000 today).

14

FAME AND ITS PRICE

THE SUCCESS OF "THE RAVEN" CHANGED EVERYTHING FOR POE. The poem was reprinted in newspaper after newspaper, and his lines seemed to be on everyone's lips. There were parodies galore, and the poem became a common reference in conversation and commentary, especially the refrain, "Nevermore." Poe may not have awakened quite as famous as Byron claimed for himself, but in 1845 he was almost certainly the most talked about poet in North America. At least one biographer has described New York as "raven-mad" in 1845.

Though Poe was only associated with the Young America movement briefly in 1845, that connection proved significant in his career, even though he opposed many of the claims of the Young Americans. The central figures of the group included John O'Sullivan, Evert Duyckinck, and David Field. O'Sullivan had founded the magazine the *Democratic Review* in Washington in 1837, with the support of President Martin Van Buren and the Democratic Party. Later he would coin the phrase *Manifest Destiny*. His ambition was to celebrate the United States, its people, its culture, its independence from Europe, and, most important, its future, and to regenerate the culture, especially literary culture. O'Sullivan promised to take "control of American culture from Boston, from the Whigs, and from old conservatives everywhere."

In late January 1845 Poe had moved his family from the relative isolation of the Brennan farm to 154 Greenwich Street. Then, in May of that year, they relocated to a second-story apartment at 195 East Broadway. Near the end of the summer of 1845, they moved again, to 85 Amity Street, only two blocks from Washington Square. Poe had left his position on the *Evening Mirror* and begun writing for a weekly called the *Broadway Journal,* edited by Charles Frederick Briggs. After remaining sober for almost two years, Poe started drinking again. The *Broadway Journal* had begun publication on January 4, 1845, with John Bisco as publisher. At first Briggs was much impressed by Poe's character and abilities and wrote to his friend James Russell Lowell, "Poe is a much better fellow than you have any idea of." Later Briggs would revise that opinion.

Instead of paying Poe for his contributions to the *Broadway Journal,* Briggs and Bisco agreed to give him one-third of the profits, which turned out to be little, and later nothing at all. On May 4, 1845, Poe wrote to Thomas, "I am as poor now as ever I was in my life—except in hope, which is by no means bankable." With the new freedom of his position on the *Broadway Journal,* Poe continued his attacks on Longfellow and on Lewis Gaylord Clark, editor of the *Knickerbocker.* But his praise for Tennyson reached new heights of hyperbole: "not only the greatest Poet in England, at present, but the greatest one, in many senses, that England, or any other Country ever produced." In "Marginalia" Poe would claim that Tennyson "seems to *see with his ear.*"

Soon Briggs would decide that Poe's scholarship was shallow and his character glib and superficial. In an article published in 1877, Briggs "declared that Poe, when drunk, was a terror to his wife and mother-in-law." And yet Briggs would concede there was something unusual about Poe's gifts: "He was a genius. As a writer, he was like an opal—all the more beautiful and full of play of color by reason of refracted light from internal strains and fractures." The biographer Mary Phillips observed that if Poe had understood those strains and fractures better, he might have shed some of his crushing burden of "conscience misery."

The author of "The Raven" found himself invited to fashionable literary parties and salons in New York. There were intellectual gatherings to discuss important issues in literature, art, and ideas, called *conversaziones.* One of the most prominent salonistes was Anne Charlotte Lynch (1815–91), who taught at the Brooklyn Female Academy (fig. 24).

Miss Lynch hosted conversations each Saturday evening at the home

FIG. 24. Anne Charlotte Lynch (1815–91). A teacher and a poet, Anne Lynch presided over a prestigious salon in New York City in the 1840s. It was considered an honor to be invited to her Saturday gatherings. She dropped Poe from her guest list because of the accusations about Mrs. Ellet's letters in 1846. (Courtesy of the Edgar Allan Poe Museum, Richmond, Virginia)

she shared with her mother at 116 Waverly Place, near Poe's residence. Guests were served only tea and cookies and cakes, but her gatherings sometimes drew as many as eighty or more guests. Often poets read their work or musicians played. Sometimes there was dancing. Celebrities such as Emerson, Melville, and Matthew Arnold attended the gatherings. At the Lynch salon and at others, Poe was often asked to recite poems, especially "The Raven."

As a critic, Poe always favored women writers, especially women poets. In the salons of New York, he appeared to be in his element. As Mrs. Elizabeth Oakes Smith would recall, "He delighted in the society of superior women, and had an exquisite perception of all the graces of manner and shades of expression." Poe's looks were striking and memorable. Those who saw him never forgot his face, especially his eyes. Years later Susan Weiss would recall: "'What *awful* eyes Mr. Poe has!' said a lady to me. 'It makes my blood run cold to see him slowly turn and fix them upon me when I am talking.'" Many referred to him simply as "The Raven."

Women writers especially admired him, adored him. And his response to one of the most talented and beautiful brought about his social downfall. She was Frances Sargent Osgood, whose poems Poe had published in *Graham's Magazine.* Two years younger than Poe, she was in awe of his accomplishments. Married to the well-known portrait painter Samuel Stillman Osgood, Frances was the mother of two daughters. She had published a number of books in both prose and verse, including *The Poetry of Flowers* in 1841, and a version of the classic children's story *Puss in Boots.* She was accomplished at literary flirtations, with many admirers, including Rufus Griswold.

On February 28, 1845, Poe delivered a lecture on American poetry called "The Poets and Principles of Poetry" at the New York Society Library. Though disparaging some popular male poets, he heaped praise on several women poets, including Frances Sargent Osgood. And for once he refrained from scorning Griswold, possibly for Osgood's sake.

The month before, on January 16, Poe had written a letter of apology to Griswold, apparently regretting some of the things he'd said about the editor. "Your letter occasioned me first pain and then pleasure . . . because I saw in it a hope of reconciliation." Reviewing the lecture in the *Weekly Mirror,* Willis wrote of Poe: "He becomes a desk—his beautiful head showing like a statuary embodiment of Discrimination."

There were particular reasons Poe was smitten with Fanny Osgood. She was childlike in her manner and enthusiasms. She was petite, and her name reminded Poe of Fanny Allan. Her girlish appearance was much like Virginia's. Even more important, her beauty and liveliness and figure no doubt reminded him of Eliza Poe. Her hair was very black and long, like Ligeia's. Poe may have sensed, even then, that she was suffering from the consumption that would kill her in 1850.

Whatever sexual relations had existed between Poe and Virginia had likely ceased when Sissy fell ill in 1842. For more than three years, Poe had not had any sexual life that we know of. From the evidence of his actions, his letters, and his writing, it would seem that Poe's sexuality was not unlike his emotional bipolarism. When drinking, he probably was impotent and asexual. When sober, he could be consumed with desire he was scarcely able to check by writing and long solitary walks in the woods. D. H. Lawrence may have had a relevant insight into Poe's sexual nature, reading "Ligeia" as a dark "battle of wills." Because of Poe's extreme desire, he felt he was damned.

Fanny's husband was often away on commissions for portraits. Mr. Osgood had also had a number of affairs with women admirers. With many suitors of her own, Fanny filled her time with writing, socializing, and flirtations. She may or may not have taken lovers, but her writing was romantic and teasingly erotic. In a letter after Poe's death, Fanny would write of Poe: "I think no one could know him—no one *has* known him personally—certainly no woman—without feeling the same interest."

Poe and Fanny began a coy exchange of poems in the *Broadway Journal.* Some biographers think Fanny was more serious about the affair than Poe. One has described her as "a weird, tender child whom one wanted to shelter." It appears Poe was less smitten, at first, and then more so as the flirtation inspired rumors and mild scandal, and she withdrew, first to Providence and then to Albany.

One poem Poe wrote to Osgood, printed in the *Broadway Journal,* included the lines:

I would not lord it o'er thy heart,
  Alas! I cannot rule my own,
Nor would I rob one loyal thought,
  From him who there should reign alone.

That Poe idealized Fanny in poems and conducted a flirtation with her is beyond dispute. It is also likely that he hoped to marry Fanny after Virginia's death. It is said that when Fanny moved to Albany, he visited her there. At the same time, Poe knew Fanny was "safe" because she was already married. He could imagine marrying her, even as he was threatened by the married state. He could fantasize some ideal union with Fanny that could never happen.

For nine years Poe had worked relentlessly, fought poverty and drink, depression, and mania. Suddenly in 1845 in New York City, he was a celebrity, admired by talented and beautiful women. As Poe recited poems and held forth with opinions at parties, Fanny sat nearby, enthusiastic and devoted. She would recall: "For hours I have listened to him entranced by strains of such pure and almost celestial eloquence as I have never read nor heard elsewhere." In a story called "Ida Grey" published in *Graham's* July 1845 issue, Fanny described her infatuation with Poe in terms many readers would recognize. Gossip in the literary community mostly blamed Poe for leading the childlike Fanny astray.

On June 25, 1845, Wiley & Putnam had published *Tales* by Edgar A. Poe, a volume containing many of his masterpieces. He was famous for his fiction as well as for "The Raven." Meanwhile, his war with Longfellow over the issue of plagiarism continued. Poe's attacks on Longfellow had more than a touch of the irrational.

To study the Poe of 1845 is to watch a man begin to lose his bearings. The affair with Fanny Osgood unsettled him, as did his apparently personal crusade to discredit Longfellow. But more than anything else, including the terrifying illness of Virginia, it was the fame of "The Raven" that wrenched Poe from his moorings. The quiet life on Spring Garden Street in Philadelphia and at the Brennan farm was over. Far from the woods and fields and solitude where he was most himself, he began to lose his direction.

As the rumors spread, Fanny fled to Providence, Rhode Island, and Poe followed her there. Some biographers think it was in Providence that Poe fathered the daughter, Fanny Fay, born about nine months later. From Providence she removed herself to Albany. Perhaps in the hope of stemming the rumors, Fanny visited Poe at home and befriended Virginia. And Samuel Osgood painted a portrait of Poe, probably at this time. Virginia was wasting away with disease, and she encouraged Poe's friendship with Fanny, who influenced Poe to remain sober. It was well known that Virginia could not live much longer.

After Poe's death, Fanny would write a long letter, published in the December 8, 1849, issue of *Saroni's Musical Times,* implicitly defending Poe (and herself) against the rumors that were common knowledge. Griswold would later reprint her words in his "Memoir" of 1850: "At his desk beneath the romantic picture of his loved and lost Lenore, he would sit, hour after hour. . . . I recollect, one morning, towards the close of his residence in this city . . . he seemed unusually gay and light-hearted. Virginia, his sweet wife, had written me a pressing invitation to come to them; and I, who never could resist her affectionate summons . . . hastened to Amity-street."

What did she mean by "the romantic picture of his loved and lost Lenore" over his desk? We can only speculate. One guess is that it was a pencil sketch of Elmira Royster. With the fame of "The Raven," many were curious about the model for the Lost Lenore. Poe may have been happy for visitors to assume the picture was the Lost Lenore of the poem.

Frances Sargent Osgood may have been an accomplished flirt and something of a coquette, but her later defense of Poe suggests a woman who deserves our respect and admiration. She described Poe's romances with her, and later with Helen Whitman and Annie Richmond, as "little poetical episodes," revealing a profound understanding of Poe. She remembered Poe's eyes as "flashing with the electric light of feeling and of thought." One of the more severe comments about Poe in this period comes from Margaret Fuller: "I did not know him, though I saw and talked with him often, but he always seemed to me shrouded in an assumed character."

BECAUSE THE *TALES*, PUBLISHED IN JUNE 1845, HAD SOLD reasonably well, Wiley & Putnam agreed to bring out a volume called *The Raven and Other Poems* in November 1845. It was Poe's first collection of poems in fourteen years. In a short preface to the poems, Poe sounded a note of diffidence, no doubt to suggest a charming modesty. If so, it was a fake modesty. "These trifles are collected and republished chiefly with a view to their redemption from the many improvements to which they have been subjected while going at random 'the rounds of the press.' . . . Events not to be controlled have prevented me from making, at any time, any serious effort in what, under happier circumstances, would have been the field of my choice. With me poetry has been not a purpose, but a passion . . . [poets] must not—they cannot at will be excited with an eye to the paltry compensations, or the more paltry commendations, of mankind."

Poe loved to affect the pose of aristocratic amateur, dismissing the judgment of public opinion. One of the ironies of Poe's career, as stated before, is that as much as he claimed to disdain a large audience, he would become after his death one of our most popular authors, and he had sought to be such.

A note was added to the first page of "Poems Written in Youth." Again, his purpose was complex, to defend himself against charges of imitating Tennyson, to excuse his youthful naïveté and ambition, and to brag that he'd written such impressive verse while in his teens. Poe was telling less than the truth, for many of the poems had been much revised. In fact, Poe kept revising his poems throughout his life, no matter how many times a poem had been reprinted. And he knew full well that poems such as "Sonnet—To Science" and "To Helen" were anything but apprenticeship compositions.

FIG. 25. Henry Wadsworth Longfellow (1807–82). The most popular American poet of his time, Longfellow drew from Poe a series of critical attacks. It's possible both Poe and Longfellow considered the charges an elaborate hoax. (Courtesy of the Edgar Allan Poe Museum, Richmond, Virginia)

Poe dedicated *The Raven and Other Poems* to Elizabeth Barrett Barrett, "The Noblest of Her Sex." Barrett thanked him and mentioned that the poet Robert Browning was much taken with the rhythm of "The Raven." Barrett also referred to the fuss made about "The Case of M. Valdemar" in London literary circles.

But the reviewers in both the United States and Britain were not as kind to *The Raven and Other Poems* as they had been to the *Tales* earlier that year. Then as now there might have been a prejudice against a writer with the audacity to publish both prose fiction and verse, and in the same year. As Poe would observe in "Marginalia," "Thus a poet . . . should be cautious not to distinguish himself in any other walk of Letters." And northern critics have sometimes been more willing to praise fiction from the South than poetry associated with that region. And yet to the reading public, Poe would always be remembered as the author of "The Raven" *and* such stories as "The Tell-Tale Heart" and "The Pit and the Pendulum." It was the critics, not the reading public, who cared so much for specialization.

Poe's new fame seemed to exacerbate his animosity toward Longfellow (fig. 25). As an esteemed poet, he could now attack the Harvard professor with even more authority. The so-called Longfellow War is one of the oddest episodes in Poe's career and one of the hardest to explain. It had begun years earlier and gathered momentum during the Philadelphia residency, to culminate in the *Broadway Journal* in 1845.

Poe would accuse Longfellow of stealing much of his drama "The Spanish Student" from Poe's unfinished play "Politian." Is the Longfellow War evidence of Poe's instability, periods of paranoia and madness? The critic Sandra Tomc has argued that Longfellow represented for Poe one of the worst examples of the "'clique' mentality" in American letters of the time.

A writer calling himself "Outis," meaning, in Greek, "nobody," published a letter in the *Evening Mirror* in March 1845 defending Longfellow's art and integrity. Some scholars have wondered if Outis might be Poe himself, fighting on both sides of the war to stimulate even more interest. Poe especially enjoyed demonstrating cleverness, his ability to outthink and outwit others. Is it possible that Poe conducted most of the feud with Longfellow as a hoax, a play war to amuse readers? Poe may have expected intelligent readers to understand that he was engaging in the old English and Scottish game of "flyting," exchanging insults to call attention to himself and to his opponent. And once the "war" got underway, it was too much fun to stop.

The biographer Mary Phillips was pretty sure that Poe, in the Longfellow War, "started his hoax of double tilting." Of Poe's review of "The Waif" and in the Outis letters, Phillips saw "neither more nor less than an attempt to engage someone of high authority in a *literary* discussion of plagiarism."

But in the course of the Longfellow War, Poe made at least two valid points among the aspersions he cast on Longfellow's work. He demonstrated that Longfellow's attempts to imitate Greek hexameters in English were mostly unsuccessful, and he did reveal an actual, but unintended, plagiarism in Longfellow's poetry. Poe made some important enemies in the process, though Longfellow was not one of them. After Poe's death, Longfellow would offer support and hospitality to Muddy.

Throughout his life Poe experienced periods of profound depression, alternating with stretches of intense activity. On July 2, 1844, he'd written to James Russell Lowell: "I can feel for the 'constitutional indolence' of which you complain—for it is one of my own besetting sins. I am excessively slothful, and wonderfully industrious—by fits."

In 1845, the year of "The Raven," a new note of frenzy enters Poe's behavior. Far from the natural world and solitude that had restored his stability often before, a heightened strain of the irrational colored his behavior with a hint of megalomania. For artists of all kinds, failure is hard to negotiate day after day, the shame of poverty and obscurity, the long periods of rejection when nothing seems to work and nobody cares. But sudden success can be even harder to surmount, to be abruptly thrust into the public view, with opportunities previously denied easily available. And healing solitude is no longer an option.

For all his sniping at the Transcendentalists and Frog-Pondians, Poe had hoped to be invited to speak at the Boston Lyceum or one of the other literary societies of his birth city. And for October 16, 1845, just such an invitation arrived. Poe agreed to lecture about American poets and poetry and to recite a poem composed for the occasion. Poe probably did not know he was the Lyceum's second or third choice.

At the Boston Odeon he would speak on a stage where Ralph Waldo Emerson had lectured and Eliza and David Poe had performed. After all his carping about the Frog-Pondians, Poe must have been a bit intimidated by the invitation. Who wouldn't be? In the vortex of his newfound fame, he could not compose a new poem. The words would not come forth, and in frustration he sought to quench his anguish with the bottle.

As the date of the lecture for the Lyceum neared, it would have been logical for Poe to stay sober, sit down, and write a new poem or, failing that, ask the Lyceum to postpone the lecture until his inspiration returned. In a calmer mood, Poe might even have realized that appearing in Boston, after all his disparagement of the literati of that city, was not the best idea, especially in his unstable state.

A week before the scheduled lecture, he visited T. D. English, editor of the *Aristidean,* visibly intoxicated and disheveled. English, who had mocked Poe in the novel *The Doom of the Drinker,* urged Poe to postpone the Boston lecture until he could deliver the promised poem. But Poe answered that he needed the fifty-dollar honorarium (about $1,500 today) and, besides, he had a scheme for dealing with the proud Boston community.

At the Boston Odeon, Caleb Cushing, an American diplomat, was scheduled to speak before Poe. Poe asked members of the platform committee to meet him at his hotel and accompany him to his room to retrieve his manuscript. In the room he rummaged through his trunk for the text. He had written neither a lecture nor a new poem. Cushing spoke for an hour and a half, in the elevated style of nineteenth-century oratory. Finally, it was Poe's turn. Dressed in black, as always, he stood in front of the audience he had so often disparaged and began with a long apology for the inferiority of the poem he was about to read, pronouncing it a work of "general imbecility" and "unworthy a *Bostonian* audience." Thomas Wentworth Higginson, then a student at Harvard, later mentor to Emily Dickinson, would recall that Poe attacked didactic poetry of the kind expected on such occasions and promised that the poem he was going to recite was not didactic.

Poe began to read "Al Aaraaf," now retitled "The Messenger Star," published when he was twenty years old, a poem hard enough to follow with a text in front of you but often impenetrable when only heard. Later Poe would claim (rightly) he was drunk when he read the poem. Some listened respectfully, but others began to leave. When he finished the 264-line poem, Poe was asked to recite "The Raven," and the recitation was well-received, as it almost always was.

Poe may have felt he'd saved the evening by reciting his most famous work, but the Boston newspapers the next morning described an audience exhausted by the length and obscurity of "The Messenger Star," offended by his remarks about didactic poetry, unimpressed by Poe's professed humility and comments about a "Bostonian audience." Poe did not improve the impression he'd made by asserting, at the reception following the lecture, that "The Messenger Star" had been written before he was twelve years old. A columnist for the *Boston Evening Transcript* mocked him as Poe had mocked Longfellow.

Yet Higginson and his friends remembered the evening as a happy event. Of the verses of "Al Aaraaf," he recalled: "They produced no very distinct impression on the audience until Poe began to read the maiden's song . . . the audience became hushed, and, as it were, breathless; there seemed no life in the hall but his. . . . I felt that we had been under the spell of some wizard."

Poe poured gasoline on the flames of resentment in Boston by bragging about his scheme to put one over on the Bostonians. "We have been quizzing the Bostonians," he wrote, "and one or two of the more stupid of their editors and editresses have taken it in high dudgeon." Newspapers across the country noticed his remarks about the Bostonians and questioned the logic of his assertions. The sources of Poe's absurd behavior when under attack go back to his days in the house of John Allan. When Allan belittled him or accused him, his refuge was his sense of intellectual and artistic superiority. Poe retreated further into his Byronic pose of contempt for the opinions of the Bostonian world. His father had responded with similar rage to critics in Boston. A writer in the *St. Louis Reveille* observed that "if [Poe] had as much tact as talent, he would make success for half a dozen papers."

Nothing in Poe's career elicits our sympathy more than this episode of the Boston lecture and its aftermath. Again and again, Poe would try to rewrite his life as he might revise a story. His imagination was his best sanctuary, as he entangled himself deeper in a fabric of illusions.

15

"THE DOMAIN OF ARNHEIM"

IN THE TURBULENCE OF HIS NEW FAME, POE WOULD BECOME sole editor and owner of the *Broadway Journal,* from October 24, 1845, to January 1846. Then, for lack of funds, he would see the magazine fold. For years he'd dreamed of having his own magazine, but when he actually found himself in the editor's chair, he was unable to secure the necessary backers or loans to sustain the weekly. Poe's downward spiral with the *Broadway Journal* can be traced in the letters his partner Briggs wrote to James Russell Lowell. At first Briggs had been dazzled by Poe's brilliance. But by June 29, 1845, he wrote to Lowell of Poe, "He has some good points, but, taken altogether, he is badly made up."

Some who worked with Poe on the *Broadway Journal* had kinder memories of the poet. Alexander T. Crane, an office boy, would later recall: "Not a great while after I had gone to work on the paper, on a hot August afternoon, while wrapping and addressing Journals, I was overcome with the heat and fainted dead away. . . . When I recovered consciousness . . . Poe was bending over me bathing my wrists and temples in cold water."

In the frenzy of editing the *Broadway Journal* and the aftermath of the Boston Lyceum debacle, Poe had written to Fanny Osgood near the end of October 1845: "Business, of late, has made of me so great a slave that I shall not be able to spend an evening with you until Thursday next." On November 13, 1845, Poe would write to his friend Evert Duyckinck, "I

FIG. 26. Elizabeth Fries Ellet (1818–77). A successful poet, writer, and translator, Mrs. Ellet sought a close relationship with Poe in 1846 but became his enemy when offended by a remark he made in anger in 1846. For the rest of his life, she denounced him as immoral and dishonorable. (Courtesy of the Edgar Allan Poe Museum, Richmond, Virginia)

really believe that I have been mad—but indeed I have had abundant reason to be so."

The consequences of his rumored affair with Frances Osgood did not end with her removal to Albany. Poe began another flirtation with twenty-seven-year-old Mrs. Elizabeth Fries Ellet (fig. 26). Mrs. Ellet was a writer and scholar, wealthy, ambitious. She had married a professor of chemistry at South Carolina College in Columbia. Mrs. Ellet remained in New York City and was a frequent guest at the same salons Poe attended. Some who knew her considered Mrs. Ellet a busybody and hypocrite. She revenged herself on Rufus Griswold for some critical comments about her by writing poison letters to both his second wife and his third.

As Poe presided over the *Broadway Journal* in its closing days, he featured Elizabeth Ellet again and again and praised her sentimental and conventional verse. She wrote flirtatious invitations to Poe, suggesting he visit her at home. Like many prudes, Mrs. Ellet judged her own behavior by different standards than those she demanded of others. As Fanny Osgood had retreated to Albany, pregnant with her third child, Poe may have felt drawn to Mrs. Ellet, whose husband was far away in South Carolina.

Poe found himself entangled in a romantic web too complex for us to sort out. Early in the new year of 1846, Mrs. Ellet visited Poe at his home on Amity Street. It seems she wanted to follow Fanny Osgood's example and become friends with the ailing and innocent Virginia. Mrs. Elizabeth Oakes Smith would later give her version of what happened: "A certain lady of my acquaintance [Mrs. Ellet] fell in love with Poe and wrote a love-letter to him. . . . This lady went to his house one day; she heard Fanny Osgood and Mrs. Poe having a hearty laugh . . . as they read over a letter. The lady listened and found it was hers, when she walked into the room and snatched it from their hands." Mrs. Ellet accused Fanny Osgood of indiscretion, embarrassing her in the eyes of other women writers.

Ellet persuaded Fanny Osgood that her reputation was in danger and that the two women authors should descend on the Poe apartment and demand all of Fanny's letters. Surprised and angered by their intrusion, Poe snarled that Mrs. Ellet should "look after her own letters." Two years later Poe would explain to Helen Whitman what happened: "I permitted myself to say what I should not have said—I had no sooner uttered the words, than *I felt* their dishonor."

Poe returned Mrs. Ellet's letters, but she pretended he hadn't. According to Poe's friend-then-enemy T. D. English, Mrs. Ellet's brother threatened Poe if he didn't yield up the already returned letters. Frightened, Poe called on English to borrow a pistol, but English urged him to apologize and put the wretched episode behind him. They argued and fought, and English beat Poe up. Poe was driven under a sofa, and English hit his face repeatedly with a signet ring. Later Poe would brag that he had given English "a flogging which he will remember to the day of his death." As his magazine foundered, Poe apologized to Mrs. Ellet and sought comfort in the bottle.

The *Broadway Journal,* the only magazine Poe would ever (briefly) own himself, ceased publication on January 3, 1846. In his valedictory notice to readers, he explained: "Unexpected engagements demanding my whole attention, and the objects being fulfilled, so far as regards myself personally . . . I now, as its editor, bid farewell—as cordially to foes as to friends."

Poe lay in bed for weeks recovering, and when Valentine's Day came, Virginia composed a valentine to cheer Edgar. It is our only example of her writing. The first letters of the lines would spell his name.

Ever with thee I wish to roam—
Dearest my life is thine.
Give me a cottage for my home
And a rich old cypress vine,
Removed from the world with its sin and care
And the tattling of many tongues.
Love alone shall guide us when we are there
Love shall heal my weakened lungs;
And Oh, the tranquil hours we'll spend,
Never wishing that others may see!
Perfect ease we'll enjoy, without thinking to lend
Ourselves to the world and its glee—
Ever peaceful and blissful we'll be.

By February 1846 Anne Lynch and other fashionable hostesses had dropped Poe from their guest lists. Before the fame of "The Raven" he'd been an outsider, and now he was an outsider again. His behavior in Boston and afterward had further isolated him from the polite world of letters, and the collapse of the *Broadway Journal* left him in debt and without a forum for his reviews. Poe's comments on contemporary writers in "The Literati of New York" and "Marginalia" had also alienated former acquaintances in the magazine world.

Yet Mary E. Hewitt remained loyal to Poe, even as rumors of scandal spread. On April 14, 1846, she wrote to him: "All Bluedom misses you from its charmed circle, and we often ask when are we to have Mr. Poe back again among us." It was also around this time that Wiley & Putnam reissued *The Raven and Other Poems* and his *Tales* combined in a single volume.

Muddy wrote to Thomas Holley Chivers about Poe: "I do believe that the poor boy is deranged! His wife is now at the point of death . . . and cannot bear to see him! Oh! my poor Virginia! She cannot live long! She is wasting away day by day. . . . seeing this continually in poor Eddy, would kill her—for she dotes upon him! . . . would to God that she died before she had ever seen him." Muddy may have been hoping Chivers would send her some money.

Miraculously, in this period of feuds and flirtations, Poe was able to finish two pieces that are among his most important tales, "The Cask of

Amontillado" and "The Domain of Arnheim." The latter would become one of Poe's most memorable statements on aesthetics, nature, and art. The opening sentence of "The Cask of Amontillado" is often quoted by creative writing instructors as the perfect beginning of a story of intrigue and mystery: "The thousand injuries of Fortunato I had borne as best I could; but when he ventured upon insult, I vowed revenge." The name Fortunato adds color and a touch of the exotic.

For Carnival, Fortunato is wearing a fool's cap with bells and a motley costume. He is merry and seemingly unaware of the narrator's malice. We discover from the conversation that the narrator's name is Montresor, meaning "My treasure." So the friend-enemies are "fortune" and "treasure," suggesting kinship, even close identity. With a torch they descend into the tunnels and caverns under Montresor's ancient family home. The alert reader is already thinking of returning to the womb of Mother Earth.

"The Cask of Amontillado" is one of Poe's most perfect stories or prose poems. The atmosphere of cold and dripping cellars entices the reader as well as Fortunato into a dead-end trap. For Daniel Hoffman, Montresor and Fortunato are two sides of the same person. Montresor, the Schemer, and Fortunato, the Dreamer, are in deadly conflict, though Fortunato doesn't realize it. It is a narrative of Montresor, analytical, acquisitive, controlling, imagining slights and insults from the unsuspecting Fortunato, more passive, dreaming, playful, fun-loving, poet, whose weakness is pride in his discrimination and taste.

Montresor carries a trowel, which occasions a joke about Freemasonry. "You are not of the masons," Fortunato says. "Yes, yes," I said, "yes, yes." But Fortunato answers, "You? Impossible! A mason?" The Anti-Masonic movement of Poe's time was supposedly democratic, opposing the wealth and power of the Masons. Some of Poe's acquaintances, including William Wirt, belonged to the Anti-Masonic Party. Montresor taunts Fortunato, suggesting he might consult Luchesi for an opinion on the newly purchased amontillado. Poe loved to play with names, in this case perhaps pitting *fortune* against *luck*.

After Montresor has led Fortunato into a hole in the wall and chained him to the rock, the reveler begins to sober up, waking to his possible fate. "'The Amontillado!' ejaculated my friend, not yet recovered from his astonishment. . . . 'True,' I replied, 'the Amontillado.'" As Montresor quickly begins to seal the opening in the wall with stones and mortar, Fortunato yells, and the narrator answers with even louder yells, exulting in his cruelty. The story ends: "I forced the last stone into its position. . . . For the half of a century no mortal has disturbed them. *In páce requiescat!*" The analytical mind has suppressed the offending poetic imagination and exults in triumph.

In the words of Thomas O. Mabbott, it "is perhaps the most moral of [Poe's] Tales. The murderer at the end remembers that his victim rests in peace. That is something the criminal had been unable to do for fifty years." In mortal years the rational is the victor, exulting in hubris and efficiency. In eternity the poetic spirit of play and imagination is always the winner.

It was in "The Domain of Arnheim," written in 1846 and published in *Columbian Lady's and Gentleman's Magazine* in March 1847, that Poe defined his aesthetics most fully. He had published the essay "The Landscape Garden" earlier but was not satisfied until he had expanded the story of Ellison and his attempt to build the ultimate work of art, a paradise on earth. In "The Landscape Garden," published in *Lady's Companion* in October 1842, Poe had discussed at length the fabulously rich character named Ellison and his ideas of landscape architecture. Drawing on the discussions of landscape design that had been popular in Britain and Europe for the past century, Poe made the case that the perfection of design is not to be found in nature alone, nor in geometrical forms, but in art that is made to *appear* perfectly natural. Two landscape painters who had a profound influence on Poe's thought were Claude Lorrain and Salvator Rosa. In his fiction Poe liked to dissolve the boundary between fact and fantasy, between life and death; in his aesthetics he liked to blur the distinction between nature and art. Making use of ideas from the essays of Hazlitt on landscape painting, the writings of Andrew Jackson Downing, and Hermann von Pückler-Muskau's *Tour of England, Ireland and France,* Poe had Ellison define his aesthetics: "My friend could not fail to perceive that the creation of the Landscape-Garden offered to the true muse the most magnificent of opportunities. . . . In the multiform of the tree, and in the multicolor of the flower, he recognized the most direct and the most energetic efforts of Nature at physical loveliness."

It has been suggested that Thomas Jefferson, who expended so much effort and wealth perfecting Monticello, may have been the prototype for Ellison. Poe also remembered the enchantment of the Ellis garden in Richmond and calls his character Ellison. The natural-seeming landscape can include the strange, the surprising. In the twentieth century the historian A. O. Lovejoy would work out these concepts in an essay called "The Chinese Origin of a Romanticism," arguing that the Romantic movement in Europe was partly inspired by the idea of the artificial though "natural"-appearing landscape in Asian garden design.

As we have seen, the name Arnheim had special associations for Poe. In a letter to Helen Whitman on October 18, 1848, he wrote: "Meantime I enclose . . . 'The Domain of Arnheim' which . . . expresses *much of my soul*. . . . This story contains more of myself and of my inherent tastes and habits of thought than anything I have written."

Mr. Ellison, the theorist and creator of "The Landscape Garden," had inherited unexpectedly a fortune vast almost beyond reckoning. He gives a certain portion of it to charity but devotes the rest of the 450 million dollars (about 13.5 billion dollars today) to building his own Xanadu. Ellison believed there were four conditions for individual happiness: life in the open air, the love of a beautiful woman, freedom from ambition, and a large and consuming project. Ellison has the spirit of a poet, but he wants to make something that transcends mere words.

Ellison realizes that while natural species, trees, shrubs, and flowers cannot be improved on, it is in the arrangement that one might "convey the sentiment of spiritual interference." In "The Domain of Arnheim" Poe shows the influence of the Hudson River school of painters, so popular in his time. For them the rivers, the Catskills, the Adirondacks, the sunsets and storms and twilights, were hieroglyphs of the soul. In his writing about landscape and the natural world, Poe was very much a part of that spirit of his times. He theorized that marriage was the ultimate culmination of Ellison's art. Poe's narrator describes the grandeur of Ellison's plan: "Above all, it was in the sympathy of a woman, not unwomanly, whose loveliness and love enveloped his existence in the purple atmosphere of Paradise, that Ellison thought to find, *and found*, exemption from the ordinary cares of humanity." The happy marriage is definitive, essential, to paradise.

As noted, Poe loved to quote Bacon's epigram that there is nothing beautiful without some element of the strange. The traveler to Arnheim is, "moreover, enwrapt in an exquisite sense of the strange." An ivory canoe bears the visitor through a gate to the vista of Arnheim, then "commences a rapid descent into a vast amphitheatre entirely begirt with purple mountains. . . . Meantime the whole Paradise of Arnheim bursts upon the view . . . and, upspringing confusedly from amid all, a mass of semi-Gothic, semi-Saracenic architecture, sustaining itself as if by miracle in mid air; glittering in the red sunlight with a hundred oriels, minarets, and pinnacles; and seeming the phantom handiwork, conjointly, of the Sylphs, of the Fairies, of the Genii, and of the Gnomes."

Those familiar with Poe's work will remember the red setting orgasmic moon that flares through the splitting House of Usher as it crumbles into the tarn. And everywhere in Arnheim there are circles, basins, amphitheaters, lined with walls of shrubbery. "The Domain of Arnheim" is a culmination of Poe's thought about aesthetics, from the exotic eastern trees and architecture to the synesthetic climax, implying the kinship of the horrific and the ecstatic.

By stopping the tale where he does, Poe avoids any details of Ellison's life with his bride inside the magic castle. He gives us a clue in the last sentence, moving from Sylphs to Fairies to the Genii of Eastern tales to the Gnomes of Norse fables and horror stories. Left out of this parable of the creation of paradise and the perfect marriage is any mention of the thousands of laborers, perhaps enslaved men and women, needed to construct and maintain such an ultimate Eden.

IN EARLY MARCH 1846 POE HAD MOVED HIS FAMILY FROM 85 Amity Street to a house at Turtle Bay on the East River. Rumors were abroad that he was being treated at an asylum in Utica, New York. The move was an attempt to escape the scandals and literary gossip that had grown up around him and troubled Virginia. And it was hoped fresh air would benefit her declining health. The Miller family, who owned the house at Turtle Bay, provided the Poes with fresh eggs and milk and other products from their farm.

Virginia was now unable to leave the house, and the Millers' daughter later recalled that she promised to serve as Poe's "guardian angel" after her death. To Elizabeth Oakes Smith, Virginia said, "I know I shall die soon . . . but I want to be as happy as possible, and make Edgar happy." Poe was not well either, but he sometimes rowed on the river in his host's boat and went for refreshing swims. On a trip to Baltimore, presumably to lecture, he was observed drinking in a tavern, and his return was delayed by illness. Papers as far away as St. Louis and New Orleans reported that he was deranged. His Baltimore friend Joseph E. Snodgrass, a temperance lecturer, wrote that Poe was suffering from "brain fever." Poe turned down invitations to read poems at the University of Vermont and Dickinson College in Pennsylvania.

In May 1846 the Poes rented a cottage at Fordham, thirteen miles north of the city, owned by the Valentine family. It would be Virginia's last residence, and Poe's also, in an area of woods and fields, with hills and views of Long Island. There were orchards nearby and the Bronx River. The rent was one hundred dollars a year (about three thousand dollars today). The house had a porch, a smooth lawn, and cherry trees. There were three rooms downstairs, kitchen, bedroom for Virginia, and a small parlor. The second floor was divided into two snug rooms, one with a fireplace. Mrs. Mary Gove Nichols, a writer as well as a homeopathist and phrenologist, visited the Poes there in 1846 and left this description: "Poe's voice was melody itself. He always spoke low, even in a violent discussion, compelling his hearers to listen if they would know his opinion. . . . The cottage had an air of taste and gentility that must have been lent to it by the presence of its inmates. So neat, so poor, so unfurnished, and yet so charming a dwelling I never saw."

Visitors to the Fordham cottage would later remember that there were songbirds in cages at the house. Writing years later, Muddy would recall a somewhat idealized portrait of Poe at Fordham: "He passed the greater part of the morning in his study, &, after he had finished his task for the day, he worked in our beautiful flower-garden or read and recited poetry to us." Another visitor remembered Poe picking cherries from a tree in the yard and throwing them down to Virginia. When a sudden hemorrhage stained the front of Virginia's white gown, Poe jumped from the tree and carried her inside.

If Virginia had not been dying, the Poes' time at Fordham might indeed have been an idyl. There was a hill with a "rocky ledge" nearby where Poe liked to sit and look out over the countryside. Poe also strolled along the Croton Aqueduct and paused at the High Bridge to view the distant city. The cottage was not far from St. John's College (later Fordham University), and Poe became friends with some of the faculty there, especially Father Edward Doucet, who invited Poe to use the college library. Poe was much impressed by the charm and sophistication of the Jesuits. "'They were highly cultivated gentlemen and scholars,' he said, 'smoked, drank, and played cards like gentlemen, and never said a word about religion.'"

In this period, when Poe was ill and unable to work, while Sissy was dying, he could still summon his courage and assert to Philip Pendleton Cooke on August 9, 1846: "I have *magnificent* objects in view—may I but live to accomplish them!" It was while living at Fordham that Poe revised "The Landscape Garden" as "The Domain of Arnheim." Walking in the fields and orchards, along the river, he dreamed of the ultimate work of art, a new Eden.

As already observed, some Poe scholars have believed that Poe suffered from a weak heart as early as his West Point days. His binges had hurt him, along with inadequate nutrition, and perhaps the use of tobacco. But the overwhelming stress of his life at this time was the continuing decline and approaching death of Virginia. Week after week and month after month, he watched his cherished child-bride, now twenty-four, suffer, coughing, struggling to breathe, vomiting blood. Added to Poe's anguish about his own health and Virginia's struggle to breathe was the perennial shortage of money. The final months of Virginia's life were among the most agonizing he would ever know. It was believed that Poe suffered from consumption also.

To make matters even worse, Poe had let himself go much too far in the sketches called "The Literati of New York." The idea was to make money by penning thumbnail, entertaining portraits of well-known writers. But Poe used some of the sketches to repay those who had offended him. He chastised acquaintances for their grammar and mocked the writing style of others, including his former partner at the *Broadway Journal*, Charles F. Briggs. Briggs retaliated by publishing a lampoon of Poe's looks and manners.

Poe also used the "Literati" controversy to vent his resentment at the treatment of southern and western writers by critics and editors in the Northeast: "Political sectional animosities . . . result [in] a depreciation of Southern and Western talent, which upon the whole is greater, more vivid, fresher, than that of the North."

At Fordham, Poe, isolated from the literary world, told Mrs. Mary Gove Nichols: "I write from a mental necessity—to satisfy my taste and my love of art. Fame forms no motive power with me." When asked about compromising his critical standards in reviews of those who had helped him, Poe shot back, "Would you blame a man for not allowing his sick wife to starve?" On Mrs. Nichols's next visit, Poe apologized for claiming to despise fame. "I love fame . . . I would drink to the very dregs the glorious intoxication. . . . No man lives, unless he is famous!"

"The Literati of New York" illustrates Poe's curious sense of humor. Supremely sensitive about his own appearance, his writing, he seemed genuinely surprised when others took offense at his derision of their looks, their work, their reputations. It was Poe's sketch of Thomas D. English, his former friend, that caused the most trouble. Poe accused English of trying to cover up his inferior knowledge of grammar by blaming printers and proofreaders. No doubt Poe was remembering his fight with English at the time of the Ellet affair and the novel English had written satirizing Poe.

English published a stinging reply, describing "Literati" as especially fit for toilet paper, and he reported that Poe had been too drunk to give a lecture at New York University or write a new poem for the Boston Lyceum appearance. English had known Poe for years and had much ammunition in his arsenal. Of Poe's drinking, he added, "The kennels [gutters] of Philadelphia streets, from which I once kindly raised him, have frequently had the pleasure of his acquaintance." English hinted he knew even more damning facts about Poe that he hesitated to reveal. Then he added two accusations that had legal implications. He said Poe had secured a loan from him "under false pretenses" and that Poe had been guilty of forgery, against Poe's own uncle.

The fury of English's attack surprised even seasoned journalists like Horace Greeley and frenemies such as Rufus Griswold. Weak and ailing in his isolation, Poe cobbled together a rejoinder, "Mr. Poe's Reply to Mr. English and Others," filling fifty pages with vituperation and insult. Poe admitted he had made some mistakes and was subject to one weakness English had accused him of, namely intoxication. Poe explained he was also dealing with a "terrible evil" he could not name: "The errors and frailties which I deplore, it cannot at least be asserted that I have been the coward to deny."

Poe sued not English but the owner of the *Mirror,* in which English's accusations had appeared. Poe's lawyer, Enoch L. Fancher, asked for $5,000 in damages (about $150,000 today). Newspapers accused Poe of maligning others while unable to accept criticism of himself. On July 20, 1846, Poe saw himself described in the *Mirror:* "A poor creature . . . called at our office the other day, in a condition of sad, wretched imbecility, bearing in his feeble body the evidences of evil living . . . we could not even entertain a feeling of contempt for one who was evidently committing a suicide upon his body, as he had already done upon his character."

A number of friends advised Poe to calm down and put the vendetta behind him. On July 30, 1846, William Gilmore Simms wrote: "Suffer me to tell you frankly . . . that you are now perhaps in the most perilous period of your career. . . . You are no longer a boy. 'At thirty wise or never!'" But English was just beginning his attack on Poe. As a serial in the *Mirror,* he published another novel called *1844, or The Power of the S.F.*, portraying Poe as Marmaduke Hammerhead, not just a drunk but also a lunatic. The novel was so popular it was later reprinted in book form.

In the depths of despair and ostracization, Poe thought of expanding the "Literati" into a book, called *Phases of American Literature,* breaking new ground in American criticism and revenging himself on his contemporaries. Some scholars have thought Poe completed that work and that it was later destroyed, possibly by Rufus Griswold.

16

VIRGINIA'S LAST DAYS

ON JUNE 12, 1846, POE HAD WRITTEN A LETTER TO SISSY, HIS only letter to just her that has survived. This document gives further evidence of the enduring affection and responsibility he felt for Virginia and the guilt for his involvement in her life: "My Dear Heart, My dear Virginia! our mother will explain to you why I stay away from you this night . . . keep up your heart in all hopefulness, and trust yet a little longer—In my last great disappointment, I should have lost my courage *but for you*—my little darling wife."

Sissy's sickness, vulnerability, her childlike innocence, unnerved Poe. Guilt for marrying her so young, perhaps for the sexual demands he'd made before, or even after, her illness, drove him away from their home periodically on binges. Even in her illness, Sissy had continued to sew, when she was strong enough, to bring in extra pennies. On her better days she "was always laughing, and loved to have children about her." On her worst days Sissy coughed and gasped for breath, too weak to speak or stand. When she felt well enough, she played with the Valentine children. A neighbor named Susan Cromwell would recall that Poe also entertained the children: "Sometimes he would play ball with us children while his wife laughed and looked on."

On June 17, 1846, Poe received a letter from Nathaniel Hawthorne that may have cheered him a little. "I confess . . . that I admire you rather as a writer of tales than as a critic upon them, I . . . could never fail to recognize your force and originality in the former."

That fall more women visited Virginia and Edgar at Fordham and brought money and other gifts. Poe himself was ill much of the time, while Muddy, strong as ever, looked after both her children and kept the house immaculate. As he watched Sissy dying, Poe experienced further humiliation. Besides his war of words with T. D. English and his lawsuit with the *Mirror*, he had the shame of seeing his poverty exposed in the newspapers and a public appeal for assistance to the Poe family. On December 15, 1846, the *New York Morning Express* published a feature headlined "Illness of Edgar A. Poe": "We regret to learn that this gentleman and his wife are both dangerously ill with the consumption. . . . We are sorry to mention the fact that they are so far reduced as to be barely able to obtain the necessaries."

On December 20, 1846, the poet Mary Hewitt wrote to Fanny Osgood: "The Poe's [*sic*] are in the same state of physical & pecuniary suffering . . . the matter has got into print—very much to my regret, as I fear it will hurt Poe's pride." Other newspapers reprinted the notice. Even the *Mirror*, which Poe had sued, asked readers to help the unfortunate author and his family. Poe's friend Willis wrote an editorial for the *Home Journal* praising Poe and asking the public to assist him and his family. Willis acknowledged Poe's struggles with alcohol and promised to forward any contributions he received to the poet. Willis's intentions were kind and generous, but for a man of Poe's pride, such appeals, publishing to the world his desperate poverty, must have been torture.

On December 30, 1846, Poe wrote to Willis: "That I am 'without friends' is a gross calumny, which I am sure *you* never could have believed . . . I am getting better, and may add—if it be any comfort to my enemies—that I have little fear of getting worse. The truth is, I have a great deal to do; and I have made up my mind not to die till it is done." Grieved by Virginia's approaching death, sick himself, broke and unable to work, Poe gathered up the will power to remind his friend that he still had things to accomplish. The *Morning Express* feature said that *both* Poe and his wife were suffering from consumption. Given Poe's many periods of disability, that is one credible explanation for his illness, along with a weak heart, and for his death three years later.

As Sissy's end approached, Poe's cousin from Baltimore, Elizabeth Herring Smith, visited, as did Mary Starr Jennings. Eliza White, daughter of the first editor of the *Southern Literary Messenger,* also came. But the woman who did the most for the Poes at this time, and would continue to aid Poe and Muddy after Virginia's death, was the widow Mrs. Marie Louise Shew, author of *Water-Cure for Ladies,* promoting health for women through exercise, correct diet, clean water, and avoidance of tobacco and alcohol. (See fig. 7.)

As she lay dying, Sissy was warmed by Poe's old West Point overcoat and the cat Catterina, which rested on her chest. Marie Louise Shew brought a feather coverlet to keep the patient warm and also ordered a case of wine to revive Sissy's spirits. Poe did not drink any of the medicinal wine. Marie Louise, called "Loui," was twenty-five years old and lived in Greenwich Village, where she painted watercolors. She was a country doctor's daughter and had a special interest in medicine herself. Loui Shew began coming to Fordham several times a week. On January 29, 1847, both Loui Shew and Mary Starr Jennings were at the Fordham cottage. Very near her end, Sissy took a picture of Poe from beneath her pillow and, after kissing the likeness, handed it to Loui.

According to Mary Starr's later account, Sissy waited until Muddy was out of the room, then placed Mary's hand in Poe's and said, "Mary, be a friend to Eddie, and don't forsake him; he always loved you, didn't you, Eddie?" Before she left for the city, Loui urged Poe to remain calm as Sissy's death was very near. Struggling for breath, Sissy passed a painful night. As the extremities of her body grew icy, Poe rubbed Sissy's hands and Muddy her feet.

Sissy died the next day, January 30. Notices of her passing appeared in the New York newspapers on the first of February. It was Loui Shew who made the funeral arrangements, bought a coffin and funeral clothes. It was possibly Loui who made a watercolor portrait of Sissy after her death, our only likeness of her from "life." It is said that Mary Starr Jennings provided a mourning suit for Poe. Muddy offered to sell Virginia's gold thimble for ten dollars, but Mary could not afford it.

On February 2 Sissy was buried in the vault of the Valentine family. It was a bitter cold day, but even so, Willis, Duyckinck, and several friends attended and accompanied the coffin to the Dutch Reformed church half a mile from the cottage. For the burial Poe wrapped the down comforter Loui had given Sissy around his shoulders. As he had promised Loui, he remained calm, perhaps numb now that the worst he'd feared so long had happened.

In gratitude Poe wrote three poems to Marie Louise Shew. Of "The Beloved Physician" only fragments remain. The second, "To M.L.S.," given to Loui on Valentine's Day, 1847, lacked inspiration but expressed sincere sentiment. The poems were in blank verse, which suggests Poe was writing quickly, since he highly valued rhyme. The third poem, written later the same year, is something of an anomaly among Poe's poems. Without the irony or guilt or the symbolism of his major poems and seemingly dashed off, it still has a charge of inspiration, revealing the intensity of Poe's attachment to the nonliterary and supposedly plain-looking Loui Shew. He called the poem simply "To ——."

> The pen falls powerless from my shivering hand.
> With thy dear name as text, though bidden by thee,
> I cannot write—I cannot speak or think,
> Alas, I cannot feel; for 'tis not feeling,
> This standing motionless upon the golden
> Threshold of the wide-open gate of dreams,
> Gazing, entranced, adown the gorgeous vista,
> And thrilling as I see upon the right,
> Upon the left, and all the way along
> Amid empurpled vapors, far away
> To where the prospect terminates—*thee only.*

"To ——" gives us a hint of the poems Poe might have written in a more confident, "natural" voice had his circumstances been different. The critic Patrick Quinn believed Poe's tales were much better than his poems because the stories were written quickly and the poems were overworked. Had Poe lived longer, he might have combined his great prose gifts with other blank verse poems.

Poe came to rely on Loui Shew's kindness and her visits, as did Muddy. He stayed at Loui's house in Greenwich Village more than once. Week after week she made her way to Fordham, bringing her cheer and practicality, money, and other gifts. The legend arose that Poe often haunted Virginia's grave in the months after her death, as he was said to have visited Jane Stanard's years earlier. In the nineteenth century such mourning was considered honorable and dignified, a sign of character and unceasing devotion.

According to one source, Poe visited Fanny Osgood in Albany after Virginia's death and asked her to marry him, but she refused. While he mourned Virginia, Poe had the satisfaction, probably the surprise, of winning his lawsuit against the publishers of the *Mirror.* He was awarded $225 (about $6,750 today) in damages for the libel and court costs of $101.72 (approximately $3,000 today). Unexpectedly, Poe had more money in his pocket than he'd seen in years. He ordered a fine black suit and some furnishings for the Fordham cottage. And he began or continued work on a new poem.

Some critics have called "Ulalume—A Ballad" Poe's finest poem. It is certainly one of his most memorable, and it serves as a fitting companion to "The Raven." Both poems are intended to create a mesmeric effect, though "Ulalume" is more explicitly a poem of guilt, anger, and remorse. It has been observed that the name Ulalume suggests "ululation, or wailing."

> The skies they were ashen and sober;
> The leaves they were crispéd and sere—
> The leaves they were withering and sere:
> It was night, in the lonesome October
> Of my most immemorial year:
> It was hard by the dim lake of Auber,
> In the misty mid region of Weir:—
> It was down by the dank tarn of Auber,
> In the ghoul-haunted woodland of Weir.

One of the strengths of "Ulalume—A Ballad" is that readers can read into it whatever they are looking for. It is another of Poe's poems about marriage, or guilt about marriage, and the dangers of passion. Even those who admire the poem have been puzzled by the last stanza. Some editors have dropped the final stanza, as Helen Whitman recommended to Poe, concluding the poem:

Then my heart it grew ashen and sober
  As the leaves that were crispéd and sere—
  As the leaves that were withering and sere—
And I cried—"It was surely October,
  On *this* very night of last year,
  That I journeyed—I journeyed down here!—
  That I brought a dread burden down here—
  On this night, of all nights in the year,
  Ah, what demon hath tempted me here?
Well I know, now, this dim lake of Auber—
  This misty mid region of Weir:—
Well I know, now, this dank tarn of Auber—
  This ghoul-haunted woodland of Weir."

But the virtues of "Ulalume—A Ballad" are obvious, the haunting repetitions and echoes, the deliciously sad imagery of All Hallows' Eve, when the spirits of the dead rove about, "the dank tarn of Auber" and "the ghoul-haunted woodland of Weir." The biographer George Woodberry pulled out all the stops when describing "Ulalume": "We have, in this poem, the most spontaneous, the most unmistakably genuine utterance of Poe, the most clearly self-portraying work of his hand."

Why does Poe call "Ulalume" a ballad? Ballads are often about superstition, strange shiftings, ghosts, murders, hangings. The ballads Poe was most familiar with would have been Scottish Border ballads, folk ballads such as "Barbara Allen," "The Two Sisters," "Sweet William's Ghost." Ballads were often "narratives of wonder and superstition."

One feature of Poe's genius, as said, was taking popular forms and subjects and elevating them to high art. In "The Rationale of Verse" Poe would compare repetition in poetry to the facets of a gem: "Let us examine a crystal . . . the equality of the sides pleases us; that of the angles doubles the pleasure . . . this pleasure seems to be squared; on bringing to view a third it appears to be cubed, and so on."

In "Ulalume" there is a death so awful the speaker must suppress it. But on Halloween he roams with his soul and is attracted by the planet Astarte (Venus), or romantic sexual love, which he hopes will guide him through the bleak landscape better than the cold Dian, or the moon of chastity. But his soul, or his conscience, warns him there is great danger in following the path of the erotic. The narrator fails to heed the admonition and stumbles on the very thing he sought to avoid: the tomb of his lost love. For like Berenicë and the wife in "The Black Cat," Ulalume must be buried and forgotten. Some think the poem was inspired by Poe's visits to Virginia's grave.

We should not forget that *tomb* rhymes with *womb,* and part of the horror of "Ulalume" is that the speaker lets himself be enticed right back to the place he has struggled to escape, as he yearns for yet another love. But that symbol of new love, which tricks him back to confront the first love, wears horns, like the Devil.

Buried deep in this misty mid-region of Weir is the tomb at the heart of all Poe's most powerful poems and stories about marriage, the body in an unmarked grave of Eliza Arnold Poe. Poems such as "The Raven" and "Ulalume," though somewhat like the magazine verse they resemble, overwritten, with wordplay carried to rococo or parodic extremes, are still haunting and enduring. Poe was playing games, but the games tap into a deeper stratum of terror and guilt at the core of his being, and ours. The more he tried to evade and forget that hypnotic torture of marriage, the more he was tricked back to face it, in the eerie graveyard light just before dawn. The mention of cypresses in the poem suggests a southern setting.

Poe admitted to Helen Whitman that the poem was "in some sense autobiographical." In "Ulalume" Poe had soared to the stratosphere and beyond and into the darkest Hell he carried within himself. The great secret he'd been on the verge of discovering and disclosing he would neither confirm nor define. The Daly daguerreotype of this period seems to show Poe with renewed confidence (fig. 27).

FIG. 27. The Daly daguerreotype, 1847. The origin and subsequent history of this daguerreotype are something of a mystery, but its authenticity is beyond dispute, and it is one of the finest portraits we have of Poe. It was probably taken in the months after Virginia's death. (Courtesy of the Edgar Allan Poe Museum, Richmond, Virginia)

17

LOUI SHEW AND *EUREKA*

MUCH OF WHAT IS KNOWN ABOUT POE IN THE MONTHS AFTER Virginia's death comes from a series of letters Loui Shew wrote to John Ingram, Poe's first major biographer, in the 1870s. From London, Ingram kept up a vast correspondence with anyone who had known Poe, relentless in seeking every scrap of information he could uncover. Loui Shew, now Mrs. Roland S. Houghton, sent him gossipy, disorganized, ungrammatical letters, filled with otherwise lost details about Poe in 1847 and 1848. On January 23, 1875, she wrote about Poe's illness at the time of Virginia's death: "I saved Mr. Poe's life at this time, having been educated medicaly [*sic*] . . . I decided that in his best health, he had leasion [*sic*] on one side of the brain, and as he could not bear stimulants or tonics, without producing insanity, I did not feel much hope."

Twenty-eight years after the events described, her memory may not have been perfect, but the details in her letters sound authentic. Even though several years younger, Mrs. Shew became a mother figure to Poe. We have only a few letters written by Poe to Marie Louise Shew. But each missive shows the intensity of Poe's dependence on this kind daughter of a country doctor. Though she was not beautiful, he may have sought to marry her.

It was after the publication of *Eureka* that Loui began to withdraw from Poe. Poe was devastated by the loss of her friendship and support. In June 1848, sixteen months after Virginia's death, he poured out his loneliness and disappointment in a letter to Loui: "Can it be true Louise that you have the *idea fixed* in your mind to desert your unhappy and unfortunate friend and patient. You did not say so, I know, but for months I have known you were deserting me, not willingly, but none the less surely." Poe's dependence on Loui for more than a year and a half had become deep and essential, as he navigated between grief for Virginia and his obsessive work on *Eureka,* his study of the origin and end of time and matter.

In August 1847 Poe had traveled to Philadelphia, likely to see friends and consult with editors. Once there, he fell ill, probably caused by drinking, and returned to Fordham to be nursed by Muddy. Of the Philadelphia visit, Louis A. Godey wrote to Poe's Maine admirer George Eveleth on August 6, 1847, that Poe "has been here—but it were better for his fame to have staid [*sic*] away." Poe wandered over the grounds of St. John's College for recreation as he recovered. On February 29, 1848, he wrote Eveleth, discussing his hopes for the *Stylus* and describing his reclusive lifestyle: "I rise early, eat moderately, drink nothing but water, and take abundant and regular exercise in the open air. But this is my private life—my studious and literary life—and of course [it] escapes the eye of the world. . . . I am done drinking, forever." According to Dr. Appleton Morgan, who knew Poe at Fordham, Poe did at times break his vow. "It is true, that rarely and infrequently he did give way while here. . . . A gentle word invariably controlled him."

In Muddy's later testimony, Poe began work on *Eureka* near the end of 1847 or at the beginning of 1848. He was entering one of his most extraordinary manic phases. Night after night he sat up scribbling as Muddy brought him cups of coffee. He was so excited he couldn't sleep as he poured onto paper a river of cascading thoughts and images about creation, God, and the end of time. With the old West Point overcoat wrapped around his shoulders, he rushed to get it all down, reworking and expanding ideas from previous letters and stories. Muddy would recall: "He never liked to be alone, and I used to sit up with him, often until four o'clock in the morning, he at his desk, writing, and I dozing in my chair . . . I . . . gave him a cup of hot coffee every hour or two."

Eureka was the work Poe believed he had prepared for all his life, since he'd written the cosmic poem "Al Aaraaf." The treatise or poem he was writing would "revolutionize the world of Physical & Metaphysical Science. I say this calmly—but I say it." As section after section and image after image and insight after insight streamed from Poe's pen in the cold nights of 1847–48, he experienced an eerie confidence, for he was writing the book that only he was destined to write. He'd become the mouthpiece of creation and time, of God, as Milton had taken dictation from the Holy Spirit, as had William Blake. All his life Poe loved and distrusted science by turns. He'd studied Newton and Laplace. Now it was his turn to put it all together.

Eureka has been described as a treatise on creation and cosmology. Poe himself would end by labeling it a prose poem. More accurately, it may be thought of as Poe's longest tale, with elements of his hoaxes of balloon flight, travel to the moon, and the manufacture of gold. The difference is that in his excited state, he lost his sense of irony and perspective. Whatever we choose to label it, *Eureka* is an ambitious work, a dramatic monologue in which a character named Edgar A. Poe searches for, and believes he *finds*, the secret of the universe. It is Poe at his most manic and driven, demonstrating step by step how to break the code of God's creation. He is M. C. Auguste Dupin solving the riddles Aristotle and the Bacon of *Novum Organum* only attempted. John T. Irwin observes that *Eureka* is "at once pre-Socratic and post-Newtonian."

Strangely, many of the insights of *Eureka* resemble ideas of modern physics, including the Big Bang theory, the expansion and contraction of the universe, dark matter and dark energy, and the uncertainty of quantum physics, not to mention the concepts of multiverse and the curvature of space-time. "Space and duration are one," Poe asserted.

Critics and biographers have wrestled with *Eureka* since it was published in 1848. The power of imagination in the work cannot be denied. Its narrative entwining physics and theology and poetry make it kin to Emerson and Thoreau's essays, the poetry of Walt Whitman, and the prophetic poems of William Blake. Poe's knowledge of Laplace's nebular hypothesis, contemporary astronomy, Bacon's scientific method, and Humboldt, is impressive. His images of radiation and condensation of atoms, planets, stars, have a wonderful poetic symmetry.

The special weakness of *Eureka* is its length. As a study of decryption, it should be about 30 pages, not 150. Poe broke his rule of unity of effect with this essay-tale and made *Eureka* much too long to read at one sitting. There is a glitter to *Eureka* that reminds us of someone inspired by amphetamines, talking far into the night long after they have lost their listeners. It is an example of how even genius can be boring, for Poe, the literary histrio, had forgotten that he was, first and last, an entertainer, not a prophet or philosopher, though he had the talent to impersonate either but not for 150 pages.

Another weakness of *Eureka* is that Poe undercuts the seriousness of the work with attempts at burlesque. He cannot resist winking at his reader, even as he holds forth on the origins and secrets of the universe. John Tresch suggests Poe believed "the fabric of reality is an enormous hoax held together by endless smaller hoaxes."

Poe formulated the thesis of *Eureka* in one sentence: *"In the Original Unity of the First Thing lies the Secondary Cause of All Things, with the Germ of their Inevitable Annihilation."* Poe was concerned about the interplay between centrifugal forces and centripetal forces, the combination the poet Ronald Johnson, in the poem "The Unfoldings," once stated "Centripetal, / Centrifugal: / fugue and petal." The narrator of *Eureka* compares the course of events, as the stars are compelled to coalesce, to the construction of a plot in a work of fiction. The irony is that we are reading just such a constructed plot: "The Universe is a plot of God."

As we read the last pages of *Eureka,* we wonder if Whitman, as he composed the 1855 *Leaves of Grass,* might not have read them also. "Electricity, heat, light, magnetism; and more—of vitality, consciousness, and thought—in a word, of spirituality. . . . The Universe has no conceivable end." As Poe concludes his tale, he reveals the great secret toward which he has been tending: "And now—this Heart Divine—what is it? *It is our own.*" And then he waxes even more manic, or Whitmanic: "Nothing is, or can be, superior to any one soul—that each soul is, in part, its own God—its own Creator."

It is surprising, and pleasing, to see that, for all the differences of their careers and reputations, just how deep the artistic and spiritual kinship of the great poets of the American Renaissance was. Poe concludes his prose poem-sermon: "In the meantime bear in mind that all is Life—Life—Life within Life—the less within the greater—and all within the *Spirit Divine.*" The route to Oneness is death. Poe adds in his final note: "That God may be all in all, *each* must become God." We merge in Abraham's bosom.

About Poe's treatise the biographer Jeffrey Meyers is succinct and damning: "Despite recent efforts to explain, justify, and revive *Eureka,* it remains a rambling, incoherent and excruciatingly boring book."

Poe was exhilarated to have finished *Eureka,* and George P. Putnam did agree to bring out the treatise. Putnam has left us an account of Poe's pitch for his book: "Seated at my desk, and looking at me a full minute with his 'glittering eye,' he at length said, 'I am Mr. Poe.' I was 'all ear.' . . . It was the author of 'The Raven' and of 'The Gold Bug!' 'I hardly know,' said the poet, after a pause, 'how to begin what I have to say. It is a matter of profound importance.' . . . An edition of fifty thousand copies might be sufficient to begin with. . . . We *did* venture, not upon fifty thousand, but five hundred." Poe was paid $14 for *Eureka* (roughly $420 today).

Eureka did not sell well. Some admired the ambition and artistry of the book. Others were mystified, and some mocked the grandiosity. Poe himself, especially in his cups, would expound on his cosmic masterpiece to anyone who would listen.

On the night of February 3, 1848, Poe presented a lecture on "The Universe" for the New York Society, quoting and summarizing much of the content of *Eureka.* Maunsell B. Field attended the lecture and left us this impression: "He appeared inspired, and his inspiration affected the scant audience almost painfully . . . his eyes seemed to glow like those of his own raven, and he kept us entranced for two hours and a half."

Poe would continue to revise *Eureka* until the end of his life. A copy of the work owned by the prominent collector and scholar Susan Jaffe Tane has more than four hundred emendations in Poe's own hand. *Eureka* struck some as a threatening work. The book was banned in Russia from 1912 to 1996 as a dangerous and subversive treatise.

18

ANNIE, ELMIRA, AND HELEN

LOUI SHEW'S ADVICE TO POE WAS THAT HE NEEDED A STRONG woman to take charge of him and set his life in order. For the rest of his life, Poe would search for that helpmeet, muse, and beauty who could guide him and make it possible to publish his own magazine, the *Stylus*. Meanwhile, rumors continued to circulate that the "sweet, trusting Fanny had been cruelly seduced . . . by the arrogant Mr. Poe, while his own poor wife lay on a sickbed at home." No longer welcome at Loui's house or in the salons of New York, he looked both north to New England and south to Richmond.

One of the poets who wrote to Poe was Jane Locke of Lowell, Massachusetts, who sent him a number of letters expressing admiration and awe as well as sympathy for his loss and struggle. Jane Locke, born Ermina Starkweather in 1805, was married to Boston attorney John G. Locke, and she published under the name Jane. Poe answered her, not sure if she was married or a widow, matching her poetic sentiment with his own. Poe traveled to Lowell, Massachusetts, where Jane Locke had arranged for him to lecture about "The Women Poets of America." In the talk he singled out Fanny Osgood once more for special praise and gave his de rigueur recitation of "The Raven."

Whatever plans Poe had for finding a new wife, he saw that Jane Locke was not the solution. But the journey to Lowell was not for naught, for at the lecture he met Jane Locke's relative, Mrs. Nancy Richmond, who lived nearby. Nancy, born in 1820, was eleven years younger than Poe. He seemed to fall in love with her instantly, and he would always call her "Annie." Nancy Richmond was tall, lively, good-looking, though not conventionally "pretty," and much involved in local charities. She had light-brown hair and was an enthusiastic lover of music, art, and poetry. She was married to a prosperous paper manufacturer, Charles B. Richmond. She and Poe seemed mutually smitten. Poe spent the evening after the lecture and the next day at the Richmonds' large house on the Concord River. Mrs. Richmond was the mother of a three-year-old daughter. Mrs. George P. Lawrence, Mr. Richmond's niece, would later recall of Annie: "She was a woman of strong character, very determined, with a vein of sentimentality and very enthusiastic about everything. . . . All her life she was given to new fads."

Long after Poe's death, Annie Richmond would recall her first impression of him: "He seemed so *unlike* any other person, I had ever known, that I could not think of him in the same way—he was incomparable—not to be measured by any ordinary standard." Poe would place the gray-eyed Annie Richmond at the climactic moment of his last great landscape story, "Landor's Cottage." (See fig. 9.)

A gathering of admirers at the Richmond house listened to Poe describe the sublime wonders of *Eureka*. There was piano music and ice cream. To Annie's brother Bardwell, Poe told the story of his life and described the long, lingering death of Virginia. Bardwell would recall that Poe stressed that the love between himself and Virginia had been that of "brother and sister." Others had persuaded him to marry Virginia, for her sake. It was an account of his marriage he would repeat to Helen Whitman, at odds with the desperate, suicide-threatening letter written to Muddy in 1835 pleading not to lose Virginia forever. Poe tried to rewrite the narrative of his marriage as he might revise a story.

In the period after Virginia's death, Poe seemed especially drawn to older married or widowed women. Part of the attraction must have been that these women had money and could stabilize his life and help him found the *Stylus*. Still, there is an irony in his courtship of older women we cannot ignore. In the words of the biographer Jeffrey Meyers: "If Poe had been impotent, as Krutch, Auden, and others have suggested, then he would surely have courted innocent virgins . . . rather than experienced wives and worldly widows."

Jane Locke, who seemed poised for a passionate, or at least a poetic, romance, found herself displaced by the younger relative. Anyone who reads the letters Poe wrote to Annie can see the depth of the connection. Annie seemed to intuitively understand Poe. The sincerity and unconditional affection she appeared to offer him became an emotional polestar for Poe in the turmoil of his last year.

Later in the summer of 1848, while Poe was in Richmond, Annie traveled to Fordham from Lowell to spend time with Muddy and listen to stories of Virginia's angelic beauty and personality. Poe would never forget the visit to Muddy as a mark of Annie's devotion and affection for him. Meanwhile, Jane Locke, stirred by Poe's visit to Lowell, even though he had snubbed her by spending more time with the Richmonds, poured her passion into a thirty-one stanza poem called "Ermina's Tale": "I felt as in the presence of a god!"

Reviews of *Eureka* had begun to appear. At first some notices seemed inclined to give the treatise the benefit of the doubt. But in the *Albion* of July 15, 1848, a reviewer began to put some teeth into the response to Poe's new disquisition. "Passing over the manifest tone of self-complacency that runs through this introduction . . . we turned over a few pages, but found to our surprise that all the poetry was in the preface." In the *Boston Evening Transcript* for July 20, Epes Sargent waxed even more skeptical: "The mocking smile of the hoaxer is seen behind his grave mask."

Probably the review that bothered Poe the most was written by Loui Shew's friend Rev. John Henry Hopkins Jr. In the *Literary World* for July 29, Hopkins went into some detail about Poe's theories of gravitation and radiation but attacked "the system of Pantheism which is more or less inwoven into the texture of the whole book."

Following his adventures in Lowell, Poe took a long-planned trip to Richmond in late July. The ostensible purpose was to solicit subscriptions for his repeatedly delayed *Stylus*. Also, he hoped to visit old friends, renew his contacts with the city of his youth, and look in on his sister, Rosalie. And somewhere in the back of his mind, he must have been aware that his sweetheart from 1826, Elmira Royster, was now a wealthy widow, Mrs. Alexander B. Shelton. In 1826 Poe had been penniless. In 1848 Poe was still more or less penniless, but he was also a celebrity, especially in the South. Through the Mackenzies, Poe would have known that Elmira had never lost interest in him. Susan Weiss, who lived in Richmond at that time, would later write: "After his wife's death [Mrs. Shelton] was continually inquiring about him of Thos. MacKenzie [*sic*]."

It's possible that Poe's primary reason for journeying to Richmond in the summer of 1848 was to contact the love of his youth. Now that Virginia was dead and Elmira a widow, it would make sense that his thoughts turned back to his first serious love and to marriage. And it is also possible there had already been letters exchanged between them.

If Poe's main purpose in traveling to Richmond was to find subscribers for the *Stylus* and to renew his romance with Elmira Shelton, he made a poor beginning. He did visit with Rosalie at the Mackenzie's home, Duncan Lodge, and he did call on the new editor of the *Southern Literary Messenger,* John R. Thompson, and sell him the essay "The Rationale of Verse." But after Poe's death, Thompson would recall that Poe also frequented the taverns along the riverfront in Richmond and soon made a spectacle of himself, drunkenly declaiming the wisdom and importance of *Eureka,* stumbling from bar to bar, losing his coat, explaining the origins and end of all creation.

Thompson recorded later that in his drunkenness Poe also tried to fight a duel with John M. Daniel, editor of the *Semi-Weekly Examiner.* Daniel had criticized Poe in his paper, and Poe demanded satisfaction. Luckily, Thompson was able to talk Poe around, and the episode ended without bloodshed. But news of Poe's sprees in the dives of Richmond that summer would add to his notoriety long after his death. Thompson would recall: "Once I found him in a saloon called 'The Alhambra.' . . . He was mounted on a marble-top table, declaiming passages from his then unpublished [*sic*] 'Eureka' to a motley crowd, to whom it was as unintelligible as so much Hebrew."

After Poe's death, John Daniel would offer a harsh assessment of him: "Thousands have seen him drunk in the streets of this city . . . in a state approaching mania." But at some date while in Richmond, Poe must have sobered up. Mrs. Jane Clark would remember that in the summer of 1848, Poe visited her: "There were some other people present, and he read *The Raven* for us. He shut out the daylight and read by an astral lamp." Besides the stories of Poe's drinking in Richmond, J. R. Thompson would later recall of Poe: "As a converser I have never heard his equal except Macaulay."

In late July or early August, Poe gathered the courage to call on Elmira Shelton at her home at 2407 East Grace Street in Richmond. Contacting her must have been one of the main purposes for returning to Richmond, but that first drink had thrown him far off course. There has been some controversy among biographers about whether Poe did or did not visit Elmira in the summer of 1848. The confusion is caused in part by the jumble of Elmira's memories recorded years later, in which she merged events of 1848 and 1849. The preponderance of evidence suggests that Poe first visited her in the summer of 1848.

Though Elmira would later claim to have been surprised when he called on her, we know from Susan Weiss's memoir that Elmira was very much aware of Poe's fame and that she'd asked the Mackenzies repeatedly about Poe's activities. In a letter to Muddy written on September 22, 1849, after she and Poe had become engaged, Elmira would admit that she had been jealous when she saw Poe and Virginia together soon after their marriage in 1836. Elmira had become a devout Episcopalian, and Mr. Shelton had left her a fortune of $70,000 ($2.1 million today). His business had included a line of steamboats on the James River as well as land transportation, and he owned a number of properties, which she supervised.

According to Elmira's later account, Poe called on her on a Sunday morning:

> I was ready to go to church and a servant told me that a gentleman in the parlour wanted to see me. I went down and was amazed to see him—but knew him instantly—He came up to me in the most enthusiastic manner and said: "Oh! Elmira, is this you?" That very morning I told him I was going to church, that I never let anything interfere with that, that he must call again and when he did call again he renewed his addresses. I laughed at it. . . . Then I found out that he was very serious and I became serious. I told him if he would not take a positive denial he must give me time to consider of it. And he said a love that hesitated was not a love for him. But he sat there a long time and was very pleasant and cheerful. He [continued] to visit me frequently but I never engaged myself to him. He begged me when he was going away to marry him. Promised he would be everything I could desire. He said when he left that he was going to New York, to wind up some business and that he would return to Richmond as soon as he ac-

complished it, though he said at the same time that he had a presentment [*sic*] he never should see me any more.

These remarks, recorded by the sculptor Edward Valentine on November 19, 1875, for John Ingram, have confused generations of Poe scholars. Some of the mistakes may be ascribed to Elmira's memory, blending together different events and dates. And Valentine may have misunderstood some of her remarks also. A decade later, Elmira would concede to Dr. John J. Moran, who had treated Poe before his death, that she had indeed been engaged to Poe in 1849 and that Poe was the love of her life. In the statement to Valentine, she is conflating the fact that Poe first called on her on a Sunday morning in the summer of 1848 with his return visit in the summer of 1849. The first clue is in the phrase *renewed his addresses.* While she was hurrying off to church, he had made no addresses. But when he visited her soon after, he did press his case for marriage. But it would be in the summer of 1849 before he "renewed his addresses."

More evidence that Poe had courted Elmira in 1848 is found in Helen Whitman's letters to John Ingram, in which she states that Poe said several times in the fall of 1848 that he *had* visited Elmira that summer. It is understandable that many years later Elmira would confuse the events of 1848 with the visit in the final summer of 1849.

Shaken by Poe's sudden appearance in her parlor, Elmira may have pleaded her church attendance as an excuse to cover her emotions. She did ask him to call again, which he did several times. Mrs. Shelton was a reserved, respectable widow with two children, Southall Bohannan, aged twelve, and Ann Elizabeth, aged nineteen, already married. More than twenty years since their teenage courtship and informal engagement had been broken, Poe and Elmira must have experienced some awkwardness as they renewed their acquaintance. If he proposed marriage to her in 1848, she would have hesitated. Elmira was thought to be practical. She'd known Edgar since he was a boy and knew his temper, imagination, and wayward tendencies.

Though Poe would assure Elmira, according to her later statements, that she was his "lost Lenore," he did not pay her the kind of poetic compliments, as far as we know, he did to Fanny Osgood, Loui Shew, Annie Richmond, and especially Helen Whitman. Had Poe persisted in his courtship of Elmira in the summer of 1848, she might well have agreed to become his wife then. But we will never know, for suddenly Poe received a message from Helen Whitman, a well-known poet and author in Providence, Rhode Island. He packed his trunk and hurried back to New York. We can only guess at Elmira's feelings, having been courted warmly, after so many years, and then suddenly abandoned.

It's possible that if Poe had stayed in Richmond and continued his calls on Elmira, his future might have been very different. As we shall see later, Elmira had some of the same influence over his behavior that Virginia and Muddy had. By leaving Richmond in August 1848, Poe entered the final downward spiral of his life. Maybe it was inevitable, possibly not.

The message Poe received that precipitated his abrupt departure from Richmond was twelve lines of verse from the somewhat mysterious and mystical Helen Whitman:

A low bewildering melody
Is murmuring in my ear—
Tones such as in the twilight wood
The aspen thrills to hear
When Faunus slumbers on the hill
And all the entranced boughs are still.

The jasmine twines her snowy stars
Into a fairer wreath—
The lily through my lattice bars
Exhales a sweeter breath—
And, gazing on Night's starry cope,
I dwell with "*Beauty which is Hope.*"

Poe's fascination with Helen Whitman had been building before his visit to Lowell in June 1848. He'd seen her poems and reviews in newspapers and magazines. Helen Whitman was one of the established poets and critics of her time, a friend of Margaret Fuller and Longfellow, an enthusiastic admirer of Emerson and the Transcendentalists. She was also drawn to contemporary fashions such as spiritualism, hypnosis, and a variety of mystical and occult subjects. Maria Jane McIntosh would later tell Helen

Whitman that when she met Poe at Fordham in June 1848, "on just such a night as this one month ago . . . his whole talk was about you."

Helen Whitman was known in the literary world as a somewhat mysterious, romantic figure. She was very beautiful. Sarah S. Jacobs of Providence remembered that she always seemed to look "above and beyond, but never at you. . . . Her spell was on you from the moment she appeared (and she generally kept you waiting a little)." Another acquaintance would remember: "At one time she wore constantly around her throat a black velvet ribbon pinned with a tiny coffin which a friend had carved for her." Mrs. Whitman preferred flowing colored scarves and veils and carried handkerchiefs soaked in ether "to calm herself." (See fig. 8.)

When Poe had pursued Fanny Osgood to Providence in 1845, at the height of his fame for "The Raven," and perhaps fathered Fanny's child, he'd walked the streets of that city unable to sleep and seen Helen Whitman standing in the moonlight in front of her house. That seemed to him later a portent of a special bond with the Rhode Island poet. When he wrote the second poem called "To Helen," Poe would place Helen Whitman in moonlight in a rose garden, conflating his memory of Elmira among the roses with the poet of Providence.

Mrs. Whitman, on her part, had read Poe's stories and been thrilled by the horror and dramatic power of his writing. She was fascinated by the weird hold the stories and "The Raven" had on the reader. She had inquired about Poe from Fanny Osgood and Anne Lynch. Later she would speak of the "strange spiritual energy or effluence which seemed to surround or ensphere the 'Raven.'" In early 1848 Anne Lynch asked a number of her poet friends to write poems to be read at a Valentine's Day party at her house. Helen Whitman sent a piece called "To Edgar A. Poe," which was read at the gathering on February 14.

Oh, thou grim and ancient Raven,
  From the Night's Plutonian shore,
Oft, in dreams, thy ghastly pinions
  Wave and flutter round my door—
Oft thy shadow dims the moonlight
  Sleeping on my chamber floor!

Helen Whitman was a gifted writer of romantic verse, with delicately erotic, even voluptuous, overtones. When Fanny Osgood saw this poem in the *Home Journal,* she wrote to Helen Whitman, "I see by the *Home Journal* that your beautiful invocation has reached the Raven in his eyrie and I suppose, ere this, he has *swooped* upon your little *dove cote* in Providence. May Providence protect you if he has!"

Poe was excited by the valentine with its delicate suggestiveness. His response was to cut out a page containing the first poem "To Helen" and mail it to Whitman. While he waited for a reply or acknowledgment from Providence, he wrote the longer poem also called "To Helen," describing his first glimpse of Mrs. Whitman at her home in 1845. The second "To Helen," sent to Whitman on June 1, 1848, is not as good as the poem of 1831. It sounds hurried and strident, direct, lacking the classical distance, inspiration, and mystery of the earlier work.

This poem set the tone for the courtship and brief engagement to Helen Whitman. Because of his long feverish letters to her and her later extensive account of their relationship, biographers have devoted considerable ink to the Poe-Whitman affair. And yet there is something strained and hyperbolic about the relationship from the beginning. Neither Poe nor Helen Whitman really needed the other. Each was gifted and accomplished, with stature and recognition in the literary community. It's understandable that they would be drawn to each other, nearing middle age, each strikingly attractive. Poe saw them as the ideal "power couple," him editing the *Stylus,* each a well-known poet and critic, pursuing a vein of the mystical and transcendental. There is more than a hint of the theatrical in their writing and conduct throughout. Yet there is also something about the performance we have to admire, though it eventually degenerated into farce. That Poe could work up such intense addresses to a woman he hardly knew gives us some indication of the power of his imagination and his desperate fantasy of having a wife to comfort and look after him. He hated and feared marriage but could not resist the dream of security and respectability.

Mrs. Whitman, whose maiden name was Power, was born January 19 (Poe's birthday) in 1803 in Providence to Nicholas Power and Anna Marsh Power. In 1828 Helen married John Winslow Whitman, a young Boston lawyer, who died in 1833. As a widow, she lived with her mother and sister at 76 Benefit Street in Providence. As a poet and writer, she had formed friendships with many other authors, including Fanny Osgood, Anne Lynch, and Rufus Griswold.

Suffering supposedly from a weak heart and sensitive nerves, Helen depended on her mother for financial support and had a number of suitors, including her neighbor William Pabodie, also an admirer of Poe's writing. From her portraits we can see that Helen had a haunted, spiritual expression that Poe must have found irresistible. There was much about Helen that was otherworldly. Like Emily Dickinson after her, she dressed mostly in white, with flowing scarves and ribbons. Given Poe's tastes and predilections, Helen Whitman may have seemed more a figure of the next world than of this. In a letter Poe would declare that Helen would be as attractive to him in death as in life: "If you *died*—then at least would I clasp your dear hand in death, and willingly—*oh, joyfully—joyfully—joyfully*—go down *with* you into the night of the Grave."

If much about the Poe-Whitman courtship seems to us artificial, even farcical, it did not seem so to them. Their poems and letters, their recorded conversations, are so overwrought they seem parodic to modern eyes and ears. Both were gifted with words and imagination. But Poe's behavior in the fall of 1848 with both Helen Whitman and Annie Richmond reveals his desperation for a woman to calm him and love him. His imagined feelings for Annie Richmond were deeper, because she was already married happily and out of reach. He could project onto Annie whatever ideals he might need. Helen Whitman was a widow, living, breathing, and ostensibly as much in need of love as he.

Helen had asked Rufus Griswold for information about the poet of "The Raven" and the rumors of his bad behavior. Surprisingly, Griswold replied that Poe had done nothing "exceptionally *wrong*. . . . He had *always* said Poe was not so much to blame in his literary embroilments as were his enemies."

Poe set out for Providence and called on Helen Whitman at 76 Benefit Street on September 21. When he finally encountered her in the flesh, she seemed just as sensitive and ethereal as he had imagined her to be. She put her hand in his and spoke as though short of breath. Helen's life had been troubled also. Her father, Nicholas Power, had deserted his family when Helen was ten, then returned years later, like Hawthorne's Wakefield, but did not live at the house on Benefit Street. Because she believed she suffered from a weak heart, the ether-soaked handkerchiefs were used to ease her nerves when she felt faint. It was thought she was subject to angina pectoris. Helen had never remarried. Her mother, who controlled the family purse strings, discouraged matrimony. In her later years Helen would befriend talented undergraduates at nearby Brown, including John Hay.

On Poe's first visit to Helen, he would stay three days and meet both Mrs. Power and sister Anna. Helen invited a number of friends to a reception for the celebrated poet. She and Poe took long walks, and he told her of the kindness of Fanny Allan. One of the marks of Poe's state of mind is the assertion to Helen that he'd married Virginia not out of love but obligation. "I did violence to my own heart, and married, for another's happiness, where I knew that no possibility of my own existed," he further explained in a letter of October 18, 1848.

Both Poe and Helen were performers, and he was attempting a role he was not prepared for. But he'd taken on the part and would play it to some inevitable end. To be married to a notable New England poet would be a particular victory for Poe. He indulged himself in fantasies of editing his powerful *Stylus* from the Power house in Providence, supported by Power money. On November 26, 1848, he wrote to Helen: "Would it *not* be 'glorious,' *darling,* to establish, in America, the sole unquestionable aristocracy—that of intellect—to secure its supremacy."

When they visited the local Atheneum library, Helen asked if he knew a strange poem published in the *American Review* called "Ulalume." Poe admitted he'd written the poem and said he preferred it to "The Raven." Helen likely knew the poem was Poe's and was flattering him. We wonder if she understood then just how dark that ballad was and what it implied about the lover-narrator. One of their walks took them all the way to Swan Point Cemetery. For poets with their melancholy temperament, no place could be more inspiring or even erotic. Helen would later recall that it was in the cemetery that Poe talked of Jane Stanard and what she had meant to him. Poe explained that he had visited Jane's grave every night for months.

After knowing Helen for one or two days, he proposed marriage. He swore she was the only woman he'd ever loved. He put his arm around her waist and looked into her eyes. At a reception at the Power house, Poe kissed Helen in front of company, an unusually bold gesture for an unmarried couple in Victorian times: "Of a sudden the company perceived that

Poe and Helen were greatly agitated. Simultaneously both arose from their chairs and walked toward the center of the room. Meeting, he held her in his arms, kissed her; they stood for a moment, then he led her to her seat."

But for all her airs of transcendentalism and spiritualism, Helen was a practical woman and a professional writer. She explained that she could not accept Poe's proposal now. She knew of his drinking and the rumors of his behavior with Fanny Osgood. Helen had met many poets and writers, but no one had affected her as Poe did. His manners, his intensity, his expressions of affection, made him seem like the brother-lover she'd yearned for. She imagined that Power and Poe must be the same name. If they were not brother and sister, they were at least cousins, with the same birthday.

Back at Fordham, Poe expressed his disappointment that no marriage had been planned, and he wrote also to Annie Richmond and Jane Locke, continuing those flirtations. When Helen answered him a few days later, she explained that in spite of the great attraction she felt for him, marriage was unlikely. For one thing, she was older than he. And with her weak heart, she was in no condition to fulfill the physical obligations of a wife. Poe replied with one of his longest missives ever, twelve single-spaced pages of emotional extravagance. In his comments about the marriage to Virginia, we see just how far afield Poe had gone in his delusions. As Regan in *Lear* comments about the king, "He hath ever but slenderly known himself."

"I saw that you were *Helen—my* Helen—the Helen of a thousand dreams—she whose visionary lips had so often lingered upon my own in the divine trance of passion. . . . I heard no words—only the soft voice, more familiar to me than my own, and more melodious than the songs of the angels." The critic Leland S. Person, speaking of "Ligeia," observed that "Poe enjoyed what might be called a cryptographic relationship with women." The special character of his letters to Helen Whitman is that of a smitten adolescent who happens to have unusual literary gifts.

To answer her fears about the risks of sexual activity, Poe assured Helen he would make no demands on her of that nature. Their love was far too pure for such conventional passion. "I would cast from me, forever, all merely human desire, and clothe myself in the glory of a pure, calm, and *unexacting* affection." In the fever of his infatuation, Poe may have believed that such an assurance would persuade Helen to the altar and marriage bed. For all her protestations of a weak heart, her swooning and inhaling of ether, and writing of ethereal realms, Helen was healthy enough to live until the age of seventy-five, remaining active as a writer almost to the end. The promise of a sexless marriage may not have been the attraction Poe imagined it to be. Instead of being persuaded by Poe's high-flown language and claims, Helen replied that gossip about Poe kept cropping up, spread throughout the literary community by Mrs. Ellet and others.

Both W. H. Auden and the biographer Jeffrey Meyers have used the word *operatic* to describe the Poe-Whitman correspondence and romance. There is certainly that aura of performance on both their parts, at times melodramatic, grandiloquent, at times silly. Yet we do not feel inclined to laugh at their theatrics, because of the intensity and desperation, especially on Poe's part. He'd lost his way, playing a semi-duplicitous role, but was driven to carry it through anyway. Poe probably half-believed what he wrote to Helen. But there is also a hint of greasepaint and flickering footlights in his letters.

In October, Poe returned to Providence, even though he'd vowed to never seek her hand in marriage again. Helen promised to give him an answer, in a letter sent to Lowell, where he would be visiting Annie Richmond and lecturing. In Lowell, Poe stayed with Jane Locke and her husband again. But the real attraction in Lowell was Annie Richmond, and when that became clear to Jane Locke, she was not shy about showing her displeasure. Poe later claimed Mrs. Locke "insulted" him, and he stormed out of the Locke house to stay with the Richmonds.

Poe proclaimed that his affection for Annie was deeper and purer than his love for Helen. Annie was also seventeen years younger than Helen. Annie had shown her devotion to Poe by visiting Muddy at Fordham the previous summer. More important, she was *safe,* a married woman with a daughter. Her husband, Charles, was tolerant, perhaps amused by Poe's histrionic attentions to his wife. Annie's younger sister would later remember Poe sitting beside Annie, before the fireplace, holding her hand as they looked into the flames. "For a long time no one spoke, and the only sound was the ticking of the tall old clock." Annie, actually Nancy, was so thrilled by Poe's attentions that she later changed her name legally to Annie after her husband's death.

When Poe met Nancy Richmond in the summer of 1848, he was certain he'd found the ideal woman for whom he had been searching. He planned to move to Lowell just to be near her, like an acolyte. In his imagination he would be "married" to her, his Mother Confessor with infinite compassion and pity for him in his fallen state. He projected onto her all he had needed. With his horror about marriage, he would not be threatened. With Annie he could have it both ways.

Surprisingly, or perhaps not so surprisingly, Helen Whitman, the astute critic, came to understand Poe better than many of his contemporaries. Out of the embarrassment and anguish of their courtship, she evolved a profound insight into the man and his work. In his poetry Helen saw "a lingering pity and sorrow for the dead;—an ever-recurring pang of remorse in the fear of having grieved them by some involuntary wrong." Helen may not have realized the depth of Poe's guilt, and the violence of repression, but she put her finger on the very heart of his anguish and one source of his great achievement.

As Poe waited at Lowell for Helen's letter, he spent several days at nearby Westfield, on the farm of Annie's parents. When a note finally arrived around November 2, it told him little. She could not make up her mind. Poe decided he must return to Providence and demand a decisive answer. He poured out his dilemma to Annie, who told him he needed a wife to look after him and urged him to marry Helen Whitman. Before leaving Lowell, Poe asked Annie to come to him when he was dying.

Poe traveled to Providence on November 4 in a flurry of conflicting emotions and hopes. Part of him knew he didn't want to marry Helen Whitman; part of him knew he had to follow through with his protestations of eternal love. He'd not been able to deliver his lecture in Lowell because of the distraction of the national election, propelling Zachary Taylor, Old Rough and Ready, to the White House. What Poe felt on the train to Providence was anything but rough and ready.

According to Poe's later account, he did not call on Helen at Benefit Street but spent a night of despair in a hotel. Then, in desperation, he took the train to Boston, planning to end his life in the city where it had begun. From his native city, Poe supposedly wrote to Annie saying he could not marry anyone, even though she advised it, and that he had come to the end of his endurance. He reminded Annie that she'd pledged to come to him on his deathbed. Poe purchased two ounces of laudanum, planning suicide. A normal dose might contain thirty milligrams of morphine. In his fevered

FIG. 28. The "Ultima Thule" daguerreotype, 1848. Taken by Edwin H. Manchester, November 9, 1848, in Providence, Rhode Island, after Poe's supposed attempt at suicide, this notorious portrait shows Poe at his most troubled and exhausted. It quickly became part of his legend after his death. (Courtesy of the Edgar Allan Poe Museum, Richmond, Virginia)

state, Poe said he drank about three hundred milligrams of morphine. He imagined that Annie would reach him as he died and perhaps join him on the voyage to eternity.

Poe hurried to the post office to mail his letter to Annie but threw up the laudanum on the way and reeled in derangement. A friend kindly helped him, though he later said he felt a perfect calm in his illness, as if outside himself, observing his suffering from a position of detachment. Annie never got the letter, and on November 7 Poe turned up in Providence again.

Several biographers, including Mary Phillips and James H. Whitty, have believed the whole laudanum and suicide attempt was a creation of Poe's delirium. The person who supposedly rescued him in Boston has never been identified. In Poe's overheated imagination, he fantasized taking the train to Boston and willing himself to die but may have stayed drunk all that time in Providence, where he was next seen.

Poe wrote a note to Helen saying he was ill but could explain his three-day absence. They did meet that afternoon at the Providence Atheneum, where Poe told her he'd taken laudanum and in confusion caught the train to Boston. We might expect him to say goodbye and return to Lowell or Fordham. Instead, he appeared at Helen's house the next day, pleading with her to consent to his proposal. When she read him excerpts from a letter accusing him of bad behavior, Poe expressed his hurt but promised to return in the evening.

Poe spent the evening in the hotel bar and sent Helen an angry note. The next day, November 9, he had a daguerreotype taken, now a notorious portrait, showing his distress, confusion, exhaustion, and sinister determination (fig. 28). Many scholars have noticed the dividedness in Poe's countenance, one side calm, healthy, the other disturbed, volatile. This portrait shows Poe in such a disturbed state it has been called the "Ultima Thule" daguerreotype.

When Poe appeared at the Power house that morning, he spoke wildly and incoherently. As he shouted, Helen hid in her room. Mrs. Power and Anna tried to calm him. When Helen finally came downstairs to face him, he begged her to rescue him. She was "an angel sent to save him from perdition." He clung to Helen so excitedly he ripped away a piece of her dress.

Mrs. Power called a local physician, A. H. Okie, who examined and diagnosed "cerebral congestion." Poe was taken to the home of William J.

Pabodie, Helen's admirer, where he stayed for several days, slowly calming down. Pabodie was said to have high regard for Poe as a writer but thought a marriage between Poe and Helen would be a calamity.

As Poe began to act more rationally, Helen relented and gave her "conditional" consent to marry him. One of the most important conditions was that he abstain from alcohol forever. Another was that her mother grant her consent. Yet Mrs. Power had been explicit all along about her opposition to the match, asserting that she would rather see Helen in her grave than married to a man like Poe.

Before he left Providence, once he recovered some equilibrium, Poe had another daguerreotype made as a gift to Helen. This one, called the "Whitman daguerreotype," of November 13, 1848, was perhaps the best likeness Poe ever had taken. (See the frontispiece to this volume.) It would become the classic image of the poet and critic. With his gray West Point coat over his shoulders, smooth-shaven except for a mustache, he looks with confidence and disdain at the camera, conveying to the viewer and to the world the persona he chose to present, assured, superior, remote, both poet and arbiter. Perhaps he was relieved to be about to escape from Providence.

After Poe was gone, Mrs. Power continued to berate Helen about her agreement to marry him. Like Poe, Helen wanted to wed, at least in principle. She could imagine she needed Poe in her arms and in her bed. But she probably knew she needed him most in her imagination.

Back in Fordham, Poe wrote fervent letters to Helen about their planned nuptials. But he penned even more passionate letters to Annie Richmond: "So long as I think that you *know* I love you, as no man ever loved woman. . . . But oh, *my darling, my* Annie, my own sweet *sister* Annie, my *pure* beautiful angel—*wife* of my soul—to be mine hereafter & *forever in the Heavens.*" If Poe had been raised a Roman Catholic, we might guess that he sought in Annie Richmond an embodiment of the Blessed Virgin, of infinite mercy and compassion, to worship and to petition for intercession and absolution for his many sins. Out of Annie Richmond, housewife of Lowell, Massachusetts, he fashioned the Mary he craved.

Poe's hyperbole in his letters to both Annie and Helen, but especially to Annie, are evidence of his emotional desperation, reaching for something stable, forgiveness, from the damnation he was certain he'd earned, and the refuge of an imagined marriage. The depth of Poe's writing came in part from the guilt he carried, the Imp of the Perverse. He recognized the bleak underside of human nature, and his own nature, and the complexity of the human condition. It is this undercurrent in Poe's poetry and fiction that makes him the exception, and so popular. In many ways he wrote magazine verse similar on the surface to a thousand others. Only Poe's work had a black electricity of guilt. Baudelaire, also obsessed with evil in the world and duplicity in his own nature, seized on Poe as a model. Poe understood that just when you expect it least, the Imp of the Perverse will appear. Therefore, you attempt, again and again, to escape to an artificial paradise, a Valley of Many-Colored Grass, an Arnheim, an ideal sanctuary of marriage.

Poe was invited to give a lecture in Providence, at the Franklin Lyceum, on December 20, 1848. Meanwhile, word of Poe's impending marriage to Helen had spread throughout the literary cohort. Muddy wrote to Annie Richmond: "I so much fear *she* is not calculated to make him happy. . . . I *know* I shall never love her as I do *you*, my own darling." Since she was already happily married, Annie was no threat to Muddy, who likely feared being displaced if Eddie took a new wife, any wife.

When Fanny Osgood learned of Poe's engagement to Helen, she traveled all the way to Providence to seek confirmation. Helen later wrote: "She threw herself at my feet & covered my hands with tears & kisses; she told me all the enthusiasm she had felt for him & her unchanged & unchanging interest in him & his best welfare. . . . I told her . . . of [his] letters of ten or twelve pages, she seemed almost incredulous. She said his letters to her were all very brief." There is reason to believe that Poe was much more attracted to Fanny physically than he ever was to Helen Whitman or the tall Annie. Fanny was petite and pretty, like the young Virginia, like Eliza Poe, with long black hair. Poe and Fanny had conducted much of their affair in person, not in letters. For the women Poe wrote the long "operatic" letters to, he probably felt little physical attraction. The impotence some biographers have ascribed to him may have been real enough, with these women. With women he was genuinely attracted to sexually, Elmira Shelton, Virginia, Fanny Osgood, he did not need to write such hyperbole.

Around December 15 Mrs. Power had all her financial assets moved out of Helen's reach, and Poe's. Helen signed the document, giving up all claim to the family wealth. Poe, too, would sign away all rights to the Power money.

As Poe was leaving New York later to give the lecture in Providence, he called on the writer Mary E. Hewitt. When she mentioned that he was to be married, Poe said, "That marriage will never take place." On December 20 Poe gave his finest lecture, "The Poetic Principle," to an audience of about two thousand in Providence. He also recited "The Raven" and the newly completed "The Bells." The appearance was so successful Poe was emboldened to ask Helen to marry him immediately, and she agreed.

Poe had to find a way to break out of the quagmire he'd created for himself, and he did it in his accustomed way, with the bottle. On December 22, when he arrived at a reception at Helen's house, he had been drinking but kept very quiet. He promised Helen once more that he would never drink again. But the next morning he had at least one glass of wine at the hotel before appearing at the Power house. Poe wrote a note to the local Episcopalian clergyman, Rev. Nathan Bourne Crocker, asking him to publish the banns for their wedding. He gave the note to William Pabodie, who didn't deliver it. On the same day, he wrote to Muddy, "We shall be married on Monday [Christmas Day] and will be at Fordham on Tuesday. on [*sic*] the first train."

Poe and Helen continued making plans for their wedding. Both seemed in a state of numbness, if not panic. They visited a local library, and it was there that Helen was handed a note, probably from Pabodie, warning her against the marriage and containing more damning evidence of Poe's bad behavior. This gave Helen the excuse she needed to end the engagement. Their conversation became so animated the librarian rebuked them and asked for quiet.

At the Power house Poe argued and at least pretended to be deeply offended. Helen was so distraught she held an ether-soaked handkerchief to her face and collapsed on a couch. Poe approached her on his knees and said, "Say that you love me, Helen." She answered, "I love you." Poe continued his pleas and protestations until Mrs. Power ordered him to leave. "Mr. Pabodie, you hear how I am insulted," Poe blurted. The good Mr. Pabodie escorted Poe to the train station. We don't have to try very hard to imagine the relief Poe felt as he made his way back to New York and Fordham, arriving on Christmas Eve. He may have had a few drinks on the train or boat to celebrate.

Though Helen was also relieved that the marriage was off, recovering for her was harder. She was experienced at literary flirtations, romantic, even suggestive amours, but she'd never remarried. For weeks after Poe left Providence, she was prostrate with chills and fever, probably embarrassed, as all the literary community gossiped about her upcoming nuptials and then the abrupt cancellation.

Poe claimed to suffer headaches after he returned to Muddy, but from his letters we can sense a millstone had been lifted. To Annie Richmond he wrote on January 11, 1849: "Indeed, indeed, Annie, there is *nothing* in this world worth living for except love. . . . I need not tell you, Annie, how great a burden is taken off my heart by my rupture with Mrs. W."

But there were consequences to Poe's escapade in Providence. Word was passed around in the literary fellowship that he had behaved abominably to Mrs. Whitman. She had many friends and was highly respected. Even Annie was irritated that he'd not followed through on her instructions to marry. Gossip about his behavior in Providence reached Charles Richmond, causing a coolness between Poe and the Richmonds. Rumors of Poe's conduct in Providence were added to stories of his seduction of the innocent, childlike Fanny Osgood.

Poe vowed to avoid literary women in the future, all except Fanny Osgood. Meanwhile, Helen wrote to Fanny Osgood asking for news about Poe but got no answer. In later years Helen Whitman held many séances to contact Poe's spirit after his death. She would write at least sixteen poems to or about Poe.

19

"FOR ANNIE" AND "THE BELLS"

WHILE INVOLVED IN COURTSHIPS WITH JANE LOCKE, ANNIE Richmond, Helen Whitman, and Elmira Shelton, Poe wrote or completed some of his finest poetry and prose. He continued producing installments of "Marginalia" and gathered most of his best ideas about poetry into the lecture called "The Poetic Principle." He had written an early version of the poem called "The Bells" at the suggestion of Loui Shew. It would become one of his most popular works and one of his most robust experiments with sound.

"The Bells" is a poem of theme and variation, repetition, ringing changes on all its controlling figures. It is said "The Bells" has been one of Poe's most popular poems in translation because its images and sound patterns can be readily carried across to other languages. With its brisk trochaic meter and ringing repetitions, the poem moves from sleigh to wedding bells, "Golden bells" to alarm bells, "brazen bells" to the tolling of funeral bells, "Iron bells," pealing out its narrative of birth, marriage, struggle, and death. This is poetry that is the opposite of prose—pure poetry, or *poésie pure,* as Mallarmé would say.

Another poem Poe finished in this period was "A Dream Within a Dream," drawing on images and ideas he'd been experimenting with throughout his life, with echoes from *The Tempest,* Calderón's play *Life Is a Dream,* and even a line from Shelley's "Adonais."

Take this kiss upon the brow!
And, in parting from you now,
Thus much let me avow—
You are not wrong, who deem
That my days have been a dream;
. . . .

I stand amid the roar
Of a surf-tormented shore,
And I hold within my hand
Grains of the golden sand—
How few! yet how they creep
Through my fingers to the deep,
. . . .
Is *all* that we see or seem
But a dream within a dream?

The poem was originally titled "For Annie," but in the summer of 1849, Poe may have intended it for Elmira Shelton when he sent it to the *Richmond Examiner* simply titled "To ——."

Another late poem that has proven to be enduringly popular was also called "For Annie." It is one of Poe's oddest poems, both in its rhythm and in its content. Poe was fond of anapestic meter and used it here and in several later poems, including "Ulalume" and "Annabel Lee." The intensity of Poe's idealization of Mrs. Richmond comes through in "For Annie." Though much younger than Poe, she was a mother to him, and like the Blessed Virgin, she seemed to offer safety, refuge, and absolution for his confessions, his searing guilt. He fantasized living in a cottage near her for the rest of his days. In his mind he must have seen an image of the Pietà, the mother of Christ holding the body of her beloved son. In loose anapestic dimeter, he dreamed of sanctuary and nurture at her breast, shriven and "married" for all eternity:

Thank Heaven! the crisis—
  The danger is past,

And the lingering illness
  Is over at last—
And the fever called "Living"
  Is conquered at last.

. . . .

She tenderly kissed me,
  She fondly caressed,
And then I fell gently
  To sleep on her breast—
Deeply to sleep
  From the heaven of her breast.

There is something authentically infantile about the poem, Mother Goose rhyme–like, unusual even in Poe's work. It's a strange lullaby, suggesting the speaker is dead and undead at once in the narrow bed. It is like a memory of the loving Eliza Poe putting the two-year-old Edgar to bed. But this time the bed is less the grave than the womb. In an odd way it is a poem of an ideal marriage. Horror of the womb is common in Poe's work, but here there is a longing, even a jubilation, to be safe in the sanctuary of Annie's (Eliza's) love and body. He has "died" sexually back into her arms or in her womb.

Poe's celebration and idealization of Annie were not limited to poetry in verse. He also wrote a landscape tale called "Landor's Cottage," exploring the poetry and splendors of the natural world. And even when writing about northern forests, he included vegetation more familiar in the Carolinas and Virginia. Poe called "Landor's Cottage" "A Pendant to 'The Domain of Arnheim.'" It's a celebration of a paradise on earth more domestic, on a more modest scale, than Ellison's majestic estate of Arnheim.

The speaker of "Landor's Cottage" takes a ramble in the countryside up the Hudson north of New York City, with a dog named Ponto and a gun, hoping to reach an unnamed village in this world of Rip Van Winkle and Sleepy Hollow, among the old Dutch farmhouses. Each detail is significant as the reader is drawn into the dreamy landscape: "A smoky mist, resembling that of the Indian summer, enveloped all things, and, of course, added to my uncertainty." The vagueness and uncertainty are important in the approach to reverie and recognition.

The valley is very narrow and opens out into a grove of elms, then sassafras and locusts, succeeded by "the softer linden, redbud, catalpa, and maple." We recall that Poe had once walked under the lindens with Elmira Royster. The narrator takes special note of a giant tulip poplar, somewhat like the mammoth tree in "The Gold-Bug," except this tulip tree has three trunks coming out of a common base, a trinity joined in unity. Poe describes the enormous tree in detail, giving the Latin name, *Liriodendron tuliperum* (more correctly, the word is *tulipifera*). The narrator exults in the majesty of the tulip trees, many over 120 feet tall.

Above the valley, cliffs loom, and a stone wall can be seen and below that a wandering stream, and where the stream makes a loop, there is a cottage. With great care Poe describes an idealized version of the cottage at Fordham, even giving its precise dimensions and birds in cages, including a mockingbird, sometimes called the southern nightingale. The narrator raps on the door with his cane. It is here that we realize why all the description has been charged with such romantic intensity, for who should come to the door but Annie Richmond: "I said to myself, 'Surely here I have found the perfection of natural, in contradistinction from artificial *grace.*' . . . So intense an expression of *romance* . . . or of unworldliness. . . . The eyes of Annie (I heard some one from the interior call her 'Annie, darling!') were 'spiritual gray'; her hair, a light chestnut."

In the poem "For Annie" and in "Landor's Cottage," we have symbolic journeys back to and into a woman's body. The terror of the earlier poems and stories has subsided, replaced by a calm reaching, through winding routes, to and into the paradise of a female body. The turmoil and confusion of the Helen Whitman affair seem to have released in Poe a catharsis of a new understanding of himself, inspired by the kindness and graciousness he found in Annie Richmond, or in his imagination of her.

It is also possible that seeing Elmira, his first love, in the summer of 1848, awakened something in Poe that had been dormant for years. And it's almost certain he'd been exchanging letters with Elmira over the winter. Poe had a peculiar talent for seeing in one individual woman the ideal, the archetype. When he saw Elmira after so many years, something in him apparently altered, as though bringing back his youth.

As far as we know, Poe had never learned that his letters to Elmira from Charlottesville in 1826 had been intercepted by Mr. Royster. But at some point in the summer of 1848, or in the letters she wrote to Poe in the months afterward, Elmira must have informed Poe that their messages to each other had been seized by her father. For more than twenty years, Poe had blamed himself and borne the guilt for the loss of Elmira. Now he came to understand he'd been absolved, at least partially. In his last works, "Landor's Cottage," "Hop-Frog," and "Annabel Lee," the pain is as real as ever, but he does not have to assume all the accountability.

The sensitivity and excitement about the natural world had always been there, but now he could again see the woman's flesh as an essential component of both nature and spirit and that nature and spirit are one. We cannot know with certainty what caused this transformation. There is no one "Lost Lenore," but it is Elmira who may have the best claim. Somehow Poe had found forgiveness and begun to forgive himself.

20

"THE POETIC PRINCIPLE"

ON DECEMBER 11, 1848, ELMIRA ROYSTER SHELTON WROTE TO her cousin Philip Fitzhugh from Miller's Landing in Essex County, Virginia, where she was staying with friends. The previous summer she'd seen Poe in Richmond for the first time in more than a decade. He'd paid court to her and then abruptly left for New York. Mrs. Shelton was a strong but soft-spoken woman. This letter is a unique glimpse into her personality and emotions at this time.

She tells Cousin Philip that she writes because she thinks he might enjoy hearing from her. She is visiting friends in the country, recovering from the very low spirits she suffered in Richmond, and asks if he has seen anyone who might ask after her. The implication is that he knows why she was depressed. She worries that some might be relieved that she has been away: "I am fearful Cousin Philip, that I shall never be a happy woman again, time will certainly do a great deal in obliterating past events from my feelings, but I am certain that I shall never feel like myself again . . . I believe you Philip to be my friend, else I would not speak so candidly, or make thus free with you."

There is not a single mention of Poe in this letter, and we would not expect there to be. Elmira was a woman of stoic dignity and poise, yet in this surprising missive, she unburdens herself of fears that no one cares for her. If Poe had awakened her affection the previous summer, he had also dealt an injury with his sudden departure, leaving her to go on with her life as a widow, to make the best of her loneliness. She begs that no one else see the letter, for she has confessed her depression, her "very low and distressing condition," when she left home in Richmond.

Elmira had been brought up in a society in which decorum was almost everything. But she is bursting to confide in Cousin Philip her struggle with depression, and her words imply that he will understand something about the cause of such low spirits. In this bleak December, she reaches out to Cousin Philip, who may be her only confidant.

Meanwhile, Poe at Fordham, basking in the affection of Annie Richmond, was almost as busy as ever. The headlines in newspapers, and the talk on everyone's lips, were about the discovery of gold in California. Men abandoned families, spent their savings, mortgaged houses, to reach the goldfields. Poe had no interest in heading to California himself, but he saw both the comic and tragic aspects of the gold fever. He satirized the old alchemical dream of turning base metals into gold in "Von Kempelen and His Discovery." To Evert Duyckinck, Poe wrote on March 8, 1849: "Of course, there is *not one* word of truth in it from beginning to end. I thought that such a style, applied to the gold-excitement, could not fail of effect." Perhaps remembering the "Balloon Hoax" and its aftermath, Duyckinck rejected the story for the *Literary World,* and it was published in *The Flag of Our Union* on April 14, 1849, causing hardly a ripple of response.

Poe also wrote one of his finest lyrics, "Eldorado," inspired by the gold rush. It's shorter than the ideal poem, which should be about the length of "The Raven" or "Ulalume." It's a poem of lapidary concision and precision. The metrics are irregular but predominantly iambic dimeter and trimeter.

> Gaily bedight,
> A gallant knight,
> In sunshine and in shadow,
> Had journeyed long,
> Singing a song,
> In search of Eldorado.
>
> But he grew old—
> This knight so bold—

And o'er his heart a shadow
  Fell, as he found
  No spot of ground
That looked like Eldorado.

And, as his strength
  Failed him at length
He met a pilgrim shadow—
  "Shadow," said he,
  "Where can it be—
This land of Eldorado?"

  "Over the Mountains
  Of the Moon,
Down the Valley of the Shadow,
  Ride, boldly ride,"
  The shade replied,—
"If you seek for Eldorado!"

The spareness and dialogue format of "Eldorado" are a triumph. It's a poem that looks back to the allegorical lyrics of Blake, and forward to the Symbolist poetry of the nineteenth and early twentieth centuries. It reminds us of Don Quixote and the Spanish conquistadors' relentless pursuit of gold. It suggests that if such a country exists, it can only be reached through the valley of the shadow, that is, through death. "Eldorado" was published in *Flag of Our Union* April 21, 1849.

Poe had said that the ideal subject for a poem was the death of a beautiful woman. In 1849 he would take up the theme again and write one of his most memorable lyrics, "Annabel Lee." He called it a ballad. Like "Ulalume" and "For Annie," it is metrically irregular, at times iambic, sometimes dactylic, sometimes anapestic, measures of enchantment and mystical ceremony. There are two versions of the final line, but many critics agree that the earlier version is the more effective.

It was many and many a year ago,
  In a kingdom by the sea,

That a maiden there lived whom you may know
  By the name of Annabel Lee;—
And this maiden she lived with no other thought
  Than to love and be loved by me.

I was a child and *she* was a child,
  In this kingdom by the sea;
But we loved with a love that was more than love—
  I and my Annabel Lee—
With a love that the wingéd seraphs in Heaven
  Coveted her and me.

And this was the reason that, long ago,
  In this kingdom by the sea,
A wind blew out of a cloud, chilling
  My beautiful Annabel Lee;
So that her high-born kinsmen came
  And bore her away from me,
To shut her up in a sepulchre,
  In this kingdom by the sea.

The angels, not half so happy in Heaven,
  Went envying her and me—
Yes!—that was the reason (as all men know,
  In this kingdom by the sea)
That the wind came out of the cloud by night,
  Chilling and killing my Annabel Lee.

But our love it was stronger by far than the love
  Of those who were older than we—
  Of many far wiser than we—
And neither the angels in Heaven above,
  Nor the demons down under the sea,
Can ever dissever my soul from the soul
  Of the beautiful Annabel Lee:—

For the moon never beams without bringing me dreams
  Of the beautiful Annabel Lee;
And the stars never rise, but I feel the bright eyes
  Of the beautiful Annabel Lee:—
And so, all the night-tide, I lie down by the side
Of my darling—my darling—my life and my bride,
  In her sepulchre there by the sea—
  In her tomb by the sounding sea.

One thing we notice immediately about "Annabel Lee," in contrast to "The Raven" and "Ululume," is the apparent absence of guilt on the part of the speaker. The change reflected in "For Annie" and "Landor's Cottage" is confirmed in this last poem. The tenor of Poe's imagination has altered. Something had been reborn in him, something physical as well as ethereal. Poe was pondering his youth, not quite so much crushed by guilt as before and contemplating a return and new life in Richmond.

What has been hardest to explain about "Annabel Lee" is why it sticks in the mind and auditory memory so tenaciously. The poem should not have the hold on readers that it does. One reason we're fascinated with poetry is that we can never entirely explain its power. We may discuss the necrophilia implied by the ending, but it's hard to account for the effect of those images and that sound.

In the final version of the poem, Poe changed the last line to "In her tomb by the side of the sea," which is more metrically perfect but lacks the resonance of "In her tomb by the sounding sea." "Sounding sea" is about the pounding of the surf, the pulse and heartbeat, about the rhythm heard in the womb, echo and distance, about pain and sorrow throughout time and beyond time. The tomb by the sounding sea implies a poetic marriage, in which the lover can lie down at her side by the lamenting waves forever. Children who hardly understand the lines memorize and recite this poem and carry the sound deep in their auditory memory, of love and the rhythmic enchantment of the sea, and timelessness. The only perfect marriage is in death.

In the last year of his life, Poe continued writing, but many literary people held him up to ridicule. James Russell Lowell, who'd written one of the first appreciations of Poe in 1844, lampooned his former friend in his *A Fable for Critics* of October 1848.

There comes Poe, with his raven, like Barnaby Rudge,
Three-fifth of him genius and two-fifths sheer fudge,
Who talks like a book of iambs and pentameters,
In a way to make people of common sense damn metres.

Poe had alienated Lowell by his drinking and by his attacks on Longfellow and claiming in "The Philosophy of Composition" that he'd written "The Raven" in a coldly calculating manner, forgetting that he'd carried the rhythm and images in his mind for years. Poe's lack of ease in the literary community and society caused him to make extravagant claims that put off writers more confident of their place in the world. Poe would die after being found in a gutter in Baltimore. Lowell would be rewarded with ambassadorships, a professorship at Harvard, and the editorship of the *Atlantic Monthly*.

In the *Southern Literary Messenger* for March 1849, Poe would tell the world what he thought of Lowell's *A Fable for Critics:* "The 'Fable' is essentially 'loose'—ill-conceived and feebly executed, as well in detail as in general."

"Mr. Lowell is one of the most rabid of the Abolition fanatics; and no Southerner who does not wish to be insulted, and at the same time revolted by a bigotry the most obstinately blind and deaf, should ever touch a volume by this author." Writing for a southern audience, Poe used the terms he thought would be most damning. And Poe touches on the real sore point in his relations with Lowell and other New England authors: "It is a fashion among Mr. Lowell's set to affect a belief that there is *no such thing* as Southern Literature." On January 13, 1849, when the news of Poe's engagement to Helen Whitman had spread throughout the community of editors and writers, Horace Greeley wrote to the pious Griswold, "Has Mrs. Whitman no friend within your knowledge that can faithfully *explain* Poe to her?" Poe had never paid back the fifty dollars Greeley had loaned him for the *Broadway Journal.*

It was in this period that Poe wrote what would be his last important story, "Hop-Frog." Like "The Cask of Amontillado," it's a story of revenge, sadistic behavior in high places, and retaliation by an entertainer. Hop-Frog is a dwarf and the jester at the king's court. This tyrant lives for pranks and joking, especially jokes on those at his court. It's the job of Hop-Frog to keep the king and his courtiers amused. Because the jester is a cripple as well as a dwarf, the king has named him Hop-Frog. (Poe, in his last year, is said to have walked with a pronounced limp.) It especially amuses the king to force Hop-Frog to drink alcohol, knowing that, like Poe, the fool is allergic to booze.

There is also at the court a beautiful midget named Tripetta, who is required to entertain the king and his courtiers. Poe leaves to our imagination how the petite Tripetta might entertain the dissolute king. One day the king forced Hop-Frog to drink bumper after bumper of wine. He and his courtiers laugh at the poor fool, and when Tripetta tries to intervene, the king throws a goblet of wine in her face. Hop-Frog pretends to laugh, but the fool vows to prepare a capital amusement for the king. For a large gathering at the palace, the king and his courtiers will dress as orangutans, in suits made of flax and tar, in chains, and pretend to attack the guests. Heavy orangutan suits are made, and on the night of the banquet, the king and his seven courtiers are chained together. A great chandelier is lowered from the ceiling.

At the moment of highest merriment, Hop-Frog hooks the chained courtiers and king to the chandelier, which is then drawn up by Tripetta. The orangutan suits are set on fire, and the king and his courtiers burn as the crowd below freezes in horror and Hop-Frog addresses them: "'As for myself, I am simply Hop-Frog, the jester—and this is my last jest.' . . . The eight corpses swung in their chains, a fetid, blackened, hideous, and indistinguishable mass. The cripple hurled his torch at them, clambered leisurely to the ceiling, and disappeared through the sky-light."

What a satisfying fantasy "Hop-Frog" must have been for Poe in 1849. For years he'd entertained with hoaxes and burlesques, with mysteries, yet he was no longer welcome in the leading magazines and drawing rooms. He'd been insulted while Virginia was dying, and his poverty had been advertised. Worst of all, some fate forced him to drink, though he hated alcohol and drunkenness. He dreamed of escaping to his own country, though it remained to be seen whether that was Lowell or Richmond or a place of his imagination.

The critic Agnieszka Soltysik Monnet and others connect "Hop-Frog" to the Nat Turner slave uprising of 1831. Dressed like orangutans, the king and courtiers suffer a lynching. There is no doubt that the sympathy of the reader (and presumably the author) is with the humiliated dwarf and the vulnerable Tripetta, who represent another "marriage." Unlike most of Poe's earlier stories, the character Hop-Frog is without guilt, more evidence that some burden of shame has been shifted from the narrator and the author in the last year of his life. On February 14, 1849, Poe wrote to his friend Frederick Thomas, expressing a renewed confidence in himself and his work: "Depend upon it, after all, Thomas, Literature is the most noble of professions."

IN APRIL 1849 POE RECEIVED A LETTER FROM EDWARD HOWARD Norton Patterson of Oquawka, Illinois. Patterson was a novelist and editor of the Oquawka *Spectator,* and he proposed to publish Poe's projected and long-delayed magazine. The letter, written the December before, had been delayed in reaching Poe. Having just turned twenty-one, Patterson was anxious to form a partnership with Poe in which Patterson would pay all costs for the magazine; profits would be shared equally with Poe. Out of the blue, this young man in a small town in northwestern Illinois had offered to make the *Stylus* possible.

Poe described to Patterson his extraordinary ambitions for the *Stylus:* "We must aim high—address the intellect—the higher classes. . . . My plan . . . would be to take a tour through the principal States—especially West & South—visiting the small towns more particularly than the large ones—lecturing as I went, to pay expenses." In the correspondence that ensued, they discussed where the magazine was to be issued. Oquawka was too remote from the cultural centers of Philadelphia, New York, and Boston. Poe suggested a compromise: St. Louis.

Poe was a celebrity, especially below the Mason-Dixon Line. Wherever he recited "The Raven" and lectured on poetry, he would find subscribers. But first he had to go to Lowell to visit the Richmonds. After a cooling in the relationship earlier in the year, due to gossip about his behavior in Providence, all was now supposedly smoothed over.

And yet, even as Poe wrote to Patterson about launching the *Stylus,* he did little to actually make it happen. In either April or May 1849, Poe had written to Annie Richmond of his deep depression. "No, my sadness is *unaccountable,* and this makes me the more sad. I am full of dark forebodings. *Nothing* cheers or comforts me. My life seems wasted."

In Massachusetts, Poe was feted and fussed over for a week. All of Annie's family seemed to gather and admire him. A local minister gave Poe a cryptogram, which the poet quickly solved. Annie's brother Bardwell took Poe to his school, where Poe flirted with a pretty young teacher named Eliza Jane Butterfield. While he was in Lowell, Annie had two daguerreotypes made of Poe. In these portraits he looks older than he had six months earlier. His thinning hair is combed forward to cover advancing baldness (fig. 29).

Poe seemed at a loss and more wearied by this visit than relieved. The infatuation with Annie Richmond might have cooled, as he saw her face to face. Poe had other things on his mind when he returned to Fordham. He'd behaved badly toward Elmira Shelton the summer before. Poe had likely been writing to Elmira over the winter and spring, attempting to regain her respect. If so, such letters have disappeared. It's likely Elmira had written to Poe, because in the summer of 1849 she would demand that her letters be returned.

At Fordham, Poe delayed his travel to Richmond yet again, for he didn't have money for the journey. He asked Patterson to send fifty dollars to him care of the *Southern Literary Messenger,* but he wouldn't have those funds until he reached Richmond. He was not well physically or emotionally. Some think that in his depression, he even asked Rufus Griswold to serve as his literary executor in case of his death. At least that's what Muddy would claim.

For years Poe had complained about his health. Some scholars think he'd had a weak heart all along. One possibility, mentioned earlier, is that Poe, after all the exposure to tuberculosis throughout his life, had contracted the disease himself. It is known that heavy drinkers are especially vulnerable to attacks from tubercles they may have carried for years. A cholera epidemic that summer had swept through cities such as New York and Philadelphia, and Poe, in his weakened state, feared he might be in-

FIG. 29. The Annie daguerreotype, 1849. Taken in the summer of 1849 in Lowell, Massachusetts, as a gift to Annie Richmond, this portrait shows the strain Poe felt as he planned a lecture trip to raise money for his planned *Stylus* magazine and his intense infatuation with the married Mrs. Richmond. (Courtesy of the Edgar Allan Poe Museum, Richmond, Virginia)

FIG. 30. Sarah Anna "Stella" Lewis (1824–80). Mrs. Lewis was a modestly talented poet whose lawyer husband paid Poe to promote her writing. She provided much-needed support for Mrs. Clemm and Poe near the end of his life. (Courtesy of the Edgar Allan Poe Museum, Richmond, Virginia)

fected. Later Muddy would write: "[He] left in such wretched spirits. Before he left home he arranged all his papers, and told me what to do with them *should he die.*" To Annie Richmond, on August 4, 1849, Muddy explained that it was she who had raised the money for Poe's journey to Richmond: "I sold everything I could to get him the means to go with and a few articles that he could not do without."

At this time Poe's main source of support seemed to be Sarah Anna "Stella" Lewis (fig. 30). Mr. Lewis had paid him one hundred dollars (about three thousand dollars today) to promote is wife's writing. Poe urged Griswold to give her more space in his *Female Poets of America,* wrote a biographical sketch of Stella himself, and promised a favor to Griswold in exchange for printing it. Muddy, who was also the beneficiary of Mrs. Lewis's largesse, wrote to Griswold: "If you will do so I will promise you a favorable review of your books as they appear. You know the influence I have with Mr. Poe."

No wonder Poe longed to escape to the South, to his lecture tour and friendly admirers. If things worked out with Elmira, he might just stay in Richmond and edit his magazine there, with her support. But Poe's dependence on and idealization of women remained intact. Before leaving for Richmond, he wrote to the editor J. R. Thompson: "But women do not argue logically as to one's merits, or demerits . . . they have been angels of mercy to me, and have tenderly led me from the verge of ruin while men stood aloof and mocked."

Poe packed his trunk with lectures and manuscripts, books, and flyers for the *Stylus*. He also took a case of clothes. With great care he included the miniature portrait of Eliza Poe, his most prized possession. According to Loui Shew, the miniature was found after Poe's death in his "satchel . . . given up by the Railroad Company."

Poe arrived in Philadelphia at the end of June 1849, just as cholera was raging in the city. Poe may have first gotten drunk and then sick or was first sick and then treated himself with liquor. This stay in Philadelphia was nothing short of a catastrophe, even compared to his earlier binges. The cholera in Philadelphia was so bad when Poe arrived that the hospitals were filled. In summer heat, the disease worked rapidly, causing vomiting and diarrhea, quick dehydration and death. In despair Poe wrote to Muddy on July 7 one of his darkest letters: "I have been *so* ill—have had the cholera, or spasms quite as bad, and can now hardly hold the pen. . . . The very instant you get this, *come* to me. . . . We can but die together. It is no use to reason with me *now;* I must die. I have no desire to live since I have done 'Eureka.' . . . I have been taken to prison once since I came here for getting drunk; but *then* I was not. It was about Virginia."

He sent this letter of despair care of Mrs. Lewis in Brooklyn, but the letter was not given to Muddy for several days. Yet even if Muddy had gotten the letter, she had no money to travel to Philadelphia, and she would not have known where to look for Poe. He would not write her again until he was on the boat approaching Richmond on July 14: "I never wanted to see any one half so bad as I want to see my own darling mother. . . . I do not think that any circumstances will ever tempt me to leave you again. When I am with you I can bear anything, but when I am away from you I am too miserable to live."

We can feel the fear in Poe's words as he neared Richmond. The uncertainty, about the *Stylus,* about his tour, about his health, about his reception by Elmira, was overwhelming. His drinking and wild behavior in Philadelphia had almost cost him his life. Something was critically wrong

FIG. 31. John Sartain (1808–97). One of the best engravers of his time, Sartain founded *Sartain's Magazine* in 1849. Among other works by Poe, he published "Annabel Lee" and "The Poetic Principle" after Poe's death. When Poe was delusional in Philadelphia in July 1849, Sartain cared for him and gave him money. (National Portrait Gallery)

with Poe, both mentally and physically. He had apparently been arrested for public drunkenness and spent a night in Moyamensing Prison. The next morning he was recognized and released without being charged. Freed from prison, Poe appeared at John Sartain's office, probably on Monday, July 2 (fig. 31).

Looking weak and ill, Poe begged Sartain to help him, claiming that two men on the train to New York had plotted to kill him. To escape them, he'd gotten off the train at Bordentown, New Jersey, then taken another train back to Philadelphia. Sartain's account was written many years later and is confusing. Why would Poe have been traveling *to* New York when he had just left there on his way to Richmond? Whatever the facts behind Poe's description of his travels, his fear was palpable, and Sartain's description of the next two days is harrowing.

Pale and frightened, Poe told Sartain that he sought refuge, a hiding place. When asked to explain, Poe claimed he had been on the train to New York when he overheard men behind him planning to kill him. He had escaped and returned to Philadelphia. When Sartain asked why they would want to murder him, Poe answered it was for "revenge" for "a woman trouble." Poe was terrified; as he talked, he decided that he should kill himself. Later Poe said he wanted to go out to the Schuylkill, and Sartain accompanied him.

While they sat in total darkness at the reservoir, Poe described a "vision" he'd had while detained in Moyamensing Prison one or two nights before. A luminous figure of a woman had directed questions at him, as the Sphinx had interrogated Oedipus. If he gave the wrong answer, he would be plunged into a cauldron of boiling liquid. He had also witnessed a terrible scene in which Muddy was cut to pieces.

After two days Poe was able to go out on his own. Within two hours he returned, explaining he had lain in the grass, and realized he had suffered hallucinations. He borrowed the price of a train ticket from Sartain and left. In his desperation Poe had sought to escape to the natural world to calm himself and heal himself. Before, when near despair, he'd treated his threatened derangement with solitude, long walks in the country. Cholera alone, and drink alone, can't explain Poe's behavior in Philadelphia in July 1849. He must have already been suffering from an advancing disease. His fantasy that two men were stalking him because of a woman trouble probably shows his guilt about women in general.

If Poe left Sartain's apartment on July 4, he must have spent a week wandering around Philadelphia. Eventually, he would turn up at the office of the *Quaker City,* a weekly edited by the young novelist George Lippard. By then it was July 12. When he called on Lippard, Poe's clothes were dirty and disheveled, and he was wearing only one shoe. He'd also lost his suitcase or valise. "You are my last hope," Poe said to Lippard. "If you fail me, I can do nothing but die." That very day Lippard had paid his rent and had no money left over. But he thought he might collect some funds for Poe from other editors and writers in Philadelphia.

Leaving Poe in the *Quaker City* office, Lippard knocked on the doors of newspapers but found them all closed because of the epidemic. Feeling he might be coming down with the fever himself, Lippard went on home to bed and only saw Poe the next morning, still in the office, sitting in the corner, his head between his hands. Weeping, Poe said, "I thought you had deserted me." Poe explained that he desperately needed to get to Virginia. "I am heart-sick for Virginia," he said. Some have suggested that *Virginia* may refer to Sissy rather than to the state.

Lippard again went knocking on doors and raised enough dollars from five different editors to get Poe off their hands and on to Richmond. Sartain contributed, along with Louis Godey and Samuel Patterson. On Friday, July 13, Poe finally caught the 10:00 p.m. train to Baltimore. Lippard and the editor Rev. C. Chauncey Burr accompanied him to the station and helped him find his valise. Lippard later said Poe held his hand for a long time, as though reluctant to leave, and that he seemed to feel a "presentiment" that his life was nearly over. While in Philadelphia, Poe sold the newly completed poem "Annabel Lee" as well as the longer "The Bells" to *Sartain's Union Magazine.* The extended version of "The Bells" would be published in the December 1849 issue and "Annabel Lee" in January 1850.

On July 9, 1849, Muddy had written to Annie Richmond: "If Eddy comes home in trouble and sick, I know not what is to become of us." Poe arrived in Richmond more than two weeks late. He checked into the American Hotel on Main Street weak and haggard and immediately sat down to write to Muddy: "Oh, my darling Mother, it is now more than three weeks since I saw you, and in all that time your poor Eddy has scarcely drawn a breath except of intense agony. Perhaps you are sick or gone from Fordham in despair, or dead . . . if I but *see you again,* all the rest is nothing. I love you better than ten thousand lives. . . . I got here with two dollars over—of which I inclose you one."

There is no reason to doubt his wretchedness, following the disaster in Philadelphia. Poe claimed to have taken calomel for the cholera, and the mercury in that may have poisoned him also. He sent Muddy one of his last two dollars. And yet we recall that a letter from Patterson with fifty dollars enclosed (about fifteen hundred dollars today) was waiting for him at the office of the *Southern Literary Messenger.* On July 19, 1849, Poe wrote to Patterson, "Your letter is only this moment received—or rather your two letters with the enclosures ($50 etc.)" If we added up all the money collected for Poe in Philadelphia, from Sartain, Lippard, Godey, and Burr, and perhaps others, it would come to far more than the train and boat fare to Richmond. The discrepancy between what he was given and paid for his work and his penniless destitution is sometimes hard to account for.

There is some disagreement about the kind of new clothes Poe wore in Richmond that summer. Many witnesses asserted that he was always seen in a black suit coat buttoned to the throat, even in hot weather, dressed somewhat like a clergyman. Others said he shed his black wool suit in the oppressive heat and sported a fashionable white linen suit and expensive panama hat. As Jeffrey Meyers tells us: "His handsome, slender and erect figure—dressed in a white suit and Panama hat—was frequently seen in the fashionable parts of the city."

There is a similar mystery about the lectures supposedly lost from his valise or trunk. He gave at least two lectures in Richmond and one in Norfolk, perhaps more. Did he rewrite them from notes or from memory? Susan Talley Weiss remembered that he lectured in Richmond on "The Poetic Principle" without a manuscript, apparently reciting poems and commentary extempore.

With help from the Mackenzies, with rest at the hotel, Poe partially regained his strength. In the meantime, Muddy had finally received his first desperate letter from Philadelphia. When she did get the outcry of despair, she answered at once, and her letter worked like a miracle to calm Poe. On July 19, 1849, he wrote: "You will see at once, by the handwriting of this letter, that I am better—much better in health and spirits. . . . Most of my suffering arose from that terrible idea which I could not get rid of—the idea that you were dead. For more than ten days I was totally deranged. . . . All was hallucination, arising from an attack which I had never before experienced—an attack of *mania-à-potu*. May Heaven grant that it prove a warning to me for the rest of my days."

Poe's dependence on Muddy had always been great, but it had grown over the years, especially since Virginia's death. Mothering Poe was Muddy's destiny and privilege, and she begged, borrowed, and flattered to keep him alive. One of Poe's last poems was the sonnet "To My Mother," not one of his better efforts, but nonetheless deeply felt. His dependence on Muddy could be seen as another kind of marriage.

Once he recovered somewhat in Richmond, Poe wrote to Edward Patterson about their plans for the *Stylus*. Poe was still weak and ill, but he kept up a brave front, and he needed to perform well at lectures to raise money. In a letter to Patterson on August 7, 1849, he would plead, "As yet, I am too feeble to travel." It is significant that Poe described his condition as "congestion of the brain."

In late July or early August 1849, Poe began to drink again and became extremely ill. Susan Weiss would remember: "Assiduous attention saved him, but it was the opinion of the physicians that another such attack would prove fatal." Dr. George Rawlings, who also treated Poe at this time, later said that in his delirium Poe drew a pistol and threatened to shoot him.

Among all the setbacks and debacles, and even knowing the sad ending, we can also view Poe's final ten weeks in Richmond as something of a victory lap. He was back in the city of his childhood and youth, a celebrity, author of "The Raven," much admired for his critical writing. The South, for better or worse, was in his blood. He insisted on dressing like a gentleman, walking with a cane, behaving toward women like a gallant. For all his pleading to Muddy, Poe had come home to Richmond.

His childhood playmate Catherine Poitiaux left this reminiscence: "I asked, alluding to his marriage, when I should see him again . . . a gray shadow such as I had never seen before, save on the face of the dying, passed across his as . . . he answered slowly: 'In the words of my Raven, perhaps—nevermore,' and in a moment he had gone."

Though Poe loved solitary rambles in the woods and countryside, he was wined and dined in Richmond, invited to teas and receptions. Through the Mackenzies he met the twenty-seven-year-old Susan Archer Talley, who later, as Susan Weiss, left us a detailed (but not always reliable) account of Poe's activities in the summer of 1849. Like so many others, she was delighted to meet and socialize with the great man. To add to the thrill, he had praised some of her poems. She would later write: "I would illustrate, if possible, the manner peculiar to him, and also the indescribable charm, I might almost say magnetism, which his eyes possessed above any others that I have ever seen." Susan Weiss would also recall that Poe "expressed his conviction that he had written his best poems, but that in prose he might yet surpass what he had already accomplished."

Poe saw a good deal of the local editors and writers, including the editor of the *Southern Literary Messenger*, John Reuben Thompson, who gave him an advance on future work, and also John M. Daniel, editor of the *Semi-Weekly Examiner*, with whom he had almost fought a duel the summer before.

One of Poe's main purposes in coming to Richmond in 1849 was to contact Elmira Royster Shelton again. Over the years Poe had written a number of poems about the loss of Elmira in 1827, associating Elmira with the natural world, with trees and the open air, with flowers and landscapes, his paradise. As Miss Chaworth was to Byron, Elmira represented to Poe youth and the innocence youth believes in.

To save money, Poe moved out of the Exchange Hotel to the Swan Tavern. We don't know exactly when he first called on Elmira Shelton. All we are sure of is that he began to visit her frequently, sometimes with his sister, Rosalie. We can imagine that she would be reserved at first, given the way he'd wooed her the summer before, then disappeared. But soon there were rumors that the two were engaged and planning a wedding.

When Mr. Shelton died, in 1844, at the age of thirty-six, he'd left Elmira at least seventy thousand dollars, the house in Richmond, and other properties of which Elmira was the manager. Likely his transportation business continued to bring income. Poe was penniless, with a reputation for drinking and much else. Mrs. Shelton was a member of St. John's Episcopal Church and a woman of property. Poe was known for stories of horror and cruelty, the Imp of the Perverse. Even his looks suggested something sinister.

Elmira's living children, Ann Elizabeth, Bettie, and Southall Bohannon, were adamantly opposed to any union between Poe and their mother. Southall mocked Poe's speech and imitated the way Poe walked with a limp. No doubt Elmira's brothers and neighbors found it hard to believe she would consider marriage to the notorious Mr. Poe. Attending his lectures was one thing, but giving her hand to a penniless libertine quite another.

In the last few months of his life, Poe demonstrated again his yearning for the haven of marriage *and* his resistance to the institution. He sought a family, respectability, and security. He needed someone with money to help launch the *Stylus*. While he claimed to be madly in love and spiritually devoted to Annie Richmond, he aggressively courted Elmira, who seems to have always been in love with him. She was both his first love and his last hope for a comfortable old age for himself and Muddy. Even as he planned a wedding with Elmira, he told others the marriage would never take place. When he left Elmira to bring Muddy to Richmond, he told his fiancée he thought he would never see her again. Just days before his death, Poe feared marriage but could not resist seeking it. Marriage might suggest sanity and security, safety, but, he knew, was often more nightmare than sanctuary. Attraction and repulsion, centripetal, centrifugal, fugue and petal. Poe could not resist, nor could he accept.

The descriptions of Elmira Shelton by those who remembered her are contradictory. In Susan Weiss's memory: "She was a tall, rather masculine looking woman, with good features, hollow cheeks, thin lips and large blue eyes, with purplish shadows around them, which had once probably been handsome. She . . . had not a particle of grace or *style,* and her countenance was wholly expressionless. She impressed me as being hard and cold."

Yet Edward M. Alfriend, who recalled Elmira in her old age, would say: "When I knew Mrs. Shelton she had a lovely, almost saintly face. Her eyes were deep blue, her hair dark brown, touched with grey, her nose thin and patrician. . . . intellectually she was a woman of education and force of character. . . . She was just the woman in which such a perturbed spirit as that of Poe would have sought rest and found it." In the photographs we have of her, Elmira looks austere, tense, a little cold. But we should remember that a subject had to remain perfectly still while a daguerreotype was made. In fact, she was beautiful, though restrained before the camera. (See fig. 3.)

Something happened in early August to interrupt the courtship. Possibly Poe learned of Mr. Shelton's will, which stipulated that Elmira would lose three-quarters of her estate if she remarried. But Elmira was in love, and she seems to have always been in love with Poe. According to Edward Alfriend, "She more than once said to me, 'I married another man, but the love of my life was Edgar Poe. I never loved anyone else.'" It's more than likely that the break with Poe in August 1849 was caused by his drinking. Elmira asked for her letters to be returned, proving that she *had* been writing to Poe.

But the break in the courtship did not deter Elmira from attending the lecture on "The Poetic Principle" at the Concert Room of the Exchange Hotel on Friday, August 17. Ostensibly, it was the kickoff of Poe's speaking tour to raise money for the *Stylus.* The lecture was an event in Richmond, as citizens turned out to welcome the celebrated native son. The local newspapers covered the lecture, and tickets were sold for twenty-five cents (about $7.50 today). Elmira sat in the first row, directly in front of the lectern.

Poe stood gracefully beside a table while he spoke, one hand on the table. The evening was one of the triumphs of his life. He was now a veteran performer. Some might criticize his "sing-song" delivery of poems, but it appears his recitation of poems was mesmeric. Dr. B. L. Gildersleeve would remember: "Like most poets he was sensitive to the music of his own verse; and that was the element he emphasized in his delivery." Poe had given the same lecture in Providence the previous December, and he'd continued to polish it. "The Poetic Principle" is the summation of Poe's lifetime of writing poetry, thinking about poetry. Along with his essays on Hawthorne, it is his most significant critical writing. The essay was also a showcase for his delivery, the literary *histrio* as poet.

One special memory of the lecture comes to us from Bishop O. P. Fitzgerald: "I was in Richmond in 1849, and remember Mr. Poe, with his white linen coat and trousers, black velvet vest, and broad Panama hat." Later, when found dying in Baltimore, Poe was wearing the ruins of a lighter suit and straw hat. Poe began the lecture by reminding his audience that "a long poem is simply a contradiction in terms." Poetry relies on "unity of effect," and long works such as *Paradise Lost* are really collections of shorter poems linked by filler. "If, at any time, any very long poem *were* popular in reality, which I doubt, it is at least clear that no very long poem will ever be popular again." But a poem can also be too brief to achieve the desired effect.

As early as 1831, Poe had been echoing Coleridge's claim that the purpose of poetry was pleasure. Therefore, moralistic poetry, didactic poetry, was by definition inferior. "I allude to the heresy of *The Didactic.*" "An immortal instinct, deep within the spirit of man, is thus, plainly, a sense of the Beautiful." Beyond all the beauties and satisfactions of the natural world, we long for something more: "We have still a thirst unquenchable, to allay which he has not shown us the crystal springs. This thirst belongs to the immortality of Man. . . . It is the desire of the moth for the star. . . . Inspired by an ecstatic prescience of the glories beyond the grave, we struggle, by multiform combinations among the things and thoughts of Time, to attain a portion of that Loveliness whose very elements, perhaps, appertain to eternity alone."

As many poets and theorists of the nineteenth century often did, Poe compares poetry to music, music being the purest and most ideal and spiritual of all the arts. "It is in Music, perhaps, that the soul most nearly attains the great end for which, when inspired with the Poetic Sentiment, it struggles—the creation of supernal Beauty."

Not only didacticism but passion can mar the perfect beauty of poetry. Yet Poe concedes that these features need not be entirely excluded from poetry. After reciting a number of examples to illustrate his point, Poe reminds us that the Poetic Principle "is, strictly and simply, the Human Aspiration for Supernal Beauty . . . always found in *an elevating excitement of the Soul*—quite independent of that passion which is the intoxication of the Heart—or of that Truth which is the satisfaction of the Reason." Then Poe gives us a stirring catalog of things that inspire the poetic sensibility:

> We shall reach, however, more immediately, a distinct conception of what the true Poetry is, by mere reference to a few of the simple elements which induce in the Poet himself the true poetical effect. He recognizes the ambrosia which nourishes his soul, in the bright orbs that shine in Heaven—in the volutes of the flower—in the clustering of low shrubberies—in the waving of the grain-fields—in the slanting of tall, Eastern trees—in the blue distance of mountains—in the grouping of clouds—in the twinkling of half-hidden brooks—in the gleaming of silver rivers—in the repose of sequestered lakes—in the star-mirroring depths of lonely wells. He perceives it in the songs of birds—in the harp of Aeolus—in the sighing of the night-wind—in the repining voice of the forest—in the surf that complains to the shore—in the fresh breath of the woods—in the scent of the violet—in the voluptuous perfume of the hyacinth—in the suggestive odour that comes to him, at eventide, from far-distant, undiscovered islands, over dim oceans, illimitable and unexplored. He owns it in all noble thoughts—in all unworldly motives—in all holy impulses—in all chivalrous, generous, and self-sacrificing deeds. He feels it in the beauty of woman—in the grace of her step—in the lustre of her eye—in the melody of her voice—in her soft laughter—in her sigh—in the harmony of the rustling of her robes. He deeply feels it in her winning endearments—in her burning enthusiasms—in her gentle charities—in her meek and devotional endurances—but above all—ah, far above all—he kneels to it—he worships it in the faith, in the purity, in the strength, in the altogether divine majesty—of her *love.*

Notice that Poe includes among the sources of inspiration "generous self-sacrificing deeds."

Edmund Wilson, one of the most distinguished American critics of the twentieth century, credited Poe with the "only first-rate classical prose of this period. . . . His literary articles and lectures, in fact, surely constitute the most remarkable body of criticism ever produced in the United States."

Poe concluded the lecture by reciting Robert Motherwell's "The Song of the Cavalier" to celebrate heroism in a South that prided itself on chivalry and possibly to warn the region of the "absurdity and impiety of warfare," as if Poe might foresee the cataclysm of the coming Civil War. It was Poe's greatest triumph, his finest moment, as he looked directly into Elmira's blue eyes and recited the litany of poetic inspiration, acknowledging the woman who had inspired him first and last, and then implicitly warned the South of the danger of a cult of heroic warfare, in the future capital of the Confederacy. If only we could stop there, as the audience applauded the native son, who then recited "The Raven" to even greater applause, as his first and final love gazed at him in admiration.

21

THE OATH AND CONSENT

IN 1882 DR. JOHN J. MORAN, THE PHYSICIAN WHO ATTENDED Poe in his final illness in Baltimore, wrote to a friend about his recent visit to Richmond. Dr. Moran had become a successful lecturer, touring the country to deliver his evolving account of the last days and hours of Poe. While in Richmond, he'd met the seventy-two-year-old Elmira Shelton and wrote: "I had returned from a lecture tour to Richmond, the home of his *Annabel Lee,* who yet lives, is near her three score and ten. Yet she was at the lecture, 32 years have intervened since his death, and she and I, met for the first time after that period, it was a meeting I shall never forget—so deeply were we impressed, that our tears could not be restrained."

Poe renewed his suit to Elmira and told Muddy that he had already bought a ring. But a significant factor in Elmira's change of attitude must have been Poe's attendance at a Sons of Temperance meeting in late August, where he took a solemn pledge to never drink again. As far as we know, Poe had never made such a formal commitment before, and he almost certainly did it to please Elmira.

The Sons of Temperance was an organization somewhat like the YMCA or Salvation Army. In order to take the pledge, Poe would have had to make a declaration of Christian faith. Since Poe himself left no statement about this event, we can only speculate on its meaning for him. But for Elmira his oath seems to have been decisive. There was talk in Richmond that they were engaged again. Poe mailed a copy of his pledge to Muddy, who then forwarded it to Annie Richmond.

It appears that Poe came to church services in Richmond, either before or after he'd taken the pledge. He may have attended with Elmira. According to one observer, Poe was so absorbed by the choir music he seemed oblivious to his surroundings. "The cessation of the music alone awakened him from his ecstacy [*sic*]. He instantly resumed the air of cold hauteur."

Susan Weiss would recall that Poe was especially pleased by his time in Richmond that last summer: "He spoke of his future, seeming to anticipate it with an eager delight, like that of youth."

With his engagement to Elmira on again and his oath to never more bend an elbow in a tavern, Poe traveled to Norfolk to repeat his lecture. The appearance in Richmond had been a resounding success, though one reviewer criticized his singsong delivery of the poems. John Daniel's comment in the *Semi-Weekly Examiner* that if Poe had talent instead of genius, he would have been a greater success probably did not please him.

Among Poe's friends made in Norfolk was young Susan V. C. Ingram, who many years later would write an account of Poe's visit of September 9, 1849, at the Hygiea Hotel at Old Point Comfort: "Mr. Poe sat there in that quiet way of his which made you feel his presence. After a while my aunt, who was nearer his age, said: 'This seems to be just the time and place for poetry, Mr. Poe.' . . . And it was. We all felt it. . . . And when we seconded the request that he recite for us he agreed readily. . . .This was only a little more than two weeks, as I remember, before Poe's death, but I saw him again before he went to Baltimore, where he died."

At Richmond Poe renewed friendships with several from childhood, including Robert Stanard, son of his ideal "Helen." Poe spent over two months in Richmond or nearby, and he was so busy socially he composed little except letters. On September 10, 1849, Poe wrote to Muddy: "[Elmira pro]poses for me to go, immediately after the marriage, to one of her houses—the one she is in now—and send for you to join us at once. . . . I confess that my heart sinks at the idea of this marriage. *I think,* however, that it will certainly take place & that immediately."

As with almost everything else in Poe's life, there would be contradictory accounts of the engagement. At one point in her later life, Elmira would claim to have never been actually betrothed to Poe. Whatever her reasons for the denial, the evidence suggests otherwise. On September 22, 1849, Elmira wrote a letter to Muddy that gives the impression that she and Poe were very close, indeed, and that her future would include Muddy as well. Elmira was not an author, but she knew how to be gracious and diplomatic: "You will no doubt be much surprised to receive a letter from one whom you have never seen. . . . I am fully prepared to *love* you, and I do sincerely hope that our spirits may be congenial—There shall be nothing wanting on my part to make them so—I have just spent a very happy evening with your dear Edgar. . . . I remember seeing Edgar, & his lovely wife, very soon after they were married—I met them—I shall never forget my feelings at the time—They were indescribable, almost agonizing."

Notice that Poe did not deny his intense love for Virginia to Elmira, as he had to Helen Whitman and Annie Richmond. Elmira was almost family, and besides, she understood him, his excitability, quick temper, his flights from responsibility.

Biographers have tended to see Poe as at least partially mercenary in his courtship of Elmira. Even with a much-reduced income after she married, she would still have a house and enough to live on and could help him establish the *Stylus*. And it was likely she had considerable savings.

That summer Poe gave Elmira an oval-shaped brooch that contained a lock of his hair. The brooch was framed in gold filigree and on its back was engraved "E.A.P. to S.E.S." In her subsequent photographs, Elmira would wear the brooch, or one like it, fastened at her throat.

Could he revive the desire he'd felt at sixteen, in the days of garden walks and kisses? He could not resist the idea of being married to his long-lost love, any more than she could resist the man she'd admired for so long. From her letter of December 1848 to her cousin Philip, it's clear Elmira suffered aching loneliness and fear that she would never be loved again.

As Poe knew what it meant to marry a smart, mature, practical woman who would expect him to be a husband in every sense of the word, he must have felt in Elmira's presence a renewed desire, such as he may not have known since his affair with Fanny Osgood. Marriage had been his ideal, all his life, and his horror. As long as he remained sober, he could be the man she expected him to be. Everything, in several senses, depended on his sobriety. Yet Elmira would have known how unlikely it was that Poe could refuse a drink in a culture in which juleps and toddies were an everyday feature of social life. Still, she was willing to hope, cherishing the idea of marriage to her first love. Even as they planned their wedding for October 17, after Poe returned from New York with Muddy, somewhere in the back of their minds, each must have known it was almost too good to be true. They were in love, but that didn't mean they could ever be happily wed. That's why the courtship has been so confusing to biographers over the years. As outlined in *Eureka,* the forces of attraction and resistance are intense.

Poe did deliver "The Poetic Principle" again on September 24, and it was another success. It is said there were about five hundred people in the audience. Since tickets sold for fifty cents this time, Poe must have made a substantial profit, enough to pay his hotel bill, with some left over for the trip north. But what became of that money or the money he received from Thompson of the *Southern Literary Messenger* for promised articles and reviews? William Winston Valentine, who attended Poe's last lecture in Richmond, noted that his face was pale and gave an impression "of scorn and discontent. He gait was firm and erect, but his manner was nervous and emphatic." Poe was performing though quite ill.

One challenge of writing about Poe, especially of his later years, is the complexity and multifacetedness of his mind. I do not doubt that his visits with Elmira had reawakened his deepest love, and hers. But from his letters to Muddy that summer, we also see his ambivalence, even toward Elmira. Writing to Muddy on August 29, he had made explicit his dividedness:

> And now let me tell you about Elmira as well as I can in a letter.—We are solemnly engaged to be married within the coming month (Septr). . . . I got angry with her for wishing to defer it till January & wrote her a cross letter. . . . We made it up & she now sanctions my writing to you, announcing the marriage in a month. She went nearly frantic when I told her I would nt [*sic*] have her. . . . Her relations—her married daughter especially—are opposed to it—because their pecuniary interests will be injured—but she defies them & seems resolved.
>
> You are to live with us *always & to take charge of the house. She says she already loves you as a mother—& I am sure you will love *her*—for she is so amiable, gentle, domestic, and affectionate. She agrees to live where I choose, but would prefer the North. . . . Mr. Shelton left property to the

> amount of $60,000 [about $1.8 million today], and since his death it has increased in value and is now worth at least 70,000 [$2.1 million]. He left it to her sole charge and management so long as she remains his widow, but if she marries, she retains only a house, furniture, carriage &c, servants (slaves) and an income from 12 to 1400$ [$360,000–$420,000]. But she has had charge of the estate now for 9 years; and as she is said to be a notable manager, no doubt she has laid by many thousand dollars in money. . . . Her son (Southall, 10 years old) is to have 20,000$ [$600,000] on coming of age. He is to live with her, if she pleases, and she is to receive an annual allowance (an ample one) for his board and education. . . . At all events, my *dear,* dear mother, you will no longer have to suffer as you have done . . .
>
> It is now 4 weeks since I have touched *anything* to drink. . . . there is *one other thing,* dear mother, which drives me frantic—*my love for Annie*—I worship her beyond all human love. My passion for her grows stronger every day. I *dare not,* at this crisis, either speak or think of her—if I did I should go mad. . . . My love for her will *never, never cease, either in this world or the next.*

The first three pages of this long letter were lost until recently. They make clear Poe's financial straits and that plans for the marriage to Elmira were well underway. His trunk had been held until he could pay his bill at the Swan Tavern. This letter is one of the clearest expressions we have of Poe's compartmentalized mind, especially about marriage. It continues: "Elmira talks about visiting Fordham. . . . Could we be happier in Richmond or Lowell?—for I suppose we could never be happy at Fordham . . . and, Muddy, I *must* be somewhere where I can see Annie."

If we are to believe Susan Weiss's memoir of 1904, there was some tension between Elmira and Rosalie about the care of Poe. Once she became engaged, Elmira took charge of Poe in his weakened condition: "One day [Rosalie] went to that lady's house when she knew her brother was there. She was shown into the parlor, where she found him lying on a sofa with a headache from his long walk. Mrs. Shelton called her into the hall and said, 'He does not need you here, and I will take care of him myself,'—and so dismissed her, to her great indignation."

While courting his past and new love and contemplating marriage,

Poe tells his mother-in-law that he must always be somewhere he can see Annie Richmond. We see not only the ambivalence of Poe's mind but the extent to which he lived in fantasy. It was such illusions that had sustained him through defeat after defeat and failure after failure. But his imagination hampered him in the actual business of living. Elmira was real and far more beautiful than Annie Richmond and probably far more in love with him. But the fact that Elmira was real, in the flesh, was also the problem. Annie Richmond was an ideal, a beacon, far away, and married, and no threat to his dream of ideal marriage.

Later, in the same letter of August 29, 1849, Poe wrote: "But I want to live *near Annie*. . . . Do not tell me anything about Annie—I cannot bear to hear it now—unless you tell me Mr. R. is dead—I have got the wedding ring and shall have no difficulty, I think, in getting a dress-coat." It should be remembered that Poe was also playing a role with Muddy. Muddy had become devoted to Annie, since Annie had visited her at Fordham the summer before and given her money and other gifts. After Poe's death, Muddy would live with the Richmonds for an extended period. Annie was a daydream Poe cherished to inspire and sustain him. Elmira was a living, breathing woman, ready to marry him, and Poe was both thrilled and frightened.

Poe was also anxious to reassure Muddy that Elmira could never replace Virginia in his heart and to promise Muddy that the marriage to Elmira was just a practical matter, no threat to her, while his real love was for Annie Richmond far away in Massachusetts. Poe had reached the dilemma he'd encountered with Helen Whitman. Again, an intelligent, beautiful woman was willing to take him into her life and into her bed. But Elmira Shelton loved the *man* Edgar Allan Poe and was willing to risk her future, against the rigid opposition of her children and family. Other women adored the celebrated poet.

In his next letter to Muddy, of September 18, 1849, Poe wrote: "Elmira has just got home from the country. I spent last evening with her. I think she loves me more devotedly than any one I ever knew & I cannot help loving her in return—Nothing is yet definitely settled." In this final letter to Muddy, we have the whole story of Poe's courtship of Elmira. Poe understands well that she loves him more than any other woman ever has. There is no nonsense about Mrs. Shelton, but she does love him, with all his flaws and self-destructiveness. Her commitment to him is the thing Poe wants most, and fears most. The wedding is now scheduled for October 17, when he returns from New York with Muddy.

Poe's last days in Richmond, after the second lecture on "The Poetic Principle," were frantically busy. He met with J. R. Thompson, editor of the *Southern Literary Messenger,* and gave him a copy of "Annabel Lee," without mentioning that the poem had been sold to *Sartain's Union Magazine.* He also had a new daguerreotype made, this one also showing him more aged since November 1848 (fig. 32). He spent the evening of September 25 with Rosalie at the Talley house and the evening of September 26 with Elmira at her home on Grace Street.

Later, after the horror of Poe's death and the rancorous attacks on Poe's character, Elmira, effectively twice widowed, told E. V. Valentine, a Richmond neighbor and sculptor: "He [continued?] to visit me frequently but I never engaged myself to him. . . . He said when he left that he was going to New York, to wind up some business and that he would return to Richmond as soon as he accomplished it, though he said at the same time that he had a presentment [*sic*] he never should see me any more."

Immediately after Poe's death, Elmira wrote to Muddy in a very different tone: "He came up to my house on the evening of the 26th Sept. to take leave of me. He was very sad, and complained of being quite sick. I felt his pulse, and found he had considerable fever, and did not think it probable he would be able to start the next morning (Thursday) as he anticipated. I felt so wretched about him all of that night, that I went up early the next morning to enquire after him, when, much to my regret, he had left in the boat for Baltimore."

Many years later Dr. John J. Moran would record: "I have the testimony from the pen of the lady herself, written to me thirty-two years ago, of the fact, and from her own lips in June last, that she was engaged to be married to POE at the time of his death."

A number of other people saw Poe on his last day and night before he left for Baltimore, and no others mentioned Poe being ill. Yet Elmira recalled clearly that he was sick, feverish, and very sad. The others may not have been as observant as she. Poe's activities after he left Elmira's house at nine o'clock on the evening of September 26 are the beginning of the mystery surrounding his death. The boat for Norfolk was scheduled to leave

FIG. 32. The Pratt daguerreotype, 1849. A few weeks before his death on October 7, 1849, Poe sat for this daguerreotype by William Pratt in Richmond. An excellent likeness, the picture suggests Poe's weariness after a summer away from home and his struggle to refrain from drinking while enjoying the hospitality accorded a native son in Richmond and seeking the hand of Elmira Shelton. (Courtesy of the Edgar Allan Poe Museum, Richmond, Virginia)

at 4:00 a.m. From Norfolk he would take another boat up the Chesapeake to Baltimore. It's not clear why Poe chose to go by boat and not the faster train to Baltimore.

Before dining, Poe stopped by the office of Dr. John Carter, a young physician. Carter would later remember that Poe was nervous but not intoxicated. When Poe left the doctor's office, he took the doctor's cane, leaving his own cane and other items. Years later Dr. Carter penned a reminiscence of the evening: "From this manner of departure I inferred that he expected to return shortly, but did not see him again, and was surprised to learn next day that he had left for Baltimore by the early morning boat. I then called on Saddler, who informed me that Poe had left his house [restaurant?] at exactly twelve that night, starting for the Baltimore boat in company with several companions whom he had met at Saddler's." One acquaintance he met at Saddler's that night, J. M. Blakey, later said Poe was not drinking. Meanwhile, Elmira worried throughout a sleepless night. In the morning she had servants hitch up her buggy and she drove to Poe's hotel, only to find that he had left hours before.

We can imagine the stress Poe felt as he stood on the deck of the boat churning up the Chesapeake on September 28 from Norfolk to Baltimore. He may have hoped to delay his arrival and the job of editing Mrs. Loud's book of poems in Philadelphia. (Mr. Loud had promised him a hundred dollars [three thousand dollars today] for preparing his wife's poems for publication.) Again he faced a decision with someone he loved and who loved him. By his own declaration, Elmira loved him more devotedly than anyone else ever had. She did not need to breathe through ether-scented handkerchiefs. She did not have to believe he was a god. Elmira could have lived and loved him in her Richmond house, or in the Virginia countryside, for another thirty or forty years. The prospect thrilled and alarmed him.

An essential clue to the mystery of Poe's death is Elmira's statement that he was feverish when he left her house. There was something very wrong, physically, with him. Poe had been exposed all his life to people suffering and dying from tuberculosis. With the trauma of his drunken days in Philadelphia, his DT's, the bacteria had probably broken free and entered his bloodstream, causing both the pallor and fever Elmira had described. According to *The Complete Medical Encyclopedia* of the American Medical Association: "Some TB bacteria usually remain dormant in the lungs even if active disease does not occur. In later years, the dormant bacteria can sometimes cause active TB infection if a person's immune system is impaired." The entry goes on to say, "People with alcoholism and those who abuse . . . illegal drugs are also at increased risk."

Meningitis, an infection of the brain covering and the spinal cord, can be caused by tubercular bacteria or some other bacteria. Someone who has shown no signs of TB can be suddenly and fatally struck with TB of the brain. We are told this is what happened to Thomas Wolfe in 1938. Wolfe had been carrying the bacillus for years, and suddenly it tore loose from a tubercle in his lungs and attacked his brain and killed him in a matter of days or weeks.

We can't prove at this late date that Poe died of tubercular meningitis or encephalitis, but given the symptoms and the history of TB among his close family members, it seems the most plausible explanation for his illness and sudden death, as Mark Dawidziak and others have suggested. Dr. Carter remembered him as nervous, distracted. Poe knew he was ill and growing disoriented.

The boat from Norfolk would have arrived in Baltimore early on the twenty-ninth, a Saturday. Poe left his trunk at the Bradshaw Hotel near the train station, where it was later found. A train conductor named Rollins would claim that he found Poe in the baggage car on his train between Baltimore and Philadelphia and then put him on another train headed back to Baltimore. As sick as he was, Poe might have done almost anything. It would make sense that he was on the train to Philadelphia, but we don't know why his trunk was left at the hotel in Baltimore, unless he was too ill to remember it. As the disease advanced, Poe may have become so weakened and confused he could not remember where he was. He had money from the sale of tickets at his last lecture, plus what Thompson had paid him for articles to be written.

Beginning in the nineteenth century, a favorite explanation for what happened to Poe in Baltimore was that he was rounded up by a political gang and kept drunk and drugged for repeated voting at different polling places around the city. But scholars such as Arthur Hobson Quinn have proven that to be most unlikely. When found on Election Day, October 3, Poe was in no condition to cast one vote. Others have suggested he had been bitten by a rabid animal and died of rabies. Those who have suspected that Poe died of meningitis or encephalitis are probably closer to the truth, and tubercular meningitis is the most likely diagnosis of all. The bacteria were eating up his brain.

What Poe actually did in those days between September 29 and October 3, 1849, we can't know. Most likely, he checked his trunk at the hotel in Baltimore while he waited for the train to Philadelphia. Poe did not call on his Baltimore relatives. In his desperate condition, they would have assumed he was drunk. But he did not forget that he needed to get to Philadelphia to earn the one hundred dollars for editing Mrs. Loud's poems, and at some point he boarded the Philadelphia train, where conductor Rollins found him unconscious in the baggage car, probably on October 2. Knowing that Poe had relatives in Baltimore, Rollins put the sick poet back on the Baltimore train at Havre de Grace. After arriving again in Baltimore on the night of the second, Poe appears to have been beaten and robbed by thugs. When found the next afternoon, he was lying on boards laid across two barrels near a lumberyard, delirious, hardly conscious.

When discovered, Poe was described as wearing filthy, cast-off clothes. But he may have been wearing the remains of a fine summer suit—not of linen, as the bishop had remembered, but of alpaca and worsted cashmere, thin for the summer heat in Richmond—and the wreck of his fine panama hat. Likely, he'd been robbed of all his money and watch and personal possessions. The clothes would have been ill fitting because he had lost so much weight.

On Wednesday, October 3, a cold, rainy, windy day, Poe reappeared in verifiable accounts. Joseph W. Walker, a local printer, found Poe not far from Gunner's Hall, a tavern at 44 East Lombard Street in Baltimore, owned by Cornelius Ryan. Walker helped Poe into the tavern, and Poe, who could barely speak, mentioned not one of his relatives but his old friend the doctor and temperance lecturer Joseph Evans Snodgrass. Walker sent a quick note to Snodgrass, who lived nearby: "There is a gentleman, rather the worse for wear, at Ryan's 4th ward polls, who goes under the cognomen of Edgar A. Poe, and who appears in great distress, & he says he is acquainted with you, and I assure you, he is in need of immediate assistance."

We don't know how long it took for the note to reach Snodgrass or how long it took the doctor-editor to come to the tavern.

> The intellectual flash of his eye had vanished, or rather had been quenched in the bowl; but the broad, capacious forehead of the author of "The Raven"

> . . . was still there, with a width, in the region of ideality, such as few men have ever possessed. But perhaps I would not have so readily recognized him had I not been notified of his apparel. His hat—or rather the hat of somebody else, for he had evidently been robbed of his clothing, or cheated in an exchange—was a cheap palm-leaf one, without a band, and soiled; his coat, of commonest alpaca, and evidently "second hand"; and his pants of gray-mixed cassimere, dingy and badly fitting. He wore neither vest nor neck-cloth, if I remember aright, while his shirt was sadly crumpled and soiled. He was so utterly stupefied with liquor that I thought it best not to seek recognition or conversation. . . . I immediately ordered a room for him, where he could be comfortable until I got word to his relatives—for there were several in Baltimore. Just at that moment, one or two of the persons referred to, getting information of the case, arrived at the spot. They declined to take private care of him, assigning as a reason, that he had been very abusive and ungrateful on former occasions, when drunk, and advised that he be sent to a hospital. . . . So insensible was he, that we had to carry him to the carriage as if a corpse. The muscles of articulation seemed paralyzed to speechlessness, and mere incoherent mutterings were all that were heard.

Why would Snodgrass think cashmere and alpaca cheap? That remains a mystery. Poe had known Snodgrass for years and knew the doctor was a fervent advocate of temperance. It is quite possible that Poe named Snodgrass because he had *not* been drinking and was only very sick and needed a doctor. But because Poe was found in a tavern and in such a wretched state, Snodgrass assumed Poe had been on a binge. Because of Dr. Snodgrass's assumption, biographers ever since have believed Poe was drunk when found. Many years later chemical tests of Poe's hair taken from his corpse revealed it unlikely Poe had consumed alcohol for at least a month before his death. Poe seems to have kept his pledge to Elmira to not drink. Dr. Moran, who treated him at the end, said his patient showed no signs of intoxication when brought to his care.

After Poe was admitted to the hospital, Dr. Moran found the cabdriver who had driven him waiting outside for his fare. When asked if Poe was drunk when found, the driver answered, "No, sir, he was a sick man, a very sick man." Because he assumed Poe was drunk when found in the tavern on Election Day, Snodgrass would make extensive use of Poe's death in his temperance lectures. And the good doctor was "willing to alter details for what he considered a greater cause."

It was Henry Herring, formerly married to Poe's late aunt Eliza, who came to the tavern and suggested Poe be taken to a hospital. Poe had indeed offended the Herrings before when in his cups. In a carriage Poe was driven to Washington College Hospital, at Broadway and Hampstead Street. A little over a month later, Dr. Moran wrote to Muddy describing Poe's last four days:

> When brought to the Hospital he was unconscious of his condition—who brought him or with whom he had been associating. He remained in this condition from 5. *Ock* in the afternoon—the hour of his admission—until 3 next morning . . .
>
> To this state succeeded tremor of of [*sic*] the limbs, and at first a busy but not violent or active delirium—constant talking—and vacant converse with spectral and imaginary objects on the walls. His face was pale and his whole person drenched in perspiration—We were unable to induce tranquility before the second day [5 October] after his admission.

Poe certainly demonstrated signs of hallucinations, but the stupor, the near coma, suggest meningitis or encephalitis. He was suffering delirium but also from something Dr. Moran later called "congestion of the brain."

Our only account of Poe's last two days comes from Dr. Moran:

> I was summoned to his bedside so soon as conscious[ness] supervened, and questioned him in reference to his family—place of residence—relatives &c. But his answers were incoherent & unsatisfactory. He told me, however, he had a wife in Richmond (which, I have since learned was not the fact) that he did not know when he had left that city or what had become of his trunk of clothing. Wishing to rally and sustain his now fast sinking hopes I told him I hoped, that in a few days he would be able to enjoy the society of his friends here, and I would be most happy to contribute in every possible way to his ease & comfort. At this he broke out with much energy, and said the best thing his best friend could do would be to blow out his brains with a pistol—that when he beheld his degradation

> he was ready to ["]sink in the earth &c." Shortly after giving expression to these words Mr. Poe seemed to dose & I left him for a short time. When I returned I found him in a violent delirium, resisting the efforts of two nurses to keep him in bed. This state continued until Saturday evening (he was admitted on Wednesday) when he commenced calling for one "Reynolds," which he did through the night up to *three* on Sunday morning. At this time a very decided change began to affect him. Having become enfeebled from exertion he became quiet and seemed to rest for a short time, then gently moving his head he said "*Lord help my poor Soul*" and expired!

Every word of Dr. Moran's account has been examined by Poe biographers like an excerpt from the Dead Sea Scrolls. Each has found evidence of something he or she was looking for. It seems Poe's delirium might have gone away, but the disease in his body took over. In his confusion Poe remembered his engagement to Elmira in Richmond and thought the wedding had already taken place. Scholars have pointed out he was possibly thinking of Jeremiah Reynolds and the voyage to the Antarctic in *The Narrative of Arthur Gordon Pym* and the embrace of the tall white figure where that story breaks off.

Later Dr. Moran would record another detail of the days before Poe's death: "Just at this moment my friend, Professor J.C.S. Monkur, one of the oldest physicians of the faculty . . . came into the sick chamber. . . . After a careful examination, Dr. Monkur gave it as his opinion that POE would die from excessive nervous prostration and loss of nerve power, resulting from exposure, affecting the encephalon, a sensitive and delicate membrane of the brain."

We can only hope that at the end Poe found peace and absolution as an Eliza-Virginia-Elmira figure in white welcomed him to a country with lakes and forests, shrubbery, and cliffs, and flowers. Poe had always healed himself by solitude in forests and along streams. As he had foreseen many times, his vision of paradise, his own landscape garden, would lie beyond the grave.

22

BURIAL AND AFTERLIFE

DR. MORAN TOOK CHARGE OF FUNERAL ARRANGEMENTS AFTER Poe's death on Sunday, October 7. The rites were scheduled for the following day, with Rev. W. T. D. Clemm, a cousin of Virginia's, officiating. Mrs. Moran made a shroud for Poe's slender body and washed and laid out the corpse. It was Henry Herring who paid for the mahogany coffin, and Neilson Poe provided the hearse to carry the coffin to the Presbyterian cemetery, where several veterans of the American Revolution were buried, including Gen. David Poe.

October 8 was a cold wet afternoon, the same prematurely wintery weather that had affected Poe adversely as he lay outside all night five days earlier. The crowd attending was small, including, besides the Rev. Clemm, Z. Collins Lee, a Baltimore lawyer who had known Poe at the University of Virginia. There was Dr. Snodgrass, Neilson Poe, Henry Herring, and Joseph H. Clarke, who had taught Poe in Richmond many years before. Also present were Poe's cousin Elizabeth Herring Smith and her husband, Edmund Morton Smith, the church sexton George W. Spence, and the undertaker Charles Suter.

Report of Poe's death spread by telegraph to New York and other cities, but Muddy and Elmira would not learn of it until later, when newspapers carried the death notice. The ceremony at the Presbyterian Cemetery in the chilling wind lasted only three minutes or so. Reverend Clemm may have been reluctant to say much about the character of Poe, recently rescued from skid row. Poe's remains were interred in Lot 27, near the graves of his brother Henry and his grandfather. Given the many adversities Poe had faced in his life, the hurried rites on the damp cloudy afternoon could seem appropriate. Bleakness had always pleased him. A passerby, J. Alden Weston, would recall the abridged rite: "The burial ceremony . . . was so cold-blooded and unchristianlike as to provoke on my part a sense of anger difficult to suppress."

Report of Poe's death reached all the leading newspapers. At Fordham, Muddy wrote to Neilson Poe asking for confirmation of the terrible report. In her sorrow and panic, Muddy went to stay with the Lewises in Brooklyn and later moved to Lowell to live with the Richmonds. Depressed and unwell, she received letters of condolence from many in the literary community, including Longfellow, who invited her to stay at his mansion in Cambridge, Massachusetts, and, according to her report, "spoke of Poe as the greatest man living."

Elmira knew Poe had been seriously ill when he left, and day after day she had worried and waited. On the morning of October 9, as she scanned the columns of the *Richmond Whig,* Elmira's eye caught a short article: "DEATH OF EDGAR A. POE—We regret to learn that Edgar A. Poe, Esq., the distinguished American poet, scholar and critic, died in this city yesterday morning, after an illness of four or five days. This announcement, coming so sudden and unexpected, will cause poignant regret among all who admire genius, and have sympathy for the frailties too often attending it. Mr. Poe . . . was in the 38th year of his age."

The announcement told Elmira nothing of the circumstances of Poe's death besides suggesting he had been on a binge. Though Elmira would later deny it, neighbors would recall that she wore mourning clothes in the aftermath of Poe's death. Anna Cora Mowatt would remember, "Mrs. Shelton went into widow's mourning." Shattered by grief, Elmira wrote Muddy, her only confidante in her love for Poe, on October 11.

> Oh! how shall I address you, my dear, and deeply afflicted friend under such heart-rending circumstances! I have no doubt, ere this, you have heard of the death of *our dear Edgar!* yes, he was the *dearest object* on earth to me . . .
>
> Oh! my dearest friend! I cannot begin to tell you what my feelings

> were, as the horrible truth forced itself upon me! It was the most severe trial I have ever had; and God alone knows how I can bear it! My heart is overwhelmed—yes, ready to burst! . . .
>
> The pleasure I had anticipated on his return with you, dear friend! to Richmond, was too great ever to be realized, and should teach me the folly of expecting bliss on earth. If it will be any consolation to you, my dear friend! to know that there is *one* who feels for you all that human can feel, then be assured that person is *Elmira.*

Muddy wrote to Annie Richmond: "I have received a letter from poor Elmira; oh, how you will pity her when you read it!"

Dr. Moran would later write that he received a letter from Elmira soon after Poe's death: "His affianced, Mrs. Shelton, wrote to me four days after his death, inquiring particularly and specifically as to how he died, the nature of his disease, and the cause." Yet within a few days, Elmira would avoid all mention of Poe and refuse requests for interviews about her famous fiancé. In the years after Poe's death, Elmira did everything she could to avoid any association with Poe. Because of the Civil War, she would lose most of her fortune. It is said she gave the wedding ring in which Poe's name was inscribed to Rosalie Poe. Not until 1875, twenty-six years after Poe's death, would Elmira consent to talk to anyone about the poet to whom she had been twice betrothed.

Before he left for Richmond in June 1849, Poe had supposedly asked that Griswold serve as his literary executor. As soon as Poe was dead, Griswold began to blacken his reputation, first in an obituary column signed "Ludwig" and later in a lengthy memoir published along with Poe's collected works. On October 9, 1849, in the *New York Tribune,* Griswold wrote: "Edgar Allan Poe is dead. He died in Baltimore the day before yesterday. This announcement will startle many, but few will be grieved by it."

Griswold was a master of the art of damning with hints and apparent praise. Because of the difficulties of Poe's life, "harsh experience had deprived him of all faith in man or woman." Griswold even hinted that there had been a "criminal" sexual relationship between Poe and Muddy. Next Griswold launched into a detailed accusation of villainy, quoting at length from Edward Bulwer-Lytton's novel *The Caxtons,* in which the author describes the character of Francis Vivian: "Irascible, envious—bad enough, but not the worst, for these salient angles were all varnished over with a cold repellant cynicism."

Helen Whitman would write to George Eveleth on December 15, 1864: "He [Griswold] could not forgive Poe the interest which he inspired in the person [F. Osgood] he [Griswold] most wished to please." Griswold's obituary was quickly reprinted in newspapers across the country. On October 13 it appeared in the *Richmond Enquirer*, where Elmira undoubtedly read it or had it read to her. Two days after writing her letter of devotion and grief to Muddy, she learned that in the eyes of the world, in the black-and-white of print, her fiancé had been known as a plagiarist, a liar, a poltroon, with many enemies and no friends. She vowed to never discuss Poe again.

Griswold's attacks on his late acquaintance would tarnish Poe's image for more than half a century. Yet the reading public would not be turned away by the stories of Poe's drinking and bad behavior. In fact, many readers would seem all the more fascinated by the gossip of his struggles, rebellion, and supposed misdeeds. As the Poe scholar Jeffrey A. Savoye would observe, "Griswold's malevolent attack on Poe had the unintended effect of raising Poe's public image to that of a literary icon."

Reverend Griswold forged passages in Poe's published letters to make Poe look dishonest, hateful, a villain, playing slyly on regional prejudice. Griswold's attacks began a debate, a controversy about Poe's character and place in American literature, that continues to this day. Scott Peeples has observed: "[Poe] knew the value of negative publicity. While it still seems unlikely that Poe would have actually wanted Griswold to malign him when he died, he might have appreciated his rival's cunning."

But there's a chance that Poe *never* asked that Griswold become his executor. The source of the request was Muddy, who after Poe's death *told* Griswold that Poe had chosen him as his executor. Muddy hoped (rightly) that Griswold would bring out an edition of Poe's work and that she, as heir, would receive the royalties. In fact, Griswold wrote to James Russell Lowell on October 18 or 25, 1849: "Poe was not my friend—I was not his—and he had no right to devolve upon me this duty of editing his works." As far as we know, Griswold never received a penny for editing Poe's works and writing his extensive "Memoir." Muddy was given several copies of the volumes to dispose of as she saw fit. Sister Rosalie received nothing. Before its copyright lapsed, in 1876, Griswold's edition of Poe's works would go through about thirty printings. Griswold did an important service by collecting Poe's writing.

Later Dr. Moran would tour the country, giving a lecture about Poe's final hours. He had changed his account so much over the years that many Poe scholars discounted whatever the doctor had to say. In June 1884, while in Richmond on a lecture tour, Dr. Moran called on Elmira at her house on Grace Street. At the age of seventy-four, in failing health, she was anxious to talk with him: "It was only last summer, during an interview with Mrs. Shelton, that I learned from her the strength of the attachment between the poet and herself—in plain words, how much they loved. She talked freely with me of their childhood and riper years when they were in each other's company." Elmira would die in 1888 at the age of seventy-eight. The Richmond paper would refer to her as "Poe's first and last love" and also mention her years of silence about the notorious author of "The Raven" and "Annabel Lee," to whom she had twice been pledged.

When the monument to Poe was dedicated in Baltimore on November 17, 1875, a bleak, raw, windy day, Dr. Snodgrass, J. H. Hewitt, Joseph H. Clarke, and others who had known Poe were present. Letters and poems of tribute were read. Among those who sent words honoring Poe were Mallarmé, Swinburne, Paul Hamilton Hayne, John Neal, Helen Whitman, Bryant, Longfellow, Tennyson, Whittier, Lowell, Aldrich, and Oliver Wendell Holmes. Besides Mallarmé's sonnet, it was Swinburne's words that were most memorable: "Widely as the fame of Poe has already spread, and deeply as it is already rooted in Europe, it is even now growing wider and striking deeper as time advances; the surest presage that Time, the eternal enemy of small and shallow reputations, will prove in this case also the constant and trusty friend and keeper of a poet's full-grown fame."

CODA

WHEN WILLIAM DEAN HOWELLS PUBLISHED THE CAMPAIGN biography for Abraham Lincoln in 1860, he wrote that the candidate "suffers no year to pass without a perusal of Poe's stories of detection." In the eleven years since Poe's death, his reputation had not faded but flourished. Given Lincoln's love of memorable prose and vigorous argument, we should not be surprised that the Great Emancipator returned to Poe's stories annually for pleasure and inspiration.

The horror and fear in Poe's work appeal to us because we recognize those emotions in ourselves. Reading Poe releases both conscious and unconscious anxieties. We feel reassured that someone else fears death and the loss of loved ones as much as we do. In a culture in which we are taught to be optimistic and forward-looking, to believe in progress, positive thinking, the solutions of technology, and improvement of ourselves and the world around us, Poe's dark view of time and nature and human nature seems oddly reassuring, as if he is speaking the truth that will make us free of illusion. His bleak narratives and laments answer our own experiences of frustration, failure, cruelty, mortality, betrayal, guilt, grief, and fear. His visions of menace thrill us because we sense he is looking at time and the human condition as they are, not as we are told they should be. Poe's horror balances the exuberance of Emerson and Whitman. We turn to him because he reminds us of deep truths about nature and human nature, our own nature, confirming our anxieties, our sense of alienation, uncertainty, the failures about us and in ourselves. Poe was not fooled by the culture of boosterism, expansionism, exploitation of labor, slavery, militarism, financial and governmental corruption, and religious hypocrisy all around him in the period after the Second Great Awakening. His work was a slap in the face to readers to wake up, for all its romance and hoaxes and yearning for a world beyond space and time. And we enjoy horror most from the comfort of an easy chair.

One extraordinary aspect of Poe's work is the way it seems to foreshadow what is called postmodernism, defined by the critic Margarida Vale de Gato as "signaling a rupture . . . dismantling the idea of art as elevated and elitist, instead placing it alongside mass and popular culture." For the critic Mark Neimeyer, Poe's work belongs to "meta-popular culture." As he seemed to anticipate concerns in modern astrophysics and semiotics, Poe also appears to be a forerunner of contemporary anti-elitist aesthetics. Brian McHale has described postmodernist fiction as portraying "worlds in collision." This may help explain why Poe appeals to us in our own unsettled and unsettling times. Jonathan Elmer has suggested that Baudelaire saw Poe as a nineteenth-century John the Baptist "wandering in the wilderness of American mediocrity." Poe referred to himself as a "literary *histrio*," but we now see him as a "visionary *histrio*" also. He would serve as a model for such popular writers as Jules Verne but also inspire rarefied esthetes like Raymond Roussel.

At least two biographical essays about Poe were published in his lifetime. After his death, Griswold, Gill, Didier, and others would publish extended narratives about the life of the author of "The Raven." Beginning with the Englishman John Ingram, and others, a torrent of longer Poe biographies would appear in the century and a half after his death.

This hunger for Poe biography suggests that Poe is unique, different, that his work and life are entwined, a mystery needing documentation and decoding, that his life story must have a ratiocinator to unlock the secrets of his poems and tales, his character, his loves and conflicts. It also suggests that while there is something uncanny about Poe, readers feel a profound kinship with that alienness. He is different from the other writers of his time, yet he is similar too. He may have loved and celebrated the world of nature like Emerson or Thoreau, and yet he was different. He may have written about the ocean as well as Melville, and yet he was different. He may have been as skilled at rhyme and meter as Longfellow or Bryant, but he was also different. It is this *difference* that keeps readers going back to his tales and poems, rhymes and images, and to his life story, cherishing the difference. Poe's gifts are so multiple, his range so wide, his psychological penetration so thorough, we feel we must know his strange life to get a purchase on the scope and depth and strangeness of his art.

Because we love the work, we want to love the man. Because the work is mysterious *and* familiar, we want to understand the man. Because the man is mysterious, we want to understand the work. Because the man is gone, the work is all we have—and a few facts that seem to illuminate the work and the work that seems to illuminate the man.

To the surprise of some, Poe's writing and his life have provided a significant means of examining issues in our history such as slavery, racial bias, expansionism, the rise of capitalism, literary nationalism, and sexuality. As we look more closely at Poe's poems, stories, essays, and biography, we realize that the exploration is far from over. In some important ways, Poe studies are only beginning. Poe is our delight, inviting us to further investigation.

All his life Poe yearned for a perfect, ideal marriage but never achieved it. Even the union with Virginia left him guilty and unsatisfied. His close friendships with Henry Hirst, F. W. Thomas, and others did not prevent him from feeling isolated and craving for something more. Poe's deepest bond may have been with his memories of his mother, Eliza Poe, with Mrs. Clemm, and with his readers, who seem to feel he is one of their family. If he found a sustaining and enduring intimacy, growing stronger as the years passed, it was ultimately with his readers, whose affections reach across boundaries of geography, language, race, and time.

All good writers are entertainers. We read and reread them because they please us. Of all the classic American writers of the nineteenth century, Poe may be the most entertaining. He delights us with lyrics and mysteries, hoaxes, puzzles, burlesques, and codes. Much of his best work can be read as parodies of horror fiction, romance, adventure, fantasy. He is an entertainer first and last. And readers around the world for almost two centuries have cherished his wit, ingenuity, surprises, exotic scenes, and playfulness. Poe is fun.

NOTES

Most references are to authors' names. The following abbreviations are also used.

Allen	Hervey Allen, *Israfel: The Life and Times of Edgar Allan Poe* (New York: Farrar & Rinehart, 1934)
Allen and Mabbott	Hervey Allen and Thomas Ollive Mabbott, *Poe's Brother* (New York: Farrar & Rinehart, 1926)
CL 2008	*The Collected Letters of Edgar Allan Poe,* 3rd ed., vols. I and II, ed. John Ward Ostrom, Burton R. Pollin, and Jeffrey A. Savoye (New York: Gordian Press, 2008)
Didier	E. L. Didier, *Life and Poems of Edgar Allan Poe* (New York: W. J. Whittleton, 1877)
E&R	*Essays and Reviews of Edgar Allan Poe,* ed. G. R. Thompson (New York: Library of America, 1984)
Fisher	Benjamin J. Fisher, *Poe in His Own Time* (Iowa City: University of Iowa Press, 2009)
Gill	William F. Gill, *The Life of Edgar Allan Poe* (New York: D. Appleton & Co., 1877)
Griswold	*Works of Edgar Allan Poe,* vol. I (New York: Harper and Brothers, n.d.), with a memoir by Rufus Wilmot Griswold
Hayes	Kevin J. Hayes, ed., *Cambridge Companion to Edgar Allan Poe* (Cambridge: Cambridge University Press, 2002)

H. L. Poe	Harry Lee Poe, *Evermore: Edgar Allan Poe and the Mystery of the Universe* (Waco, TX: Baylor University Press, 2012)
Hutchisson	James M. Hutchisson, *Poe* (Jackson: University Press of Mississippi, 2005)
Ingram	John H. Ingram, *Life and Letters of Edgar Allan Poe* (London: Ward, Lock, Bowden & Co., 1891)
Jackson and Thomas	David K. Jackson and Dwight Thomas, eds., *The Poe Log: A Documentary Life of Edgar Allan Poe, 1809–1849* (New York: G. K. Hall, 1987)
Kennedy, *Historical*	J. Gerald Kennedy, ed., *A Historical Guide to Edgar Allan Poe* (New York: Oxford University Press, 2001)
Kennedy and Peeples	J. Gerald Kennedy and Scott Peeples, eds., *The Oxford Handbook of Edgar Allan Poe* (New York: Oxford University Press, 2019)
Kennedy and Weissberg	J. Gerald Kennedy and Liliane Weissberg, eds., *Romancing the Shadow: Poe and Race* (New York: Oxford University Press, 2001)
Mabbott, I	Thomas Ollive Mabbott, ed., *The Poems of Edgar Allan Poe* (Cambridge: Belknap Press of Harvard University Press, 1969)
Mabbott, II and III	Thomas Ollive Mabbott, ed. *Tales and Sketches of Edgar Allan Poe* (Cambridge: Belknap Press of Harvard University Press, 1978)
Meyers	Jeffrey Meyers, *Edgar Allan Poe: His Life and Legacy* (New York: Charles Scribner's Sons, 1992)
P&T	*Poetry and Tales of Edgar Allan Poe,* ed. Patrick F. Quinn (New York: Library of America, 1984)
P. E. Phillips	Philip Edward Phillips, ed., *Poe and Place* (Cham, Switzerland: Palgrave Macmillan, 2018)
Phillips	Mary E. Phillips, *Edgar Allan Poe the Man,* vols. I and II (Chicago: John C. Winston Co., 1926)

Porte and Morris — Joel Porte and Saundra Morris, eds., *Emerson's Prose and Poetry* (New York: W. W. Norton, 2001)

Quinn, A. H. — Arthur Hobson Quinn, *Edgar Allan Poe: A Critical Biography* (Baltimore: Johns Hopkins University Press, 1998)

Silverman — Kenneth Silverman, *Edgar A. Poe: Mournful and Never-Ending Remembrance* (New York: HarperCollins, 1992)

Whitty — J. H. Whitty, "Memoir of Poe," in *The Complete Poems of Poe* (Boston: Houghton Mifflin, 1911)

Woodberry — George E. Woodberry, *The Life of Edgar Allan Poe*, vols. I and II (New York: Biblio and Tanner, 1965)

INTRODUCTION

1 **"Marriage. . . becomes a site":** Ellen Weinauer, "Undead Wives and Undone Husbands," in Kennedy and Peeples, 175.

2 **"our cousin, Mr. Poe":** Allen Tate, "Our Cousin, Mr. Poe," in *Poe: A Collection of Critical Essays*, ed. Robert Regan (Englewood Cliffs, NJ: Prentice Hall, 1967), 38.

"the most original genius": Edward Wagenknecht, *Edgar Allan Poe: The Man behind the Legend* (New York: Oxford University Press, 1963), 4.

7 **"writing is a form of nympholepsy":** J. Gerald Kennedy, *Poe, Death, and the Life of Writing* (New Haven: Yale University Press, 1987), 76.

11 **"the best-known poem":** Eric W. Carlson, *Introduction to Poe: A Thematic Reader* (Glenview, IL: Scott, Foresman, 1967), xxii.

12 **"the mark of a decidedly":** Jeffrey Meyers, *Edgar Allan Poe: His Life and Legacy* (New York: Charles Scribner's Sons, 1992), 271.

"always and for all lands": Ibid., 274.

13 **"the ether of postmodern meta-culture":** Mark Neimeyer, "Poe and Popular Culture," in *The Cambridge Companion to Edgar Allan Poe*, ed. Kevin J. Hayes (Cambridge: Cambridge University Press, 2002), 207.

14 **"Nothing highlighted freedom":** Toni Morrison, *Playing in the Dark: Whiteness and the Literary Imagination* (New York: Vintage Books, 1993), 38.

15 **"No early American writer":** Ibid., 32.

taken up by the Young America editors: Meredith L. McGill, *American Literature and the Culture of Reprinting, 1834–1853* (Philadelphia: University of Pennsylvania Press, 2001), 44.

"literary neutrality": Terence Whalen, *Edgar Allan Poe and the Masses: The Political Economy of Literature in Antebellum American* (Princeton: Princeton University Press, 1999), 31.

15 **"average racism":** Ibid., 138.
"male mother": David Greven, *Gender Protest and Same-Sex Desire in Antebellum American Literature* (Burlington, VT: Ashgate, 2014), 151.
Greven suggests that Ligeia: Ibid., 82.
"prisonhouse of gender": Ibid., 13.

1. ELIZA

17 **originally from Germany:** *CL* 2008, I, 183.
"dweller at the sign of the peacock": Elsdon C. Smith, *New Dictionary of American Family Names* (New York: Gramercy, 1988), 402.
David made furniture: Woodberry, I, 2.
18 **"I bought grain and hay":** Phillips, I, 26.
"David Poe out of his own": Ibid., 27.
David Poe provided two brass cannons: Didier, 21.
nine "free white males" . . . "fish inspector": Allen, 679–80.
near the age of seventy-two: Woodberry, I, 3.
David Poe Sr. died: Phillips, I, 29; Jackson and Thomas, 159.
Lord Montague's daughter: Phillips, I, 135.
Henry Arnold, who wrote comedies: Phillips, I, 38.
"I am profoundly excited": *CL* 2008, I, 450.
19 **Eliza joined Elizabeth:** Geddeth Smith, *The Brief Career of Eliza Poe* (London: Associated University Presses, 1988), 25.
by the age of fifteen: Hutchisson, 4.
began to play "Ophelia": G. Smith, 56.
20 **"the delicate outlines of the nose":** Mabbott, II, 312.
Jews in the eighteenth century: One of the leading Poe scholars of the twentieth century, Thomas O. Mabbott, wrote in an endnote to the story "Ligeia" that the narrator's refusal to give the heroine's last name suggests that Ligeia is Jewish. From Mabbott's note: "Maxwell Morton, in *A Builder of the Beautiful* (1928), p. 58, has pointed out that Ligeia is described as resembling the poet's mother, Elizabeth Arnold Poe, who had a Hebraic nose and large dark eyes. This is hardly accidental, for her son, despite his lack of a conscious memory of her, owned her miniature portrait, and revered her memory."

In 1932 the biographer Una Pope-Hennessey would make the same observation about Eliza's looks and heritage, adding: "The surname Arnold is not uncommon in Jewish annals. Many Jews were connected to the theater" (*Edgar Allan Poe: A Critical Biography* [London: Macmillan, 1934], 149).

Eliza's family may or may not have been Jewish, but it seems Poe believed they were. In anti-Semitic America of the nineteenth century, he did not dare to make public such a claim but couldn't resist throwing out hints.
Eliza would act with Matthew Sully: Phillips, I, 58–59.
It is believed that the miniature: Christopher P. Semtner, *The Poe Shrine* (Charleston, SC: Arcadia Publishing, 2017), 38.

20 **"Heavens, what a form!":** G. Smith, 127.
"Mrs. Hopkins's interesting figure": Ibid., 70.
had formed a Thespian Club: John H. Ingram, *Life and Letters of Edgar Allan Poe* (London: Ward, Lock, Bowdon & Co., 1891), 1.
"If industry can claim": Woodberry, I, 11–12.
21 **"Sometimes she danced a Polish":** Ibid., 13.
On April 18, 1808: Ingram, 4.
during a fierce storm: Phillips, I, 1.
David Poe Sr. disowned his son: Ibid., 62.
David and Eliza had visited the Poes: Ibid., 68.
Boston tax records of May 1809: Whitty, xx.
"She was a lovely little creature": G. Smith, 93.
22 **suffering from consumption:** Woodberry, I, 14–15.
It has been said he died: Phillips, I, 77.
"quarreled and parted": Jackson and Thomas, 13.
as a child, Edgar played Cupid: Christopher P. Semtner, *Edgar Allan Poe's Richmond* (Charleston, SC: History Press, 2021), 92.
"Mrs. Poe's name is a brilliant gem": G. Smith, 122.
the melodrama *Tekeli:* Richard Kopley, "Re-Ordering Place in Poe's *Arthur Gordon* Pym," in P. E. Phillips, 210.
an elderly Welsh woman: Jackson and Thomas, 14; Allen, 14.
23 **"Left alone, the only support":** Jackson and Thomas, 11.
last appearance in Richmond: Whitty, xxii.
"A singular fashion prevails": Jackson and Thomas, 13.
"TO THE HUMANE HEART": Ibid.
helped look after the children: Ibid., 14.
"For my little son Edgar": G. Smith, 96; John Carl Miller, *Building Poe Biography* (Baton Rouge: Louisiana State University Press, 1977), 121.
24 **Poe would wear the miniature:** Semtner, *Shrine,* 30.
"dark family troubles": Phillips, I, 92.
"Died on last Sunday morning": Jackson and Thomas, 15.
"acute pneumonia": Phillips, I, 85.
Old St. John's burial ground: Ibid., 87.
it was even hinted that Mr. Mackenzie: Ibid., 85.
26 **"Consumption . . . actually did enhance":** Kennedy, *Death,* 68.
"a chronic fear of abandonment": J. Gerald Kennedy, "Poe's Terror Analytics," in Kennedy and Peeples, 813.
"For Poe, her story could never be written": Kennedy, *Death,* 88.
"Introduction": Mabbott, I, 157.
27 **"Some scientists now believe":** Jenny Chen, "Childhood Guilt, Adult Depression," *Atlantic,* January 5, 2015, https://www.theatlantic.com/health/archive/2015/childhood-guilt-adult-depression/384176.
"connected to controls": Ibid.
28 **"In speaking of my mother":** *CL* 2008, I, 116.

28 **"The writer of this article":** Arthur Hobson Quinn, *Edgar Allan Poe: A Critical Biography* (Baltimore: Johns Hopkins University Press, 1998), 50.

2. FANNY ALLAN

29 **"strongly anti-democratic":** Edward H. Davidson, *Poe: A Critical Study* (Cambridge: Harvard University Press, 1957), 207.

six million dollars . . . in tobacco: David K. Jackson, *Poe and the Southern Literary Messenger* (Richmond: Dietz Publishers, 1934), 16.

Joseph Gallego gave the Mackenzies: Semtner, *Richmond,* 112.

31 **John Allan assumed:** Miller, *Building,* 49.

Allan wrote to the Poes in Baltimore: *CL* 2008, I, 59.

There is some evidence: Whalen, 24.

32 **John Allan had first proposed:** Susan Archer Weiss, *Independent* 57, August 25, 1904, 443.

was considered "girlish": Silverman, *Edgar A. Poe,* 14.

raised himself above his merchant status: Semtner, *Richmond,* 25.

33 **he was baptized:** Jackson and Thomas, 15.

"gave a large dinner-party to show": Phillips, I, 104.

"Lay of the Last Minstrel": Woodberry, I, 19.

"a purple jacket, velvet cape": Semtner, *Richmond,* 28.

"a lovely little fellow": Phillips, I, 105.

a dog called "Tib": Semtner, *Shrine,* 76.

Edgar first studied with: Jackson and Thomas, 21, 23.

name had been inscribed in the Allan family Bible: Silverman, 15.

he once owned roller skates: Whitty, xxiii.

34 **"'Tis the Aunt of Edgar":** Jackson and Thomas, 19.

she feared they might claim: Hervey Allen and Thomas Olive Mabbott, *Poe's Brother* (New York: George H. Dunn, 1926), 21.

John Allan strode to the school: Phillips, I, 116.

reading the newspaper to admiring adults: Ibid., 119.

35 **inspired by African and African American:** Semtner, *Richmond,* 30.

"an ice-cold hand laid upon his face": Susan Archer Weiss, *Home Life of Poe* (New York: Broadway Publishing Co., 1907), 29–30.

"In the nursery we played": Phillips, I, 120.

"Poe was in love with being in love": Semtner, *Richmond,* 40.

appearing as a ghost: Ibid., 33.

inspected the loading and unloading: Ibid., 31.

36 **even a telescope:** Silverman, 16.

"Ned cared but little": Jackson and Thomas, 24.

"I was not afraid coming across": Ibid., 26.

"reading a little Story Book": Ibid.

37 **"Your Son I am glad to say":** Silverman, 18.

reading Latin "pretty sharply": Jackson and Thomas, 36.

"his schooldays in London": Whitty, xxiii. In an essay called "The Realm of Dream and Memory: Poe's England," J. Gerald Kennedy examines the places Poe likely saw during his years in Britain, at an age when such sights could make a profound impression on an imaginative boy. Since young Poe spent time in both England and Scotland, there was much for him to take in and remember.

When Poe and the Allans arrived in London, in 1815, the city's population was more than one million, in contrast with Richmond's mere ten thousand (P. E. Phillips, 73). For a child sensitive to things weird and wonderful, it's likely the future poet was struck by the teeming crowds and the large wooden statues of Gog and Magog opposite the Guild Hall on King Street (72). Given that he spent five years in the city, Poe would almost certainly have witnessed such sights as the Inns of Temple, London Bridge, St. Paul's Cathedral, the Tower of London, Piccadilly, Westminster Abbey, and Westminster Hall, where Parliament then met.

The Allans' first rented house, at 47 Southampton Row, was near a mansion that housed the British Museum, where the young Poe would have seen the Rosetta Stone and the Elgin Marbles from the Parthenon as well as Egyptian mummies. The first probably influenced him to think about the translation and skills of code breaking. The second may have inspired awe about "the glory that was Greece," celebrated in the first "To Helen" (72). The third would be recalled in the comedy "Some Words with a Mummy."

As young Edgar made his way to the Dubourg School in 1815–18, he would have passed through some of the seediest places in London. Those streets would later be recalled in the story "The Man of the Crowd" (74). At the Manor House School at Stoke Newington, Poe must have learned he was near a house where Daniel Defoe had once lived. *Robinson Crusoe,* always a favorite of his, later helped inspire his only novel, *The Narrative of Arthur Gordon Pym.*

Kennedy points out that Poe visited Irvine, Scotland, at least twice, for several weeks after arriving in Britain in 1815 and for three months in 1819, when he stayed with Allan relatives. From his youth, Poe was very much aware of the poems of Robert Burns, and Mary Starr would later declare that Burns was a favorite of Poe's in the early 1830s.

Poe would also have seen Dean Castle in Kilmarnock, "where a zigzag [crack] ran down the façade of the keep" (75). Poe would later describe such a fissure in the House of Usher. The Allans' second address in London at 39 Southampton Row would be referred to in "Why the Little Frenchman Wears His Hand in a Sling." While in London, Poe probably read Mary Shelley's *Frankenstein* (1818) and Scott's *The Bride of Lammermoor* (1819). Both would later influence his Gothic fiction. The critic Michael Allen has suggested that in this period "Poe absorbed from Byron the defensive self-parodic tendencies that distance him from the unwashed masses" (81).

At the British Museum, Poe would have first glimpsed massive sarcophagi, later to figure dramatically in "Ligeia." He would also have encountered signs in Edinburgh for the Usher Distillery (85).

37 **"If he was not the poorest":** Ibid., 87.
"own democratic sympathies": Ibid., 89.
"in Letters as in government": *E&R,* 1078.
echoing his new Young America associates: Ibid.
tobacco market collapsed: J. Gerald Kennedy, "A Brief Biography," in Kennedy, *Historical,* 21.
owed about £35,000: Silverman, 21.

38 **"They are a little Englishised":** Jackson and Thomas, 47.
a house on Fourteenth Street: Ibid., 51.
"fiery, pedantic, pompous Irishman": Woodberry, I, 24.
"He was remarkable": Didier, 30–31; Meyers, 14.

39 **"The verses, I remember":** Didier, 31.
"inclined to be imperious": Jackson and Thomas, 53.
"He won local distinction": Killis Campbell, *The Mind of Poe and Other Studies* (Cambridge: Harvard University Press, 1933), 7.
To "cap" a verse meant: *Brewer's Dictionary of Phrases and Fables,* 16th ed. (New York: Harpers Resources, 1999), 201.
"He was, indeed, a leader": Jackson and Thomas, 49–50.
"[Edgar] never asked any": Phillips, I, 186.
a member of the Charleston Comedians: Ibid., 188.
known as a swift runner and jumper: Ibid., 197.
"Poe was a much more advanced": Didier, 33–34; Jackson and Thomas, 58.

40 **"Poe, as I recall":** Ingram, 19; Jackson and Thomas, 53.
"Not to bear the name of the father": Davidson, 47.
Ebenezer Burling taught him to swim: Whitty, xxv.
"DEAR HENRY I have just seen": Jackson and Thomas, 61–62.

41 **"an ignoble gesture":** Allen and Mabbott, *Poe's Brother,* 22.

3. JANE STANARD AND ELMIRA ROYSTER

42 **"I never knew the time Edgar":** Phillips, I, 224.
The scent would always: A. H. Quinn, 631.
"the first, purely ideal love": *CL* 2008, II, 694.

43 **as a girl had seen Eliza:** Phillips, I, 203.
may have suffered from a brain tumor: Semtner, *Richmond,* 43.
"the truest, tenderest of this world's": Wagenknecht, 176.
"Helen, thy beauty is to me": Mabbott, I, 165–66.

45 **"That Poe had a powerful intellect":** T. S. Eliot, "From Poe to Valéry," *Hudson Review* 2, no. 2 (Autumn 1949): 325.

46 **"Magazine literature [is]":** *E&R,* 1377.
one of the finest houses in Richmond: Jackson and Thomas, 64.

47 **As a boy, he'd seen enough:** Phillips, I, 201.

47 **classes with Dr. and Mrs. Ray Thomas:** Jackson and Thomas, 64.
a good friend of William Galt: Phillips, I, 175.
"was fond of all the boys": Ibid., 226.
"roamed hand in hand": Ibid.
"a trysting place": Ibid., 179.
"He was a beautiful boy": A. H. Quinn, 91.
"I married another man": Edward M. Alfriend, "Unpublished Recollection of Edgar Allan Poe, *Literary Era* 7 (January–September 1901): 490; Phillips, I, 225.
48 **Mr. Royster had loaned:** Allen and Mabbott, 30.
"With Mrs. Allan suspicious": Whitty, xxvii.
It was an error that in retrospect: Phillips, I, 228.
"to develop the reasoning": A. H. Quinn, 97.
Library privileges: Ibid., 102.
49 **It was probably the last letter:** Allen and Mabbott, 28.
Drunken students threw bricks: Silverman, 31.
"Dixon made a physical attack": *CL* 2008, I, 6.
"We have had a great many": Ibid., 8–9.
a professor cruelly horsewhipped: James M. Hutchisson, "An Orphan's Life: 1809–1831," in Kennedy and Peeples, 26.
50 **"This order however was":** *CL* 2008 I, 5.
Poe had to burn some: Semtner, *Richmond*, 57.
"I will boldly say": *CL* 2008, I, 59.
gave Poe at the university less: A. H. Quinn, 113
Poe joined the Jefferson Society: Hutchisson, "An Orphan's Life: 1809–1831," in Kennedy and Peeples, 25.
51 **the habit of chewing tobacco:** Wagenknecht, 41.
"No one could say that he *knew* him": Jackson and Thomas, 75.
"As Librarian I had": Phillips, I, 249.
"On one occasion Prof. Batterman": William F. Gill, *The Life of Edgar Allan Poe* (New York: D. Appleton, 1877), 35.
"a very attractive companion": A. H. Quinn, 108.
52 **"[Poe] was fond of quoting":** Jackson and Thomas, 69.
53 **irony and mystery in "Song":** Mabbott, I, 66.
"Yet, strangely, every prose": Phillips, I, 277.
"created a scene": Whitty, xxviii.
54 **John Allan was jealous of Poe:** Wagenknecht, 27.
"awarded the highest honors": Meyers, 23.

4. *TAMERLANE AND OTHER POEMS*

55 **"taunts & abuse that followed":** *CL* 2008, I, 20.
It is said Poe: Whitty, xxviii.

55 **"I have heard you say":** *CL* 2008, I, 10–11.
"The servants were forbidden": Weiss, *Independent*, May 5, 1904, 1011.
56 **"It depends upon yourself":** *CL* 2008, I, 11.
"every day threatened with a warrant": *CL* 2008, I, 61.
"I am in the greatest necessity": Ibid., 12–13.
Most likely, he worked his way: Jackson and Thomas, 78.
It is possible Poe stopped in Baltimore: *CL* 2008, I, 13.
"had frequent fainting spells": Whitty, xxx.
Some have thought he appeared: Jackson and Thomas, 80.
57 **listed in the *United States Review:*** Jeffrey A Savoye, "Poe and Baltimore: Crossroads and Redemption," in P. E. Phillips, 105.
"the so-called 'black tulip'": David A. Randall, *The J. A. Lilly Collection of Edgar Allan Poe* (Bloomington: Indiana University Press, 1964), 3.
"Aspiring poets bid for the title": Susan J. Wolfson, "Entertaining Byron in America," *Byron Journal* 45, no. 1 (2017): 3.
Fitz-Greene Halleck inaugurated himself: Ibid.
Byronism as "rampant": Ibid.
"No writer has done half so much": Ibid., 5.
"every city, town, and village": Ibid.
58 **"for a boy or man":** Ibid., 16.
"master poems of modern democracy": Ibid.
59 **"We walk'd together on the crown":** Mabbott I, 33–34.
60 **she was "dead" to him:** Phillips, I, 305–6.
A student Poe had known: Phillips, I, 308–9.
61 **"escape [from] his ambiguous":** Meyers, 33.
He held the rank of private: Silverman, 42.
on November 8, 1827, his company: *CL* 2008, I, 15.
the ship almost wrecked: Kennedy, "Brief Biography," *Historical*, 25.
Dr. Edmund Ravenel: A. H. Quinn, 130.
62 **"The Lake":** Mabbott, I, 85–86.
63 **he became an "artificer":** Semtner, *Richmond*, 69.
"remain as he is": Silverman, 43.
"My father do not throw me aside": *CL* 2008, I, 17.
64 **"to forgive all":** Ibid., 61.
"The said Perry": Jackson and Thomas, 90–91.
"I have to say that": Ibid.
65 **"a young gentleman of genius":** Ibid., 93.
"Frankly, Sir, do I declare": Ibid., 92.
Searching Mosher's clothes: *CL* 2008, I, 33.
66 **Poe's spelling of *Quaterly* for *Quarterly:*** Ibid., 31.
"irrecoverably a poet": Ibid., 27.
"I am not particularly anxious": Silverman, 52.
On December 10, 1829, Poe sold: *CL* 2008, I, 25.
67 **"Science! true daughter of Old Time thou art!":** Mabbott, I, 91.

68 **"His deep familiarity with science":** John Tresch, *The Reason for the Darkness of Night: Edgar Allan Poe and the Forging of American Science* (New York: Farrar, Straus and Giroux, 2021), 11.
"a medium between Heaven & Hell": *CL* 2008, I, 26.
"Ligeia! wherever": Mabbott, I, 109–10.
"For what (to them) availeth": Ibid., 111.
69 **"What guilty spirit, in what shrubbery dim":** Ibid., 112.
"Far from being signs": Michael C. Cohen, "Echoes of 'The Raven': Unoriginality in Poe's Verse," in Kennedy and Peeples, 104.
70 **"asserts its originality":** Ibid., 109.
"though nonsense, rather exquisite": Jackson and Thomas, 98.
"the very first words of encouragement": *CL* 2008, I, 47.
"a pile of brickbats": Silverman, 58–59.
"A part are exceedingly boyish": Jackson and Thomas, 103.
71 **"We view the production":** Silverman, 59.
Allan's records show him buying: Jackson and Thomas, 105.
It is said that Gen. Winfield Scott: Ingram, 65.
a copy of Poe's early poems: Woodberry, I, 67n.
"Mr. A. is not very often sober": *CL* 2008, I, 54.
Poe supported Aunt Nancy: Woodberry, I, 68.

5. WEST POINT

72 **"nothing except what I considered":** *CL* 2008, I, 55.
73 **"very polite and attentive":** Ibid., 57.
One cadet would quote: Jackson and Thomas, 114; Silverman, 62.
That poem would be reprinted: Mabbott, I, 90.
"respects to Mrs. A.": *CL* 2008, I, 58.
74 **Benny Haven's nearby tavern:** Meyers, 44; Phillips, I, 380.
"He was very shy and reserved": Woodberry, I, 70.
"From childhood's hour I have not been": Mabbott, I, 146–47.
76 **He simply lacked the strength:** Allen, 221.
"no further communication with yourself": Silverman, 63.
77 **"Did I, when an infant":** *CL* 2008, I, 59–60.
"If she had not have died": Ibid., 61–62.
"From the time of writing this": Ibid., 62.
"I do not think the Boy has one": Jackson and Thomas, 112–13.
78 **"What would I not give":** Whalen, 24.
79 **confined in the guardhouse:** Phillips, I, 384–85.
with only twenty-four cents: Hutchisson, 26.
"a marble doorway, inscribed": Scott Peeples, *The Afterlife of Edgar Allan Poe* (Rochester: Camden House, 2004), 17.
Poe collected $170 (about $5,100 today): Jackson and Thomas, 117.

79 **"The cadets, especially from the South":** Ibid.; Phillips, I, 392.
some threw their copies into the Hudson: Semtner, *Shrine,* 54.
hurriedly and cheaply produced: Ingram, 85.
80 **"A poem, in my opinion":** *E&R,* 11.
"definition of the work": Rachel Polonsky, "Poe's Aesthetic Theory," in Hayes, 45.
"Romance who loves to nod and sing": Mabbott, I, 156.
81 **"could not love except":** Ibid.
"If I could dwell": Ibid., 175–77.
82 **"A passionate poem is":** *E&R,* 1354.
"Lo, Death has reared himself a throne": Mabbott, I, 201–2.
83 **which creates the radical and new:** Davidson, 58–59.
the sea devours the human: Patrick Quinn, *The French Face of Edgar Poe* (Carbondale: Southern Illinois University Press, 1957), 25.

6. MARIA CLEMM AND BALTIMORE

84 **labored for a short while:** Weiss, *Home Life of Poe,* 63; Hutchisson, 34; John Carl Miller, *Poe's Helen Remembers* (Charlottesville: University Press of Virginia, 1979), 454.
Poe's letters of wretchedness: Kennedy, *Death,* 92.
85 **the city was more culturally diverse:** *Columbia Encyclopedia,* 5th ed. (New York: Columbia University Press, 1993), 218.
"She was the ever-vigilant guardian": Jackson and Thomas, 410; Meyers, 60.
he soon "went West": Phillips, I, 415–16.
"I was intimate with Poe's brother": Whitty, xxi.
87 **"a small annuity":** Phillips, I, 417.
"Dear Sir,—I am almost ashamed": *CL* 2008, I, 66–67.
"entirely given up to drink": Ibid., 43.
88 **seventy-two periodicals:** A. H. Quinn, 187.
"a surprising number and variety": John C. French, "Poe's Literary Baltimore," *Maryland Historical Magazine* 32 (June 1937): 104.
"was at high tide": Ibid., 105.
had previously edited: Ibid., 107.
89 **Seven Stars Tavern:** Ibid., 102
"long and frequent walks together": Didier, 50–51.
90 **He would describe it to James Russell Lowell:** *CL* 2008, I, 450.
"At midnight, in the month of June": Mabbott, I, 186–87.
91 **"The point of the story is always":** lecture at Cornell University, early 1980s.
"mount to paradise": Ralph Waldo Emerson, "Merlin I," *Emerson's Prose and Poetry,* ed. Joel Porte and Saundra Morris (New York: W. W. Norton, 2001), 449.
92 **"Achieving proprietary control":** McGill, 44.
"best AMERICAN TALE": Jackson and Thomas, 120.
"A lofty name shall have": Mabbott, II, 19.

93 **a story about sexual impotence:** Marie Bonaparte, *The Life and Works of Edgar Allan Poe* (New York: Humanities Press, 1971), 374.
"Thou wretch!—thou vixen!": Mabbott, II, 62.
"the institution of marriage": Weinauer, 174.
"Poe's black humor": Daniel Royot, "Poe's Humor," in Hayes, 68.
Mary would recall her relations: Phillips, I, 430.
94 **"My intimacy with Mr. Poe":** Augustus Van Cleef, "Poe's Mary," *Harper's New Monthly Magazine* 78 (March 1889); 635–38 (italics mine); Allen, 268–71.
95 **modeled in part on Benjamin Disraeli's *Vivian Grey:*** Alexander Hammond, "Early Experiments in Genre: Imitations, Burlesques, Satires," in Kennedy and Peeples, 149.
an inventor and lawyer: Miller, *Building,* 209.
Latrobe was the son: Tresch, 69.
"was in Roman characters": Allen, 281.
96 **"I had not proceeded far":** Ibid.
Poe confronted Hewitt: Jackson and Thomas, 134.
"His figure was remarkably good": Allen, 283; Jackson and Thomas, 133–34.
"We . . . can not refrain from": Jackson and Thomas, 133.
97 **"The hulk flew at a rate":** Mabbott II, 138.
"To conceive the horror": Ibid., 145.
"Oh, horror upon horror!": Ibid., 146.
The ship spins faster: Tresch, 157.
Hoffman points out: Daniel Hoffman, *Poe Poe Poe Poe Poe Poe Poe* (Garden City, NY: Doubleday, 1972), 149.
98 **a drunken fantasy:** Royot, "Poe's Humor," in Hayes, 63.
"A very fine piece of work": Meyers, 66–67.
"I attended to his literary business": Wagenknecht, 91; Miller, *Poe's Helen,* 241.
100 **"Mrs. Clemm also spoke vaguely":** Van Cleef, 636.
"Dear Sir,—I cannot come": *CL* 2008, I, 83.
"Mr. Kennedy . . . was the first": *CL* 2008, I, 292; Phillips, I, 484.
"He was debauched": Meyers, 68.
"I feel at the very bottom of my heart": *CL* 2008, I, 71.
Miss Valentine sent money: Weiss, *Independent,* August 25, 1904, 443.
the older Allan servants, who informed: Whitty, xxxv.
101 **"When I think of the long":** *CL* 2008, I, 67–68.
Mrs. Allan stepped into the sickroom: Jackson and Thomas, 137.
"Blessed with every social": Ibid., 138.
102 **"I have accordingly":** *CL* 2008, I, 100.

7. RETURN TO RICHMOND

103 **"Dear Sir,—Poe did right in referring":** Gill, 73.
between four and five thousand magazines: Silverman, 99.

103 **"meant to be consumed":** Sandra M. Tomc, "Poe and His Circle," in Hayes, 27.
104 **"to stimulate the pride":** Silverman, 100.
105 **"It is indeed a subject":** Ibid., 102.
already suffering from the frail heart: Phillips, I, 490.
"Antebellum readers' avidity": David Leverenz, "Spanking the Master: Mind-Body Crossings in Poe's Sensationalism," in Kennedy, *Historical*, 104.
"Slavery serves as": Teresa A. Goddu, "Poe, Sensationalism, and Slavery," in Hayes, 92.
106 **"both analyst and symptom":** Ibid., 99.
"Whilst we confess": Ingram, 93.
an incestuous relationship: *New Standard Jewish Encyclopedia*, 7th ed., ed. Geoffrey Wigoder and Cecil Roth (New York: Facts on File, 1992), 136.
"Misery is manifold": Mabbott, II, 209.
107 **"emaciation was excessive":** Ibid., 215.
A story had appeared: Jeffrey A. Savoye, "Poe in Baltimore," in P. E. Phillips, 98.
threatens castration: Bonaparte, 218.
108 **"sado-necrophilia":** P. Quinn, 21; Bonaparte, 218.
"Marriage, in short": Weinauer, 175.
"The history of all Magazines": *CL* 2008, I, 84–85.
analysis and obsession: Patrick Quinn, 226.
a story of "self-detection": Kennedy, *Death*, 128.
"I have been desirous": *CL* 2008, I, 93.
109 **White was warned that:** Silverman, 104.
Two former schoolmates: Wagenknecht, 66.
But White would never: Kennedy, "Brief Biography," 36.
an act of manipulation: Ibid., 35.
With her mother's death: Jackson and Thomas, 159.
110 **"Mr. Poe's (Edgar's) animosity":** Miller, *Building*, 139.
111 **"I am blinded with tears":** *CL* 2008, I, 102–4.
112 **"My feelings at this moment":** Ibid., 107.
"That you are sincere": Jackson and Thomas, 171–72.
113 **"Mr. Poe was the most":** Semtner, *Richmond*, 72.
"[Poe] resisted more temptations": Phillips, I, 542.
"I have absolutely no pleasure": Didier, 101.
indeed a marriage license was: Jackson and Thomas, 171; Allen, 309, 704–5.
was never consummated: Joseph Wood Krutch, *Edgar Allan Poe: A Study in Genius* (New York: Alfred A. Knopf, 1926), 52.
114 **"Virginia once kissed Poe in public":** Wagenknecht, 181.
An acquaintance who knew the Poes: Hutchisson, 55.
115 **when Virginia was about fifteen:** Meyers, 86.
116 **But Muddy intervened:** John Evangelist Walsh, *Plumes in the Dust* (Chicago: Nelson Hall, 1980), 40, 41.
"Eddie finished Virginia's education himself": Miller, *Building*, 48.
117 **"forbidden spirit enkindling":** Mabbott, II, 230.
"And thus, joy suddenly faded": Ibid.

117 **Poe would refer to Kabbalah:** Mabbott, III, 1190.
"We dote upon records": *E&R,* 1322.
118 **the barrier between life and death:** Patrick Quinn, 266–67.
"Where the gentler sex is concerned": *E&R,* 1317.
119 **the chess player had defeated:** Semtner, *Richmond,* 68.
A man named William Schlumberger: E&R, 1275; "William Schlumberger," Wikipedia, accessed June 22, 2021, www.wikipedia.org/wiki/William__Schlumberger.
destroyed by fire in 1854: A. H. Quinn, 248.
derived from David Brewster's: Burton R. Pollin, *Discoveries in Poe* (Notre Dame: University of Notre Dame Press, 1970), 171.
120 **"investment in literary derivation":** Stephen Rachman, "The Marginal Center," in Kennedy and Peeples, 463.
"conscious adoption and adaptation": Ibid., 464.
"a process in which": Ibid.
"Check this lying hospitality": Ralph Waldo Emerson, "Self-Reliance," in Porte and Morris, 130.
"unworthy of a school-boy": *E&R,* 547.
"In the four quarters of the globe": Hutchisson, 58.
121 **"We . . . often find ourselves":** *E&R,* 506.
the division and asymmetry: Michael J. Deas, *The Portraits and Daguerreotypes of Edgar Allan Poe* (Charlottesville: University Press of Virginia, 1988), 9.
"the first original literary theorist": Hutchisson, 64.
"*The Southern Literary Messenger* is equal": Silverman, 123.
"two blocks away": Colin (Joan) Dayan, "Poe, Persons, and Property," in Kennedy and Weissberg, 110.
122 **"even, and especially":** Morrison, 46–47.
"for distribution of slaves": Christopher P. Semtner, "Poe's Richmond and Richmond's Poe," in P. E. Phillips, 43.
"average racism": Ibid., 124.
"gradual elimination": Ibid., 129.
"sidestep the entire question": Ibid., 178.
"Poe endeavored to ignore": J. Gerald Kennedy and Liliane Weissberg, "Introduction: Poe, Race, and Contemporary Criticism," in Kennedy and Weissberg, xiv.
issue of "amalgamation": Leland S. Person, "Poe's Philosophy of Amalgamation: Reading Racism in the Tales," in Kennedy and Weissberg, 206.
"race lurks behind walls": Ibid.
"buried corpses": Ibid.
"He clearly embedded": Ibid., 212.
123 **"the revenge of blackness":** Ibid., 221.
"lamentable system upon": Kennedy, "Trust No Man," in Kennedy and Weissberg, 236.
"Washington Poe of Macon, Georgia": Harry Lee Poe, *Evermore: Edgar Allan Poe and the Mystery of the Universe* (Waco, TX: Baylor University Press, 2012), 46.
"For in that short ceremony": Phillips, I, 532.

124 **Virginia "ran out on the sidewalk":** Semtner, *Shrine,* 72.
"The MS. however, has an air": Mabbott, II, 286.
Nothing came of the plan: Miller, *Building,* 143.
He applied, without success: *CL* 2008, I, 145–46.

125 **It was claimed that when Poe:** Silverman, 126.
He told others that he *had* been adopted: *CL* 2008, I, 100.
"No will was found": Ibid.
Poe would weave the *al* sound: Silverman, 126.
Mr. Shelton stepped forward: Allen, 305–6.
Mary Winfree, told Poe: Semtner, *Shrine,* 156.
Poe's flirtation with White's daughter: Woodberry, I, 185.

126 **She and Poe would remain friends:** Phillips, I, 517.
"I think it one of the finest specimens": Gill, 75.

8. NEW YORK AND PHILADELPHIA

127 **Subscriptions had increased:** Scott Peeples, "A Life in Print, 1931–1849," in Kennedy and Peeples, 37.

128 **"illiterate and vulgar":** *CL* 2008, I, 236.
"I wish you to fall in": Gill, 83.
But the *New York Review* folded soon: Phillips, I, 548; Pope-Hennessey, 187.
The Poes first lived: Jackson and Thomas, 242, 244.
"I never saw him": Phillips, I, 554; A. H. Quinn, 267.
The critic Louis Renza: Peeples, 89.

130 **writing was an effort to escape silence:** Kennedy, *Death,* 116.
"The *Monthlies* of Gotham": Jackson and Thomas, 243.
At first the Poes lived: Ibid., 248, 255.
Pedder helped the Poes: Whitty, xli.
But in 1995 the scientist: H. L. Poe, 48.

131 **Poe considered learning the trade:** Silverman, 132.
"the earth was hollow and inhabited": John T. Irwin, *American Hieroglyphics* (New Haven: Yale University Press, 1980), 77.
escaping enslaved men and women often hid: Kennedy, "Brief Biography," 31.

132 **"passionate and frenzied search":** Patrick Quinn, 188.
"Pym's voyage to the pole": Irwin, 91.
Much of Poe's depiction: Lauren Coats, "Poe's Novel Explorations," in Kennedy and Peeples, 390.
"the unreadability of lived experience": Kennedy, *Death,* 146.
"a voyage to the end": Ibid., 147.
"extraordinary combination of": Irwin, 115.

133 **as David Greven suggests:** Greven, 161.
"'Tsalal is Hell,' because": Peeples, 96.

133 **"entombed alive":** *P&T,* 1153.
"We alone had escaped": Ibid., 1156.
"Tekeli-li! Tekeli-li!": Ibid., 1162.
134 **"And now we rushed":** Ibid., 1179.
"evokes the transfiguration": Irwin, 148–49.
"that ultimate vision": Richard Kopley, "Re-ordering Place in Poe's *Arthur Gordon Pym,*" P. E. Phillips, 210.
horror of origins, and endings: Davidson, 178.
"fatal and foetal": Hoffman, 221.
in a world where slavery was a way of life: Some of the most profound work in recent years has been devoted to Poe's only novel and its issues of race and slavery of African men and women. The exploration of *Pym* is ongoing and so extensive it's hard to keep up. Here I will include just a few examples of the scholarship and commentary.

Terence Whalen, in *Edgar Allan Poe and the Masses,* points out that "the chasm opened up by the ambush forms the letters of the Ethiopian verb root *to be shady,* while a wall within the chasm contains the Arabic verb root *to be white* and the Egyptian word designating 'the region of the south,'" illustrates in a coded way the vast divide in the United States over issues of African American slaves and race (170).

Betsy Erkkila, in "The Poetics of Whiteness," suggests *Pym* reveals "Poe's own grim vision of democratic history as a triumph of Blacks, blood, and dark apocalypse" (57). Lindon Barrett, in "Presence of Mind: Detection and Racialization in 'The Murders in the Rue Morgue,'" argues, "In landscapes, in seascapes, as well as in human anatomies, the closing details of the narrative contrast images of blackness and whiteness, marking out a world of irreconcilable divisions fixed ultimately as the clash of people and civilizations" (157).

J. Gerald Kennedy, in "'Trust No Man': Poe, Douglass, and the Culture of Slavery," observes, echoing other recent commentators, that the landscape of *Pym* "tells us all we need to know about the novel's symbolic geography, and Pym's demonizing of the black-skinned natives makes plain Poe's own unbridled bigotry" (242). Kennedy reads *Pym* as a "cultural critique exposing the blindness of white 'colonial knowledge.'" Kennedy believes that Poe "ultimately questions the Anglo-Saxon prejudices of his narrator, thus implicitly defying the political censorship of the antebellum South" (253).

David Greven, in *Gender Protest and Same Sex Desire in Antebellum American Literature,* emphasizes the queer theory implications of *Pym.* He argues, "The Pym-Augustus relationship constitutes a narrative of same-sex love's inevitably grim fate in the social order, communion ceding to cannibalism, Eros to Thanatos, love to horror.". Greven adds that "Dirk Peters embodies doubleness of race, physicality, personality, and sexuality, as his double-phallic name suggests" (143).

Continuing his argument about the fluidity of gender, Greven states: "A determinedly hoaxical work, *Pym,* foregrounds identity as the ultimate hoax" (149). Greven's most radical statement must be: "Poe takes Dirk Peters's hybridic qualities to a new, gender-bending level, depicting him as a male mother whose body emits blood from his groin" (151).

About the white image looming over the abyss at the end of Pym's account, Greven suggests: "The white figure signals gender ambiguity, male sexuality, and a privileged racial category" (161). Later Greven states: "If patriarchy remains intact, the novel yet manages to memorialize a revolt, however haphazard and finally ineffectual" (163).

135 **"One notice in the *New Yorker*":** Jackson and Thomas, 250; Silverman, 137.
"Plot, . . . properly defined": *E&R,* 148.

136 **"In the greenest of our valleys":** Mabbott, I, 315.
"Man doth not yield himself": Mabbott, II, 310.

137 ***Ligeia* rhymes with and suggests *idea:*** Hoffman, 247.
"I cannot, for my soul": Mabbott, II, 310.
He depicts her as a connoisseur: Alexandra Urakova "Undying Enigmas in 'Ligeia,'" in Kennedy and Peeples, 311.
"[created] female characters": Leland S. Person, "Poe and Nineteenth-Century Gender Constructions," in Kennedy, *Historical,* 138.
"some large, old, decaying city": Mabbott, II, 310.
her "majesty, the quiet ease": Ibid., 311.
"There is no exquisite beauty": Ibid., 311–12.
"the raven-black, the glossy": Ibid., 312.
"I looked at the delicate": Ibid.

138 **In an unpublished self-portrait:** Mabbott, II, 298.
"the beauty of the fabulous Houri": Ibid., 313.
"remains forever beyond": NSJE, 536.
"She was the most violently": Mabbott II, 315.
"And of such passion": Ibid.
"[Ligeia's] lack of remembered": Ibid., 331.

139 **Poe knew well a novel:** *E&R,* 1451.
Byron's grandmother was named: Pollin, 96.
"Rebecca as the 'sensual Jewess'": Greven, 84.

140 **"And there streamed forth":** Mabbott, II, 330.
Throughout his career Poe had shown: *CL* 2008, I, 544.
she haunts the narrator forever: Modern scholars and theorists have given us a number of alternate ways of approaching "Ligeia." David Greven, studying the story from the angle of queer theory, sees the character Ligeia as "*phallic feminine:* a male fantasy of femininity that seeks to endow femininity with powers traditionally associated with masculinity while also preserving a feminine ideal" (72). He then asserts that Ligeia "gives birth to herself" at the end of the tale (73). Ligeia resists the limits placed on her by gender and returns as "a figure of power untouchable as she is intimidating . . . existing for herself alone . . . the phallic mother" (82).

Greven describes "Ligeia" as "a fantasy of Black woman's triumphant usurpation of the white woman's position and her claims to marital sexuality" (85). E. J. Hansen stresses the exotic Egyptian theme in "Ligeia" as her "reincarnation in a room full of Egyptian sarcophagi" (Emily James Hansen, "Poe, Egypt, and 'Egyptomania,'" in P. E. Phillips, 268).

9. WILLIAM BURTON

141 **though their poverty could not be disguised:** Jackson and Thomas, 313.
Mary would sing: Van Cleef, 639.
The Poes were also visited: Jackson and Thomas, xxviii; Woodberry, I, 296.
142 **"an enterprising man but vulgar":** Silverman, 142.
"impudent attempt at humbugging": Jackson and Thomas, 254.
143 **"I am sorry you have thought":** Woodberry, I, 240; Rufus W. Griswold, "Memoir," *Works of Edgar Allan Poe* (New York: Harper and Brothers, n.d.), I, 49.
He gave special praise to Fouqué's: *E&R,* 252–58.
"I intend to put up": *CL* 2008, I, 188.
144 **"singularly deficient in all":** *E&R,* 671.
"too palpable to be mistaken": Ibid., 678.
"When I consider . . . Mr. Emerson": Ibid., 1418.
"It would be desirable that you": *CL* 2008, I, 281.
"A furious delirium possessed": Mabbott, II, 461.
145 **"I was favorably impressed":** Phillips, I, 580–81.
Henry Beck Hirst, a writer and lawyer: Ibid., 591.
James Campbell Usher: Mabbott, II, 393.
"During the whole of a dull, dark": Ibid., 397–98.
146 **"A cadaverousness of complexion":** Ibid., 401.
"a journey into the depths of the self": Richard Wilbur, "The House of Poe," in Regan, *Poe,* 108.
"The forehead was massive and broad": Mabbott, II, 298.
"the sentience of all vegetable things": Ibid., 408.
"The now ghastly pallor": Ibid., 402.
147 **"Perhaps the eye of":** Ibid., 400.
"We have no reason to believe": *E&R,* 1314.
148 **"There were times, indeed":** Mabbott, II, 411.
"Not hear it? yes, I hear it": Ibid., 416.
149 **"Then, with a low moaning cry":** Ibid., 416–17.
"self-birthing": Leverenz, 110.
"I am much pleased with a tale": *CL* 2008, I, 195.
150 **"My earliest recollections":** Mabbott, II, 427–28.
"In truth, the ardor": Ibid., 431.
"In a few seconds I": Ibid., 447.
151 **"*You have conquered*":** Ibid., 448.
"elementary substitution ciphers": Silverman, 152.
it promised privacy: Louis A. Renza, "Poe and the Issue of American Privacy," in Kennedy, *Historical,* 181.
the most popular of all: Hutchisson, 113.
"the analytic sublime": Shawn James Rosenheim, *The Cryptographic Imagination* (Baltimore: Johns Hopkins University Press, 1998), 65.
152 **"If in many of my productions":** Mabbott, II, 473.

10. *PENN MAGAZINE*

153 **"To say we have *read* this production":** Jackson and Thomas, 282.
"a greater amount of trash": Silverman, 154.
"We have read a goodly number": Jackson and Thomas, 282.
"Why ought the author": Silverman, 155.
154 **"Appallachia *[sic]*" would be a better:** Mabbott, II, 497.
"There should be no hesitation": *E&R,* 1415.
"*Repose* speaks in all": Mabbott, II, 502.
"It appears that ownership": Kennedy, *Death,* 98.
155 **"many of the periodicals":** McGill, 149.
"A foreign theme": Ibid., 156.
"Poe calls for an investment": Ibid., 171.
"Sir: I find myself at leisure": *CL* 2008, I, 217–18. Angle brackets appear in the quoted passage in the *Collected Letters,* indicating Poe's own revision to his letter.
"The charge of 100$ I shall not": Ibid., 220.
156 **"*nothing stronger than water*":** Ibid., 263.
"buffoon and a felon": Ibid., 262–63.
"PROSPECTUS OF THE PENN": Jackson and Thomas, 301.
"Its aim, chiefly shall be": *E&R,* 1025; Jackson and Thomas, 300.
157 **"was possessed with a burning love":** *P&T,* 1190.
the hero is probably Jewish: Wagenknecht, 87.
"He was a remarkably": *P&T,* 1200.
"At the moment I seemed": Ibid., 1205.
158 **"We were all like brothers":** Ibid., 1236.
"intense excitement with": Ibid., 1237.
"carved over with": Ibid., 1247.
"rhetoric of imperial": John Carlos Rowe, "Edgar Allan Poe's Imperial Fantasy and the American Frontier," in Kennedy and Weissberg, 77.
"I need the countenance of those who stand": *CL* 2008, I, 252.
159 **"Poe belonged mainly":** Tomc, "Poe and His Circle," 24.
"There is one thing more: Phillips, I, 643.
160 **(as would Billy Burton):** Ingram, 145.
the benchmark for remuneration: Silverman, 163.
"*no* merit whatever": *E&R,* 824.
"It is a mere mass": Ibid., 493.
161 **"contain a great deal of sense":** Silverman, 165.
"Criticism is *not,* we think": *E&R,* 1031.
"A book is written": Ibid., 1032.
162 **"a kind of Dr. Jekyll":** Patrick Quinn, 229.
"We have said that the tale": "Nathaniel Hawthorne," *E&R,* 573.
"We look upon him": Ibid., 569.

162 **"They who dream by day":** Mabbott, II, 638.
163 **"giant serpents of Syria":** Ibid., 640.
"its inmost recesses": Ibid., 641.
"the censers of the angels": Ibid., 642.
"in the silence of the night": Ibid., 645.
164 **"I feel that a shadow":** Ibid., 643.
165 **"But there is one pleasure still":** Mabbott, II, 600.
"In the tranquil landscape": Emerson, "Nature," in Porte and Morris, 29.
"As we find cycle within cycle": Mabbott, II, 601.
"was all one radiant harem": Ibid., 603.
166 **"In five minutes the whole sea":** Ibid., 580.
"It is now within a few days": Ibid., 584.
167 **Virginia at her harp or piano:** H. L. Poe, 49.
168 **"I feel that *now* is the time to strike":** *CL* 2008, I, 347.

11. RATIOCINATION

170 **Or we also might consider:** Hutchisson, 139.
"a voluptuous scene, that masquerade": Mabbott II, 671.
"And Darkness and Decay": Ibid., 677.
171 **"She addressed [Poe]":** Meyers, 129.
"It is a curious fact that": Kelly Ross, "Deciphering Dupin: Poe's Racionative Plots," in Kennedy and Peeples, 206.
172 **"a powerful counter-fantasy":** Kennedy, "Poe's Terror Analytics," in Kennedy and Peeples, 820.
"You are right about the hair-splitting": *CL* 2008, I, 595.
"reflects his acts of duping": Peter Thoms, "Dupin and the Power of Detection," in Hayes, 135.
"an obscure library in the Rue Montmartre": Mabbott, II, 531.
"in a retired and desolate": Ibid., 532.
173 **"we sallied forth":** Ibid., 533.
"EXTRAORDINARY MURDERS": Ibid., 537.
174 **"denies what is and explains":** Ibid., 574.
Dupin leads us little by little to understand what occurred: Several modern critics have studied the racial implications of "The Murders in the Rue Morgue." Lindon Barrett, in "Presence of Mind: Detection and Racialization in 'The Murders in the Rue Morgue,'" examines the contrast of "whiteness" and "blackness" in the story, identifying whiteness with Dupin and Blackness with the orangutan (159). Part of the tension in the story derives from fear: "The threat of racial blackness takes the form of a threat to rational conduct and to social organization" (162). In blunt terms, the ape stands for a Black man threatening white society (167).

Elise Lemire, in the essay "Amalgamation Discourses and the Race Riots of 1838 in Poe's Philadelphia," studies the fear of race mixing, "amalgamation," called "miscegenation" later. Riots occurred during a meeting of the second Antislavery Convention of American Women, attended by numbers of white abolitionists. In the city where the country was born, angered whites attacked Blacks and Black property. Lemire points out the significance of the orangutan wielding the razor in "The Murders in the Rue Morgue": at that time many, if not most, of the barbers in the city were Black (183). The legend was that orangutans "are passionately fond of women," and Lemire addresses the sexual dimensions of the story: in effect, Madame L'Espanaye and her daughter are raped by a Black man, according to the code and fear of the time (190).

Judith Fetterly writes, altering Marie Bonaparte's interpretation, "One of the bodies has been forcibly thrust up a chimney, an image evocative of rape" (quoted in Lemire, 195).

174 **"father of the detective tale":** Phillips, I, 654.

175 **"E. A. Poe, Esq, has retired":** Jackson and Thomas, 365.

"men whose imbecility": *CL* 2008, I, 260.

"He had the docility": Ingram, 172–73.

"To coin one's brain into silver": *CL* 2008, I, 292.

"The brief, the terse, the condensed": Ibid., 274.

the Poe family moved out: Jackson and Thomas, 367.

By September 12 of that year: Ibid., 379.

paid less than a common laborer's: Hutchisson, 151.

176 **"I met Poe in Philadelphia":** Phillips, I, 760.

177 **"Robert Tyler expressed himself":** Woodberry, I, 318.

"caviar for the gourmet": Mabbott, III, 715.

"man of dark complexion": Thoms, Hayes, 140.

At this time Poe's debts totaled: *CL* 2008, I, 336.

"his wearing apparel": Tresch, 179.

178 **"No poet in America has done so much":** *CL* 2008, I, 413.

By Harnden's Express, Poe sent: Ibid., 377.

179 **"One of his eyes resembled":** Mabbott, III, 792.

Evil Eye implies an "evil I": Arthur Robinson, quoted in Paul Christian Jones, "Poe's Doubles From 'William Wilson' to "The Cask of Amontillado'": Kennedy and Peeples, 244.

"They heard!—they suspected!": Mabbott, III, 797.

"I am poor": *CL* 2008, I, 393.

181 **was the work of Judge Beverley Tucker:** Peeples, 98–100.

"average racism": Whalen, 124.

"a region infinitely more dreary": Mabbott, III, 817.

"It was a species of table land": Ibid.

182 **"We estimated the entire":** Ibid., 828.

the mother's body yielding: Bonaparte, 363.

183 **"*A good glass in the Bishop's*":** Mabbott, III, 840.

183 **the scarab beetle has symbolized:** Ibid., 845.
"of 'The Gold-Bug' (my most successful tale)": *CL* 2008, I, 441.
184 **March 7, 1842:** Tresch, 170.
Later Poe would blame Dickens: *CL* 2008, I, 450.
Predictably, this cooled: Silverman, 199–200.
the film had not yet sold: Phillips, I, 676.
"When Mr. Poe reached our house": Van Cleef, 639.
185 **"Will you be kind enough":** *CL* 2008, I, 353.

12. WASHINGTON, DC

186 **"His dark hair hung carelessly":** Jackson and Thomas, 380.
"I will *send* for you": Ibid., 384.
187 **Chivers would offer:** Damon, 173–74.
"far surpass all American journals": *E&R*, 1033.
188 **"I believe that I am making":** *CL* 2008, I, 386.
"My dear fellow—Thank you": Ibid., 389.
"seedy in his appearance": Meyers, 145.
189 **In April 1843 the Poe family:** Jackson and Thomas, 409.
"There is one thing I am anxious": Woodberry, II, 32–33.
190 **"For the most wild, yet most homely":** Mabbott, III, 849.
"From my infancy": Ibid., 850.
"It was this unfathomable": Ibid., 852.
191 **"I withdrew my arm":** Ibid., 856.
"figurative rape scene": Weinauer, 179.
"as the monks of the middle ages": Mabbott, III, 857.
"It is impossible to describe": Ibid.
"I looked upon my future": Ibid., 858.
"I rapped heavily": Ibid.
"like the sobbing of a child": Ibid., 859.
"The corpse, already greatly decayed": Ibid.
Poe seduces the reader: Leland S. Person, "Outing the Perverse: Poe's False Confessionals," in Kennedy and Peeples, 262.
"We identify with the Imp": Ibid., 266.
resentment for his marriage: Meyers, 137.
192 **the black cat symbolizes slavery:** Goddu, Hayes, 102.
193 **"the most voluptuous natural scenery":** Mabbott, III, 863.
"I saw, or dreamed that I saw": Ibid., 865.
"the most important, and perhaps": Deas, 8.
"I am ugly enough God knows": *CL* 2008, I, 381.
"noted in British naval history": Silverman, 196–97.
197 **"I followed the windings of":** Mabbott, III, 942–43

197 **"This path was excessively sinuous":** Ibid., 943.
"In an instant I seemed to rise": Ibid., 948.
"Nor was it [a dream]": Ibid.

198 **But sales were so poor:** Jackson and Thomas, 426.
"who in turn tries all the professions": Emerson, "Self-Reliance," in Porte and Morris, 132.

199 **"I have loved often and deeply":** Joy Bayless, *Rufus Wilmot Griswold: Poe's Literary Executor* (Nashville: Vanderbilt University Press, 1943), 10.
"He seems to be a kind": Tomc, "Poe and His Circle," 31.
"the infinite in the finite": Charles Baudelaire, *Les Fleurs du mal,* trans. Wallace Fowlie (New York: Bantam Books, 1964), 3.

200 **"Such quotations, allusions, phrasings":** William M. Forrest, *Biblical Allusions in Poe* (New York: Macmillan, 1928), 147.
"an ecstatic prescience": *E&R,* 77.
over twenty print editions: Phillips, I, 651.

201 **"a notorious blackmailer":** *Poe Studies* 4, no. 2 (December 1971): 1.
"*the most important addition*": *E&R,* 556.
"When once he sent for me": Griswold, "Memoir," 52; Woodberry, II, 35.
"I kiss her cold lips": Silverman, 217.

202 **"The vault where she is":** Bayless. 66.
"That he has *some* talents": Meyers, 127.
"Griswold had been reared": Bayless, 187–88.

203 **the "literary *histrio*":** *E&R,* 14.
"wander about the streets": Phillips, I, 700.
"Her life was despaired of": *CL* 2008, II, 641.
Hirst also owned a pet raven: Mabbott, I, 355.
"would come, during these early": Phillips, I, 694–95.
"'to arrange for the treatment'": Ibid., 762.
"heart failure": Ibid.

204 **he'd worked for more than ten years:** Weiss, *Home Life of Poe,* 185.
"In the summer of 1842": Allen, 433.
would later claim to have offered Poe: Jackson and Thomas, 435.

13. NEW YORK, "THE PURLOINED LETTER"

205 **"We have just this minute":** *CL* 2008, I, 437–38.

206 **published in 1843 in London:** Mabbott, III, 1065.

207 **"The last nine hours":** Mabbott, III, 1078–1079.

208 **"The unparticled matter":** *CL* 2008, I, 449.
while Poe shared a room: Phillips, II, 882.

209 **Washington had once made the house:** Gill, 148.
a rock outcrop called Mount Tom: Kent P. Ljungquist, "Poe's Landscapes, Picturesque and Ideal," in Kennedy and Peeples, 288.

209 **According to the daughter:** Phillips, II, 896.
Sometimes the Brennan children: Pollin, 163.
Muddy had a room: Hutchisson, 156.
"as a shy, solitary, taciturn": Gill, 149; Wagenknecht, 50.
"My life has been *whim*": *CL* 2008, I, 450.
"I would write on the lintels": Emerson, "Self-Reliance," in Porte and Morris, 123.
210 **"the best play ever written by an American":** *E&R*, 1129.
"In a short period both his mother": Silverman, 224.
"A more estimable man": Jacob E. Spannuth and Thomas O. Mabbott, ed. *Doings of Gotham: Poe's Contributions to "The Columbia Spy"* (Pottsville, PA: Jacob E. Spannuth, 1929), 34.
211 **"For the heart whose woes are legion":** Mabbott, I, 343–44.
212 **Poe was deeply influenced:** Mabbott, III, 1024.
"P. Is not God spirit?": Ibid., 1033.
"Yes; for mind, existing": Ibid., 1036.
213 **"No pain—I am dying":** Ibid., 1239.
"The upper lip, at the same time": Ibid.
"It impressed me": Ibid., 1240.
"For God's sake!—quick": Ibid., 1242.
"His whole frame at once": Ibid., 1243.
"As one reads them": Woodberry, II, 109–10.
214 **"'The Raven' was written in a day":** Whitty, xlviii.
"But all these things are mine": S. Foster Damon, *Thomas Holley Chivers: Friend of Poe* (New York: Harper & Brothers, 1930), 199.
Susan Weiss would later claim: Weiss, *Home Life*, 185.
"No more—no more": Mabbott, I, 311.
215 **"Once upon a midnight dreary":** Ibid., 364–65.
216 **"How *shall* the ritual then be read":** Ibid., 337.
"an exaggerated sense of wrong": Gill, 140–41.
represents a Black body: Leverenz, 122.
217 ***"Mournful and Never-Ending"*:** *E&R*, 25.
"the human thirst for self-torture": Ibid., 24.
"Be that word our sign": Mabbott, I, 369.
218 **"The bird beat the bug":** *CL* 2008, I, 505.
It is said his lifetime earnings: Meyers, 186.

14. FAME AND ITS PRICE

219 **New York as "raven-mad":** Walsh, *Plumes*, 6.
with the support of President Martin Van Buren and the Democratic Party: After the *Democratic Review* was moved to New York, in 1840, the young Walt Whitman became a supporter and contributor. William Gilmore Simms sent his writing from South Carolina. While preaching intense nationalism, O'Sullivan seemed little inter-

ested in the growing controversy about slavery. He promised that "all history has to be re-written; political science and the whole scope of all moral truth have to be considered and illustrated in the light of the democratic principle" (Widmer, 42). O'Sullivan and all his associates felt like revolutionaries and modeled themselves on the figures of the American Revolution. He saluted the "Great Nation of Futurity" (43).

In New York, O'Sullivan became allied with young writers and editors such as Evert Duyckinck. Duyckinck, from an old Dutch family, would be prominent in New York literary life for several decades. He would become a close friend of Herman Melville and in 1845 would publish a series with Wiley & Putnam called the Library of America Books.

It may have been Nathaniel Willis who introduced Poe to the Young Americans. In January 1845, just as "The Raven" made Poe famous, Poe became coeditor of the *Broadway Journal* with Charles F. Briggs, also a Young American. Earlier Poe had called Duyckinck's magazine, *Arcturus,* "one of the *very* best journals in the country" (*E&R,* 823). Both O'Sullivan and Duyckinck were searching for "the genius of American Literature" (102).

It is likely Lowell's tribute to Poe in *Graham's Magazine* in January 1845 that drew the attention of the Young Americans to Poe. Poe's posture as an "aristocrat" was useful to their cause at the time, because Poe had the proper pedigree and credibility to demonstrate the widening embrace of their program (McGill, 207). Meredith L. McGill tells us, "Poe's relative anonymity as an author was indispensable to his construction by the Young Americans as a figure with redemptive power" (204).

Suddenly, Poe, who had been looking for a publisher for his tales for years, found himself invited to join the exclusive Copyright Club, with connections to Duyckinck and the Library of America Books. Poe, who had detested literary nationalism, found himself calling the Young Americans "the choice and magnanimous few who spoke promptly in my praise" (Widmer, 108). The Young Americans were happy to recruit Poe to their cause because the brilliance of his criticism and his independence gave their movement more prestige (McGill, 204). Poe's interest in copyright was also something he shared with the Young Americans (Kennedy, "A Brief Biography," 53).

Later Poe would attack statements by Young Americans such as "We believe we are now upon the verge of an era, which will eclipse even the brilliant glory of the sixteenth century" (Widmer, 150). But for a year Poe seemed willing to lend his name and his pen to the Young American circle. John Tresch tells us that in the spirit of the Young Americans, Poe hoped that his own magazine, the *Stylus,* was "aimed at writing a literary nation into existence" ("Extra! Extra! Poe Invents Science Fiction!" 123–24). It was through Duyckinck that he published his two most important books, *Tales* and *The Raven and Other Poems,* both in 1845. The Young Americans made sure *Tales* received many positive reviews.

It is ironic that O'Sullivan, given his futuristic ideals, would later support the Confederacy in the Civil War.

219 **"control of American culture":** Edward L. Widmer, *Young America* (New York: Oxford University Press, 1999), 12.

220 **at 195 East Broadway:** Jackson and Thomas, 530.
85 Amity Street: Ibid., 572; A. H. Quinn, 475.
Poe started drinking again: Jackson and Thomas, 530.
"Poe is a much better fellow": Phillips, II, 988.
"I am as poor now as ever": *CL* 2008, I, 504.
"not only the greatest Poet": Damon, 138–39.
"seems to *see with his ear*": *E&R,* 1332.
"a terror to his wife": Miller, *Building,* 189.
"He was a genius": Phillips, II, 1025.
burden of "conscience misery": Ibid., 1026.
221 **as many as eighty or more guests:** Silverman, 279.
"He delighted in the society": Ingram, 280.
"What *awful* eyes Mr. Poe": Susan Weiss, "Last Days of Edgar Allan Poe," *Scribner's Magazine,* March 1878, 711.
222 **And for once:** Woodberry, II, 122.
"Your letter occasioned me first pain": *CL* 2008, I, 477.
"He becomes a desk": Jackson and Thomas, 510.
"battle of wills": D. H. Lawrence, *Portable Lawrence,* ed. Diana Trilling (New York: Viking Press, 1946), 672–73.
223 **"I think no one could know him":** Griswold, "Memoir," 88; Whitty, liv.
"a weird, tender child": Walsh, *Plumes,* 11.
"I would not lord it o'er thy heart": Silverman, 283.
"For hours I have listened": Griswold, 91; Philips, II, 954–55.
224 **fathered the daughter, Fanny Fay:** John Evangelist Walsh, *Midnight Dreary: The Mysterious Death of Edgar Allan Poe* (New Brunswick, NJ: Rutgers University Press, 1998), 29.
After Poe's death Fanny would write a long letter: *CL* 2008, II, 867.
"At his desk beneath": Griswold, 89; A. H. Quinn, 480.
225 **"I did not know him":** Meyers, 173.
"These trifles are collected": *P&T,* 18.
227 **"Thus a poet . . . should be cautious":** *E&R,* 1301.
"'clique' mentality": Sandra Tomc, "Edgar Allan Poe and His Enemies," in Kennedy and Peeples, 566.
228 **"started his hoax of double tilting":** Phillips, II, 956–57.
"I can feel for the 'constitutional indolence'": *CL* 2008, I, 448.
the Lyceum's second or third choice: Walsh, *Plumes,* n. 30.
Eliza and David Poe had performed: Phillips, II, 1054.
229 **"general imbecility":** "Memoir," 57; Silverman, 267.
he was drunk: Kent Ljungquist, "The Poet as Critic": Hayes, 14.
230 **"They produced no very distinct impression":** Jackson and Thomas, 578; Phillips, II, 1055.
"We have been quizzing the Bostonians": Jackson and Thomas, 581.
"If [Poe] had as much tact": Ibid., 588.

15. THE DOMAIN OF ARNHEIM

231 **"He has some good points":** Woodberry, II, 143.
"Not a great while after": Jackson and Thomas, 557; Woodberry, II, 140.
"Business, of late": *CL* 2008, I, 532.
"I really believe that I have been mad": Ibid., 533.
232 **She had married a professor:** Phillips, II, 1141.
She revenged herself on Rufus Griswold: Bayless, 224.
233 **"A certain lady of my acquaintance":** Jackson and Thomas, 622.
"I permitted myself": *CL* 2008, II, 731–32.
hit his face repeatedly: Hutchisson, 190.
"a flogging which he will remember": *CL* 2008, I, 585.
"Unexpected engagements demanding": Jackson and Thomas, 615.
234 **"Ever with thee I wish to roam—":** Ibid., 625.
"All Bluedom misses you": *CL* 2008, I, 500.
"I do believe": Meyers, 187.
235 **"The thousand injuries of Fortunato":** Mabbott, III, 1256.
Montresor and Fortunato are two sides: Hoffman, 223.
"You are not of the masons": Mabbott, III, 1260.
opposing the wealth and power: Person, Kennedy and Peeples, 263.
"'The Amontillado!' ejaculated my friend": Mabbott, III, 1262.
236 **"I forced the last stone":** Ibid., 1263.
"is perhaps the most moral": Ibid., 1252.
Two landscape painters who: Kent P. Ljungquist, "Poe's Landscapes, Picturesque and Ideal": Kennedy and Peeples, 293.
blur the distinction between: Ibid., 297.
"My friend could not fail": Mabbott, II, 707.
Monticello, may have been: Ljungquist, "Poe's Landscapes": Kennedy and Peeples, 287.
Poe also remembered: Christopher P. Semtner, "Poe's Richmond and Richmond's Poe": P. E. Phillips, 50.
237 **A. O. Lovejoy would work:** A. O. Lovejoy, "The Chinese Origin of a Romanticism": *Essays in the History of Ideas* (Baltimore: Johns Hopkins University Press, 1948), 101–35.
"Meantime I enclose": *CL* 2008, II, 712; Mabbott, III, 1266.
"convey the sentiment of spiritual": Ibid., 1276.
"Above all, it was in": Ibid., 1277.
"moreover, enwrapt": Ibid., 1279.
"commences a rapid descent": Ibid., 1283.
238 **"I know I shall die soon":** Phillips, II, 1098.
239 **"brain fever":** Jackson and Thomas, 640.
Poe turned down invitations: Ibid.
"Poe's voice was": Benjamin F. Fisher, *Poe in His Own Time* (Iowa City: University of Iowa Press, 2010), 210–12; A. H. Quinn, 508–9.

239 **"He passed the greater part":** Miller, *Building,* 47–48; Phillips, II, 1118.
When a sudden hemorrhage: Phillips, II, 1120–21.
240 **invited Poe to use the college library:** Hutchisson, 194.
"They were highly cultivated": Jackson and Thomas, 644.
"I have *magnificent* objects in view": *CL* 2008, I, 597.
Poe suffered from consumption: J. Gerald Kennedy, "A Brief Biography," 54.
"Political sectional animosities": Whitty, lxi.
"I write from a mental necessity": Mary Gove Nichols, "Reminiscences of Edgar Poe (1863)," in Fisher, 213.
241 **"I love fame":** Ibid., 214.
"The kennels [gutters] of Philadelphia": Silverman, 309.
"The errors and frailties which I deplore": Woodberry, II, 189.
242 **"A poor creature . . . called":** Jackson and Thomas, 656.
"Suffer me to tell you": Ibid., 660.
it was later destroyed: Gill, 230.

16. VIRGINIA'S LAST DAYS

243 **"My Dear Heart":** *CL* 2008, I, 578.
"was always laughing": Phillips, II, 1139.
"Sometimes he would play ball": Ibid., 1140.
"I confess": Ibid., 1138; Jackson and Thomas, 646–47.
244 **"We regret to learn":** Ibid., 672.
"The Poe's [*sic*] are in the same state": Ibid., 673–74.
"That I am 'without friends'": *CL* 2008, I, 612.
245 **Marie Louise Shew, author:** Semtner, *Shrine,* 116.
"Mary, be a friend to Eddie": Van Cleef, 640.
Poe rubbed Sissy's hands: Walsh, *Plumes,* 80.
It was possibly Loui who made: Miller, *Poe's Helen,* 264.
Muddy offered to sell: Van Cleef, 640.
246 **"The pen falls powerless":** Mabbott, I, 407–8.
Patrick Quinn believed Poe's tales: Patrick Quinn, 252.
247 **Poe visited Fanny:** Meyers, 208.
He ordered a fine black suit: Ibid., 201.
Ulalume suggests "ululation, or wailing": Meyers, 211.
"The skies they were ashen and sober": Mabbott, I, 415–19.
248 **"the most unmistakably genuine utterance":** Woodberry, II, 235.
"Let us examine a crystal": *E&R,* 33.

17. LOUI SHEW AND *EUREKA*

251 **"I saved Mr. Poe's life":** Miller, *Building*, 92.
252 **"Can it be true Louise":** *CL* 2008, II, 677–79.
"has been on here—but it were better": Ibid., 633.
Poe wandered over the grounds: Phillips, II, 1241.
"I rise early": *CL* 2008, II, 648.
"It is true, that rarely": Phillips, II, 1244.
"He never liked to be alone": Meyers, 213–14
"revolutionize the world": *CL* 2008, II, 650.
253 **"at once pre-Socratic and":** Irwin, 222.
"Space and duration are one": *P&T*, 1340.
254 **"the fabric of reality":** John Tresch, "Extra! Extra! Poe Invents Science Fiction," in Hayes, 121.
"In the Original Unity": *P&T*, 1261.
"Centripetal, / Centrifugal": Ronald Johnson, *To Do as Adam Did: Selected Poems of Ronald Johnson* (Jersey City: House Publisher, 2), 62.
"The Universe is a plot": *P&T*, 1342.
"Electricity, heat, light": Ibid., 1352.
"And now—this Heart Divine": Ibid., 1356.
"Nothing is, or can be": Ibid., 1357.
"In the meantime bear in mind": Ibid., 1358–59.
The route to Oneness is death: Irwin, 235.
"That God may be all": *P&T*, 1359.
255 **"Despite recent efforts to explain":** Meyers, 218.
"Seated at my desk": Ingram, 353–54.
Poe was paid $14: Meyers, 219.
"He appeared inspired": Jackson and Thomas, 720.
more than four hundred emendations: H. L. Poe, 56; Susan Jaffe Tane, *Nevermore: The Edgar Allan Poe Collection of Susan Tane* (Ithaca: Cornell University Library, 2006), 56.
The book was banned: H. L. Poe, 148.

18. ANNIE, ELMIRA, AND HELEN

256 **"sweet, trusting Fanny":** Walsh *Plumes*, 132.
published under the name Jane: Jackson and Thomas, xxxi.
257 **"She was a woman of strong character":** Phillips, II, 1293.
"He seemed so *unlike*": Miller, *Building*, 163.
"brother and sister": Silverman, 347.
"If Poe had been impotent": Meyers, 221.
258 **"I felt as in the presence of a god!":** Jackson and Thomas, 748.

258 **"Passing over the manifest":** Ibid., 743.
"The mocking smile": Ibid., 744.
"the system of Pantheism": Ibid., 745.
259 **"After his wife's death":** Weiss, *Independent,* August 25, 1904, 445.
"Once I found him": Jackson and Thomas, 749.
"Thousands have seen him": Meyers, 225; Jackson and Thomas, 750.
"There were some other people present": Ibid., 750.
"As a converser": Phillips, II, 1301.
260 **"I was ready to go to church":** A. H. Quinn, 628–29.
262 **"A low bewildering melody":** Jackson and Thomas, 747.
263 **"on just such a night as this":** *CL* 2008, II, 682; Miller, *Helen,* 256.
"above and beyond, but never at you": Phillips, II, 1280–81.
"At one time she wore constantly": Ibid., 1317.
"to calm herself": Semtner, *Shrine,* 130.
conflating his memory of Elmira: Phillips, II, 1284.
"strange spiritual energy": Miller, *Building,* 217; Woodberry, II, 288.
"Oh, thou grim and ancient Raven": Jackson and Thomas, 729.
264 **"I see by the *Home Journal*":** Ibid., 729–30.
265 **"If you *died*—then at least":** *CL* 2008, II, 700.
"exceptionally *wrong*": Bayless, 148.
266 **"I did violence to my own heart":** *CL* 2008, II, 708.
"Would it *not* be 'glorious'": Ibid., 735.
Poe explained that: Helen Whitman, *Edgar Poe and His Critics* (New York: Rudd & Carlton, 1860), 49.
"Of a sudden the company": Phillips, II, 1315.
267 **"He hath ever but slenderly":** Shakespeare, *King Lear,* I, i, 289–90.
"I saw that you were *Helen*": *CL* 2008, II, 696–97.
"Poe enjoyed what": Leland S. Person, "Poe and Nineteenth-Century Gender Constructions," in Kennedy, *Historical,* 143.
"I would cast from me": *CL* 2008, II, 700.
268 **the word *operatic*:** Carlson, *Introduction,* xxi; Meyers, 230.
"For a long time no one spoke": Jackson and Thomas, 763.
269 **"a lingering pity and sorrow":** Helen Whitman, 48.
Poe asked Annie to come to him: Jackson and Thomas, 764.
271 **Poe turned up in Providence again:** *CL* 2008, II, 721–22.
the whole laudanum and suicide attempt: Phillips, II, 1333.
"an angel sent to save him": Jackson and Thomas, 766.
272 **rather see Helen in her grave:** Ibid., 767.
"So long as I think that you": *CL* 2008, II, 721; Jackson and Thomas, 768.
273 **"I so much fear *she* is not":** Jackson and Thomas, 773.
"She threw herself": Ibid., 773–74; Miller, *Poe's Helen,* 154–55.
274 **"That marriage will never":** Jackson and Thomas, 778.
"We shall be married on Monday": *CL* 2008, II, 744.

274 **"Say that you love me":** Jackson and Thomas, 780; Ingram, 386.
"Mr. Pabodie, you hear how I am insulted": Miller, *Poe's Helen,* 145.
275 **"Indeed, indeed, Annie":** *CL* 2008, II, 748–49.
his seduction of the innocent: Walsh, *Plumes,* 149.
asking for news: Jackson and Thomas, 784–85.
séances to contact Poe's spirit: Semtner, *Shrine,* 108–9.

19. "FOR ANNIE" AND "THE BELLS"

276 **and even a line from Shelley's "Adonais":** Mabbott, I, 450.
277 **"Take this kiss upon the brow!":** Ibid., 451–52.
"Thank Heaven! the crisis": Ibid., 456–59.
278 **"A smoky mist, resembling":** Mabbott, III, 1328.
279 **"the softer linden, redbud":** Ibid., 1332.
"I said to myself": Ibid., 1338–39.

20. "THE POETIC PRINCIPLE"

281 **"I am fearful Cousin Philip":** Walsh, *Midnight,* 134–36.
282 **"Of course, there is *not one* word":** *CL* 2008, II, 785.
"Gaily bedight": Mabbott, I, 463.
283 **"It was many and many a year ago":** Ibid., 477–78.
286 **"The 'Fable' is essentially 'loose'":** *E&R,* 816–17.
"Mr. Lowell is one of the most rabid": Ibid., 819.
"Has Mrs. Whitman no friend": Jackson and Thomas, 788.
287 **"As for myself":** Mabbott, III, 1354.
288 **connect "Hop-Frog" to the Nat Turner:** Agnieszka Soltysik Monnet, "'The Fall of the House of Usher' and the Architecture of Unreliability," in Kennedy and Peeples, 326.
"Depend upon it": *CL* 2008, II, 770.
"We must aim high": *CL* 2008, II, 793–94.
289 **"No, my sadness is":** Ibid., 796.
she would demand that her letters: Phillips, II, 1438.
291 **"[He] left in such wretched spirits":** Ingram, 415.
"I sold everything I could": Miller, *Building,* 29.
"If you will do so": Silverman, 414.
292 **"But women do not argue logically":** *CL* 2008, II, 819.
"satchel . . . given up by": Miller, *Building,* 131–32; Silverman, 414.
"I have been *so* ill": *CL* 2008, II, 820–21.
"I never wanted to see": Ibid., 822–23.
293 **Pale and frightened:** Walsh, *Midnight,* 72–75.
294 **He borrowed the price:** Ibid., 75–76.

294 **"You are my last hope":** Jackson and Thomas, 817; Silverman, 418.
"I thought you had deserted me": Silverman, 419.
295 **he seemed to feel a "presentiment":** Jackson and Thomas, 817.
"If Eddy comes home": Woodberry, II, 311.
"Oh, my darling Mother": *CL* 2008, II, 823–24.
"Your letter is only this moment": Ibid., 828.
296 **"His handsome, slender and erect":** Meyers, 247.
Susan Talley Weiss remembered: Weiss, *Home Life of Poe,* 199–200.
"You will see at once": *CL* 2008, II, 825–26.
"As yet, I am too feeble": Ibid., 829.
"Assiduous attention saved him": Weiss, *Scribner's,* March 1878, 712.
297 **Poe drew a pistol:** Whitty, lxxiii.
"I asked, alluding": Ibid., lxxxi–lxxxii.
"I would illustrate, if possible": A. H. Quinn, 623; Weiss, *Scribner's,* 708.
"expressed his conviction": Weiss, *Scribner's,* 714.
298 **Southall mocked Poe's speech:** Walsh, *Midnight,* 27.
299 **"She was a tall, rather masculine":** Weiss, *Independent* 57, August 25, 1904, 443.
"When I knew Mrs. Shelton": Alfriend, 490.
"She more than once": Ibid.
300 **"Like most poets":** Phillips, II, 1443.
"I was in Richmond in 1849": Ibid., 1446.
"If at any time": *E&R,* 72.
"I allude to the heresy": Ibid., 75.
"An immortal instinct": Ibid., 76.
"We have still a thirst": Ibid., 77.
"It is in Music, perhaps": Ibid., 78.
301 **"is, strictly and simply":** Ibid., 92–93.
"We shall reach, however": Ibid., 93–94.
the "only first-rate classical prose": Meyers, 240.

21. THE OATH AND CONSENT

303 **"I had returned from":** Allen, 718.
304 **Poe mailed a copy:** Wagenknecht, 37.
"The cessation of the music": Phillips, II, 1443.
"He spoke of his future": Weiss, *Scribner's,* 713–14.
John Daniel's comment: Jackson and Thomas, 827.
"Mr. Poe sat there in that quiet": A. H. Quinn, 630–31.
"[Elmira pro]poses for me to go": *CL* 2008, II, 836.
305 **"You will no doubt":** A. H. Quinn, 634–35.
The brooch was framed: Phillips, II, 1489.
306 **"His gait was firm and erect":** A. H. Quinn, 635.

306 **"And now let me tell you":** Edgar Allan Poe to Maria Clemm, August 29, 1849 (LTR-330), Edgar Allan Poe Society of Baltimore, accessed March 30, 2019, https://www.eapoe.org/works/letters/p4908280.htm.

307 **"Elmira talks about visiting":** *CL* 2008, II, 830–31.

"One day [Rosalie] went to that lady's": Weiss, *Independent* 57, August 25,1904, 443.

308 **"But I want to live *near Annie*":** *CL* 2008, II, 831–32.

"Elmira has just got home": Ibid., 837.

309 **"He [continued?] to visit me":** A. H. Quinn, 628–29.

"He came up to my house": Walsh, *Midnight,* 132.

"I have the testimony from": John J. Moran, *A Defense of Edgar Allan Poe* (Washington, DC: William F. Boogher, 1885), 50–51.

311 **"From this manner of departure":** Walsh, *Midnight,* 66.

One acquaintance he met: Whitty, lxxxiii.

"Some TB bacteria usually": *American Medical Association: Complete Medical Encyclopedia,* ed. Jerrold B. Leikin and Martin S. Lipsky (New York: Random House, 2003), 1242, 1244.

312 **Wolfe had been carrying the bacillus:** David Herbert Donald, *Look Homeward: A Life of Thomas Wolfe* (Boston: Little. Brown, 1987), 462–63.

as Mark Dawidziak and others: Mark Dawidziak: *A Mystery of Mysteries: Death and Life of Edgar Allan Poe* (New York: St. Martin's Press, 2023), 238–43.

A train conductor named Rollins: Walsh, *Midnight,* 81.

313 **Rollins found him unconscious:** Phillips, II, 1499.

lying on boards laid across two barrels: Ibid., 1501.

"There is a gentleman": Jackson and Thomas, 844.

"The intellectual flash": Ibid., 845.

314 **Poe seems to have kept his pledge to Elmira:** Semtner, *Shrine,* 176.

"No, sir, he was a sick man": Moran, 63.

315 **"willing to alter details for what":** *CL* 2008, II, 872.

"When brought to the Hospital": Jackson and Thomas, 845.

"I was summoned to his bedside": Ibid., 846.

316 **"Just at this moment my friend":** Moran, 70–71.

22. BURIAL AND AFTERLIFE

317 **The crowd attending was small:** Jackson and Thomas, 848–49.

318 **"The burial ceremony":** Ibid., 848.

"spoke of Poe as the greatest man": Silverman, 438.

"We regret to learn that Edgar A. Poe": A. H. Quinn, 644.

"Mrs. Shelton went into widow's mourning": Miller, *Helen,* 41.

"Oh! how shall I address you": Walsh, *Midnight,* 132–34.

319 **"I have received a letter from Poor Elmira":** Wagenknecht, 178.

"His affianced, Mrs. Shelton, wrote": Moran, 11–12.

319 **gave the wedding ring:** Semtner, *Shrine*, 161.
"Edgar Allan Poe is dead": Jackson and Thomas, 849; Fisher, 73.
"harsh experience": Fisher, 78.
"criminal" sexual relationship: Wagenknecht, 10.
"Irascible, envious—bad enough": Fisher, 79.
320 **"He [Griswold] could not forgive Poe":** Miller, *Building*, 214.
"Griswold's malevolent attack on Poe": Jeffrey A. Savoye, "The Works of the Late Edgar Allan Poe: Poe's Legacy and Griswold's Authority," in *Edgar Allan Poe Review* (Spring 2019): 7.
"[Poe] knew the value of negative publicity": Peeples, 4.
"Poe was not my friend": Savoye, *EAP Review* (Spring 2019): 5.
Before its copyright lapsed, in 1876: J. Gerald Kennedy and Scott Peeples, "The Unfolding Investigation of Edgar Allan Poe," in Kennedy and Peeples, 6.
321 **"It was only last summer":** Moran, 34–36.
"Widely as the fame of Poe": Whitty, lxxxv.

CODA

322 **"suffers no year to pass without":** William Dean Howells, *Life of Abraham Lincoln* (Springfield, IL: Abraham Lincoln Association, 1938), 31–32.
323 **"signaling a rupture . . . dismantling":** Margarida Vale de Gato, "Poe and Modern(ist) Poetry: An Impure Legacy," in Kennedy and Peeples, 618.
"meta-popular culture": Mark Neimeyer, "Poe and Popular Culture," in Hayes, 207.
"worlds in collision": Brian McHale, "Worlds in Collision," *Postmodernist Fiction* (London: Routledge, 1987), 75.
"wandering in the wilderness": Jonathan Elmer, "Poe and the Avant-Garde," in Kennedy and Peeples, 700.
"visionary *histrio*": Ibid., 632.

BIBLIOGRAPHY

Alfriend, Edward M. "Unpublished Recollections of Edgar Allan Poe." *Literary Era* 8 (January–September 1901): 489–92.

Allen, Hervey. *Israfel: The Life and Times of Edgar Allan Poe.* New York: Farrar & Rinehart, 1934.

Allen, Hervey, and Thomas Ollive Mabbott. *Poe's Brother.* New York: George H. Doran, 1926.

Allen, Michael. *Poe and the British Magazine Tradition.* New York: Oxford University Press, 1969.

Barrett, Lindon. "Presence of Mind: Detection and Racialization in 'The Murders in the Rue Morgue.'" In *Romancing the Shadow: Poe and Race,* edited by Kennedy and Weissberg, 157–76.

Baudelaire, Charles. *Les Fleurs du mal.* Edited by Wallace Fowlie. New York: Bantam Books, 1964.

Bayless, Joy. *Rufus Wilmot Griswold: Poe's Literary Executor.* Nashville: Vanderbilt University Press, 1943.

Bewley, Edward. "The True Ancestry of Edgar Allan Poe." *New York Genealogical and Biographical Record* 37 (1907): 55–69.

Bloom, Harold. *Kabbalah and Criticism.* New York: Continuum, 1975.

Bonaparte, Marie. *The Life and Works of Edgar Allan Poe.* Translated by John Rodker. 1949. Reprint. New York: Humanities Press, 1971.

Brewer's Dictionary of Phrase and Fable. 16th ed. New York: HarperResources, 1999.

Brigham, Clarence S. *Edgar Allan Poe's Contributions to Alexander's Weekly Messenger.* Worcester, MA: American Antiquarian Society, 1943.

Campbell, Killis. *The Mind of Poe and Other Studies.* Cambridge: Harvard University Press, 1933.

Carlson, Eric W., comp. *Critical Essays on Edgar Allan Poe.* Boston: G. K. Hall, 1987.

——, ed. *Introduction to Poe: A Thematic Reader.* Glenview, IL: Scott, Foresman, 1967.

Chen, Jenny. "Childhood Guilt, Adult Depression?" *Atlantic,* January 5, 2015. https://www.theatlantic.com/health/archive/2015/01/childhood-guilt-adult-depression/384176.

Coats, Lauren. "Poe's Novel Explorations." In *The Oxford Handbook of Edgar Allan Poe,* edited by Kennedy and Peeples, 384–405.

Cohen, Michael C. "Echoes of 'The Raven': Unoriginality in Poe's Verse." In *The Oxford Handbook of Edgar Allan Poe,* edited by Kennedy and Peeples, 104–20.

Columbia Encyclopedia. 5th ed. New York: Columbia University Press, 1993.

Damon, S. Foster. *Thomas Holley Chivers: Friend of Poe.* New York: Harper & Brothers, 1930.

David, Harriet Ide Eager. *Elmira: The Girl Who Loved Edgar Allan Poe.* Boston: Houghton Mifflin, 1966.

Davidson, Edward H. *Poe: A Critical Study.* Cambridge: Harvard University Press, 1957.

Dawidziak, Mark. *A Mystery of Mysteries: The Death and Life of Edgar Allan Poe.* New York: St. Martin's Press, 2023.

Dayan, Colin (Joan). "Poe, Persons, and Property." In *Romancing the Shadow,* edited by Kennedy and Weissberg, 106–26.

Deas, Michael J. *The Portraits and Daguerreotypes of Edgar Allan Poe.* Charlottesville: University Press of Virginia, 1988.

De Gato, Margarida Vale. "Poe and Modern(ist) Poetry: An Impure Legacy." In *The Oxford Handbook of Edgar Allan Poe,* edited by Kennedy and Peeples, 618–40.

Didier, E. L. *Life and Poems of Edgar Allan Poe.* New York: W. J. Whittleton, 1877.

Dietz, F. "Poe's First and Final Love." *Southern Literary Messenger* (March 1943): 38–47.

Donald, David Herbert. *Look Homeward: A Life of Thomas Wolfe.* Boston: Little, Brown, 1987.

Edgar Allan Poe Society of Baltimore. www.eapoe.org. (Website maintained by Jeffrey A. Savoye.)

Eliot, T. S. "From Poe to Valéry." *Hudson Review* 2, no. 2 (Autumn 1947): 327–42.

Elmer, Jonathan. "Poe and the Avant-Garde." In *The Oxford Handbook of Edgar Allan Poe,* edited by Kennedy and Peeples, 701–17.

Emerson, Ralph Waldo. *Emerson's Prose and Poetry.* Edited by Joel Porte and Saundra Morris. New York: W. W. Norton, 2001.

Erkkila, Betsy. "The Poetics of Whiteness: Poe, Douglass, and the Racial Imaginary." In *Romancing the Shadow: Poe and Race,* edited by Kennedy and Weissberg, 41–74.

Fisher, Benjamin F. *Poe in His Own Time.* Iowa City: University of Iowa Press, 2010.

Forrest, William M. *Biblical Allusions in Poe.* New York: Macmillan, 1928.

French, John C. "Poe's Literary Baltimore." *Maryland Historical Magazine* 32 (June 1937): 101–12.

Gill, William F. *The Life of Edgar Allan Poe.* New York: D. Appleton, 1877.

Goddu, Teresa A. "Poe, Sensationalism, and Slavery." In *The Cambridge Companion to Edgar Allan Poe,* edited by Hayes, 92–112.

Greven, David. *Gender Protest and Same-Sex Desire in Antebellum American Literature.* Burlington, VT: Ashgate, 2014.

Griswold, Rufus W. "Memoir." *Works of Edgar Allan Poe,* I, 32–94. New York: Harper and Brothers, n.d.

Hammond, Alexander. "Early Experiments in Genre: Imitations, Burlesques, Satires." In *The Oxford Handbook of Edgar Allan Poe,* edited by Kennedy and Peeples, 139–56.

Hansen, Emily James. "Poe, Egypt, and Egyptomania." In *Poe and Place,* edited by P. E. Phillips, 265–88.

Harmon, William. "'Mistah Kurtz—he dead' in Company: Redundancy and Ellipsis." *Connotations* 21, nos. 2–3 (2011–12).

Harrison, James A. *Life and Letters of Edgar Allan Poe.* Vols. I and II. New York: Thomas D. Crowell, 1902 and 1903.

Hayes, Kevin J., ed. *The Cambridge Companion to Edgar Allan Poe.* Cambridge: Cambridge University Press, 2002.

Hoffman, Daniel. *Poe Poe Poe Poe Poe Poe Poe.* Garden City, NY: Doubleday, 1972.

Howells, W. D. *Life of Abraham Lincoln.* 1860. Springfield, IL: Abraham Lincoln Association, 1938.

Hutchisson, James M. "An Orphan's Life, 1809–1831." In *The Oxford Handbook of Edgar Allan Poe,* edited by Kennedy and Peeples, 18–32.

———. *Poe.* Jackson: University Press of Mississippi, 2005.

Ingram, John H. *Life and Letters of Edgar Allan Poe.* London: Ward, Lock, Bowden & Co., 1891.

———. "Unpublished Correspondence of Edgar Allan Poe," *Appleton's Journal* (May 1878).

Irwin, John T. *American Hieroglyphics.* New Haven: Yale University Press, 1980.

Jackson, David K. *Poe and the Southern Literary Messenger.* Richmond: Dietz Publishers, 1934.

Jacobs, Robert D. *Poe: Journalist & Critic.* Baton Rouge: Louisiana State University Press, 1969.

Johnson, Ronald. *To Do as Adam Did: Selected Poems of Ronald Johnson.* Jersey City, NJ: House Publisher, 2000.

Jones, Paul Christian. "Counterparts: Poe's Doubles from 'William Wilson' to 'The Cask of Amontillado.'" In *The Oxford Handbook of Edgar Allan Poe,* edited by Kennedy and Peeples, 236–56.

Kennedy, J. Gerald. "Edgar Allan Poe, 1809–1849: A Brief Biography." In *A Historical Guide to Edgar Allan Poe,* edited by Kennedy, 19–62.

——, ed. *A Historical Guide to Edgar Allan Poe.* New York: Oxford University Press, 2001.

——. *Poe, Death, and the Life of Writing.* New Haven: Yale University Press, 1987.

——. "Poe's Terror Analytics." In *The Oxford Handbook of Edgar Allan Poe,* edited by Kennedy and Peeples, 809–27.

——. "The Realm of Dream and Memory: Poe's England." In *Poe and Place,* edited by P. E. Phillips, 71–96.

——. "'Trust No Man': Poe, Douglass, and the Culture of Slavery." In *Romancing the Shadow: Poe and Slavery,* edited by Kennedy and Weissberg, 225–57.

Kennedy, J. Gerald, and Liliane Weissberg, eds. *Romancing the Shadow: Poe and Race.* New York: Oxford University Press, 2001.

Kennedy, J. Gerald, and Scott Peeples, eds. *The Oxford Handbook of Edgar Allan Poe.* New York: Oxford University Press, 2001.

Kopley, Richard. "Re-Ordering Place in Poe's *Arthur Gordon Pym.*" In *Poe and Place,* edited by P. E. Phillips, 193–213.

Krutch, Joseph Wood. *Edgar Allan Poe: A Study in Genius.* New York: Alfred A. Knopf, 1926.

Lawrence, D. H. *The Portable D. H. Lawrence.* New York: Viking Press, 1947.

Lemire, Elise. "'The Murders in the Rue Morgue': Amalgamation Discourses and the Race Riots of 1838 in Poe's Philadelphia." In *Romancing the Shadow: Poe and Race,* edited by Kennedy and Weissberg, 177–204.

Leverenz, David. "Spanking the Master: Mind-Body Crossings in Poe's Sensationalism." In *A Historical Guide to Edgar Allan Poe,* edited by Kennedy, 95–127.

Ljungquist, Kent P. "Poe as Critic." In *The Cambridge Companion to Edgar Allan Poe,* edited by Hayes, 7–20.

——. "Poe's Landscapes: Picturesque and Ideal." In *The Oxford Handbook of Edgar Allan Poe,* edited by Kennedy and Peeples, 286–303.

Lovejoy, A. O. *Essays in the History of Ideas.* Baltimore: Johns Hopkins University Press, 1948.

Mabbott, Thomas Ollive. *Complete Works of Edgar Allan Poe.* 3 vols. Cambridge: Belknap Press of Harvard University Press, 1978.

McGann, Jerome. *The Poet Edgar Allan Poe: Alien Angel.* Cambridge: Harvard University Press, 2014.

McGill, Meredith L. *American Literature and the Culture of Reprinting, 1834–1853.* Philadelphia: University of Pennsylvania Press, 2001.

McHale, Brian. "Worlds in Collision." *Postmodernist Fiction.* London: Routledge, 1987, 59–72.

Meyers, Jeffrey. *Edgar Allan Poe: His Life and Legacy.* New York: Charles Scribner's Sons, 1993.

Miller, John Carl. *Building Poe Biography.* Baton Rouge: Louisiana State University Press, 1977.

———. *Poe's Helen Remembers.* Charlottesville: University Press of Virginia, 1979.

Monnet, Agnieszka Soltysik. "'The Fall of the House of Usher' and the Architecture of Unreliability." In *The Oxford Handbook of Edgar Allan Poe,* edited by Kennedy and Peeples, 320–37.

Moran, John J. *A Defense of Edgar Allan Poe.* Washington, DC: William F. Boogher, Publisher, 1885.

Morrison, Toni. *Playing in the Dark: Whiteness and the Literary Imagination.* New York: Vintage Books, 1993.

Muller, John P., and William J. Richardson, eds. *The Purloined Poe: Lacan, Derrida & Psychoanalytical Reading.* Baltimore: Johns Hopkins University Press, 1988.

New Standard Jewish Encyclopedia. 7th ed. Edited by Geoffrey Wigoder et al. New York: Facts on File, 1992.

Nichols, Mary Gove. "Reminiscences of Edgar Poe (1863)." In *Poe in His Own Time,* edited by Fisher, 210–16.

Niemeyer, Mark. "Poe and Popular Culture." In *The Cambridge Companion to Edgar Allan Poe,* edited by Hayes, 718–34.

Ober, Warren U., Paul S. Burtness, and William R. Seat Jr. *The Enigma of Poe.* Boston: D. C. Heath, 1960.

Ocker, J. W. *Poe-Land.* New York: Countryman Press, 2015.

Ostrom, John Ward. *The Collected Letters of Edgar Allan Poe.* Vols. I and II. 3rd ed. Revised, corrected, and expanded by Burton R. Pollin and Jeffrey A. Savoye. Staten Island, NY: Gordian Press, 2008.

Peeples, Scott. *The Afterlife of Edgar Allan Poe.* Rochester, NY: Camden House, 2004.

———. "A Life in Print: 1831–1849." In *The Oxford Handbook of Edgar Allan Poe,* edited by Kennedy and Peeples, 33–49.

Person, Leland S. "Outing the Perverse: Poe's False Confessionals." In *The Oxford Handbook of Edgar Allan Poe,* edited by Kennedy and Peeples, 252–68.

———. "Poe and Nineteenth Century Gender Constructions." In *A Historical Guide to Edgar Allan Poe,* edited by Kennedy, 129–65.

———. "Poe's Philosophy of Amalgamation: Reading Racism in the Tales." In *Romancing the Shadow: Poe and Race,* edited by Kennedy and Weissberg, 205–24.

Phillips, Mary E. *Edgar Allan Poe the Man.* Vols. I and II. Chicago: John C. Winston, 1926.

Phillips, Philip Edward, ed. *Poe and Place.* Cham, Switzerland: Palgrave Macmillan, 2018.

Poe, Edgar Allan. *The Collected Letters of Edgar Allan Poe.* 3rd ed. 2 vols. Edited by John Ostrom, Ward, Burton R. Pollin, and Jeffrey A. Savoye. New York: Gordian Press, 2008.

———. *Essays and Reviews.* Edited by G. R. Thompson. New York: Library of America, 1984.

———. *Poetry and Tales.* Edited by Patrick F. Quinn. New York: Library of America, 1984.

Poe, Harry Lee. *Evermore: Edgar Allan Poe and the Mystery of the Universe.* Waco, TX: Baylor University Press, 2012.

Poe Studies. Washington State University, 1968–.

Pollin, Burton R. *Discoveries in Poe.* Notre Dame, IN: University of Notre Dame Press, 1970.

Polonsky. Rachel. "Poe's Aesthetic Theory." In *The Cambridge Companion to Edgar Allan Poe,* edited by Hayes, 42–56.

Pope-Hennessy, Una. *Edgar Allan Poe: A Critical Biography.* London: Macmillan, 1934.

Quinn, Arthur Hobson. *Edgar Allan Poe: A Critical Biography.* 1941. Reprint. Baltimore: Johns Hopkins University Press, 1998.

Quinn, Arthur Hobson, and Richard H. Hart. *Edgar Allan Poe's Letters and Documents.* New York: Scholars Facsimiles and Reprints, 1945.

Quinn, Patrick. *The French Face of Edgar Poe.* Carbondale: Southern Illinois University Press, 1957.

Rachman, Stephen. "The Marginal Center: 'Pinakidia,' 'Marginalia,' and 'Fifty Suggestions.'" In *The Oxford Handbook of Edgar Allan Poe,* edited by Kennedy and Peeples, 462–78.

Randall, David A. *The J. K. Lilly Collection of Edgar Allan Poe.* Bloomington: Indiana University, 1964.

Regan, Robert. *Poe: A Collection of Critical Essays.* Englewood Cliffs, NJ: Prentice Hall, 1967.

Rein, David M. "Poe and Mrs. Shelton." *American Literature* 28, no. 2 (May 1956): 225–27.

Renza, Louis A. "Poe and the Issue of American Privacy." In *A Historical Guide to Edgar Allan Poe,* edited by Kennedy, 167–88.

Rose, Alexander G., III, and Jeffrey Alan Savoye. *Such Friends as These.* Baltimore: Enoch Pratt Free Library Centennial Publication, 1985.

Rosenheim, Shawn James. *The Cryptographic Imagination.* Baltimore: Johns Hopkins University Press, 1997.

Ross, Kelly. "Deciphering Dupin: Poe's Ratiocinative Plots." In *The Oxford Handbook of Edgar Allan Poe,* edited by Kennedy and Peeples, 205–24.

Rowe, John Carlos. "Edgar Allan Poe's Imperial Fantasy and the American Frontier." In *Romancing the Shadow: Poe and Race,* edited by Kennedy and Weissberg, 75–105.

Royot, Daniel. *The Formal Center in Literature: Explorations from Poe to the Present.* Rochester, NY: Camden House, 2018.

———. "Poe's Humor." In *The Cambridge Companion to Edgar Allan Poe,* edited by Hayes, 57–71.

Savoye, Jeffrey A. "Poe and Baltimore: Crossroads and Redemption." In *Poe and Place,* edited by P. E. Phillips, 97–122.

———. "The Works of the Late Edgar Allan Poe: Poe's Legacy and Griswold's Authority." *EAP Review* (Spring, 2019): 1–13.

Semtner, Christopher P. *Edgar Allan Poe's Richmond.* Charleston: History Press, 2012.

———. *The Poe Shrine: Building the World's Finest Edgar Allan Poe Collection.* Charleston, SC: Arcadia Publishing, 2017.

———. "Poe's Richmond and Richmond's Poe." In *Poe and Place,* edited by P. E. Phillips, 43–70.

Silverman, Kenneth. *Edgar A. Poe: Mournful and Never-Ending Remembrance.* New York: HarperCollins, 1992.

Smith, Elsdon C. *New Dictionary of American Family Names.* New York: Gramercy, 1988.

Smith, Geddeth. *The Brief Career of Eliza Poe.* London: Associated University Presses, 1988.

Spannuth, Jacob E., and Thomas Ollive Mabbott, eds. *Doings of Gotham: Poe's Contributions to "The Columbia Spy."* Pottsville, PA: Jacob E. Spannuth, 1929.

St. Armand, Barton Levi. "Poe's Unnecessary Angel." In *Ruined Eden of the Present: Hawthorne, Melville, and Poe,* edited by G. R. Thompson and Virgil L. Lokke, 283–302. West Lafayette, IN: Purdue University Press, 1981.

Tane, Susan Jaffe. *Nevermore: The Edgar Allan Poe Collection of Susan Tane.* Ithaca: Cornell University Library, 2006.

Tate, Allen. "Our Cousin, Mr. Poe." In *Poe: A Collection of Critical Essays,* edited by Robert Regan, 38–50. Englewood Cliffs, NJ: Prentice Hall, 1967.

Thomas, Dwight, and David K. Jackson. *The Poe Log: A Documentary Life of Edgar Allan Poe, 1809–1849.* New York: G. K. Hall, 1987.

Thoms, Peter. "Dupin and the Power of Detection." In *The Cambridge Companion to Edgar Allan Poe,* edited by Hayes, 133–47.

Ticknor, Caroline. *Poe's Helen.* New York: Charles Scribner's Sons, 1916.

Tomc, Sandra. "Edgar Allan Poe and His Enemies." In *The Oxford Handbook of Edgar Allan Poe,* edited by Kennedy and Peeples, 559–75.

——. "Poe and His Circle." In *The Cambridge Companion to Edgar Allan Poe,* edited by Hayes, 21–41.

Traubel, Horace. *With Walt Whitman in Camden.* Vol. IV. Reprint. Carbondale: Southern Illinois University Press, 1959.

Tresch, John. "Extra! Extra! Poe Invents Science Fiction!" In *The Cambridge Companion to Edgar Allan Poe,* edited by Hayes, 113–32.

——. *The Reason for the Darkness of the Night: Edgar Allan Poe and the Forging of American Science.* New York: Farrar, Straus and Giroux, 2021.

Urakova, Alexandra. "Undying Enigmas in 'Ligeia.'" In *The Oxford Handbook of Edgar Allan Poe,* edited by Kennedy and Peeples, 304–19.

Van Cleef, Augustus. "Poe's Mary." *Harper's New Monthly Magazine* 78 (March 1889): 634–40.

Van Leer, David. Introduction. *Edgar Allan Poe: Selected Tales.* New York: Penguin, 1998.

——. *The Queening of American.* New York: Routledge, 1998.

Wagenknecht, Edward. *Edgar Allan Poe: The Man behind the Legend.* New York: Oxford University Press, 1963.

Walsh, John Evangelist. *Midnight Dreary: The Mysterious Death of Edgar Allan Poe.* New Brunswick, NJ: Rutgers University Press, 1998.

——. *Plumes in the Dust.* Chicago: Nelson Hall, 1980.

Weinauer, Ellen. "Undead Wives and Undone Husbands: Poe's Tales of Marriage." In *The Oxford Handbook of Edgar Allan Poe,* edited by Kennedy and Peeples, 173–88.

Weinstock, Jeffrey Andrew. "Postmodern Poe." In *The Oxford Handbook of Edgar Allan Poe,* edited by Kennedy and Peeples, 718–34.

Weiss, Susan Archer. *Home Life of Poe.* New York: Broadway., 1907.

——. "Last Days of Edgar Allan Poe." *Scribner's Magazine,* March 1878, 707–16.

——. "Reminiscences of Edgar A. Poe." *Independent* 56, May 5, 1904, 1010–1014.

——. "Reminiscences of Edgar A. Poe." *Independent* 57, August 25, 1904, 443–48.

Whalen, Terence. *Edgar Allan Poe and the Masses: The Political Economy of Literature in Antebellum America.* Princeton: Princeton University Press, 1999.

Whitman, Sarah Helen. *Edgar Poe and His Critics.* New York: Rudd & Carlton, 1860.

Whitty, J. H., ed. "Memoir of Poe." *The Complete Poems of Poe,* xix–lxxxvi. Boston: Houghton Mifflin, 1911.

Widmer, Edward L. *Young America.* New York: Oxford University Press, 1999.

Wigoder, Geoffrey, et al. *New Standard Jewish Encyclopedia.* 7th new rev. ed. New York: Facts on File, 1992.

Wilbur, Richard. "Edgar Allan Poe's *Eleonora.*" *The Catbird's Song,* 104–17. New York: Harcourt Brace, 1997.

——. "The House of Poe," in Regan, 98–120.

——. "Introduction." *Poe: Complete Poems, with an Introduction and Notes.* New York: Dell, 1959. 7–39.

——. "Poe and the Art of Suggestion." *The Catbird's Song,* 7–25. New York: Harcourt Brace, 1997.

Wolfson, Susan J. "Entertaining Byron in America." *Byron Journal* (Liverpool University Press) 45, no. 1 (2017): 3–22.

Woodberry, George E. *The Life of Edgar Allan Poe.* Vols. I and II. 1909. Reprint. New York: Biblio and Tanner, 196.

INDEX